# The McDonaldization of Society
## Revised New Century Edition

*To Alan Ritzer, who helped open my eyes to McDonaldization,
and to Paul O'Connell, whose gentleness and
Shavian wit were inspirations for this book.*

# GEORGE RITZER
*University of Maryland*

# The McDonaldization of Society
## Revised New Century Edition

PINE FORGE PRESS
An Imprint of Sage Publications, Inc.
Thousand Oaks • London • New Delhi

*For information:*

 Pine Forge Press
A Sage Publications Company
2455 Teller Road
Thousand Oaks, California 91320
E-mail: order@sagepub.com

Sage Publications Ltd.
1 Oliver's Yard
55 City Road
London EC1Y 1SP
United Kingdom

Sage Publications India Pvt. Ltd.
B-42 Panchsheel Enclave
Post Box 4109
New Delhi 110 017  India

Printed in the United States of America

**Library of Congress Cataloging-in-Publication Data**

Ritzer, George.
The McDonaldization of society / George Ritzer.—Rev. new century ed.
    p. cm.
Includes bibliographical references and index.
ISBN: 0-7619-8811-4 (cloth)
ISBN: 0-7619-8812-2 (pbk.)
    1.  Social structure—United States. 2.  United States—Social conditions—1980-
3.  Management—Social aspects—United States. 4.  Fast food restaurants—Social
aspects—United States. 5.  Rationalization (Psychology) I. Title.

HM706.R58 2004
306'.0973—dc22

                                                    2003023424


This book is printed on acid-free paper.

04   05   06   07   10   9   8   7   6   5   4   3   2

| | |
|---|---|
| *Acquisitions Editor:* | Jerry Westby |
| *Editorial Assistant:* | Vonessa Vondera |
| *Production Editor:* | Denise Santoyo |
| *Copy Editor:* | Linda Gray |
| *Typesetter:* | C&M Digitals (P) Ltd. |
| *Indexer:* | Kathy Paparchontis |
| *Cover Designer:* | Edgar Abarca/Ravi Balasuriya |
| *Production Artist:* | Michelle Lee Kenny |

# Contents

# Preface

$W$hy another edition of *The McDonaldization of Society?*

- For one thing, the paradigm for this process—McDonald's—is undergoing dramatic changes and is declining in significance. This is important in itself, but it must also be addressed for what it *does* and *does not* tell us about the broader process of McDonaldization.

- Second, the fast-food industry is also changing with a variety of new trends (for example, the growing importance of non-American chains in the American market) worthy of discussion.

- Third, the tentacles of McDonaldization are continuing to spread more widely and more deeply into various social institutions, such as education, medicine, the criminal justice system, and so on.

- Fourth, broader processes that subsume McDonaldization, at least in part, are growing in importance. The most notable of these broader processes is globalization, and it needs to be discussed in greater detail, as does its relationship to McDonaldization.

- Fifth, the topic of McDonaldization has, by now, attracted the attention of a number of journalists (most notably Eric Schlosser and his international best-seller [inspired, in part, by an earlier edition of this book], *Fast Food Nation*), and their work, as well as recent scholarly work on this topic, needs to be integrated into this discussion.

- Sixth, current events have important implications for McDonaldization, and they need to be dealt with in the text. For example, with the end of the 2003 war with Iraq, and of the rule of Saddam Hussein, clones of McDonald's—one called "MaDonal" complete with golden arches, red and yellow colors, and clowns, to say nothing of cheeseburgers and french fries—appeared there almost immediately. How long before McDonald's itself will be opening in Iraq (and forcing the clones out of business)?

Thus, there is much that is new to be discussed here, and it will be integrated into the basic structure of this book, which remains largely unchanged.

While employing basically the same format, a few major structural changes have been made in this edition. For one thing, given the thrust of the preceding discussion, an entire chapter (8) is now devoted to globalization and its relationship to McDonaldization. In addition to a broad discussion of globalization, there is also a more specific treatment of my recent work on the "globalization of nothing." As we will see, McDonaldization is one of several key forces in the globalization of nothing.

To keep the length of this book manageable, the chapter (formerly, Chapter 8) on birth, death, and death-defying acts has been eliminated. However, at least some of that material has been retained, especially in Chapters 6 and 7 where it is used to offer illustrations of some of the basic dimensions of McDonaldization.

McDonaldization has roared into a new century. It is an infinitely more mature and more powerful force today than it was when I first began thinking about it two decades ago or even when I began writing the first edition of this book over a decade ago. In spite of its recent difficulties, McDonald's has many more outlets, has become a much more powerful enterprise internationally, and has wormed its way into the hearts and minds of many more consumers and entrepreneurs. More important, there are many more clones of McDonald's, not only in the fast-food industry but in many other settings as well. Many other nations have been invaded by McDonaldized American businesses, and many have created indigenous versions of those enterprises. Most important, McDonaldization has become even more deeply ingrained not only in the culture of the United States but also in many other cultures around the world. At the same time, the global opposition to McDonald's and McDonaldization has also expanded dramatically.

This book is essentially a work in social criticism. McDonald's clearly has many advantages that contributed to its expansion, and they will be mentioned throughout the book. However, McDonald's and its many clones have plenty of opportunity, and spend huge sums of money, to tell you about their good points. The book seeks to give the public discourse a little balance by focusing on the problems created, and the dangers posed, by McDonaldization.

As a theoretically based work in social criticism, this book is part of a historical tradition in the social sciences in which social theory is used to critique society and thereby to provide the base for its betterment. This tradition animated the most important theoretical source of this book— the work of Max Weber—as well as that of other social theorists, such as Georg Simmel, Emile Durkheim, Karl Marx, C. Wright Mills, and Jürgen Habermas.

I should point out that I bear no particular animus toward McDonald's. It is no better or worse than most other fast-food restaurants and other manifestations of the rationalization process. I have labeled the process of concern here "McDonaldization" because McDonald's was, and is, the most important manifestation of this process. Besides, it has a better ring to it than some of the alternatives—"Burger Kingization," "Starbuckization," "Seven Elevenization," "Fuddruckerization," "H&R Blockization," "KinderCareization," "Jiffy Lubeization," or "NutriSystemization."

As the preceding list makes clear, a wide array of social phenomena are linked in this book under the heading of McDonaldization. Some have been directly affected by the principles of the fast-food restaurant, whereas in other cases, the effect is more indirect. Some have all the basic dimensions of McDonaldization, but others only one or two. In any case, in my view, they all are part of what Weber called the rationalization process, or to make Weber more timely, McDonaldization.

The major themes of this book, especially the critiques of the irrationalities of McDonaldization, are likely to be highly controversial. My experience in lecturing on this theme is that audiences generally support McDonaldization and feel protective toward it. Critiques of McDonaldization inevitably spawn heated debate in the lecture hall. I hope this book will spark a similar debate in a larger arena. The generation of such debate, as well as the insights to be derived from it, is the essence not only of good teaching but also of good sociology. Whether or not the reader agrees with my conclusions, I will have succeeded in achieving my goal if the reader has been provoked into rethinking this significant aspect of everyday life.

This book is written to be accessible to a wide readership. However, it is firmly based on one of the strongest social theories, Weber's theory of rationalization. It is also an "empirical" study, albeit a highly informal one. The "data" are drawn from a wide range of available sources and deal with the full range of social phenomena that fall under the heading of McDonaldization. However, although it is theory based and relies on data, this is not written as a dry theoretical and empirical study; it is not weighted down by many of the requirements of scholarly monographs. Rather, it is designed to be read by many people and inform them of a wide-ranging social development occurring all around them. More important, it is written as a warning that the seductions and attractions of McDonaldization should not blind us to its many dangers.

I hope this book offers readers some new insight into the society they are constructing. If they are as alarmed as I am by the dangers posed by McDonaldization, perhaps they can do what Weber thought virtually impossible—act to reverse the trend toward McDonaldization. Although I do not think such a reversal is likely, or even necessarily desirable, I do think there are steps that people can take to ameliorate the problems, to humanize a McDonaldized society. I hope this book will not only inform but also serve as a warning and, perhaps most important, point the reader in directions that can help make the "iron cage of McDonaldization" a more human setting in which to work and live.

I have received a wealth of valuable comments toward improving this new edition and would like to thank the following for their help:

Angelo Fanelli, University of Florida, Gainesville

Celestino Fernandez, University of Arizona

Peter R. Hoffman, Loyola Marymount University

Marybeth C. Stalp, Western State College

Linda Morrison, Oakland University

F. Kurt Cylke, SUNY Geneseo

Jennifer Jones-Corley, University of Illinois

Eric T. Metzler, Indiana University

Douglas J. Adams, University of Arkansas

Philip Cohen, University of California, Irvine

I am especially grateful to my assistant, Mike Ryan, for his invaluable help with this revision. Deep thanks to Jerry Westby, my editor at Pine Forge Press, who continues to believe in, and support, my work. It is a joy to work with him. I would also like to thank Linda Gray for her close copyediting and for offering several additions and useful suggestions that have been integrated into the text of the book.

In anticipation of the possibility of yet another revision of this book, and in an effort to de-McDonaldize the relationship between author and reader, I would appreciate receiving feedback on this book as well as additional examples of McDonaldization (with documentation, if possible), by e-mail (Ritzer@socy.umd.edu).

# 1

# An Introduction to McDonaldization

◆───────────────────────────────

R ay Kroc (1902–1984), the genius behind the franchising of McDonald's restaurants, was a man with big ideas and grand ambitions. But even Kroc could not have anticipated the astounding impact of his creation. McDonald's is the basis of one of the most influential developments in contemporary society. Its reverberations extend far beyond its point of origin in the United States and in the fast-food business. It has influenced a wide range of undertakings, indeed the way of life, of a significant portion of the world. And in spite of McDonald's recent and well-publicized economic difficulties, that impact is likely to expand at an accelerating rate.[1]*

However, this is *not* a book about McDonald's, or even about the fast-food business,[2] although both will be discussed frequently throughout these pages. I devote all this attention to McDonald's (as well as the industry of which it is part and that it played such a key role in spawning) because it serves here as the major example of, and the paradigm for, a wide-ranging process I call *McDonaldization*,[3]—that is,

the process by which the principles of the fast-food restaurant are coming to dominate more and more sectors of American society as well as of the rest of the world.[4]

───────────

*Notes may be found at the back of the book, beginning on p. 251.

1

As you will see, McDonaldization affects not only the restaurant business but also education, work, the criminal justice system, health care, travel, leisure, dieting, politics, the family, religion, and virtually every other aspect of society.[5] McDonaldization has shown every sign of being an inexorable process, sweeping through seemingly impervious institutions and regions of the world.

The success of McDonald's (in spite of recent troubles; see the closing section of this chapter) itself is apparent: In 2002, its total sales was over $41 billion, with operating income of $2.1 billion.[6] McDonald's, which first began operations in 1955, had 31,172 restaurants throughout the world as of early 2003.[7] Martin Plimmer, a British commentator, archly notes: "There are McDonald's everywhere. There's one near you, and there's one being built right now even nearer to you. Soon, if McDonald's goes on expanding at its present rate, there might even be one in your house. You could find Ronald McDonald's boots under your bed. And maybe his red wig, too."[8]

McDonald's and McDonaldization have had their most obvious influence on the restaurant industry and, more generally, on franchises of all types:

1. According to the International Franchise Association there were 320,000 small franchised businesses in the United States in 2000 and they did about $1 trillion in annual sales. Although accounting for less than 10% of retail businesses, over 40% of all retail sales come from franchises and they employ more than 8 million people. Franchises are growing rapidly with a new one opening every 8 minutes in the United States.[9] Over 57% of McDonald's restaurants are franchises.[10]

2. In the restaurant industry, the McDonald's model has been adopted not only by other budget-minded hamburger franchises, such as Burger King and Wendy's, but also by a wide array of other low-priced fast-food businesses. Yum! Brands, Inc. operates nearly 33,000 restaurants in 100 countries[11] under the Pizza Hut, Kentucky Fried Chicken, Taco Bell, A&W Root Beer, and Long John Silver's franchises and has more outlets than McDonald's, although its total sales ($24 billion in 2002) is not nearly as high.[12] Subway (with almost 19,000 outlets in 72 countries[13]) is one of the fastest-growing fast-food businesses and claims to be—and may actually be—the largest restaurant chain in the United States.[14]

3. Starbucks, a relative newcomer to the fast-food industry, has achieved dramatic success of its own. A local Seattle business as late as

1987, Starbucks had over 6,000 company-owned shops (there are no franchises) by 2003, more than ten times the number of shops in 1994.[15] Starbucks has been growing rapidly internationally and is now a presence in Latin America, Europe (it is particularly omnipresent in London), the Middle East, and the Pacific Rim.

4. Perhaps we should not be surprised that the McDonald's model has been extended to casual dining—that is, more upscale, higher-priced restaurants with fuller menus (for example, Outback Steakhouse, Chili's, Olive Garden, and Red Lobster). Morton's is an even more upscale, high-priced chain of steakhouses that has overtly modeled itself after McDonald's: "Despite the fawning service and the huge wine list, a meal at Morton's conforms to the same dictates of uniformity, cost control and portion regulation that have enabled American fast-food chains to rule the world."[16] In fact, the chief executive of Morton's was an owner of a number of Wendy's outlets and admits: "My experience with Wendy's has helped in Morton's venues."[17] To achieve uniformity, employees go "by the book": "an ingredient-by-ingredient illustrated binder describing the exact specifications of 500 Morton's kitchen items, sauces and garnishes. A row of color pictures in every Morton's kitchen displays the presentation for each dish."[18,19]

5. Other types of business are increasingly adapting the principles of the fast-food industry to their needs. Said the vice chairman of Toys "R" Us, "We want to be thought of as a sort of McDonald's of toys."[20] The founder of Kidsports Fun and Fitness Club echoed this desire: "I want to be the McDonald's of the kids' fun and fitness business."[21] Other chains with similar ambitions include Gap, Jiffy Lube, AAMCO Transmissions, Midas Muffler & Brake Shops, Great Clips, H&R Block, Pearle Vision, Bally's, Kampgrounds of America (KOA), KinderCare (dubbed "Kentucky Fried Children"[22]), Jenny Craig, Home Depot, Barnes & Noble, PETsMART.

6. McDonald's has been a resounding success in the international arena. Over half of McDonald's restaurants are outside the United States (in the mid-1980s, only 25% of McDonald's were outside the United States). The majority (982) of the 1,366 new restaurants opened in 2002 were overseas (in the United States, the number of restaurants increased by less than four hundred).[23] Well over half of McDonald's revenue comes from its overseas operations. McDonald's restaurants are now found in 118 nations around the world, serving 46 million customers a day.[24] The

leader, by far, is Japan with almost 4,000 restaurants, followed by Canada with over 1,300, and Germany with over 1,200. As of 2002, there were 95 McDonald's in Russia,[25] and the company plans to open many more restaurants in the former Soviet Union and in the vast new territory in Eastern Europe that has been laid bare to the invasion of fast-food restaurants. Great Britain has become the "fast-food capital of Europe,"[26] and Israel is described as "McDonaldized," with its shopping malls populated by "Ace Hardware, Toys 'R Us, Office Depot, and TCBY."[27]

7. Many highly McDonaldized firms outside of the fast-food industry have also had success globally. Although most of Blockbuster's 8,500 sites are in the United States, more than 2,000 of them are to be found in twenty-eight other countries.[28] Wal-Mart is the world's largest retailer with 1.3 million employees and $218 billion in sales. Over three thousand of its stores are in the United States (as of 2002). It opened its first international store (in Mexico) in 1991, but it now has more than one thousand units in Mexico, Puerto Rico, Canada, Argentina, Brazil, China, Korea, Germany, and the United Kingdom. In any week, more than 100 million customers visit Wal-Mart stores worldwide.[29]

8. Other nations have developed their own variants of this American institution. Canada has a chain of coffee shops, Tim Hortons (merged with Wendy's not long ago), with 2,200 outlets (160 in the United States).[30] Paris, a city whose love for fine cuisine might lead you to think it would prove immune to fast food, has a large number of fast-food croissanteries; the revered French bread has also been McDonaldized.[31] India has a chain of fast-food restaurants, Nirula's, that sells mutton burgers (about 80% of Indians are Hindus, who eat no beef) as well as local Indian cuisine.[32] Mos Burger is a Japanese chain with over fifteen hundred restaurants that in addition to the usual fare, sells Teriyaki chicken burgers, rice burgers, and "Oshiruko with brown rice cake."[33] Perhaps the most unlikely spot for an indigenous fast-food restaurant, war-ravaged Beirut of 1984, witnessed the opening of Juicy Burger, with a rainbow instead of golden arches and J. B. the Clown standing in for Ronald McDonald. Its owners hoped that it would become the "McDonald's of the Arab world."[34] Most recently, in the immediate wake of the 2003 war with Iraq, clones of McDonald's (sporting names like "MaDonal" and "Matbax") opened in that country complete with hamburgers, french fries, and even golden arches.[35]

9. And now McDonaldization is coming full circle. Other countries with their own McDonaldized institutions have begun to export them to the United States. The Body Shop, an ecologically sensitive British cosmetics

chain had, as of early 2003, over nineteen hundred shops in fifty nations,[36] of which three hundred were in the United States. Furthermore, American firms are now opening copies of this British chain, such as Bath & Body Works.[37] Pret A Manger, a chain of sandwich shops that also originated in Great Britain (interestingly, McDonald's purchased a 33% minority share of the company in 2001), has over 130 company-owned and -run restaurants, mostly in the United Kingdom but now also in New York, Hong Kong, and Tokyo.[38]

10. Ikea, a Swedish-based (but Dutch-owned) home furnishings company, did about 12 billion euros in business in 2002 derived from the over 286 million people (equal to about the entire population of the United States) visiting their 150-plus stores in 29 countries. Purchases were also made from the 118 million copies of their catalog printed in over 45 languages. In fact, that catalog is reputed to be the second largest publication in the world, just after the Bible.[39] An international chain to watch in the coming years is H&M clothing, founded in 1947 and now operating over 900 stores in 17 countries with plans to open another 110 stores by the end of 2003. It currently employs over 39,000 people and sells more than 500 million items a year.[40]

## ◆ MCDONALD'S AS A GLOBAL ICON

McDonald's has come to occupy a central place in American popular culture, not just the business world.[41] A new McDonald's opening in a small town can be an important social event. Said one Maryland high school student at such an opening, "Nothing this exciting ever happens in Dale City."[42] Even big-city newspapers avidly cover developments in the fast-food business.

Fast-food restaurants also play symbolic roles on television programs and in the movies. A skit on the legendary television show *Saturday Night Live* satirized specialty chains by detailing the hardships of a franchise that sells nothing but Scotch tape. In the movie *Coming to America* (1988), Eddie Murphy plays an African prince whose introduction to America includes a job at "McDowell's," a thinly disguised McDonald's. In *Falling Down* (1993), Michael Douglas vents his rage against the modern world in a fast-food restaurant dominated by mindless rules designed to frustrate customers. *Moscow on the Hudson* (1984) has Robin Williams, newly arrived from Russia, obtain a job at McDonald's. H. G. Wells, a central character in the movie *Time After Time* (1979), finds himself transported to the modern world of a McDonald's, where he tries to order the tea he was accustomed to drinking in Victorian England. In *Sleeper* (1973), Woody Allen awakens in the future only to encounter a McDonald's. *Tin Men* (1987) ends with the early 1960s heroes driving off into a future represented by a huge golden arch looming in the distance. *Scotland, PA* (2001) brings *Macbeth* to the Pennsylvania of the 1970s. The famous murder scene from the Shakespeare play involves, in this case, plunging a doughnut king's head into the boiling oil of a deep fat fryer. The McBeths then use their ill-gotten gains to transform the king's greasy spoon café into a fast-food restaurant featuring McBeth burgers.

Further proof that McDonald's has become a symbol of American culture is to be found in what happened when plans were made to raze Ray Kroc's first McDonald's restaurant. Hundreds of letters poured into McDonald's headquarters, including the following:

> Please don't tear it down! . . . Your company's name is a household word, not only in the United States of America, but all over the world. To destroy this major artifact of contemporary culture would, indeed, destroy part of the faith the people of the world have in your company.[43]

In the end, the restaurant was rebuilt according to the original blueprints and turned into a museum.[44] A McDonald's executive explained the move: "McDonald's . . . is really a part of Americana."

Americans aren't the only ones who feel this way. At the opening of the McDonald's in Moscow, one journalist described the franchise as the "ultimate icon of Americana."[45] When Pizza Hut opened in Moscow in 1990, a Russian student said, "It's a piece of America."[46] Reflecting on the growth of fast-food restaurants in Brazil, an executive associated with Pizza Hut of Brazil said that his nation "is experiencing a passion for things American."[47] On the popularity of Kentucky Fried Chicken in Malaysia, the local owner said, "Anything Western, especially American, people here love. . . . They want to be associated with America."[48]

One could go further and argue that in at least some ways McDonald's has become *more important* than the United States itself. Take the following story about a former U.S. ambassador to Israel officiating at the opening of the first McDonald's in Jerusalem wearing a baseball hat with the McDonald's golden arches logo:

> An Israeli teen-ager walked up to him, carrying his own McDonald's hat, which he handed to Ambassador Indyk with a pen and asked: "Are you the

Ambassador? Can I have your autograph?" Somewhat sheepishly, Ambassador Indyk replied: "Sure. I've never been asked for my autograph before."

As the Ambassador prepared to sign his name, the Israeli teen-ager said to him, "Wow, what's it like to be the ambassador from McDonald's, going around the world opening McDonald's restaurants everywhere?" Ambassador Indyk looked at the Israeli youth and said, "No, no. I'm the American ambassador—not the ambassador from McDonald's!"

Ambassador Indyk described what happened next: "I said to him, 'Does this mean you don't want my autograph?' And the kid said, 'No, I don't want your autograph,' and he took his hat back and walked away."[49]

Two other indices of the significance of McDonald's (and, implicitly, McDonaldization) are worth mentioning. The first is the annual "Big Mac Index" (part of "burgernomics") published by a prestigious magazine, *The Economist*. It indicates the purchasing power of various currencies around the world based on the local price (in dollars) of the Big Mac. The Big Mac is used because it is a uniform commodity sold in many different nations. In the 2003 survey, a Big Mac in the United States cost an average of $2.71; in China it was $1.20; in Switzerland it cost $4.52.[50] This measure indicates, at least roughly, where the cost of living is high or low, as well as which currencies are undervalued (China) and which are overvalued (Switzerland). Although *The Economist* is calculating the Big Mac Index tongue-in-cheek, at least in part, the index represents the ubiquity and importance of McDonald's around the world.

The second indicator of McDonald's global significance is the idea developed by Thomas Friedman that "no two countries that both have a McDonald's have ever fought a war since they each got McDonald's." Friedman calls this the "Golden Arches Theory of Conflict Prevention."[51] Another half-serious idea, it implies that the path to world peace lies through the continued international expansion of McDonald's. Unfortunately, it was proved wrong by the NATO bombing of Yugoslavia in 1999, which had sixteen McDonald's as of 2002.

To many people throughout the world, McDonald's has become a sacred institution.[52] At that opening of the McDonald's in Moscow, a worker spoke of it "as if it were the Cathedral in Chartres . . . a place to experience 'celestial joy.'"[53] Kowinski argues that indoor shopping malls, which almost always encompass fast-food restaurants, are the modern "cathedrals of consumption" to which people go to practice their "consumer religion."[54] Similarly, a visit to another central element of McDonaldized society, Walt Disney World,[55] has been described as "the middle-class hajj, the compulsory visit to the sunbaked holy city."[56]

McDonald's has achieved its exalted position because virtually all Americans, and many others, have passed through its golden arches on innumerable occasions. Furthermore, most of us have been bombarded by commercials extolling McDonald's virtues, commercials tailored to a variety of audiences and that change as the chain introduces new foods, new contests, and new product tie-ins. These ever-present commercials, combined with the fact that people cannot drive very far without having a McDonald's pop into view, have embedded McDonald's deeply in popular consciousness. A poll of school-age children showed that 96% of them could identify Ronald McDonald, second only to Santa Claus in name recognition.[57]

Over the years, McDonald's has appealed to people in many ways. The restaurants themselves are depicted as spick-and-span, the food is said to be fresh and nutritious, the employees are shown to be young and eager, the managers appear gentle and caring, and the dining experience itself seems fun-filled. People are even led to believe that they contribute through their purchases, at least indirectly, to charities such as the Ronald McDonald Houses for sick children.

## ◆ THE LONG ARM OF MCDONALDIZATION

McDonald's strives to continually extend its reach within American society and beyond. As the company's chairman said, "Our goal: to totally dominate the quick service restaurant industry worldwide. . . . I want McDonald's to be more than a leader. I want McDonald's to dominate."[58]

McDonald's began as a phenomenon of suburbs and medium-sized towns, but in more recent years, it has moved into smaller towns that supposedly could not support such a restaurant and into many big cities that are supposedly too sophisticated.[59] You can now find fast-food outlets in New York's Times Square as well as on the Champs-Elysées in Paris. Soon after it opened in 1992, the McDonald's in Moscow sold almost thirty thousand hamburgers a day and employed a staff of twelve hundred young people working two to a cash register.[60] (Today McDonald's controls an astounding 83% of the fast-food market in Russia.[61]) In early 1992, Beijing witnessed the opening of the world's largest McDonald's, with seven hundred seats, twenty-nine cash registers, and nearly one thousand employees. On its first day of business, it set a new one-day record for McDonald's by serving about forty thousand customers.[62]

Small satellite, express, or remote outlets, opened in areas that cannot support full-scale fast-food restaurants, are also expanding rapidly. They are found in small storefronts in large cities and in nontraditional settings such as department stores, service stations,[63] and even schools. These satellites typically offer only limited menus and may rely on larger outlets for food storage and preparation.[64] McDonald's is considering opening express outlets in museums, office buildings, and corporate cafeterias. A flap occurred not long ago over the placement of a McDonald's in the new federal courthouse in Boston.[65] Among the more striking sites for a McDonald's restaurant are the Grand Canyon, the world's tallest building (Petronas Towers in Malaysia), a ski-through on a slope in Sweden, and in a structure in Shrewsbury, England that dates back to the 13th century.

No longer content to dominate the strips that surround many college campuses, fast-food restaurants have moved onto many of those campuses. The first campus fast-food restaurant opened at the University of Cincinnati in 1973. Today, college cafeterias often look like shopping-mall food courts (and it's no wonder, given that campus food service is a $9.5 billion-a-year business[66]). In conjunction with a variety of "branded partners" (for example, Pizza Hut and Subway), Marriott now supplies food to many colleges and universities.[67] The apparent approval of college administrations puts fast-food restaurants in a position to further influence the younger generation.

We no longer need to leave many highways to obtain fast food quickly and easily. Fast food is now available at many, and in some cases all, convenient rest stops along the road. After "refueling," we can proceed with our trip, which is likely to end in another community that has about the same density and mix of fast-food restaurants as the locale we left behind. Fast food is also increasingly available in hotels,[68] railway stations, and airports.

In other sectors of society, the influence of fast-food restaurants has been subtler but no less profound. Food produced by McDonald's and other fast-food restaurants has begun to appear in high schools and trade schools; over 20% of school cafeterias offer popular brand-name fast foods such as Pizza Hut or Taco Bell at least once a week.[69] Said the director of nutrition for the American School Food Service Association, "Kids today live in a world where fast food has become a way of life. For us to get kids to eat, period, we have to provide some familiar items."[70] Few lower-grade schools as yet have in-house fast-food restaurants. However, many have had to alter school cafeteria menus and procedures to make fast food readily available.[71] Apples, yogurt, and milk may go straight into the trash can, but hamburgers, fries, and shakes are devoured. The attempt to hook school-age children on fast food reached something of a peak in Illinois, where McDonald's operated a program called, "A for Cheeseburger." Students who received As on their report cards received a free cheeseburger, thereby linking success in school with rewards from McDonald's.[72]

The military has also been pressed to offer fast food on both bases and ships. Despite the criticisms by physicians and nutritionists, fast-food outlets increasingly turn up inside hospitals. Although no homes yet have a McDonald's of their own, meals at home often resemble those available in fast-food restaurants. Frozen, microwavable, and prepared foods, which bear a striking resemblance to meals available at fast-food restaurants, often find their way to the dinner table. There are even cookbooks—for example, *Secret Fast Food Recipes: The Fast Food Cookbook*—that allow one to prepare "genuine" fast food at home.[73] Then there is also home delivery of fast foods, especially pizza, as revolutionized by Domino's.

Another type of expansion involves what could be termed "vertical McDonaldization."[74] That is, the demands of the fast-food industry, as is well documented in Eric Schlosser's *Fast Food Nation,* have forced industries that service it to McDonaldize in order to satisfy its insatiable demands. Thus, potato growing and processing, cattle ranching, chicken raising, and meat slaughtering and processing have all had to McDonaldize their operations, and this has led to dramatic increases in production. However, that growth has not come without costs. Meat and poultry are more likely to be disease-ridden, small (often non-McDonaldized) producers and ranchers have been driven out of business, and millions of people have been forced to work in low-paying, demeaning, demanding, and sometimes outright dangerous jobs. For example, in the meatpacking industry, relatively safe, unionized, secure, manageable, and relatively high-paying jobs in firms with once-household names like Swift and Armour have been replaced by unsafe, nonunionized, insecure, unmanageable, and relatively low-paying positions with largely anonymous corporations. While some (largely owners, managers, and stockholders) have profited enormously from vertical McDonaldization, far more have been forced into a marginal economic existence.

McDonald's is such a powerful model that many businesses have acquired nicknames beginning with Mc. Examples include "McDentists" and "McDoctors," meaning drive-in clinics designed to deal quickly and efficiently with minor dental and medical problems;[75] "McChild" care centers, meaning child care centers such as KinderCare; "McStables," designating the nationwide race horse-training operation of Wayne Lucas; and "McPaper," describing the newspaper *USA TODAY*.[76]

McDonald's is not always enamored of this proliferation. Take the case of We Be Sushi, a San Francisco chain with a half dozen outlets. A note appears on the back of the menu explaining why the chain was not named "McSushi":

> The original name was *McSushi*. Our sign was up and we were ready to go. But before we could open our doors we received a very formal letter from the lawyers of, you guessed it, McDonald's. It seems that McDonald's has cornered the market on every McFood name possible from McBagle [sic] to McTaco. They explained that the use of the name McSushi would dilute the image of McDonald's.[77]

So powerful is McDonaldization that the derivatives of McDonald's in turn exert their own influence. For example, the success of *USA TODAY* has led many newspapers across the nation to adopt, for example, shorter stories and colorful weather maps. As one *USA TODAY* editor said, "The same newspaper editors who call us McPaper have been stealing our McNuggets."[78] Even serious journalistic enterprises such as the *New York Times* and *Washington Post* have undergone changes (for example, the use of color) as a result of the success of *USA TODAY*. The influence of *USA TODAY* is blatantly manifested in *The Boca Raton News*, which has been described as "a sort of smorgasbord of snippets, a newspaper that slices and dices the news into even smaller portions than does *USA TODAY*, spicing it with color graphics and fun facts and cute features like 'Today's Hero' and 'Critter Watch.'"[79] As in *USA TODAY*, stories in *The Boca Raton News* usually start and finish on the same page. Many important details, much of a story's context, and much of what the principals have to say is cut back severely or omitted entirely. With its emphasis on light news and color graphics, the main function of the newspaper seems to be entertainment.

Like virtually every other sector of society, sex has undergone McDonaldization.[80] In the movie *Sleeper*, Woody Allen not only created a futuristic world in which McDonald's was an important and highly visible element, but he also envisioned a society in which people could enter a machine called an "orgasmatron," to experience an orgasm without going through the muss and fuss of sexual intercourse.

Similarly, real-life "dial-a-porn" allows people to have intimate, sexually explicit, even obscene conversations with people they have never met and probably never will meet.[81] There is great specialization here: Dialing numbers such as 555-FOXX will lead to a very different phone message than dialing 555-SEXY. Those who answer the phones mindlessly and repetitively follow "scripts" that have them say such things as, "Sorry, tiger, but your Dream Girl has to go. . . . Call right back and ask for me."[82] Less scripted are phone sex systems (or Internet chat rooms) that permit erotic conversations between total strangers. The advent of the webcam now permits people even to see (though still not touch) the person with whom they are having virtual sex. As Woody Allen anticipated with his orgasmatron, "Participants can experience an orgasm without ever meeting or touching one another."[83] "In a world where convenience is king, disembodied sex has its allure. You don't have to stir from your comfortable home. You pick up the phone, or log onto the computer and, if you're plugged in, a world of unheard of sexual splendor rolls out before your eyes."[84] In New York City, an official called a three-story pornographic center "the McDonald's of sex" because of its "cookie-cutter cleanliness and compliance with the law."[85] These examples suggest that no aspect of people's lives is immune to McDonaldization.

## ◆ THE DIMENSIONS OF MCDONALDIZATION

Why has the McDonald's model proven so irresistible? Eating fast food at McDonald's has certainly become a "sign"[86] that, among other things, one is in tune with the contemporary lifestyle. There is also a kind of magic or enchantment associated with such food and its settings. However, the focus here is the four alluring dimensions that lie at the heart of the success of this model and, more generally, of McDonaldization. In short, McDonald's has succeeded because it offers consumers, workers, and managers efficiency, calculability, predictability, and control.[87]

### Efficiency

One important element of McDonald's success is *efficiency*, or the optimum method for getting from one point to another. For consumers, McDonald's offers the best available way to get from being hungry to being full. In a society where both parents are likely to work or where a single parent is struggling to keep up, efficiently satisfying hunger is very attractive. In a society where people rush from one spot to another, usually by car, the efficiency of a fast-food meal, perhaps even a drive-through meal, often proves impossible to resist.

The fast-food model offers, or at least appears to offer, an efficient method for satisfying many other needs, as well. Woody Allen's orgasmatron offered an efficient method for getting people from quiescence to sexual gratification. Other institutions fashioned on the McDonald's model offer similar efficiency in losing weight, lubricating cars, getting new glasses or contacts, or completing income tax forms.

Like their customers, workers in McDonaldized systems function efficiently following the steps in a predesigned process. They are trained to work this way by managers who watch over them closely to make sure that they do. Organizational rules and regulations also help ensure highly efficient work.

### Calculability

Calculability is an emphasis on the quantitative aspects of products sold (portion size, cost) and services offered (the time it takes to get the product). In McDonaldized systems, quantity has become equivalent to quality; a lot of something, or the quick delivery of it, means it must be good. As two observers of contemporary American culture put it, "As a culture, we tend to believe deeply that in general 'bigger is better.'"[88] Thus, people order the Quarter Pounder, the Big Mac, the large fries. More recent lures are the "double" this (for instance, Burger King's "Double Whopper with Cheese") and the "super-size" that. People can quantify these things and feel that they are getting a lot of food for what appears to be a nominal sum of money (best exemplified by McDonald's current "dollar menu"). This calculation does not take into account an important point, however: The high profit margin of fast-food chains indicates that the owners, not the consumers, get the best deal.

People also tend to calculate how much time it will take to drive to McDonald's, be served the food, eat it, and return home; then, they compare that interval to the time required to prepare food at home. They often conclude, rightly or wrongly, that a trip to the fast-food restaurant will take less time than eating at home. This sort of calculation particularly supports home delivery franchises such as Domino's, as well as other chains that emphasize time saving. A notable example of time saving in another sort of chain is LensCrafters, which promises people, "Glasses fast, glasses in one hour."

Some McDonaldized institutions combine the emphases on time and money. Domino's promises pizza delivery in half an hour, or the pizza is free. Pizza Hut will serve a personal pan pizza in five minutes, or it, too, will be free.

Workers in McDonaldized systems also tend to emphasize the quantitative rather than the qualitative aspects of their work. Since the quality of the work is allowed to vary little, workers focus on things such as how quickly tasks can be accomplished. In a situation analogous to that of the customer, workers are expected to do a lot of work, very quickly, for low pay.

## Predictability

McDonald's also offers *predictability,* the assurance that products and services will be the same over time and in all locales. The Egg McMuffin in New York will be, for all intents and purposes, identical to those in Chicago and Los Angeles. Also, those eaten next week or next year will be identical to those eaten today. Customers take great comfort in knowing that McDonald's offers no surprises. People know that the next Egg McMuffin they eat will not be awful, although it will not be exceptionally delicious, either. The success of the McDonald's model suggests that many people have come to prefer a world in which there are few surprises. "This is strange," notes a British observer, "considering [McDonald's is] the product of a culture which honours individualism above all."[89]

The workers in McDonaldized systems also behave in predictable ways. They follow corporate rules as well as the dictates of their managers. In many cases, what they do, and even what they say, is highly predictable. McDonaldized organizations often have scripts (perhaps the best-known is McDonald's, "Do you want fries with that?") that employees are supposed to memorize and follow whenever the occasion arises.[90] This scripted behavior helps create highly predictable interactions between workers and customers. While customers do not follow scripts, they tend to develop simple recipes for dealing with the employees of McDonaldized systems.[91] As Robin Leidner argues,

> McDonald's pioneered the reutilization of interactive service work and remains an exemplar of extreme standardization. Innovation is not discouraged . . . at least among managers and franchisees. Ironically, though, "the object is to look for new, innovative ways to create an experience that is exactly the same no matter what McDonald's you walk into, no matter where it is in the world."[92]

### Control through Nonhuman Technology

The fourth element in McDonald's success, *control*,[93] is exerted over the people who enter the world of McDonald's. Lines, limited menus, few options, and uncomfortable seats all lead diners to do what management wishes them to do—eat quickly and leave. Furthermore, the drive-through (in some cases, walk-through) window leads diners to leave before they eat. In the Domino's model, customers never enter in the first place.

The people who work in McDonaldized organizations are also controlled to a high degree, usually more blatantly and directly than customers. They are trained to do a limited number of things in precisely the way they are told to do them. The technologies used and the way the organization is set up reinforce this control. Managers and inspectors make sure that workers toe the line.

McDonald's also controls employees by threatening to use, and ultimately using, technology to replace human workers. No matter how well they are programmed and controlled, workers can foul up the system's operation. A slow worker can make the preparation and delivery of a Big Mac inefficient. A worker who refuses to follow the rules might leave the pickles or special sauce off a hamburger, thereby making for unpredictability. And a distracted worker can put too few fries in the box, making an order of large fries seem skimpy. For these and other reasons, McDonald's and other fast-food restaurants have felt compelled to steadily replace human beings with machines. Technology that increases control over workers helps McDonaldized systems assure customers that their products and service will be consistent.

### ◆ THE ADVANTAGES OF MCDONALDIZATION

This discussion of four fundamental characteristics of McDonaldization makes it clear that McDonald's has succeeded so phenomenally for good, solid reasons. Many knowledgeable people such as the economic columnist, Robert Samuelson, strongly support McDonald's business model. Samuelson confesses to "openly worship[ing] McDonald's," and he thinks of it as "the greatest restaurant chain in history."[94] In addition, McDonald's offers many praiseworthy programs that benefit society, such as its Ronald McDonald Houses, which permit parents to stay with children undergoing treatment for serious medical problems; job-training programs for teenagers; programs to help keep its employees in school;

efforts to hire and train the handicapped; the McMasters program, aimed at hiring senior citizens; an enviable record of hiring and promoting minorities; and a social responsibility program with social goals improving the environment and animal welfare.[95]

The process of McDonaldization also moved ahead dramatically undoubtedly because it has led to positive changes.[96] Here are a few specific examples:

- A wider range of goods and services is available to a much larger portion of the population than ever before.
- Availability of goods and services depends far less than before on time or geographic location; people can do things, such as obtain money at the grocery store or a bank balance in the middle of the night, that were impossible before.
- People are able to get what they want or need almost instantaneously and get it far more conveniently.
- Goods and services are of a far more uniform quality; at least some people even get better quality goods and services than before McDonaldization.
- Far more economical alternatives to high-priced, customized goods and services are widely available; therefore, people can afford things they could not previously afford.
- Fast, efficient goods and services are available to a population that is working longer hours and has fewer hours to spare.
- In a rapidly changing, unfamiliar, and seemingly hostile world, the comparatively stable, familiar, and safe environment of a McDonaldized system offers comfort.
- Because of quantification, consumers can more easily compare competing products.
- Certain products (for example, diet programs) are safer in a carefully regulated and controlled system.
- People are more likely to be treated similarly, no matter what their race, gender, or social class.
- Organizational and technological innovations are more quickly and easily diffused through networks of identical operators.
- The most popular products of one culture are more easily diffused to others.

## ♦ A CRITIQUE OF MCDONALDIZATION: THE IRRATIONALITY OF RATIONALITY

Although McDonaldization offers powerful advantages, it has a downside. Efficiency, predictability, calculability, and control through nonhuman technology can be thought of as the basic components of a rational system.[97]

However, rational systems inevitably spawn irrationalities. Another way of saying this is that rational systems serve to deny human reason; rational systems are often unreasonable. The downside of McDonaldization will be dealt with most systematically under the heading of the irrationality of rationality; in fact, paradoxically, the irrationality of rationality can be thought of as the fifth dimension of McDonaldization.

For example, McDonaldization has produced a wide array of adverse effects on the environment. One is a side effect of the need to grow uniform potatoes from which to create predictable french fries. The huge farms of the Pacific Northwest that now produce such potatoes rely on the extensive use of chemicals. In addition, the need to produce a perfect fry means that much of the potato is wasted, with the remnants either fed to cattle or used for fertilizer. The underground water supply in the area is now showing high levels of nitrates, which may be traceable to the fertilizer and animal wastes.[98] Many other ecological problems are associated with the McDonaldization of the fast-food industry: the forests felled to produce paper wrappings, the damage caused by packaging materials, the enormous amount of food needed to produce feed cattle, and so on.

Another unreasonable effect is that fast-food restaurants are often dehumanizing settings in which to eat or work. Customers lining up for a burger or waiting in the drive-through line and workers preparing the food often feel as though they are part of an assembly line. Hardly amenable to eating, assembly lines have been shown to be inhuman settings in which to work.

Such criticisms can be extended to all facets of the McDonaldizing world. For example, at the opening of Euro Disney, a French politician said that it will "bombard France with uprooted creations that are to culture what fast food is to gastronomy."[99]

As you have seen, McDonaldization offers many advantages. However, this book will focus on the great costs and enormous risks of McDonaldization. McDonald's and other purveyors of the fast-food model spend billions of dollars each year outlining the benefits of their system. However, critics of the system have few outlets for their ideas. For example, no one is offering commercials between Saturday-morning cartoons warning children of the dangers associated with fast-food restaurants.

Nonetheless, a legitimate question may be raised about this critique of McDonaldization: Is it animated by a romanticization of the past and an impossible desire to return to a world that no longer exists? Some critics do base their critiques on nostalgia for a time when life was slower and offered more surprises, when people were freer, and when one was more likely to deal with a human being than a robot or a computer.[100] Although they have a point, these critics have undoubtedly exaggerated the positive aspects of a world without McDonald's, and they have certainly tended to forget the liabilities associated with earlier eras. As an example of the latter, take the following anecdote about a visit to a pizzeria in Havana, Cuba, which in many respects is decades behind the United States:

> The pizza's not much to rave about—they scrimp on tomato sauce, and the dough is mushy.
>
> It was about 7:30 P.M., and as usual the place was standing-room-only, with people two deep jostling for a stool to come open and a waiting line spilling out onto the sidewalk.
>
> The menu is similarly Spartan. . . . To drink, there is tap water. That's it— no toppings, no soda, no beer, no coffee, no salt, no pepper. And no special orders.
>
> A very few people are eating. Most are waiting. . . . Fingers are drumming, flies are buzzing, the clock is ticking. The waiter wears a watch around his belt loop, but he hardly needs it; time is evidently not his chief concern. After a while, tempers begin to fray.
>
> But right now, it's 8:45 P.M. at the pizzeria, I've been waiting an hour and a quarter for two small pies.[101]

Few would prefer such a restaurant to the fast, friendly, diverse offerings of, say, Pizza Hut. More important, however, critics who revere the past do not seem to realize that we are not returning to such a world. In fact, fast-food restaurants have begun to appear even in Havana.[102] The increase in the number of people crowding the planet, the acceleration of technological change, the increasing pace of life—all this and more make it impossible to go back to the world, if it ever existed, of home-cooked meals, traditional restaurant dinners, high-quality foods, meals loaded with surprises, and restaurants run by chefs free to express their creativity.

It is more valid to critique McDonaldization from the perspective of the future.[103] Unfettered by the constraints of McDonaldized systems, but using the technological advances made possible by them, people would have the potential to be far more thoughtful, skillful, creative, and well-rounded than they are now. In short, if the world were less McDonaldized, people would be better able to live up to their human potential.

We must look at McDonaldization as both "enabling" and "constraining."[104] McDonaldized systems enable us to do many things that we were not able to do in the past. However, these systems also keep us from doing things we otherwise would do. McDonaldization is a "double-edged" phenomenon. We must not lose sight of that fact, even though this book will focus on the constraints associated with McDonaldization—its "dark side."

## ◆ WHAT ISN'T MCDONALDIZED?

This chapter should give you a sense not only of the advantages and disadvantages of McDonaldization but also of the range of phenomena discussed throughout this book. In fact, such a wide range of phenomena can be linked to McDonaldization that you may be led to wonder what isn't McDonaldized. Is McDonaldization the equivalent of modernity? Is everything contemporary McDonaldized?

Although much of the world has been McDonaldized, at least three aspects of contemporary society have largely escaped the process:

- ◆ Those aspects traceable to an earlier, "premodern" age. A good example is the mom-and-pop grocery store.
- ◆ New businesses that have sprung up or expanded, at least in part, as a reaction against McDonaldization. For instance, people fed up with McDonaldized motel rooms in Holiday Inns or Motel 6s can instead stay in a bed-and-breakfast, which offers a room in a private home with personalized attention and a homemade breakfast from the proprietor.
- ◆ Those aspects suggesting a move toward a new, "postmodern" age. For example, in a postmodern society, "modern" high-rise housing projects would make way for smaller, more livable communities.

Thus, although McDonaldization is ubiquitous, there is more to the contemporary world than McDonaldization. It is a very important social process, but it is far from the only process transforming contemporary society.

Furthermore, McDonaldization is not an all-or-nothing process. There are degrees of McDonaldization. Fast-food restaurants, for example, have been heavily McDonaldized, universities moderately McDonaldized, and mom-and-pop grocers only slightly McDonaldized. It is difficult to think of social phenomena that have escaped McDonaldization totally, but some local enterprise in Fiji may yet be untouched by this process.

# ♦ MCDONALD'S TROUBLES: IMPLICATIONS FOR MCDONALDIZATION

McDonald's has been much in the news in the early 21st century, and most of the time, the news has been bad (at least for McDonald's)—bombings (some involving fatalities) and protests at restaurants overseas, lawsuits claiming that its food made people obese and that it mislabeled some food as vegetarian, declining stock prices, and its first-ever quarterly loss. McDonald's has responded by withdrawing from several nations, settling lawsuits, closing restaurants, reducing staff, cutting planned expansions, replacing top officials, and remodeling restaurants.

It is hard to predict whether the current situation is merely a short-term downturn to be followed by renewed expansion or the beginning of the end of McDonald's (after all, even the Roman Empire, to say nothing of A&P and Woolworth's, among many others, eventually declined and disappeared). For the sake of discussion, let's take the worst-case scenario—McDonald's imminently turning off the griddles in the last of its restaurants.

This would clearly be a disastrous event as far as stockholders, franchisees, employees, and devotees of Big Macs and Chicken McNuggets are concerned, but what of its broader implications for the McDonaldization of society? The hypothetical demise of McDonald's would spell the end of the model for this process, but it would be of *no consequence* to the process itself. We might need to find a new model and label—"Starbuckization" suggests itself at the moment because of Starbucks' great current success and its dramatic expansion around the globe—but whatever we call it, the process itself will not only continue but grow more powerful. Can we really envision an alternative future of increasing *in*efficiency, *un*predictability, *in*calculability, and *less* reliance on new technology?

In the restaurant industry, the decline and eventual disappearance of McDonald's would simply mean greater possibilities for its competitors (Subway, Wendy's) and open the way for more innovative chains (In-N-Out Burger). However, which fast-food chains dominate would be of little consequence to the process of McDonaldization since *all of them* are highly McDonaldized and all are based on the model pioneered by McDonald's. What would be of consequence would be a major revival of old-fashioned, non-McDonaldized alternatives like cafes, "greasy spoons," diners, cafeterias, and the like.[105] However, these are not likely to undergo significant expansion unless some organization finds a way to successfully McDonaldize them. And if they do, it would simply be the McDonaldization of yet another domain.

What is certainly *not* going to happen is a return to the pre-McDonald's era dominated by the kinds of alternatives mentioned above. Can we really envision the approximately 13,000 sites currently occupied by McDonald's restaurants in the United States being filled by a like number of independently owned and operated cafes and diners? The problem of finding skilled short-order cooks to staff them pales in comparison to the difficulty in finding people who will frequent them. It's been nearly fifty years since the franchise revolutionized the fast-food industry with the opening of the first of the McDonald's chain. The vast majority of Americans have known little other than the McDonaldized world of fast food, and for those born before 1955, the alternatives are increasingly dim memories. Thus, McDonaldized systems for the delivery of fast food (e.g., drive-through lanes, home-delivered pizzas), and the McDonaldized food itself (Whoppers, Taco Bell's watered-down version of the taco), have become the standards for many people. A hamburger made on the grill at a diner or a taco from an authentic taco stand are likely to be judged inferior to the more McDonaldized versions. Furthermore, those who are accustomed to the enormous efficiency of the fast-food restaurant are unlikely to put up with the relative inefficiencies of diners or taco stands. Those who have grown used to great predictability are not likely to be comfortable with food served in wildly different quantities and shapes. The greater human involvement in preparing and serving food in non-McDonaldized alternatives is likely to be off-putting to most consumers who have grown acclimated to the dehumanization associated with the nonhuman technologies and scripted counter people found throughout today's fast-food industry. The key point is that McDonald's current difficulties do not auger a return to earlier non-McDonaldized alternatives or even to the widespread creation (if one could even envision such a thing) of some new non-McDonaldized form.

McDonald's is doing better outside the United States, and it is there that we are likely to see a continued expansion of it, and other American fast-food chains, for the foreseeable future (by all accounts, the American market for fast-food restaurants is saturated, and this is a big source of McDonald's problems). More important, as pointed out earlier, many other nations have witnessed the emergence of their own fast-food chains modeled, naturally, after McDonald's. Not only are they expanding within their own borders, but they are also increasingly interested in global expansion (Britain's Pizza Express is expanding into Eastern European countries as San Marzano restaurants), even into the American market. Interesting recent examples include the opening in Manhattan of a number of Pret A Manger (the British chain that, as we have seen, is partly owned by McDonald's) shops offering higher-quality, prewrapped sandwiches and Pollo Capero (from Guatemala) fried-chicken restaurants in Los Angeles and Houston (with plans for big expansion in the United States). In fact, the center of McDonaldization, as was previously the case with many forms of factory production, is increasingly shifting outside the United States. Whether it occurs under the name of Mos Burger (Japan) or Nirula's (India), it is still McDonaldization.

If the principles have proven successful and have proliferated so widely, why is McDonald's in trouble? There are obviously a number of reasons, including many bungled opportunities and initiatives such as efforts to be more attractive to adults, to create new menu items, and to restructure restaurants as well as the chain as a whole. While McDonald's could have done better, the fact is that in the end it has been undercut by its own success. Many competitors have adopted its principles and entered the niche created by McDonald's for fast food. Like many other innovators, McDonald's now finds itself with many rivals who learned not only from McDonald's successes but also from its failures. (One could say that these competitors are "eating McDonald's lunch.") McDonald's, too, may now be better able to overcome its problems and learn from the hot new companies in the fast-food industry. However, whether or not it does, fast-food restaurants and, more generally, the process of McDonaldization are with us for the foreseeable future.

## ♦ A LOOK AHEAD

Because this book is a work in the social sciences, it cannot merely assert that McDonaldization is spreading throughout society; it must present evidence for that assertion. Thus, after a discussion of the precursors to McDonaldization in Chapter 2, Chapters 3 through 6 provide evidence in the context of a discussion of the four basic dimensions of McDonaldization outlined in this chapter: efficiency, calculability, predictability, and control. Numerous examples in each chapter show the degree to which McDonaldization has penetrated society and the accelerating rate of that penetration.

The remainder of the book is more analytical. In Chapter 7, the fifth and paradoxical element of McDonaldization—the irrationality of rationality—is explored. Although much of the book criticizes McDonaldization, this chapter presents the critique most clearly and directly, discussing a variety of irrationalities, the most important of which is dehumanization. Chapter 8 discusses the relationship between McDonaldization and possibly the most important social change of our times—globalization. This is followed by a discussion, in Chapter 9, of the place of McDonaldization in other aspects of our changing world, whether there are any limits to the process, its future prospects, and even the possibility of "de-McDonaldization." In the concluding chapter (10), individuals and groups bothered, if not enraged, by McDonaldization are offered ways of dealing with an increasingly McDonaldized world.

# 2

# McDonaldization
# and Its Precursors

◆

## From the Iron Cage to the Fast-Food Factory

McDonaldization did not emerge in a vacuum; it was preceded by a series of social and economic developments that not only anticipated it but also gave it many of the basic characteristics touched on in Chapter 1.[1] In this chapter, I will look briefly at a few of these developments. First, I will examine the notion of bureaucracy and Max Weber's theories about it and the larger process of rationalization. Next, I will offer a discussion of the Nazi Holocaust, a method of mass killing that can be viewed as the logical extreme of Weber's fears about rationalization and bureaucratization. Then, I will look at several intertwined socioeconomic developments that were precursors of McDonaldization: scientific management as it was invented at the turn of the century by F. W. Taylor, Henry Ford's assembly line, the mass-produced suburban houses of Levittown, the shopping mall, and Ray Kroc's creation of the McDonald's chain. These are not only of historical interest; most continue to be important to this day.

## ◆ BUREAUCRATIZATION:
## MAKING LIFE MORE RATIONAL

A *bureaucracy* is a large-scale organization composed of a hierarchy of offices. In these offices, people have certain responsibilities and must act in accord with rules, written regulations, and means of compulsion exercised by those who occupy higher-level positions.

The bureaucracy is largely a creation of the modern Western world. Although earlier societies had organizational structures, they were not nearly as effective as the bureaucracy. For example, in traditional societies, officials performed their tasks because of a personal loyalty to their leader. These officials were subject to personal whim rather than impersonal rules. Their offices lacked clearly defined spheres of competence, there was no clear hierarchy of positions, and officials did not have to obtain technical training to gain a position.

Ultimately, the bureaucracy differs from earlier methods of organizing work because of its formal structure, which, among other things, allows for greater efficiency. Institutionalized rules and regulations lead, even force, those employed in the bureaucracy to choose the best means to arrive at their ends. A given task is broken down into components, with each office responsible for a distinct portion of the larger task. Incumbents of each office handle their part of the task, usually following preset rules and regulations, and often in a predetermined sequence. When each of the incumbents has, in order, handled the required part, the task is completed. In handling the task in this way, the bureaucracy has used what its past history has shown to be the optimum means to the desired end.

### Weber's Theory of Rationality

The roots of modern thinking on bureaucracy lie in the work of the turn-of-the-century German sociologist Max Weber.[2] His ideas on bureaucracy are embedded in his broader theory of the *rationalization* process. In the latter, Weber described how the modern Western world managed to become increasingly rational—that is, dominated by efficiency, predictability, calculability, and nonhuman technologies that control people. He also examined why the rest of the world largely failed to rationalize.

As you can see, McDonaldization is an amplification and extension of Weber's theory of rationalization. For Weber, the model of rationalization was the bureaucracy; for me, the fast-food restaurant is the paradigm of McDonaldization.[3]

Weber demonstrated in his research that the modern Western world had produced a distinctive kind of rationality. Various types of rationality had existed in all societies at one time or another, but none had produced the type that Weber called formal rationality. This is the sort of rationality

I refer to when I discuss McDonaldization or the rationalization process in general.

What is formal rationality? According to Weber, *formal rationality* means that the search by people for the optimum means to a given end is shaped by rules, regulations, and larger social structures. Individuals are not left to their own devices in searching for the best means of attaining a given objective. Weber identified this type of rationality as a major development in the history of the world: Previously, people had been left to discover such mechanisms on their own or with vague and general guidance from larger value systems (religion, for example).[4] After the development of formal rationality, they could use institutionalized rules that help them decide—or even dictate to them—what to do. An important aspect of formal rationality, then, is that it allows individuals little choice of means to ends. In a formally rational system, virtually everyone can (or must) make the same, optimal choice.

Weber praised the bureaucracy, his paradigm of formal rationality, for its many advantages over other mechanisms that help people discover and implement optimum means to ends. The most important advantages are the four basic dimensions of rationalization (and of McDonaldization).

First, Weber viewed the bureaucracy as the most efficient structure for handling large numbers of tasks requiring a great deal of paperwork. As an example, Weber might have used the Internal Revenue Service, for no other structure could handle millions of tax returns so well.

Second, bureaucracies emphasize the quantification of as many things as possible. Reducing performance to a series of quantifiable tasks helps people gauge success. For example, an IRS agent is expected to process a certain number of tax returns each day. Handling less than the required number of cases is unsatisfactory performance; handling more is excellence.

The quantitative approach presents a problem, however: little or no concern for the actual quality of work. Employees are expected to finish a task with little attention paid to how well it is handled. For instance, IRS agents who receive positive evaluations from their superiors for managing large numbers of cases may actually handle the cases poorly, costing the government thousands or even millions of dollars in uncollected revenue. Or the agents may handle cases so aggressively that taxpayers become angered.

Third, because of their well-entrenched rules and regulations, bureaucracies also operate in a highly predictable manner. Incumbents of a given office know with great assurance how the incumbents of other offices will behave. They know what they will be provided with and when they will receive it. Outsiders who receive the services that bureaucracies dispense know with a high degree of confidence what they will receive and when they will receive it. Again, to use an example Weber might have used, the millions of recipients of checks from the Social Security Administration know precisely when they will receive their checks and exactly how much money they will receive.

Finally, bureaucracies emphasize control over people through the replacement of human judgment with the dictates of rules, regulations, and structures. Employees are controlled by the division of labor, which allocates to each office a limited number of well-defined tasks. Incumbents must do those tasks, and no others, in the manner prescribed by the organization. They may not, in most cases, devise idiosyncratic ways of doing those tasks. Furthermore, by making few, if any, judgments, people begin to resemble human robots or computers. Having reduced people to this status, leaders of bureaucracies can think about actually replacing human beings with machines. This replacement has already occurred to some extent: In many settings, computers have taken over bureaucratic tasks once performed by humans. Similarly, the bureaucracy's clients are also controlled. They may receive only certain services and not others from the organization. For example, the Internal Revenue Service can offer people advice on their tax returns but not on their marriages. People may also receive appropriate services in certain ways and not others. For example, people can receive welfare payments by check, not in cash.

### Irrationality and the "Iron Cage"

Despite the advantages it offers, bureaucracy suffers from the *irrationality of rationality*. Like a fast-food restaurant, a bureaucracy can be a dehumanizing place in which to work and by which to be serviced. Ronald Takaki characterizes rationalized settings as places in which the "self was placed in confinement, its emotions controlled, and its spirit subdued."[5] In other words, they are settings in which people cannot always behave as human beings—where people are dehumanized.

In addition to dehumanization, bureaucracies have other irrationalities. Instead of remaining efficient, bureaucracies can become increasingly inefficient because of tangles of red tape and other pathologies. The emphasis on quantification often leads to large amounts of poor-quality work. Bureaucracies often become unpredictable as employees grow unclear about what they are supposed to do and clients do not get the services they expect. Because of these and other inadequacies, bureaucracies begin to lose control over those who work within and are served by them. Anger at the nonhuman technologies that replace them often leads employees to undercut or sabotage the operation of these technologies. All in all, what were designed as highly rational operations often end up quite irrational.

Although Weber was concerned about the irrationalities of formally rationalized systems, he was even more animated by what he called the "iron cage" of rationality. In Weber's view, bureaucracies are cages in the sense that people are trapped in them, their basic humanity denied. Weber feared most that bureaucracies would grow more and more rational and that rational principles would come to dominate an accelerating number of sectors of society. He anticipated a society of people locked into a series of rational structures, who could move only from one rational system to another—from rationalized educational institutions to rationalized workplaces, from rationalized recreational settings to rationalized homes. Society would eventually become nothing more than a seamless web of rationalized structures; there would be no escape.

A good example of what Weber feared is found in the contemporary rationalization of recreational activities. Recreation can be thought of as a way to escape the rationalization of daily routines. However, over the years, these escape routes have themselves become rationalized, embodying the same principles as bureaucracies and fast-food restaurants. Among the many examples of the rationalization of recreation[6] are Club Med,[7] chains of campgrounds, and package tours. Take, for example, a thirty-day tour of Europe. Buses hurtle through only the major cities in Europe, allowing tourists to glimpse the maximum number of sites in the time allowed. At particularly interesting or important sights, the bus may slow down or even stop to permit some picture taking. At the most important locales, a brief stopover is planned so visitors can hurry through the site, take a few pictures, buy a souvenir, then hop back on the bus to head to the next attraction. With the rationalization of even their recreational activities, people do live to a large extent in the iron cage of rationality.

## ◆ THE HOLOCAUST: MASS-PRODUCED DEATH

Weber wrote about the iron cage of rationalization and bureaucratization in the early 1900s. Zygmunt Bauman argues that Weber's worst fears about these processes were realized in the Nazi Holocaust, which began within a few decades of his death in 1920.

Bauman contends that "the Holocaust may serve as a paradigm of modern bureaucratic rationality."[8] Like the bureaucracy, the Holocaust was a distinctive product of Western civilization. In fact, Bauman argues that the Holocaust was not an aberration but "in keeping with everything we know about our civilization, its guiding spirit, its priorities, its immanent vision of the world."[9] That is, the Holocaust required the rationality of the modern world. It could not have occurred in premodern, less rationalized societies.[10] In fact, the pogroms that had occurred in premodern societies were too inefficient to allow the systematic murder of the millions of people killed in the Holocaust.

The Holocaust can also be seen as an example of modern social engineering in which the goal was a perfectly rational society. To the Nazis, a perfect society was one free of Jews, as well as gypsies, gays, lesbians, and the disabled. Hitler himself defined the Jews as a "virus," a disease that had to be eliminated from Nazi society.

The Holocaust had all the basic characteristics of rationalization (and McDonaldization). It was an effective mechanism for the destruction of massive numbers of human beings. For example, early experiments showed that bullets were inefficient; the Nazis eventually settled on gas as the most efficient means of destroying people. The Nazis also found it efficient to use members of the Jewish community to perform a variety of tasks (for example, choosing the next group of victims) that the Nazis otherwise would have had to perform themselves.[11] Many Jews cooperated because it seemed like the "rational" thing to do (they might be able to save others or themselves) in such a rationalized system.

The Holocaust emphasized things such as how many people could be killed in the shortest time. Bauman offers additional examples:

> For railway managers, the only meaningful articulation of their object is in terms of tonnes per kilometre. They do not deal with humans, sheep, or barbed wire; they only deal with cargo, and this means an entity consisting entirely of measurements and devoid of quality. For most bureaucrats, even such a category as cargo would mean too strict a quality-bound restriction. They deal only with the financial effects of their actions. Their object is money.[12]

There was certainly little attention paid to the quality of the life, or even of the death, of the Jews as they marched inexorably to the gas chambers.

In another quantitative sense, the Holocaust has the dubious distinction of being seen as the most extreme of mass exterminations:

Like everything else done in the modern—rational, planned, scientifically informed, expert, efficiently managed, coordinated—way, the Holocaust left behind and put to shame all its alleged pre-modern equivalents, exposing them as primitive, wasteful and ineffective by comparison. Like everything else in our modern society, the Holocaust was an accomplishment in every respect superior. . . . It towers high above the past genocidal episodes.[13]

The Holocaust involved an effort to make mass murder routine. The whole process had an assembly line quality about it. Trains snaked their way toward the concentration camps, victims lined up and followed a set series of steps. Once the process was complete, camp workers produced stacks of dead bodies for systematic disposal.

Finally, the victims of the Holocaust were managed by a huge nonhuman technology. Some of the components of this technological system are described below:

[Auschwitz] was also a mundane extension of the modern factory system. Rather than producing goods, the raw material was human beings and the end-product was death, so many units per day marked carefully on the manager's production charts. The chimneys, the very symbol of the modern factory system, poured forth acrid smoke produced by burning human flesh. The brilliantly organized railroad grid of modern Europe carried a new kind of raw material to the factories. It did so in the same manner as with other cargo. . . . Engineers designed the crematoria; managers designed the system of bureaucracy that worked with a zest and efficiency.[14]

Needless to say, the Holocaust represented the ultimate in the irrationality of rationality. After all, what could be more dehumanizing than murdering millions of people in such a mechanical way? Furthermore, for the murders to have occurred in the first place, the victims had to be dehumanized—that is, "reduced to a set of quantitative measures."[15] Bauman concludes, "German bureaucratic machinery was put in the service of a goal incomprehensible in its irrationality."[16]

Discussing the Holocaust in the context of McDonaldization may seem extreme to some readers. Clearly, the fast-food restaurant cannot be discussed in the same breath as the Holocaust. There has been no more heinous crime in the history of humankind. Yet I have strong reasons for presenting the Holocaust as a precursor of McDonaldization. First, the Holocaust was organized around the principles of formal rationality, relying extensively on the paradigm of that type of rationality—the bureaucracy. Second, the Holocaust was also linked to the factory system, which you will soon discover was related to other precursors of McDonaldization. Finally, the spread of formal rationality today, through the process of McDonaldization, supports Bauman's view that something like the Holocaust could happen again.

## ◆ SCIENTIFIC MANAGEMENT: FINDING THE ONE BEST WAY

A less dramatic but no less important precursor to McDonaldization was the development of scientific management. In fact, Weber at times mentioned scientific management in his discussion of the rationalization process.

Scientific management was created by Frederick W. Taylor in the late nineteenth and early twentieth centuries. His ideas played a key role in shaping the work world throughout the twentieth century.[17] Taylor developed a series of principles designed to rationalize work and was hired by a number of large organizations (for example, Bethlehem Steel) to implement those ideas, mostly in their factories.

Taylor was animated by the belief that the United States suffered from "inefficiency in almost all our daily acts" and that there was a need for "greater national efficiency"; his followers came to be known as "efficiency experts." His "time-and-motion" studies were designed to replace what Taylor called the inefficient "rule-of-thumb" methods that dominated work in his day with what he thought of as the "one best way"—that is, the optimum means to the end of doing a job.[18] Taylor outlined a series of steps to be followed in time and motion studies:

1. Find a number of workers, preferably in diverse work settings, who are particularly skillful at the work in question.

2. Make a careful study of the elementary movements (as well as the tools and implements) employed by these people in their work.

3. Time each of these elementary steps carefully (here was one of the ways in which Taylor emphasized calculability) with the aim of discovering the most efficient way of accomplishing each step.

4. Make the work efficient by eliminating inefficient steps, such as "all false movements, slow movements, and useless movements."

5. Finally, after all unnecessary movements have been eliminated, combine the most efficient movements (and tools) to create the "one best way" of doing a job.[19]

Scientific management also placed great emphasis on predictability. Clearly, in delineating the one best way to do a job, Taylor sought an approach that each and every worker could use. Taylor also believed that allowing workers to choose their own tools and methods of doing a job led to low productivity and poor quality. Instead, he sought the complete standardization of tools and work processes. In fact, he felt that poor standards were better than no standards at all because they caused at least some improvement in productivity and quality. Of course, Taylor favored the clear and detailed standards that made sure all workers did a given type of job in exactly the same way and would therefore consistently produce high-quality work.

Overall, scientific management produced a nonhuman technology that exerted great control over workers. When workers followed Taylor's methods, employers found that they worked much more efficiently, that everyone performed the same steps (that is, their work exhibited predictability), and that they produced a great deal more while their pay had to be increased only slightly (another instance of emphasizing calculability). Thus, Taylor's methods meant increased profits to those enterprises that adopted them.

Like all rational systems, scientific management had its irrationalities. Above all, it was a dehumanizing system in which people were considered expendable and treated as such. Furthermore, because workers did only one or a few tasks, most of their skills and abilities remained unused. This had disastrous consequences, and by the 1980s, American industry found itself outstripped by Japanese industry, which had found a way not only to be formally rational but also to use the abilities of its workers more fully.[20] In the 1990s, Japanese industry, and the Japanese economy as a whole, went into a tailspin, but the lessons that American industry had learned from Japan during the 1980s helped lead to the robust economy of the late 1990s.

Although one hears little these days of Taylor, efficiency experts, and time-and-motion studies, their impact is strongly felt in a McDonaldized society. For instance, hamburger chains strive to discover and implement the "one best way" to grill hamburgers, cook french fries, prepare shakes, process customers, and the rest. The most efficient ways of handling a variety of tasks have been codified in training manuals and taught to managers who, in turn, teach them to new employees. The design of the fast-food restaurant and its various technologies have been put in place to aid in the attainment of the most efficient means to the end of feeding large numbers of people.[21] Here, again, McDonald's did not invent these ideas but, rather, brought them together with the principles of the bureaucracy and of the assembly line, thus contributing to the creation of McDonaldization.

## ◆ THE ASSEMBLY LINE: TURNING WORKERS INTO ROBOTS

Like modern bureaucracy and scientific management, the assembly line came into existence at the dawn of the twentieth century. Pioneered in the bureaucratized automobile industry, the ideas of scientific management helped shape it. Henry Ford generally receives credit for the invention of the assembly line, although it was mainly a product of Ford engineers.[22]

The automobile assembly line was invented mainly because Ford wanted to save time, energy, and money (that is, to be more efficient). Greater efficiency would lead to lower prices, increased sales, and greater profitability for the Ford Motor Company.

Ford got the idea for the automobile assembly line from the overhead trolley system used at the time by Chicago meatpackers to butcher cattle. As the steer was propelled along on the trolley system, a line of highly specialized butchers performed specific tasks, so that by the end of the line, the steer had been completely butchered. This system was clearly more efficient than having a single meat cutter handle all these tasks.

On the basis of this experience and his knowledge of the automobile business, Ford developed a set of principles for the construction of an automobile assembly line, principles that to this day stand as models of efficiency:

- Workers are not to take any unnecessary steps; work-related movements are reduced to an absolute minimum.
- Parts needed in the assembly process are to travel the least possible distance.
- Mechanical (rather than human) means are to be used to move the car (and parts) from one step in the assembly process to the next. (At first, gravity was used, but later, electrical conveyor belts were employed.)
- Complex sets of movements are eliminated, and the worker does "as nearly as possible only one thing with one movement."[23]

The Japanese adopted American assembly line technology after World War II and then made their own distinctive contributions to heightened efficiency. For example, the Japanese "just-in-time" system replaced the

American "just-in-case" system. Both systems refer to the supply of needed parts to a manufacturing operation. In the American system, parts are stored in the plant until, or in case, they are needed. This system leads to inefficiencies such as the purchase and storage (at great cost) of parts that will not be needed for quite some time. To counter these inefficiencies, the Japanese developed the just-in-time system: Needed parts arrive at the assembly line just as they are to be placed in the car or whatever object is being manufactured. In effect, all the Japanese company's suppliers become part of the assembly line process.

In either system, the assembly line permits the quantification of many elements of the production process and maximizes the number of cars or other goods produced. What each worker on the line does, such as putting a hubcap on each passing car, is highly predictable and leads to identical end products.

The assembly line is also a nonhuman technology that permits maximum control over workers. It is immediately obvious when a worker fails to perform the required tasks. There would, for example, be a missing hubcap as the car moves down the line. The limited time allotted for each job allows little or no room for innovative ways of doing a specific task. Thus, fewer, less-skilled people are able to produce cars. Furthermore, the specialization of each task permits the replacement of human workers with robots. Today, mechanical robots handle more and more assembly line tasks.

As has been well detailed by many observers, the assembly line carries with it much irrationality. For example, it can be a dehumanizing setting in which to work. Human beings, equipped with a wide array of skills and abilities, are asked to perform a limited number of highly simplified tasks over and over. Instead of expressing their human abilities on the job, people are forced to deny their humanity and to act like robots.

Despite its flaws, the assembly line represented a remarkable step forward in the rationalization of production and became widely used throughout manufacturing. Like bureaucracy and even the Holocaust, the automobile assembly line is an excellent illustration of the basic elements of formal rationality.

The assembly line also has had a profound influence on the development of the fast-food restaurant. The most obvious example of this is the conveyor belt used by Burger King to cook its hamburgers. Less obvious is the fact that much of the work in a fast-food restaurant is performed in assembly line fashion, with tasks broken down into their simplest components. For example, "making a hamburger" means grilling the burgers, putting them on the rolls, smearing on the "special sauce," laying on the lettuce and tomato, and wrapping the fully dressed burgers. Even customers face a kind of assembly line, the drive-through window being the most obvious example. As one observer notes, "The basic elements of the factory have obviously been introduced to the fast-food phenomenon . . . [with] the advent of the feeding machine."[24]

In addition to being a precursor, the automobile assembly line laid the groundwork for McDonaldization in another way. Mass production gave many people ready access to affordable automobiles, which in turn led to the immense expansion of the highway system and the tourist industry that grew up alongside it.[25] Restaurants, hotels, campgrounds, gas stations, and the like arose and served as the precursors to many of the franchises that lie at the base of the McDonaldized society.[26]

## ◆ LEVITTOWN: PUTTING UP HOUSES—"BOOM, BOOM, BOOM"

The availability of the automobile helped make possible not only the fast-food restaurant but also suburbia, especially the mass-produced suburban houses pioneered by Levitt & Sons, founded by Abraham Levitt. Between 1947 and 1951, this company built 17,447 homes on former New York potato fields, thereby creating Levittown, Long Island, and an instant community of 75,000 people.[27] The first houses in the planned community of Levittown, Pennsylvania, went on sale in 1958. The Levittowns provided the model for innumerable contemporary suburban developments. With their need for and access to automobiles, suburban dwellers were, and are, a natural constituency for the fast-food restaurant.

Levitt & Sons thought of their building sites as large factories using assembly line technology. William Levitt, one of the sons, explained the system this way:

> What it amounted to was a reversal of the Detroit assembly line. . . . There, the car moved while the workers stayed at their stations. In the case of our houses, it was the workers who moved, doing the same jobs at different locations. To the best of my knowledge, no one had ever done that before.[28]

The workers performed specialized tasks, much like their compatriots on the automobile assembly line. Said Alfred Levitt, another one of the sons, "The same man does the same thing every day, despite the psychologists.

It is boring; it is bad; but the reward of the green stuff seems to alleviate the boredom of the work."[29] Thus, the Levitts rationalized the work of the construction laborer much as Ford had done with the automobile worker, with much the same attitude toward the worker.

The housing site as well as the work was rationalized. In and around the building locale, the Levitts constructed warehouses, woodworking shops, plumbing shops, and a sand, gravel, and cement plant. Thus, instead of buying these services and their resulting products from others and then shipping them to the construction site, the products and services were onsite and controlled by the Levitts. Where possible, the Levitts also used prefabricated products. However, they deemed manufacturing an entirely prefabricated house less efficient than making a partially prefabricated one.

The actual construction of each house followed a series of rigidly defined and rationalized steps. For example, in constructing the wall framework, the workers did no measuring or cutting; each piece had been cut to fit. The siding for a wall consisted of 73 large sheets of Colorbestos, replacing the former requirement of 570 small shingles. All houses were painted under high pressure, using the same two-tone scheme—green on ivory. As a result, "Once the groundwork is down, houses go up boom, boom, boom."[30] The result, of course, was a large number of nearly identical houses produced quickly at low cost.

The emphasis on quantitative factors went beyond the physical construction of the house. For example, to sell the houses, instead of empha-sizing the total cost of the house, real estate agents focused their pitches on the size of the down payment and monthly payments. The agents believed that the kinds of buyers attracted to Levittown were far more interested in such immediate numbers than the apparently more remote issue of the asking price of a house. Advertisements for Levittown houses stressed "the size and value of the house."[31] In other words, Levittown, like its many successors in the march toward increased rationalization, tried to convince consumers that they were getting the most for the least money.

These principles, once used exclusively in low-priced homes, have now been applied to high-priced homes, as well. "McMansions" are increas-ingly often little more than huge and luxuriously appointed factory-made, modular homes.[32]

Many have criticized life in identical houses in highly rationalized communities. One early critique renamed suburbia "Disturbia," describ-ing the suburban home as a "split level trap."[33] However, one can also look positively at suburban rationalization. For example, many residents of Levittown have customized their homes so that they no longer look as homogeneous as before. People now see "the Levitt box disguised as a Tudor Manor, a Swiss chalet, a Pennsylvania Dutch barn."[34] Other observers have found much of merit in Levittown and suburbia. Herbert Gans, for example, concluded his study of a third Levittown built in New Jersey by arguing that "whatever its imperfections, Levittown is a good place to live."[35] Whether or not it is a "good" place to live, Levittown is certainly a rationalized place.

### ◆ SHOPPING CENTERS: MALLING AMERICA

Another component of rationalized society whose development was fueled by the rise of automobiles, and of suburban housing, was the fully enclosed shopping mall.[36] The modern mall had precursors in the Galleria Vittorio Emanuele in Milan, Italy (completed in 1877), and the first planned outdoor shopping center in the United States (built in 1916). The original fully enclosed shopping mall, however, was Southdale Center in Edina, Minnesota, which opened in 1956, not long after the opening of Ray Kroc's first McDonald's. Today, tens of thousands of malls in the United States are visited by hundreds of millions of shoppers each month. The United States' largest shopping mall to date, The Mall of America, opened in 1992 down the road from Edina, in Bloomington, Minnesota. It included four department stores, four hundred specialty shops (many of them parts of chains), and an amusement park.[37] This has become a global phenomenon as exemplified by Wuhan Plaza in Hubei Province, China serving an estimated 1 million shoppers a day. The mall complex has about 30 department stores, with a total business floor space of over 2 million square meters. This amounts to 0.38 square meters of shopping space per permanent urban resident, a number well above that of any mall in the West.[38]

Shopping malls and McDonaldized chains complement each other beautifully. The malls provide a predictable, uniform, and profitable venue for such chains. When a new mall is built, the chains line up to gain entry. For their part, most malls would have much unrented space and not be able to exist were it not for the chains. Simultaneous products of the fast-moving automobile age, malls and chains feed off each other, furthering McDonaldization.

Ironically, malls today have become a kind of community center for both young and old. Many elderly people now use malls as places to both exercise and socialize. Teens prowl the malls after school and on weekends, seeking social contact and checking out the latest in fashions and mass entertainment. Because some parents also take their children to malls to "play," malls are offering play rooms (free ones as well as profit-making outlets that charge an entry fee and may offer things like free video games, and free movies).[39] Like many other contributors to the McDonaldization of society, malls strive to engage customers from cradle to grave.

William Kowinski argues that the mall "was the culmination of all the American dreams, both decent and demented; the fulfillment, the model of the postwar paradise."[40] One could give priority to the mall, as Kowinski does, and discuss the "malling of America." However, in my view, the fast-food restaurant is a far more powerful and influential force. Like the mall, however, McDonaldization can be seen as both "decent and demented."

## ◆ MCDONALD'S: CREATING THE "FAST-FOOD FACTORY"

Ray Kroc, the creator of the McDonald's empire, is usually credited with developing its rational principles. However, the basic McDonald's approach was created by two brothers, Mac and Dick McDonald.[41] The McDonald brothers opened their first restaurant in Pasadena, California, in 1937. They based the restaurant on the principles of high speed, large volume, and low price. To avoid chaos, they offered customers a highly circumscribed menu. Instead of personalized service and traditional cooking techniques, the McDonald brothers used assembly line proce- dures for cooking and serving food. In place of trained cooks, the broth- ers' "limited menu allowed them to break down food preparation into simple, repetitive tasks that could be learned quickly even by those step- ping into a commercial kitchen for the first time."[42] They pioneered the use of specialized restaurant workers such as "grill men," "shake men," "fry men," and "dressers" (those who put the "extras" on burgers and who wrapped them). They developed regulations dictating what workers should do and even what they should say. In these and other ways, the McDonald brothers took the lead in the development of the rationalized "fast-food factory."[43]

Kroc invented neither the McDonald's principles nor the idea of a franchise. Franchising is a system in which "one large firm . . . grants or sells the right to distribute its products or use its trade name and processes to a number of smaller firms. . . . franchise holders, although legally independent, must conform to detailed standards of operation designed and enforced by the parent company."[44] The Singer Sewing Machine company pioneered franchising after the Civil War, and automobile manufacturers and soft drink companies were using it by the turn of the twentieth century. By the 1930s, it had found its way into retail businesses such as Western Auto, Rexall Pharmacy, and the IGA food markets.

Furthermore, there had been many efforts to franchise food service before Kroc arrived on the scene in the early 1950s. The first food service franchises, the A&W Root Beer stands, made their debut in 1924. Howard Johnson began franchising ice cream and other food in 1935. The first Dairy Queen opened in 1944; efforts to franchise it nationally led to a chain of about 2,500 outlets by 1948. Other well-known food franchises predated McDonald's. Big Boy started in the late 1930s, and Burger King (then InstaBurger) and Kentucky Fried Chicken began in 1954. Thus, Kroc's first McDonald's, which opened on April 15, 1955, was a relative latecomer to the franchising business in general and the food franchise business in particular. But I am getting a bit ahead of the story.

In 1954, when Ray Kroc first visited it, McDonald's was but a single drive-in hamburger stand in San Bernardino, California (ironically the same city where Taco Bell was founded by Glen Bell[45]). The basic menu, the approach, and even some of the techniques that McDonald's is famous for today had already been created by the McDonald brothers. Although it was a local sensation, the McDonald brothers were content to keep it that way; they were doing very well and had few grand ambitions in spite of a few tentative steps toward franchising. With plenty of ambition for all of them, Kroc became their franchising agent and went on to build the McDonald's empire of franchises, thereby giving impetus to McDonaldization. At first, Kroc worked in partnership with the McDonald brothers, but after he bought them out in 1961 for $2.7 million, he was free to build the business as he wished.

Kroc took the specific products and techniques of the McDonald brothers and combined them with the principles of other franchises (food service and others), bureaucracies, scientific management, and the assembly line. Kroc's genius was in bringing all these well-known ideas and techniques to bear on the fast-food business and adding his ambition to turn it, through franchising, into a national, then international, business. *McDonald's and McDonaldization, then, do not represent something new but, rather, the culmination of a series of rationalization processes that had been occurring throughout the twentieth century.*

Kroc's major innovation lay in the way he franchised McDonald's. For one thing, he did not permit regional franchises in which a single franchisee received control over all the outlets to be opened in a given area. Other franchisers had foundered because regional franchisees had grown too powerful and subverted the basic principles of the company. Kroc maximized central control, and thereby uniformity throughout the system, by granting franchises one at a time and rarely granting more than one franchise to a specific individual. Kroc also gained control over, and profited from, franchisee's property.[46] Another of Kroc's innovations was to set the fee for a franchise at a rock-bottom $950. Other franchisers had set very high initial fees and made most of their money from them. As a result, they tended to lose interest in the continued viability of the franchisees. At McDonald's, profits did not come from high initial fees but from the 1.9% of store sales that headquarters demanded of its franchisees. Thus, the success of Kroc and his organization depended on the prosperity of the franchisees. This mutual interest was Kroc's greatest contribution to the franchise business and a key factor in the success of McDonald's and its franchisees, many of whom became millionaires in their own right.

Although Kroc imposed and enforced a uniform system, he encouraged the franchisees to come up with innovations that could enhance not only their operations but also those of the system as a whole. Take the case of product innovations. Kroc himself was not a great product innovator. One of his most notorious flops was the Hulaburger, a slice of grilled pineapple between two pieces of cheese wrapped in a toasted bun. Successful creations, such as the fish sandwich (the Filet-o-Fish), the Egg McMuffin, McDonald's breakfast meals, and even the Big Mac came from franchisees. Thus, McDonald's achieved a balance between centralized control and the independence of franchisees.

Kroc spearheaded a series of developments that further rationalized the fast-food business.[47] For one thing, he (unwittingly) served as preacher and cheerleader for the principles of rationalization as he lectured "about uniformity, about a standardized menu, one size portions, same prices, same quality in every store."[48] This uniformity allowed McDonald's to differentiate itself from its competitors, whose food was typically inconsistent. McDonald's also led the field by imposing a limited menu (at first, ten items), creating tough standards for the fat content of hamburgers, converting to frozen hamburgers and french fries, using inspectors to check on uniformity and conformity, and forming in 1961 the first full-time training center in the business (called Hamburger University and offering a "degree" in "hamburgerology"). Today, more than 65,000 managers in McDonald's restaurants have graduated from Hamburger University, now located in a 130,000 square foot, state-of-the-art facility on the McDonald's Home Office Campus in Oak Brook, Illinois, with a faculty of 30 resident professors.

Because of McDonald's international scope, translators and electronic equipment enable professors to teach and communicate in 22 languages at one time. McDonald's also manages ten international training centers, including Hamburger Universities in England, Japan, Germany, and Australia.[49] In 1958, McDonald's published an operations manual that detailed how to run a franchise.[50] This manual laid down many of the principles for operating a fast-food restaurant:

> It told operators *exactly* how to draw milk shakes, grill hamburgers, and fry potatoes. It specified *precise* cooking times for all products and temperature settings for all equipment. It fixed *standard* portions on every food item, down to the *quarter ounce* of onions placed on each hamburger patty and the *thirty-two slices per pound* of cheese. It specified that french fries be cut at *nine thirty-seconds of an inch* thick. And it defined quality *controls* that were unique to food service, including the disposal of meat and potato products that were held more than *ten minutes* in a serving bin.
>
> ... Grill men ... *were instructed* to put hamburgers down on the grill moving from left to right, creating *six rows of six* patties each. And because the first two rows were farthest from the heating element, they were instructed (and still are) to flip the third row first, then the fourth, fifth, and sixth before flipping the first two [italics added].[51]

It is hard to imagine a more rational system.

## ♦ CONCLUSION

McDonald's and McDonaldization did not occur in a historical vacuum; they had important precursors that remain important to this day. The assembly line, scientific management, and bureaucracy provided many of the basic principles on which fast-food restaurant chains were built. Furthermore, these precursors provided the environment the fast-food chains needed to thrive: large numbers of factory workers and bureaucrats driving great distances between work and their suburban dwellings in automobiles that also allowed them to visit shopping malls in their spare time.

The fast-food restaurant has become the model of rationality. Although it has adopted elements of rationality pioneered by its predecessors, it also represents a quantum leap in the process of rationalization. What we have today is sufficiently more extreme than previous forms of rationalization to legitimize the use of a distinct label—McDonaldization—to describe the most contemporary aspects of the rationalization process.

One other point: Before the fast-food restaurant, rationalization mainly applied to work settings and the production process. *What the fast-food restaurant did was to bring rationalization to consumption settings and the consumption process.* It coincided with the beginnings of a major shift in the United States, and much of the rest of the developed world, away from production and in the direction of consumption. Occurring very early in this transition, the founding of McDonald's, and its extraordinary success, made it *the* model for dramatic changes to come in the realm of consumption, many of which pointed in the direction of ever-increasing McDonaldization. With this development, people came to be confronted by progressive rationalization not only in their work settings but also in their leisure activities. That is, they confronted rationalization wherever they turned.

Just as Weber fretted over the emerging iron cage of rationality, I foresee a similar iron cage being created by the increasing ubiquity of the fast-food model. Weber was particularly upset by the irrationality of rationality, a concern that also lies at the heart of this book. As you will see in the following chapters, Weber's theory, adapted to fit the new realities of a McDonaldized world, has great relevance at the dawn of the twenty-first century.

# 3

## Efficiency

◆————————————————————————

### Drive-Throughs and Finger Foods

O f the four dimensions of McDonaldization, efficiency is the one
perhaps most often linked to the seeming increase in the pace of
life. Increasing efficiency is behind just-in-time production, faster
service, streamlined operations, and tight schedules everywhere from the
workplace to Disney World to the home.

Efficiency seems like a good thing. It is clearly advantageous to
consumers, who can obtain what they need more quickly with less
effort. Similarly, efficient workers can perform their tasks more rapidly
and easily. Managers and owners gain because more work gets done,
more customers are served, and greater profits are earned. But as is the
case with rationalization in general, and each of its dimensions,
irrationalities such as surprising inefficiencies and the dehumanization
of workers and customers emerge from the drive for increased efficiency.

*Efficiency* means choosing the optimum means to a given end. However,
the truly optimum means to an end is rarely found. People and organizations rarely maximize because they are hampered by things such as the
constraints of history, financial circumstances, and organizational realities
and by the limitations of human nature.[1] Nevertheless, organizations
continue to strive for maximization in the hopes that they will at least
be able to progressively increase their efficiency.

In a McDonaldized society, people rarely search for the best means
to an end on their own. Rather, they rely on previously discovered and

institutionalized means. Thus, when people start a new job, they are not expected to figure out for themselves how to do the work most efficiently. Instead, they undergo training designed to teach them what has been discovered over time to be the most efficient way of doing the work. Once on the job, people may discover little tricks that help them to perform the task more efficiently, and these days, they are encouraged to pass this information on to management so that all workers performing that task can perform a bit more efficiently. In this way, over time, efficiency (and productivity) gradually increases. In fact, much of the economic boom in the 1990s was attributed to dramatic increases in efficiency and productivity that permitted growth with little inflation. While that boom went bust in the early 21st century, the basis for a resurgence in the economy exists, at least in part, in those gains in efficiency and productivity.

Although the fast-food restaurant certainly did not create the yearning for efficiency, it has helped turn efficiency into an increasingly universal reality. Many sectors of society have had to change to operate in the efficient manner demanded by those accustomed to life in the drive-through lane of the fast-food restaurant. While many manifestations of efficiency can be traced directly to the influence of the fast-food restaurant; many more of them predate and helped shape the fast-food restaurant. Nonetheless, they all play a part in the preoccupation with efficiency fueled by McDonaldization.

In diverse social settings, increasing efficiency has been largely a matter of streamlining various processes, simplifying products, and having customers do work formerly done by paid employees.

## ♦ STREAMLINING THE PROCESS

Above all else, Ray Kroc was impressed by the efficiency of the McDonald brothers' operation, as well as the enormous profit potential of such a system applied at a large number of restaurant sites. Here is how Kroc described his initial reactions to the McDonald's system:

> I was fascinated by the simplicity and effectiveness of the system . . . each step in producing the limited menu was stripped down to its essence and accomplished with a minimum of effort. They sold hamburgers and cheeseburgers only. The burgers were . . . all fried the same way.[2]

But Kroc's obsession with streamlined processes predated his discovery of McDonald's. When he was selling blenders to restaurants, he was disturbed by restaurants' lack of efficiency:

> There was inefficiency, waste, and temperamental cooks, sloppy service and food whose [sic] quality was never consistent. What was needed was a simple product that moved from start to completion in a *streamlined* path [italics added].[3]

Kroc toyed with other alternatives for streamlining the restaurant meal before settling on the McDonald's hamburger as a model of efficiency:

> He had contemplated hot dogs, then rejected the idea. There were too many kinds of hot dogs—hot dogs with cereal and flour, the all-meat hot dog which is all kinds of meat, the all-beef hot dog, the kosher hot dog. And along with the different varieties, there were all sorts of different ways of cooking hot dogs. They could be boiled, broiled, rotisseried, charcoaled, and on and on. Hamburgers, on the other hand, were simplicity itself. The condiments were added to the hamburger, not built in. And there was only one way to prepare the hamburger—to grill it.[4]

Kroc and his associates experimented with each component of the hamburger to increase the efficiency of producing and serving it. For example, they started with partially sliced buns that arrived in cardboard boxes. But the griddle workers had to spend time opening the boxes, separating the buns, slicing them in half, and discarding the leftover paper and cardboard. Eventually, McDonald's found that buns sliced completely in half, separated, and shipped in reusable boxes could be used more efficiently. The meat patty received similar attention. For example, the paper between the patties had to have just the right amount of wax so that the patties would readily slide off the paper and onto the grill. Kroc's goal in these innovations was greater efficiency:

> The purpose of all these refinements, and we never lost sight of it, was to make our griddle man's job easier to do quickly and well. And the other considerations of cost cutting, inventory control, and so forth were important to be sure, but they were secondary to the critical detail of what happened there at the smoking griddle. This was the vital passage of our *assembly-line,* and the product had to flow through it smoothly or the whole plant would falter [italics added].[5]

## The Fast-Food Industry: Speeding the Way from Secretion to Excretion

Today, all fast-food restaurants prepare their menu items on a kind of assembly line involving a number of people in specialized operations (for example, the burger "dresser"). The ultimate application of the assembly line to the fast-food process is, as was pointed out in the preceding chapter, Burger King's conveyor belt: A raw, frozen hamburger placed on one end moves slowly via the conveyor under a flame and emerges in ninety-four seconds on the other end fully cooked. Then, there is Domino's system:

> Lonnie Lane starts slapping and saucing: kneading and tossing the dough and then spooning the proper measure of sauce on to it. . . .
>
> He slides the tray down . . . and Victor Luna starts reaching for the toppings. A dozen bins are arrayed in front of him: cheese, pepperoni, green pepper. . . . Luna sprinkles stuff over the tray by the handful. . . .
>
> He eases the tray onto a conveyor belt that takes it through a 12-foot oven . . . in six minutes. . . .
>
> . . . the store manager is dispatching waiting drivers and waiting drivers are folding pizza boxes. . . .
>
> . . . the crew chief and quality controller . . .
>
> . . . slices it with a pizza wheel and slides it into a box that already bears a computer label with the customer's address.[6]

Similar techniques are employed throughout the fast-food industry.

Getting diners into and out of the fast-food restaurant has also been streamlined. McDonald's has done "everything to speed the way from secretion to excretion."[7] Parking lots adjacent to the restaurant offer readily available parking spots. It's a short walk to the counter, and although customers sometimes have to wait in line, they can usually quickly order, obtain, and pay for their food. The highly limited menu makes the diner's choice easy, in contrast to the many choices available in other restaurants. ("Satellite" and "express" locations have even more streamlined menus.) With the food obtained, it is but a few steps to a table and the beginning of the "dining experience." With little inducement to linger, diners generally eat quickly and then gather the leftover paper, Styrofoam, and plastic; discard them in a nearby trash receptacle; and get back in their cars to drive to the next (often McDonaldized) activity.

Not too many years ago, those in charge of fast-food restaurants discovered that the drive-through window made this whole process far more efficient. McDonald's opened its first drive-through in 1975 in Oklahoma City; within four years, almost half its restaurants had one. Instead of requiring diners to undergo the "laborious" and "inefficient" process of parking the car, walking to the counter, waiting in line, ordering, paying, carrying the food to the table, eating, and disposing of the remnants, the drive-through window offered diners the streamlined option of driving to the window and driving off with the meal. Diners could eat while driving if they wanted to be even more efficient. The drive-through window is also efficient for the fast-food restaurant. As more and more people use the drive-through window, fewer parking spaces, tables, and employees are needed. Furthermore, consumers take their debris with them as they drive away, thereby reducing the need for trash receptacles and employees to empty those receptacles periodically.

Modern technology offers further advances in streamlining. Here is a description of some of the increased efficiency at a Taco Bell in California:

> Inside, diners in a hurry for tacos and burritos can punch up their own orders on a touch-screen computer. Outside, drive-through customers see a video monitor flash back a list of their orders to avoid mistakes. They then can pay using a pneumatic-tube like those many banks employ for drive-up transactions. Their food, and their change, is waiting for them when they pull forward to the pickup window. And if the line of cars grows too long, a Taco Bell worker will wade in with a wireless keyboard to take orders.[8]

## Home Cooking (and Related Phenomena): "I Don't Have Time to Cook"

In the early 1950s, the dawn of the era of the fast-food restaurant, the major alternative to fast food was the home-cooked meal, made mostly from ingredients purchased beforehand at various local stores and early supermarkets. This was clearly a more efficient way of preparing meals than earlier methods, such as hunting game and gathering fruits and vegetables before cooking.

The home cooking of the 1950s was made more efficient by the proliferation of refrigerators and gas and electric stoves. Cookbooks also made a major contribution to efficient home cooking. Instead of inventing a dish every time a meal was prepared, the cook could follow a recipe and thus more efficiently produce the dish.

Soon, the widespread availability of the home freezer led to the expanded production of frozen foods. The most efficient frozen food was (and for many still is) the "TV dinner." Swanson created its first TV dinner, its meal-in-a-box, in 1953 and sold 25 million of them in the first year.[9] People could stock their freezers with an array of such dinners (for example, Chinese, Italian, and Mexican dinners as well a wide variety of "American" cooking) and readily pop them into the oven. The large freezer also permitted other efficiencies, such as making a few trips to the market for enormous purchases rather than making many trips for small ones. People could readily extract from their own freezers, when needed, a wide range of ingredients for a meal. Finally, freezers allowed people to cook large portions that could then be divided up, frozen, and defrosted periodically for dinner.

However, meals from the freezer began to seem comparatively inefficient with the advent of microwavable meals.[10] Microwaves usually cook faster than other ovens, and people can prepare a wider array of foods in them. Perhaps most important, microwave ovens spawned a number of food products (including microwavable soup, pizza, hamburgers, fried chicken, french fries, and popcorn) that permit the efficient preparation of the fare people have learned to love in fast-food restaurants. For example, one of the first microwavable foods produced by Hormel was an array of biscuit-based breakfast sandwiches popularized by McDonald's with its Egg McMuffin.[11] As one executive put it, "Instead of having a breakfast sandwich at McDonald's, you can pick one up from the freezer of your grocery store."[12] In fact, many food companies now employ people who continually scout fast-food restaurants for new ideas. In some ways, "homemade" fast foods seem more efficient than the versions offered by fast-food restaurants. Instead of getting into the car, driving to the restaurant, and returning home, people need only pop their favorite foods into the microwave. On the other side, the efficiency of the microwaved meal suffers because it requires a prior trip to the market.

Supermarkets have long been loaded with other kinds of products that increase efficiency for those who want to "cook" at home. Instead of starting from scratch, the cook can use prepackaged mixes to make "homemade" cakes, pies, pancakes, waffles, and many other foods. No need to endlessly stir hot cereal; simply pour boiling water over the contents of a premeasured packet. No need to cook pudding from scratch or even to use the more efficient instant mixes; just pick up already-made pudding from the dairy cases at the supermarket. In fact, entire meals are now available right out of the box. Dinty Moore's Classic Bakes are entire casserole dinners for four to five and promise to be "hot and hearty, quick and convenient, ready in minutes."

An increasingly important competitor is the fully cooked meal consumers may now buy at the supermarket. People can merely stop on the way home and purchase all the courses of a meal, which they "prepare" by unwrapping the packages—no cooking required.

Then there are the takeout meals from chains such as Boston Market (now a wholly owned subsidiary of McDonald's with 650 company-owned restaurants in 28 states[13]) and eatZi's, which cater to the "meal replacement" market. Said one consumer, "I don't have time to cook. I just worked all day, and I have other things to do, and this is going to be quick. . . ."[14] EatZi's, for example, "sells 200 entrees and 1,500 fresh items daily, all prepared from scratch under the supervision of chefs trained at culinary schools. The meals include everything from macaroni and cheese to swordfish and sushi as well as sandwiches and salads."[15]

The McDonaldization of food preparation and consumption has also reached the booming diet industry. Diet books promising all sorts of shortcuts to weight loss are often at the top of the best-seller lists. Losing weight is normally difficult and time-consuming, but diet books promise to make it easier and quicker. For those on a diet (and many people are on more or less perpetual diets), the preparation of low-calorie food has also been streamlined. Instead of cooking diet foods from scratch, dieters may now purchase an array of prepared foods in frozen or microwavable form. Those who do not wish to go through the inefficient process of eating these diet meals can "prepare" and consume products such as diet shakes and bars (Slim-Fast, for example) in a matter of seconds. Dieters seeking even greater efficiency also have various pills that expedite weight loss—the now-banned "fen-phen" and others.

The issue of dieting points to new efficiencies outside the home as well, to the growth of diet centers such as Jenny Craig, NutriSystem,[16] and Curves (a popular new Texas-based diet and exercise company with over 5,000 studios that caters exclusively to women and features an efficient 30-minute workout).[17] NutriSystem sells dieters, at substantial cost, prepackaged freeze-dried food. In what is close to the ultimate in stream-lined cooking, all the dieter need do is add water. Freeze-dried foods are also convenient for NutriSystem, because they can be efficiently pack-aged, transported, and stored (and they are often conveniently popped into the microwave by the consumer).

Dieters' periodic visits to weight-loss clinics are also streamlined. At NutriSystem, a counselor is allotted ten minutes with each client. During that brief time, the counselor takes the client's weight, blood pressure, and measurements, asks routine questions, fills out a chart, and devotes whatever time is left to "problem solving." If the session extends beyond the allotted ten minutes and other clients are waiting, the receptionist will buzz the counselor's room.

### Shopping: Creating Ever-More Efficient Selling Machines

Shopping for all kinds of goods and services, not just food, has also been streamlined. The department store obviously is a more efficient place in which to shop than a series of specialty shops dispersed throughout the city or suburbs. In addition, the shopping mall increases efficiency by bringing a wide range of department stores and specialty shops under one roof.[18] It is cost-efficient for retailers because the collection of shops and department stores brings in throngs of people ("mall synergy"). And it is efficient for consumers because in one stop they can visit numerous shops, have lunch at a "food court" (likely populated by many fast-food chains), see a movie, have a drink, and go to an exercise or diet center.

The drive for shopping efficiency did not end with the malls. 7-Eleven and its clones (for example, Circle K, AM/PM, and Wawa) have become drive-up, if not drive-through, minimarkets. For those who need only a few items, pulling up to a highly streamlined 7-Eleven (its 25,000th shop opened in Chicago in mid-2003) is far more efficient (albeit more costly) than running to a supermarket. Shoppers have no need to park in a large lot, obtain a cart, wheel through myriad aisles in search of needed items, wait in lines at the checkout, and then tote purchases back to a sometimes distant car. At 7-Eleven, they can park right in front and quickly find what they need. Like the fast-food restaurant, which offers a highly circumscribed menu, 7-Eleven has sought to fill its shops with a limited array of commonly sought goods: bread, milk, cigarettes, aspirin, even videos, and self-serve items, such as hot coffee, hot dogs, microwaved sandwiches, cold soda, and Slurpees. 7-Eleven's efficiency stems from the fact that it ordinarily sells only one brand of each item, with many items unobtainable.

Even more efficient are the quick and convenient BrewThrus springing up all over the country. Customers simply drive into a BrewThru, which is set up like a garage lined with many convenience store products, especially beer and wine. An attendant comes out to the car to take your order, brings you what you want, takes your money, and you are back on the road in no time.[19]

For greater selection, consumers must go to the relatively inefficient supermarket. Of course, supermarkets have sought to make shopping more efficient by institutionalizing ten-item-limit, no-checks-accepted lines for consumers who might otherwise frequent the convenience stores.

People who do not feel that they have the time to visit the mall are able to shop from the comfort of their homes through catalogues (for example, L.L. Bean, Lands' End).[20] Another alternative to visiting the mall is home television shopping, although it may lead to many hours in front of the TV. Products are paraded before viewers, who can purchase them simply by phoning in and conveniently charging their purchases. The efficiency of shopping via catalogs and TV has increased even further with the advent of express package delivery systems, such as Federal Express.

The Internet has also greatly increased shopping efficiency. For example, instead of traveling to a book superstore or wandering from one small bookshop to another, you can access Amazon.com and have over a million different titles at your fingertips. After selecting and charging the titles you want, you just sit back and wait for the books to be delivered to your door. One of the more recent developments in this area is the "virtual pharmacy," which allows people to obtain prescription drugs without seeing a physician; consultations with "online doctors" are also available.[21]

An often overlooked aspect of the efficiency of cybershopping is that it can be done while you are at work.[22] Although employers are likely to feel that shopping from work adversely affects worker efficiency, it is certainly very efficient from the perspective of the worker/consumer.

Of course, the drive to make Internet shopping ever more efficient continues. Thus, we are witnessing the evolution of shopping robots, or "shopbots," which automatically surf the Web for specific products, lowest prices, and shortest delivery dates.[23] For example, shop.lycos.com offers a shopbot that does comparison shopping at over 32,000 online stores. Google.com also now has a shopbot, or what it prefers to call a spider, named Froogle (froogle.google.com): "Browse by category—apparel, computers, flowers, whatever—or enter a query term, and it will present a list of matching products, each with a thumbnail sketch on the left and description, price and retailer on the right."[24]

All types of shopping, but particularly ordering from distant merchants, have become far more efficient with the widespread use of credit cards. Shoppers need not go to the bank to load up on cash or return to the bank if they run out of cash at the mall. They can even shop in other countries without needing to purchase foreign currency. Although paying cash still might be more efficient, at least some clerks are surprised, even suspicious, when people make purchases, especially large ones, with cash. And credit cards are certainly a more efficient way of paying than writing out personal checks and being required to show several pieces of identification.

The credit card has also McDonaldized the process of obtaining credit.[25] In the past, people had to go through lengthy and cumbersome application procedures to receive credit. Now, the credit card companies have streamlined the process to the extent of mailing millions of people notices that they have been preapproved for credit. Thus, consumers now need do next to nothing to receive a line of credit amounting to several hundred or, more likely, several thousand dollars. That's efficiency, even from the point of view of the customer. Of course, credit card companies see preapproval as an efficient means of recruiting large numbers of potential debtors who will pay near-usurious interest rates in exchange for the right to run up a balance.

### Higher Education: Just Fill in the Box

The educational system, specifically the contemporary university (which has now been dubbed "McUniversity"[26]), offers many examples of the pressure for greater efficiency. One is the machine-graded, multiple-choice examination. In a much earlier era, students were examined individually in conference with their professors. This may have been a good way to find out what students knew, but it was highly labor-intensive and inefficient. Later, the essay examination became popular. Grading a set of essays was more efficient than giving individual oral examinations, but it was still relatively time-consuming. Enter the multiple-choice examination, the grading of which was a snap. In fact, graduate assistants could grade it, making evaluation of students even more efficient for the professor. Now computer-graded examinations maximize efficiency for both professors and graduate assistants. They even offer advantages to students, such as making it easier to study and limiting the effect of the subjective views of the grader on the grading process.

Other innovations in academia are further streamlining the educational process. Even the multiple-choice examination leaves the professor saddled with the inefficient task of composing the necessary sets of questions. Furthermore, at least some of the questions have to be changed each semester to foil new students who gain possession of old exams. To ease the burden, textbook publishers started providing professors with manuals (free of charge) loaded with multiple-choice questions to accompany the textbooks required for use in large classes. However, the professor still had to retype the questions or have them retyped. Now, publishers often provide these sets of questions on computer disks. All the professor needs to do is select the desired questions and let the printer do the rest. Another advance is the advent of computer-based programs to grade essay examinations and term papers.[27] Thus, professors may soon be able to return to assigning these more traditional types of school work without any loss in efficiency. Indeed, with these great advances, professors now can choose to have very little to do with the entire examination process, from question composition to grading, freeing up time for activities that many professors, but few students, value more highly, such as writing and research.

Publishers have provided other services to streamline teaching for those professors who adopt best-selling textbooks. A professor may receive many materials with which to fill class hours—lecture outlines, computer simulations, discussion questions, videotapes, movies, even ideas for guest lecturers and student projects. Professors who choose to use all these devices need do little or nothing on their own for their classes.

I've participated in an excellent example of streamlining in higher education—custom publishing.[28] In a customized textbook, the editor recruits various authors to write chapters on specific topics. The professor interested in adopting the book for class use receives a list of the available chapters. The professor may choose any subset of the chapters, which can be put together in the order the professor wishes. A customized book is produced, and the number of copies required for the professor's class is printed. This development has been made possible by the advent of new computer technology as well as ultra-high-speed printers.

Customized textbooks are more efficient than regular textbooks in at least three ways:

1. Having many experts write single chapters streamlines the process, because each chapter requires just weeks or months of work; having one author write them all can take years.

2. Because it contains only those chapters that will actually be used, a customized book is more likely to be streamlined with fewer chapters than a traditional textbook.

3. The chapters can be mixed and matched to produce textbooks for many different courses; subsets of the same collection of chapters can be used in different courses.

Another advance in efficiency in academia is the development of a relatively new type of service on college campuses. For a nominal fee, students may purchase lecture notes for their courses written by instructors, teaching assistants, and top-notch students. No more inefficient note taking; in fact, no more inefficient class attendance. Students are free to pursue more valuable activities, such as poring over arcane academic journals in the graduate library or watching the "soaps."

One last academic efficiency worth noting is the ability of students to purchase already completed term papers online. There are a variety of Web sites[29] that now promise to deliver original, made-from-scratch research papers on any topic for the "low, low fee" of between $9.95 and $19.95 per page. They even have express delivery available for those students who have put off academic dishonesty to the last moment. Beware, however, as there is also a host of other Web sites popping up that help professors detect plagiarism, thereby combating efficiency with efficiency.[30]

## Health Care: Docs-in-a-Box

It might be assumed that modern medicine is immune to the drive for efficiency and invulnerable to rationalization more generally.[31] However, medicine has been McDonaldized. In fact, instances of what may be termed "assembly line medicine" have been reported. One example is Dr. Denton Cooley (his "fetish is efficiency"), who gained worldwide fame for streamlining delicate open-heart surgery in a "heart surgery factory" that operated "with the precision of an assembly-line."[32] Even more striking is the following description of the Moscow Research Institute of Eye Microsurgery:

> In many ways the scene resembles any modern factory. A conveyor glides silently past five work stations, periodically stopping, then starting again. Each station is staffed by an attendant in a sterile mask and smock. The workers have just three minutes to complete their tasks before the conveyor moves on; they turn out 20 finished pieces in an hour.
>
> Nearly everything else about the assembly line, however, is highly unusual: the workers are eye surgeons, and the conveyor carries human beings on stretchers. This is . . . where the production methods of Henry Ford are applied to the practice of medicine . . . a "medical factory for the production of people with good eyesight."[33]

Such assembly lines are not yet the norm in medicine, yet one can imagine that they will grow increasingly common in the coming years.

Perhaps the best example of the increasing efficiency of medical practice in the United States is the growth of walk-in/walk-out surgical or emergency centers. "McDoctors" or "Docs-in-a-box" serve patients who want medical problems handled with maximum efficiency. Each center handles only a limited number of minor problems but with great dispatch. Although the patient with a laceration cannot be stitched as efficiently as a customer in search of a hamburger can be served, many of the same principles shape the two operations. For instance, it is more efficient for the patient to walk in without an appointment than to make an appointment with a regular physician and wait until that time arrives. For a minor emergency, such as a slight laceration, walking through a McDoctors is more efficient than working your way through a large hospital's emergency room. Hospitals are set up to handle serious problems for which efficiency is not (yet) the norm, although some hospitals already employ specialized emergency room physicians and teams of medical personnel.

From an organizational point of view, a McDoctors can be run more efficiently than a hospital emergency room. Docs-in-a-box can also be more efficient than private doctors' offices because they are not structured to permit the kind of personal (and therefore inefficient) attention patients expect from their private physicians.

### Entertainment: Moving People (and Trash) Efficiently

With the advent of videotapes, DVDs, and video rental stores, many people no longer deem it efficient to drive to their local theater to see a movie. Movies can now be viewed, often more than one at a sitting, in people's own dens. Blockbuster, the largest video rental firm in the United States, predictably "considers itself the McDonald's of the video business."[34] It attracts an average of 3 million customers a day.[35]

The video rental business may already be in danger of replacement by even more efficient alternatives, such as Netflix or the pay-per-view movies offered by many cable companies. For a nominal fee of $20 a month, Netflix. com customers can keep a revolving library of up to three DVDs. There are never any late fees, and they even provide you with return envelopes, postage already paid. Alternatively, instead of trekking to the video store, people can just turn to the proper channel and phone the cable company to obtain a desired movie. Satellite dishes allow people access to a wide range of video offerings, including many movie channels and pay-per-view options. Systems like TIVO even allow customers to record their favorite shows while they are watching something else or to rewind or pause live television. Video-on-demand systems, already available to an estimated 7 million customers,[36] allow people to order any of the movies available in video stores from the comfort of their homes any time they wish.[37] Said one customer at a video store, "I'd definitely get video on demand. . . . I wouldn't have to come over here to pick this up. And I wouldn't have to bring it back tomorrow, which is going to be a pain in my butt."[38] Those who are not satisfied with any single offering can buy a television set with "picture-in-a-picture," which enables them to view a movie while also watching a favorite TV show on an inset on the screen.

Keeping up with one's reading is becoming more streamlined as well. Audiobooks (books-on-tape) was a $2.4 billion a year industry in 2000 and is growing at the rate of 10% per year.[39] As of 2002, Audiobooks had at least 60 million listeners; it is estimated that almost a quarter of all American households have listened to a book-on-tape in the previous year.[40] Audiobooks allow people to engage in other activities—commuting, walking, jogging, or watching a sports event on TV with the sound off—while listening to a book. One company specializes in renting books to truckers so that they can listen while they drive.[41] Truckers can rent books at one spot and drop them off down the road at another. Cracker Barrel, a national restaurant chain, offers a similar service to all drivers (about three-quarters of those who listen to audiobooks do so in the car[42]), who can pick up a book at one restaurant and drop it off in another, perhaps three states away. However, downloading audiotapes from the Web eliminates the inefficiencies associated with picking up and dropping off tapes.[43] Further streamlining occurs when books-on-tape are recorded in abridged form. Gone are the "wasted" hours listening to "insignificant" parts of novels. With liberal cutting, *War and Peace* can be heard in one listening (perhaps while walking on a treadmill).

Another sort of efficiency in the entertainment world is the system for moving people developed by modern amusement parks, particularly Disneyland and Walt Disney World.[44] At Disney World and Epcot Center, for example, a vast highway and road system filters many thousands of cars each day into the appropriate parking lots. Once each driver has been led to a parking spot (often with the help of information broadcast over the radio), jitneys come to whisk visitors to the gates of the park. Once in the park, visitors find themselves in a vast line of people, on what is, in effect, a huge conveyor belt that leads them from one ride or attraction to another. Once they actually reach an attraction, some sort of conveyance—car, boat, submarine, plane, rocket, or moving walkway—moves them through and out of the attraction as rapidly as possible. The speed with which visitors move through each attraction enhances their experience and reduces the likelihood that they will question the "reality" of what they see. In fact, they are often not quite sure what they have witnessed, although it seems exciting.

Disney World has been victimized by its own success: Even its highly efficient systems cannot handle the hordes that descend on the park at the height of the tourist season. Visitors must face long lines at many of the most popular attractions. However, the waits would be far longer were it not for the efficiency with which Disney World processes people.

People are not the only thing that Disney World must process efficiently.[45] The throngs that frequent such amusement parks eat a great deal (mostly fast food, especially finger foods) and therefore generate an enormous amount of trash. If Disney World emptied trash receptacles only at the end of each day, the barrels would be overflowing most of the time. To prevent this (and it must be prevented since cleanliness—some would say sterility—is a key component of the McDonaldized world in general and Disney World in particular), hordes of employees constantly sweep, collect, and empty trash. To take a specific example, bringing up the rear in the nightly Disney parade, a group of cleaners almost instantly disposes of whatever trash and animal droppings have been left behind. Within a few minutes, they have eliminated virtually all signs that a parade has just passed by. Disney World also employs an elaborate system of underground tubes. Garbage receptacles are emptied into this system, which whisks the trash away at about sixty miles per hour to a central trash disposal plant far from the view of visitors. Disney World is a "magic kingdom" in more ways than one. Here is the way one observer compares another of the modern, highly rational amusement parks— Busch Gardens—to ancestors such as county fairs and Coney Island:

> Gone is the dusty midway, the cold seduction of a carnie's voice, the garish, gaudy excitement and all the harsh promise evoked by a thousand yellow lights winking in darkness. In its place is a vast, self-contained environment, as complex as a small city and endowed with the kind of *efficiency* beyond the reach of most cities of any size [italics added].[46]

### Other Settings: Streamlining Relationships with Even the Pope

Modern health clubs, including chains such as Holiday Spas (and Curves), also strongly emphasize efficiency.[47] These clubs often offer virtually everything needed to lose weight and stay in shape, including exercise machines, running track, and swimming pool. The exercise machines are highly specialized so that people can efficiently work specific areas of the body. Running machines and the StairMaster increase cardiovascular fitness; weight-lifting machines increase strength and muscularity in targeted areas of the body. Many machines are even equipped with calorie counters that keep track of exactly how many of those salty french fries are being burnt away. Another efficiency associated with many of these machines is that people can do other things while exercising. Many clubs have television sets throughout the gym. The exerciser can also read, listen to music, or listen to an audiobook (probably abridged) while working out. All this is offered in the sterile environment often associated with McDonaldization.[48]

Other examples of streamlining to increase efficiency abound. Drive-through windows streamline banking for both consumers and bankers. Drive-up kiosks receive film and send it off to a central location for development. The latest cellular phones allow people to snap pictures and send them instantaneously to others with similar phones (or to e-mail accounts). Some McDonald's now have automated kiosks in their drive-thru lanes where customers can rent and return DVDs (and it has experimented with a stand-alone kiosk in Washington, D.C., that also offers a variety of other products). At gasoline stations, customers can put their credit cards into a slot on or near the pump and have their accounts automatically charged; when they finish pumping, they retrieve the receipt and the card with no contact with, or work done by, anyone working for the gas station. For example, in the case of Mobil's "Speedpass," a transponder attached to a key tag or to a vehicle's rear window, communicates with the pump via radio frequency signals (a similar technology is used with increasing frequency on the nation's toll roads). When the car pulls up, the pump is activated and the correct amount is charged to the driver's credit-card account.

Even religion has been streamlined, through things such as drive-in churches and televised religious programs.[49] In 1985, the Vatican announced that Catholics could receive indulgences ("a release by way of devotional practices from certain forms of punishment resulting from sin") through the Pope's annual Christmas benediction on TV or radio. Previously, Catholics had to engage in the far less efficient activity of going to Rome for the Christmas benediction and manifesting the "proper intention and attitude" to receive their indulgences in person.[50] More generally, Christian bookstores are stocked with "how-to" books "claiming to be able to teach us the '10 steps to spiritual maturity' or how to be a successful parent in 60 minutes."[51]

Streamlining is a defining characteristic of the Internet. For example, search engines such as Yahoo!, Altavista, Google, Hotbot, and EuroSeek now do a lot of the work that was formerly performed by computer users.[52] In the early days of the Internet, getting the information one wanted was a difficult matter requiring a great deal of skill and knowledge of arcane computer programs. Now, all users need do is access the search engine, type in the desired topic, and they are on their way. A process of de-skilling has taken place; skills once the possession of the user are now built into the system. The Internet also renders such activities as political campaigning,[53] medical symposia,[54] student research,[55] even romance[56] more efficient. Even more obviously, e-mail is far more streamlined than "snail mail."[57] No need to write a letter, put it in an envelope, seal it, paste on a stamp, mail it, and wait days or weeks for a reply. Now, all that is needed are a few keystrokes and a click on the "send" button. Replies may be received almost instantaneously. Better yet, if both you and the person you are e-mailing are simultaneously using the same Internet chat service (AOL Instant Messenger, Yahoo Messenger, etc.), you can have a "conversation" online without any need to send even an e-mail. A similar set of advantages has attracted people to e-cards for birthdays, anniversaries, holidays, and the like.[58]

## ◆ SIMPLIFYING THE PRODUCT

Many efficiencies have been gained by streamlining various processes. But another way to increase efficiency is by simplifying products. Consider the nature of the food served at fast-food restaurants. Complex foods based on sophisticated recipes are, needless to say, not the norm at fast-food restaurants. The staples of the industry are foods that require relatively few ingredients and are simple to prepare, serve, and eat.

In fact, fast-food restaurants generally serve "finger food," food that can be eaten without utensils. Hamburgers, french fries, fried chicken, slices of pizza, and tacos are all finger foods.

Many innovations over the years have greatly increased the number and types of finger foods available. The Egg McMuffin is an entire breakfast—egg, Canadian bacon, English muffin—combined into a handy sandwich. Devouring such a sandwich is far more efficient than sitting down with knife and fork and eating a plate full of eggs, bacon, and toast. The creation of the Chicken McNugget, perhaps the ultimate finger food, reflects the fact that chicken is pretty inefficient as far as

McDonald's is concerned. The bones, gristle, and skin that are such a barrier to the efficient consumption of chicken have all been eliminated in the Chicken McNugget. Customers can pop the bite-size morsels of fried chicken right into their mouths even as they drive. Were they able to, the mass purveyors of chicken would breed a more efficiently consumed chicken free of bones, gristle, and skin.[59] McDonald's also offers an apple pie that, because it is completely encased in dough, can be munched like a sandwich.

The limited number of menu choices also contributes to efficiency in fast-food restaurants. McDonald's does not serve egg rolls (at least not yet), and Taco Bell does not offer fried chicken. In spite of what they tell people, fast-food restaurants are far from not only full-serve restaurants but also the old cafeterias that offered a vast array of foods.

Advertisements like "We do it your way" or "Your way, right away" imply that fast-food chains happily accommodate special requests. But pity the consumer who has a special request in a fast-food restaurant. Because much of their efficiency stems from the fact that they virtually always do it one way—their way—the last thing that fast-food restaurants want to do is do it your way. The typical hamburger is usually so thin that it can be cooked only one way—well done. Bigger burgers (the McDonald's Quarter Pounder, for example) can be prepared rare, but the fast-food restaurant insists, for the sake of efficiency (and these days for health reasons), that they all be cooked one way. Customers with the temerity to ask for a less well-done burger or well-browned fries are likely to cool their heels for a long time waiting for such "exotica." Few customers are willing to wait because, after all, it defeats the main advantages of going to a fast-food restaurant—speed and efficiency. The limited number of menu items also allows for highly efficient ordering of supplies and food delivery. In sum, the idea behind what Henry Ford once said about cars has been extended to hamburgers: "Any customer can have a car painted any color that he wants so long as it is black."[60]

Many products other than fast food have been simplified in the name of efficiency. AAMCO Transmissions works mainly on transmissions, and Midas Muffler largely restricts itself to the installation of mufflers. H&R Block does millions of simple tax returns in its nearly nine thousand offices. Because it uses many part-time and seasonal employees and does not offer the full array of tax and financial services available from a CPA, it is undoubtedly not the best place to have complicated tax returns completed.[61] "McDentists" may be relied on for simple dental procedures, but people would be ill-advised to have root canal work done there.

Pearle Vision centers offer eye examinations, but people should go to an eye doctor for any major vision problem.

Most "serious" newspapers (for example, the *New York Times* and the *Washington Post*) are relatively inefficient to read, when stories begin on page one and then carry over to additional pages. *USA TODAY* simplified this product by keeping whole stories on the same page—in other words, by offering "News McNuggets." *USA TODAY* ruthlessly edits stories to simplify and reduce narrative content (no words wasted), leaving a series of relatively bare facts.

In this, *USA TODAY* was anticipated by the various digests, most notably the still popular *Reader's Digest*. The original aim of *Reader's Digest* was to offer magazine articles that "could be written to please the reader, to give him the nub of the matter in the new fast-moving world of the 1920s, instead of being written at length and with literary embellishments to please the author or the editor."[62] Other precursors to *USA TODAY* are magazines such as *Time, Newsweek,* and *Business Week.* As two observers noted, "The message is that busy executives don't have time to read in depth so don't waste time reading the *Wall Street Journal* every day when one quick bite of *Business Week* once a week is sufficient to give you a step ahead of the competition."[63]

## ◆ PUTTING CUSTOMERS TO WORK

A final mechanism for increasing efficiency in a McDonaldizing world is to put customers to work. Fast-food customers perform many more unpaid tasks compared with those who dine at full-service restaurants:

> A few years ago, the fast food chain McDonald's came up with the slogan "We do it all for you." In reality, at McDonald's, we do it all for them. We stand in line, take the food to the table, dispose of the waste, and stack our trays. As labor costs rise and technology develops, the consumer often does more and more of the work.[64]

However, although it is efficient for the fast-food restaurant to have consumers wait in line, waiting in line is inefficient for consumers. It is efficient for fast-food restaurants to have the diner do much of the work done by employees in a traditional restaurant, but is it efficient for the consumer? Is it efficient to order your own food rather than having a waiter do it? Or to bus your own paper, plastic, and Styrofoam rather than having a busperson do it?

The tendency to put customers to work was underscored in 2003 by Steak n Shake (over 400 restaurants in the United States) TV advertisements describing fast-food restaurants as "workaurants."[65] In contrast, Steak n Shake emphasizes its use of china plates and the fact that the food is actually served by a wait staff.

The salad bar is a classic example of putting the consumer to work. The customer "buys" an empty plate and then ambles over to the salad bar to load up on the array of vegetables and other foods available that day. Quickly seeing the merit in this system, many supermarkets installed their own, more elaborate salad bars. The salad lover can thus work as a salad chef at lunch hour in the fast-food restaurant and then do it all over again in the evening at the supermarket. The fast-food restaurant and the supermarket achieve huge gains in efficiency because they need only a small number of employees to keep the various compartments well stocked.

In a number of fast-food restaurants, including Roy Rogers,[66] consumers are expected to take a naked burger to the "fixin' bar" to add lettuce, tomatoes, onions, and so on. In such cases, they end up logging a few minutes a week as sandwich makers. At Burger King and most other fast-food franchises, people must fill their own cups with ice and soft drinks, thereby spending a few moments as "soda jerks." Similarly, customers serve themselves in the popular breakfast buffets at Shoney's or the lunch buffets at Pizza Hut.

Once again taking the lead, at least in the fast-food industry (a similar technology is being used in airports to buy plane tickets), McDonald's is testing self-ordering kiosks in some restaurants that allow customers to use a touch screen to place their food orders. They do what counter people at McDonald's currently do—find and touch the picture on the screen that matches the food being ordered.[67]

Shopping also offers many examples of imposing work on the consumer. The old-time grocery store, where the clerk retrieved the needed items, has been replaced by the supermarket, where a shopper may put in several hours a week "working" as a grocery clerk, seeking out wanted (and unwanted) items during lengthy treks down seemingly interminable aisles. Having obtained the groceries, the shopper then unloads the food at the checkout counter and, in some cases, even bags the groceries.

Of course, some supermarket checkout stands now have the customer do the scanning, thereby eliminating the need for a checkout clerk.[68] The systems that allow customers to pay with credit cards eliminate the need for cashiers. The developer of one scanning system predicted that "self-service grocery technology could be as pervasive as the automatic cash machines used by bank customers."[69]

One customer, apparently a strong believer in McDonaldization, said of such a system, "It's quick, easy and efficient. . . . You get in and out in a hurry."[70] But as an official with a union representing supermarket clerks put it, "To say it's more convenient for the customer is turning the world upside down. . . . In general, making customers do the work for themselves is not customer service."[71]

Virtually gone are gas station attendants who fill gas tanks, check the oil, and clean windows; people now put in a few minutes a week as unpaid attendants. One exception to this rule is the state of New Jersey, where it is actually against the law to pump your own gas. Although one might think that eliminating the gas station attendant leads to lower gasoline prices (and indeed it does in the short run), a comparison of gas prices at stations with and without attendants shows little difference in price. In the end, the gasoline companies simply found another way to force the consumer to do the work they once had to pay employees to do.

In some doctors' offices, patients must now weigh themselves and take their own temperatures. More important, patients have been put to work in the medical world through the use of an increasingly wide array of do-it-yourself medical tests. Two basic types are available: monitoring instruments and diagnostic devices.[72] Monitoring devices include blood pressure monitors and glucose and cholesterol meters. Among the diagnostic tests are pregnancy detectors, ovulation predictors, HIV test kits, and fecal occult blood detectors. Thus, patients are now being asked to familiarize themselves with technologies that were formerly the exclusive province of physicians, nurses, or trained technicians. In addition, patients are being asked to sample bodily fluids (blood, urine) or byproducts (fecal matter) that were once handled (very gingerly) by professional medical people. But in an era of high medical costs, it is cheaper and more efficient (no unnecessary trips to the doctor's office or to the lab) for patients to monitor and test themselves. Such home testing may identify problems that otherwise might not be discovered, but it can also lead to unnecessary worry, especially in the case of "false positive" results. In either case, many of us are now "working," at least part-time, as unpaid medical technicians.

The automated teller machine (ATM) in the banking industry allows everyone to work, for at least a few moments, as an unpaid bank teller (and often pay fees for the privilege). Recently, to encourage the use of ATMs, some banks have begun charging a fee for the use of human tellers.[73] The growing reluctance of customers to enter the bank (possibly, for example, out of a reluctance to pay for human interaction), in turn, has led to longer lines at the ATM machines, ironically reducing their efficiency.

Phone companies now make people put in a few minutes a day as operators. Instead of asking a long-distance operator to make calls, people are urged to dial such calls themselves, thereby requiring them to keep lengthy lists of phone numbers and area codes. Instead of simply dialing "0" to make a collect long-distance call, people must now remember lengthy sets of numbers to save money. Another such effort by the phone companies involves having people look up numbers in the phone book rather than call an operator for information. To discourage people from using the operator for such information, there is now likely to be a fairly hefty charge for the service. In the state of Washington, consumers can now even install their own telephones simply by plugging them into the jacks, dialing 811, and answering a series of questions posed by a computer by punching digits on the phone.[74]

When calling many businesses these days, instead of dealing with a human operator, people must push a bewildering sequence of numbers and codes before they get, they hope, to the desired extension.[75] Here is the way one humorist describes such a "conversation" and the work involved for the caller:

> The party you are trying to reach—Thomas Watson—is unavailable at this time. To leave a message, please wait for the beep. To review your message, press 7. To change your message after reviewing it, press 4. To add to your message, press 5. To reach another party, press the star sign and enter the four-digit extension. To listen to Muzak, press 23. To transfer out of phone mail in what I promise you will be a futile effort to reach a human, press 0—because we treat you like one.[76]

Instead of being interviewed by the government census taker, people usually receive a questionnaire (one that is supposedly self-explanatory) in the mail to fill out on their own. The self-response rate for occupied housing units in the 2000 census was 75.5%. In other words, only 24.5% of the time was a real-life census taker used to obtain the information, and even then they were deployed only after residents failed to respond to the mailed questionnaire.[77]

Many of these examples may seem trivial. Clearly, trolling the salad bar or punching numbers on a computer screen is not highly burdensome. But the ubiquity of these activities means that the modern consumer spends an increasingly significant amount of time and energy doing unpaid labor. Thus, although organizations are realizing greater efficiencies, customers are often sacrificing convenience and efficiency.

## ♦ CONCLUSION

The first dimension of McDonaldization, efficiency, involves the search for the optimum means to a given end. In recent years, the fast-food restaurant has spearheaded the search for optimum efficiency and has been joined in that quest by other elements of our McDonaldizing society. There are innumerable ways to search for ever-greater efficiency, but in McDonaldizing systems, that search has taken the form primarily of streamlining a variety of processes, simplifying goods and services, and using the customer to perform unpaid work that paid employees used to do.

As with the other dimensions of McDonaldization, there is no question that greater efficiency brings advantages to all concerned. However, it is important to remember that mechanisms designed to increase efficiency are generally put in place by organizations to further their own interests, and they are not always the same as those of consumers. Furthermore, the search for increased efficiency is intensifying with the result that we will increasingly experience a world that is not necessarily organized in a way that furthers the interests of consumers. Yet the more we encounter efficiency, the more of it we crave. As a result, we often end up clamoring for that which may not be in our best interests.

# 4

# Calculability

◆————————————————————————

## Big Macs and Little Chips

McDonaldization is not simply a matter of efficiency. It also involves calculability: calculating, counting, quantifying. Quantity tends to become a surrogate for quality.[1] Numerical standards are set for both processes (production, for example) and end results (goods, for example). In terms of processes, the emphasis is on speed (usually high), whereas for end results the focus is on the number of products produced and served or on their size (usually large).

This calculability has a number of positive consequences, the most important being the ability to produce and obtain large amounts of things very rapidly. Customers in fast-food restaurants get a lot of food quickly; managers and owners get a great deal of work from their employees, and the work is done speedily. However, the emphasis on quantity tends to affect adversely the quality of both the process and the result. For customers, calculability often means eating on the run (hardly a "quality" dining experience) and consuming food that is almost always mediocre. For employees, calculability often means obtaining little or no personal meaning from their work; therefore, the work, products, and services suffer.

Calculability is intertwined with the other dimensions of McDonaldization. For instance, calculability makes it easier to determine efficiency; that is, those steps that can be clocked as taking the least time are usually considered the most efficient. Once quantified, products and processes become more predictable, because the same amounts of materials or time are used from one place or time to another. Quantification is also linked to control, particularly to the creation of nonhuman technologies that perform tasks in a given amount of time or make products of a given weight or size. Calculability is clearly linked to irrationality since, among other things, the emphasis on quantity tends to affect quality adversely.

Crucial to any discussion of calculability in contemporary society is the impact of the computer.[2] The tendency to quantify virtually everything has obviously been expedited by its development and now widespread use. The first computer, constructed in 1946, weighed thirty tons, employed nineteen thousand vacuum tubes (that were constantly blowing out), filled an entire room, and had very limited capacity. Now, because the silicon chip (invented in the 1970s) provides the necessary electronic circuitry in microscopic form, computers are being made ever smaller (for example, Palm Pilots, laptops, and notebooks), more powerful, cheaper. The resulting proliferation of personal computers allows more of us to do more calculations with increasing speed. Many aspects of today's quantity-oriented society could not exist, or would need to be greatly modified, were it not for the modern computer. Consider the following:

- The registration of masses of students at large state universities, the processing of their grades, and the constant recalculation of grade point averages.
- Extensive medical testing in which a patient takes a battery of blood and urine tests. The results are returned in the form of a series of numbers on a variety of measures as well as the normal ranges for each measure. This quantification permits efficient diagnosis of medical problems and allows the patient to be a kind of do-it-yourself physician.
- The development and widespread use of the credit card. The computer made possible the billions of transactions associated with the credit card. The growth of the credit card, in turn, made possible a massive increase in consumer spending and business sales. More generally, debit cards, direct deposits, electronic payment, and online banking in general were made possible by the computer.
- The ability of the television networks to give us almost instantaneous election results.
- Virtually continuous political polling and TV ratings.

Although society undoubtedly was already moving toward increased calculability before computer technology advanced to its current level, computers have greatly expedited and extended that tendency. Keeping in mind the centrality of the computer, let us turn in the remainder of this chapter to a discussion of the three key aspects of calculability: (1) emphasizing quantity rather than quality, (2) giving the illusion of quantity, and (3) reducing production and service to numbers.

## ◆ EMPHASIZING QUANTITY RATHER THAN QUALITY OF PRODUCTS

McDonald's has always emphasized bigness; it and the other fast chains have a "bigger-is-better mentality."[3] For a long time, the most visible symbols of this emphasis were the large signs, usually beneath the even larger golden arches, touting the millions and later billions of hamburgers sold by McDonald's. This was a rather heavy-handed way of letting everyone know about McDonald's great success. (With the wide-scale recognition of their success in recent years, there is less need for McDonald's to be so obvious; hence the decline of such signs and the decrease in the size of the golden arches.[4]) The mounting number of hamburgers sold not only indicated to potential customers that the chain was successful but also fostered the notion that the high quality of the burgers accounted for the immense sales. Hence, quantity appeared to equal quality.

McDonald's carries this emphasis on quantity to its products' names. The best-known example is the Big Mac (and McDonald's even tested a Mega Mac, 50% bigger than the Big Mac). A large burger is considered desirable simply because consumers receive a large serving. Furthermore, consumers are led to believe that they are getting a great deal of food for a small price. Calculating consumers come away with the feeling that they are getting a good deal—and maybe even getting the best of McDonald's.

### The Fast-Food Industry: Of "Big Bites" and "Super Big Gulps"

Many other fast-food restaurants mirror McDonald's emphasis on quantity. Burger King points up the quantity of meat in the "Whopper" and the "Double Whopper." Wendy's has its "Biggies," including Biggie fries. Not to be outdone, Jack in the Box has its "Colossus," Hardee's its "Monster Thickburger," Pizza Hut its "Big New Yorker," Domino's touts its "Feast Pizza," and Kentucky Fried Chicken its "Mega" meal. Taco Bell offers "Double Decker Tacos," as well as five menu items called "Big Fill": five kinds of burritos that each deliver up to a half pound of food for ninety-nine cents or less.[5] Similarly, 7-Eleven proffers its customers a hot dog called the "Big Bite" and a large soft drink called the "Big Gulp"—and now, the even larger "Super Big Gulp." In recent years, the tendency has been for the fast-food restaurants to push ever-larger servings. For example, McDonald's offers a "Super-Size" fries, 20% larger than a large order, and customers are urged to "super-size" their meals. Then there is the "Double Quarter Pounder" as well as the "Triple Cheeseburger."[6]

All this emphasis on quantity suggests that fast-food restaurants have little interest in communicating anything directly about quality.[7] Were they interested, they might give their products names such as "McDelicious," or "McPrime." But the fact is that typical McDonald's customers know they are not getting the highest-quality food:

> No one, but no one, outside of a few top McDonald's executives, knows exactly what's in those hamburger patties, and, whatever they're made of, they're easy to overlook completely. I once opened up a bun . . . and looked at a McDonald's patty in its naked state. It looked like a Brillo pad and I've never forgotten it.
>
> Let's face it. Nobody thinks about what's between the bun at McDonald's. You buy, you eat, you toss the trash, and you're out of there like the Lone Ranger.[8]

Another observer has argued that people do not go to McDonald's for a delicious, pleasurable meal but, rather, to "refuel."[9] McDonald's is a place to fill their stomachs with lots of calories and carbohydrates so that they can move on to the next rationally organized activity. Eating to refuel is far more efficient than eating to enjoy a culinary experience.

The propensity for fast-food restaurants to minimize quality is well reflected in the sad history of Colonel Harland Sanders, the founder of Kentucky Fried Chicken. The quality of his cooking techniques and his secret seasoning (which his wife originally mixed, packed, and shipped herself) led to a string of about four hundred franchised outlets by 1960. Sanders had a great commitment to quality, especially to his gravy: "To Sanders himself the supreme stuff of his art was his gravy, the blend of herbs and spices that time and patience had taught him. It was his ambition to make a gravy so good that people would simply eat the gravy and throw away 'the durned chicken.'"[10]

After Sanders sold his business in 1964, he became little more than the spokesman and symbol for Kentucky Fried Chicken. The new owners soon made clear their commitment to speed rather than quality: "The Colonel's gravy was fantastic, they agreed . . . but it was too complex, too time-consuming, too expensive. It had to be changed. It wasn't fast food."

Ray Kroc, who befriended Colonel Sanders, recalls him saying, "That friggin' . . . outfit. . . . They prostituted every goddamn thing I had. I had the greatest gravy in the world and those sons of bitches they dragged it out and extended it and watered it down that I'm so goddamn mad."[11]

At best, what customers expect from a fast-food restaurant is modest but strong-tasting food—hence, the salty/sweet french fries, highly seasoned sauces, saccharine shakes. Given such modest expectations of quality, customers do have greater expectations of quantity. They expect to get a lot of food and pay relatively little for it.

Even the more upscale McDonaldized restaurant chains are noted for the size of their portions and the mediocrity of their food. Of the Olive Garden, one reviewer said, "But what brings customers in droves to this popular chain remains a mystery. The food defined mediocrity. Nothing was bad, but nothing was especially good, and it certainly isn't authentically Italian." Of course, the reason is quantity, "Portions . . . are large. . . . So you'll probably end up leaving stuffed, which is not to say satisfied."[12]

The Cheesecake Factory, begun in Beverly Hills in 1978 and now with 63 restaurants (12 more are planned to open by the end of 2003), is another example of an upscale restaurant known for its huge portions (although many devotees consider its food to be higher in quality than, say, Olive Garden). Quantity is also in evidence in the menu consisting of over 200 highly varied items (with an average check of just under $16).[13]

### Higher Education: Grades, Scores, Ratings, and Rankings

The restaurant industry is far from being alone in its devotion to things that can be quantified. In education, most courses run for a standard number of weeks and hours per week. In the main, little attention is devoted to determining whether a given subject is best taught in a given number of weeks or hours per week. The focus seems to be on how many students (the "products") can be herded through the system and what grades they earn rather than the quality of what they have learned and of the educational experience.

An entire high school or college experience can be summed up in a single number, the grade point average (GPA). Armed with their GPAs, students can take examinations with quantifiable results, such as the PSAT, SAT, and GRE. Colleges, graduate schools, and professional schools can focus on three or four numbers in deciding whether or not to admit a student.

For their part, students may choose a university because of its rating. Is it one of the top ten universities in the country? Is its physics department in the top ten? Are its sports teams usually top ranked?

Potential employers may decide whether or not to hire graduates on the basis of their scores, their class ranking, as well as the ranking of the university from which they graduated. To increase their job prospects, students may seek to amass a number of different degrees and credentials with the hope that prospective employers will believe that the longer the list of degrees, the higher the quality of the job candidate. Personal letters of reference, however important, are often replaced by standardized forms with quantified ratings (for example, "top 5 percent of the class," "ranks 5th in class of 25").

The number of credentials a person possesses plays a role in situations other than obtaining a job. For example, people in various occupations can use long lists of initials after their names to convince prospective clients of their competence. (My BA, MBA, and PhD are supposed to persuade the reader that I am competent to write this book, although a degree in "hamburgerology" might be more relevant.) Said one insurance appraiser with ASA, FSVA, FAS, CRA, and CRE after his name, "the more [initials] you tend to put after your name, the more impressed they [potential clients] become."[14] However, the sheer number of credentials tells little about the competence of the person sporting them. Furthermore, this emphasis on quantity of credentials has led people to make creative use of letters after their names. For example, one camp director put "ABD" after his name to impress parents of prospective campers. However, as all academics know, this informal (and largely negative) label stands for "All But Dissertation," for people who have completed their graduate courses and exams but who have not written their dissertations. Also noteworthy here is the development of organizations whose sole reason for existence is to supply meaningless credentials, often through the mail.

The emphasis on quantifiable factors is common even among college professors (the "workers" if students are "products"). For example, at more and more colleges and universities, the students evaluate each course by answering questions with ratings of, for example, one to five. At the end of the semester, the professor receives what is in effect a report card with an overall teaching rating. Students have little or no room to offer qualitative evaluations of their teachers on such questionnaires. Although student ratings are desirable in a number of ways, they also have some unfortunate consequences. For example, they tend to favor professors who are performers, who have a sense of humor, or who do not demand too much from students. The serious professor who places great demands on students is not likely to do well in such ratings systems, even though he or she may offer higher-quality teaching (for example, more profound ideas) than does the performer.

Quantitative factors are important not only in teaching but also in research and publication. The "publish or perish" pressure on academicians in many colleges and universities tends to lead to great attention to the quantity of their publications rather than the quality. In hiring and promotion decisions, a resume with a long list of articles and books is generally preferred to one with a shorter list. Thus, an award-winning teacher was turned down for tenure at Rutgers University not long ago because, in the words of his department's tenure committee, his stack of publications was "not as thick as the usual packet for tenure."[15] The unfortunate consequence of this bias is the publication of less than high-quality works, the rush to publication before a work is fully developed, or publication of the same idea or finding several times with only minor variations.

Another quantitative factor in academia is the ranking of the place in which a work is published. In the hard sciences, articles in professional journals receive high marks; books are less valued. In the humanities, books are of much higher value and sometimes more prestigious than journal articles. Being published by some publishers (for example, university presses) yields more prestige than being published by others (for example, commercial presses).

In sociology, for example, a formal ratings system assigns points for publication in professional journals. A publication in the prestigious *American Sociological Review* receives ten points, the maximum in this system, and one in the far less prestigious (and in order not to hurt anyone's feelings, fictional) *Antarctic Journal of Sociology*, with a readership primarily composed of penguins, receives only one point. By this system, the professor whose journal publications yield 340 points is supposed to be twice as "good" as one who earns only 170 points.

However, as is usually the case, such an emphasis on quantity tends not to relate to quality:

- ◆ It is highly unlikely that the quality of a professor's life work can be reduced to a single number. In fact, it seems impossible to quantify the quality of an idea, theory, or research finding.
- ◆ This rating system deals with quality only indirectly. That is, the rating is based on the quality of the journal in which an article was published, not the quality of the article itself. No effort is made to evaluate the quality of

the article or its contribution to the field. Poor articles can appear in the highest-ranking journals, excellent ones in low-ranking journals.

♦ The academician who writes only a few high-quality papers might not do well in this rating system. In contrast, someone who produces a lot of mediocre work could well receive a far higher score. This kind of system tends to lead ambitious sociologists (and those in most other academic fields) to conclude that they cannot afford to spend years honing a single work because it will not pay off much in their point score.

Any system that places so much emphasis on quantity of publications will lead to the production of a great deal of mediocre work.

The sciences have come up with another quantifiable measure in an effort to evaluate the quality of work: the number of times a person's work is cited in the work of other scholars. The assumption is that high-quality, important, and influential work is likely to be used and cited by other scholars. People can use the variety of citation indexes published each year to calculate the number of citations per year for every scholar. However, once again the problem of evaluating quality arises. Can the influence of a person's academic work be reduced to a single number? Perhaps a few central uses of one scholar's ideas will influence the field more than many trivial citations of another scholar's work. Furthermore, the mere fact that a work is cited tells people nothing about how the work was used by other scholars. A worthless piece of work attacked by many people and thereby cited in their work would lead to many citations for its creator. Conversely, scholars may ignore a truly important piece of work that is ahead of its time, leading to a minuscule number of citations for the author.

Not too long ago, Donald Kennedy, then the president of Stanford University, announced a change in that university's policies for hiring, promoting, or granting tenure to faculty members. Disturbed by a report indicating "that nearly half of faculty members believe that their scholarly writings are merely counted—and not evaluated—when personnel decisions are made," Kennedy said,

> First, I hope we can agree that the quantitative use of research output as a criterion for appointment or promotion is a bankrupt idea. . . . The overproduction of routine scholarship is one of the most egregious aspects of contemporary academic life: It tends to conceal really important work by sheer volume; it wastes time and valuable resources.[16]

To deal with this problem, Kennedy proposed to limit the extent to which the number of publications would be used in making personnel decisions.

He hoped that the proposed limits would "reverse the appalling belief that counting and weighing are the important means of evaluating faculty research."[17] In spite of protestations like this one, there is little evidence that there has been much progress in reducing the emphasis on quantity rather than quality in the academic world.

In fact, in recent years there has been a massive increase in the emphasis on quantitative factors in the British academic world. For example, "League tables of universities are now produced grading research and teaching, as well as increased access by nonparticipating groups (ethnic minorities, working-class students). These make the system subject to quantitative, rather than the previous qualitative evaluations and therefore clearly *calculable*."[18]

## Health Care: Patients as Dollar Signs

In profit-making medical organizations (for example, HCA [Hospital Corporation of America] and Humana), physicians, along with all other employees, feel pressured to contribute to the corporation's profitability. For example, limiting time with each patient and maximizing the number of patients seen in a day allows the corporation to reduce costs and increase profits. This emphasis on quantity can easily threaten the quality of medical care. Profits can also be increased by pushing doctors to spend less time with patients, to see more patients, to turn down patients who probably can't pay the bills, and to see only patients who have the kinds of diseases whose treatment is likely to yield large profits.

Following the lead of profit-making medical organizations, all medical bureaucracies are now pushing medicine in the direction of greater calculability. Even nonprofit medical organizations—for example, nonprofit hospitals and health maintenance organizations, or HMOs (most HMOs are for-profit, maybe a better example would be a local clinic)—are employing professional managers and instituting sophisticated accounting systems.

The federal government, through Medicare, introduced the prospective payment and DRG (diagnostic related groups[19]) programs, in which a set amount is reimbursed to hospitals for a given medical diagnosis, no matter how long the patient is hospitalized. Prior to 1983, the government paid whatever "reasonable" amount it was billed. Outside agencies have also grown increasingly concerned about spiraling medical costs and have sought to deal with the problem by limiting what they will pay for and how much they will pay for it. Thus, a third-party payer (an insurer) might refuse to pay for certain procedures or for hospitalization or perhaps pay only a given amount.

Doctors, who have traditionally placed quality of patient care above all else (at least ideally), are complaining about the new emphasis on calculability. At least one physicians' union engaged in a strike centered on issues such as required number of visits, number of patients seen, and an incentive system tying physician salaries to productivity. As one physician union leader put it, however romantically, doctors are "the only ones who think of patients as individuals . . . not as dollar signs."[20]

### Television: Aesthetics Are Always Secondary

Television programming is heavily, if not almost exclusively, determined by quantitative factors. The ratings of a program, not its quality, determine the advertising revenue it is likely to generate and therefore its longevity. A vice president of programming for ABC made this emphasis on calculability quite clear: "Commercial television programming is designed to attract audiences to the advertisers' messages which surround the programming. . . . Inherent creative aesthetic values [quality] are important, but always secondary."[21] Over the years, the commercial networks have dropped many critically acclaimed programs because of poor ratings.

Potential programs are tested on sample audiences in an effort to predict which shows will achieve high ratings. When pilots for new shows are broadcast, those that achieve or demonstrate potential for high ratings are selected for the regular schedule. The ratings service A. C. Nielsen (founded in 1936 by Arthur C. Nielsen to measure radio audiences and which began measuring TV audiences in the 1950s) then determines the fate of television programs.[22] Nielsen places sophisticated electronic meters and hand-punched computers (as well as hand-written diaries) in the homes of a sample of American television viewers. Ratings are derived from the number of Nielsen-selected homes that tune into a particular program.

Over the years, television rating systems have grown more sophisticated. Instead of relying solely on aggregate numbers, some programs succeed or fail on the basis of their ratings within specific demographic groups. Advertisers who sell primarily to a particular demographic group will support a program with relatively low overall ratings (for example, the highly acclaimed *Homicide*, although it finally succumbed to low overall ratings and was canceled in 1999) as long as its ratings within the targeted group are high.

Of course, as is clear in the case of *Homicide,* ratings reveal nothing about a program's quality. This difference between ratings and quality has been one reason for the existence of the Public Broadcasting System (PBS). Because of its public funding, PBS can make programming decisions based more on the quality of a program than on its ratings. In fact, in at least one case, a show canceled by NBC was picked up by PBS.[23]

In spite of its power and popularity, the Nielsen system has a number of weaknesses: The sample is small (five thousand households in the national sample and approximately twenty thousand households in local samples)[24]; only a fraction of U.S. television markets are surveyed; people can lie in the ratings of those local markets where paper diaries are still used; the diary return rate varies from market to market; and so on.[25] When asked whether or not to trust Nielsen ratings, an NBC executive said, "I don't think they've given anyone a reason to trust them. The fact of the matter is, Nielsen is operating a system that is measurably deficient in reliability, accuracy and utility."[26] Nielsen continues to play a dominant role in shaping television programming, although the TV networks are moving toward creating a rival rating system.

Historically, television stations in Europe have been far more likely to be run by the government than to be owned privately. As a result, they have been less responsive to the wishes of commercial sponsors for high ratings and more interested in the quality of programs. However, even these government-run stations do program the most popular American shows. Furthermore, the advent of private European cable and satellite television networks has served to make programming decisions in European television more similar to those in American television.

### Sports: Nadia Comaneci Scored Exactly 79.275 Points

The quality of various sports has been altered by, perhaps even sacrificed to, calculability. For instance, the nature of sporting events has been changed by the needs of television.[27] Because teams in many sports earn a large part of their revenue from television contracts, they will sacrifice the interests of paid spectators, even compromise the games themselves, to increase their television income.

A good example is the so-called TV time-out. In the old days, commercials occurred during natural breaks in a game—for example, during a time-out called by one of the teams, at halftime, or between innings. But these breaks were too intermittent and infrequent to bring in the increasingly large fees advertisers were willing to pay. Now regular TV time-outs are scheduled in sports such as football and basketball. The owners of sports franchises may be maximizing their incomes from advertising, but the momentum of a team may be lost because of an inopportune TV time-out. Thus, these time-outs do alter the nature of some sports; they may even affect the outcome of games. Also, these time-outs interrupt the flow of the game for the fans who watch in person (and pay high ticket prices for the privilege). The fans at home can at least watch the commercials; the spectators at the games have little to watch until the commercial ends and the game resumes. But the owners consider such negative effects on the quality of the game insignificant compared with the economic gain from increased advertising.

Clearly though, sports continue to place a premium on the quality of both individual and team performance: the power of basketball star Shaquille O'Neill and the teamwork of the championship teams of the New York Yankees of the late 1990s and 2000. At the same time, quantitative factors have always been enormously important in sports. In many cases, quality is directly related to quantity: The better the performance, the higher the score and the greater the number of victories. However, over the years, the emphasis on the quantifiable attributes of sports has increased:

> Modern sports are characterized by the almost inevitable tendency to transform every athletic feat into one that can be quantified and measured. The accumulation of statistics on every conceivable aspect of the game is a hallmark of football, baseball, hockey, and of track and field too, where the accuracy of quantification has, thanks to an increasingly precise technology, reached a degree that makes the stopwatch seem positively primitive.[28]

Even a highly aesthetic sport such as gymnastics has been quantified:

> How can one rationalize and quantify a competition in gymnastics, in aesthetics? The answer now seems obvious. Set up an interval scale and a panel of judges and then take the arithmetic mean of the subjective evaluations. . . . Nadia Comaneci scored exactly 79.275 points in Montreal, neither more nor less. The ingenuity of Homo Mensor must not be underestimated.[29]

The growing emphasis on quantity can sometimes adversely affect the quality of play in a sport. For example, the basketball star motivated by a need to stand out individually and score as many points as possible may negatively affect the play of individual teammates and the team's overall performance. The quality of play is even more compromised by owners' attempts to maximize points scored.

Basketball, for example, was once a rather leisurely game in which a team could take as long as necessary to bring the ball down the court and get a player into position to take a good shot. Basketball fans enjoyed the strategies and maneuvers employed by the players. Toward the end of the game, a team holding a slim lead could attempt to "freeze" the ball—that is, not risk missing a shot and thereby giving their opponents a chance to take possession of the ball.

A few decades ago, however, the leadership of collegiate and professional basketball decided that fans raised in the McDonald's era wanted to see faster games and many more points scored. In other words, fans wanted from basketball what they got from their fast-food restaurant: great speed and large quantities. Hence, in college games, offensive teams were limited to thirty-five seconds in which to attempt a shot; in professional games, twenty-four-second time clocks were established. Although the "run-and-shoot" style of play generated by the time clocks has created faster-paced, higher-scoring games, it may have adversely affected the quality of play. No longer is there much time for the maneuvers and strategies that made the game so interesting to "purists." But a run-and-shoot style of basketball fits in well with the McDonaldized "eat-and-move" world of dinners purchased at drive-through windows and consumed on the run.

Interestingly, in recent years, professional basketball teams have developed new defensive strategies and the scores of game have plummeted. There is now interest in making further changes in the game to reduce the advantages of the defensive team and thereby once again inflate the scores.

Similarly, baseball owners decided long ago that fans prefer to see high-scoring games with lots of hits, home runs, and runs scored rather than the kind of game favored by "purists": pitchers' duels in which the final score might be 1–0. Thus, they took a number of steps to increase the number of runs scored. Livelier baseballs travel farther than old-fashioned "dead balls." In some baseball parks, outfield fences have been brought closer to home plate to increase the number of home runs.

The designated hitter, found in the American League but not in the more traditional National League, is the most notable effort to increase hits and runs. Instead of the often weak-hitting pitcher taking his turn at bat, someone whose main (and sometimes only) skill is hitting replaces him. Designated hitters get more hits, hit more home runs, and help produce more runs than pitchers who are allowed to bat.

Although use of the designated hitter in American League baseball has undoubtedly increased the number of runs scored, it has also affected, perhaps adversely, the quality of the game (this is why the National

League has steadfastly refused to adopt the designated hitter). For example, when pitchers bat in certain situations they often employ a sacrifice bunt, a very artful practice that is intended to advance a runner already on base. But a designated hitter rarely sacrifices an at-bat by bunting. Pinch hitters play less of a role when designated hitters replace weak-hitting pitchers.[30] Finally, if there is less need to pinch hit for them, starting pitchers can remain in games longer, which reduces the need for relief pitchers.[31] In these and other ways, baseball is a different game when a designated hitter is employed. In other words, the quality of the game has changed, some would say for the worse, because of the emphasis on quantity.

### Politics: There Were No Sound Bites in the Lincoln-Douglas Debate

The political sector offers a number of revealing examples of the emphasis on calculability—for example, the increasing importance of polls in political campaigns.[32] Candidates and incumbents, obsessed by their ratings in political polls, often adjust their positions on issues or the actions they take on the basis of what pollsters say will increase (or not lower) their rankings. How a specific political position affects ratings can become more important than whether the politician genuinely believes in it.

Television has also affected politics in various ways. It has led to shorter conventions, for one thing, as well as shorter political speeches. In the famous Lincoln-Douglas debates of 1858, the candidates "spoke for ninety minutes each on a single topic: the future of slavery in the territories."[33] Prior to television, political speeches on radio at first often lasted an hour; by the 1940s, the norm had dropped to thirty minutes. In the early years of television, speeches also lasted about half an hour, but because political campaign speeches became more tailored to television coverage and less to the immediate audience, speeches have grown shorter, less than twenty minutes on the average. By the 1970s, speeches had been largely replaced by the sixty-second advertisement. In today's televised presidential debates, candidates have a minute or two to offer their position on a given issue.

News reports of political speeches have shrunk to fit the visual demands of television as well. By the 1984 presidential campaign, only about fifteen seconds of a speech would likely find its way onto a national news program. Four years later, speaking time on such reports shrank to only nine seconds.[34] As a result, political speechwriters concentrate on creating ten- or fifteen-second "sound bites" that are likely to be picked up by the national networks. This emphasis on length has clearly reduced the quality of public political speeches and therefore the quality of public discourse on important political issues.

Not surprisingly, calculability also affected foreign policy. One area that displayed an absolute mania for numbers was nuclear deterrence.[35] Although this issue is less publicly visible now that the Cold War has ended, there are no signs that either the United States or Russia plans to give up its ability to deter the other from launching a nuclear attack. Both sides continue to possess nuclear arsenals large enough to destroy each other many times over. Nevertheless, their efforts to negotiate treaties reducing nuclear weapons often became bogged down in trying to assess accurately the size and power—"the relative throw weight"—of their respective nuclear arms. Although accurate measures were undoubtedly important in trying to achieve parity, both sides tended to get lost in the minutiae of the numbers and lose sight of the qualitative fact that both sides could eliminate most of their nuclear weapons and still retain the ability to destroy the other side, even the world as a whole. Here we have one of the clearest manifestations of the irrationality of rationality.

### Other Settings: Junk Food Journalism and Tourist Junk(ets)

An interesting example of the emphasis on quantity over quality is the newspaper *USA TODAY*.[36] *USA TODAY* is the kind of newspaper that can be read in about the time it takes a person to consume a meal at a fast-food restaurant.[37] One observer underscored the newspaper's corresponding lack of concern for quality: "Like parents who take their children to a different fast-food joint every night and keep the refrigerator stocked with ice cream, *USA TODAY* gives its readers only what they want. No spinach, no bran, no liver."[38]

The package tour is another example of calculability, with its clear emphasis on the quantity of sights visited rather than the quality of those visits.[39] A tourist can see lots of sights (often through a bus window) in many different countries, but the quality of the sight-seeing is very superficial. When tourists return from such a trip, they can crow about the large number of countries and sights visited, slides taken, and video-tapes filled. (They can even bore their friends for hours with interminable slide or video shows of their trip.) However, given the nature of such trips, devotees of packaged tours are hard-pressed to tell their friends very much about the countries they visited or the sights they saw.

A host of other enterprises are obsessed with size these days. Concerned with flagging business, in 1997 Kmart refurbished some of its stores and called them "Big Kmart." Its superstores that combine a traditional Kmart with a supermarket are called "Super Kmart Centers."[40] While Kmart is in great financial difficulties these days (in fact, it's bankrupt), other far more successful competitors have moved in this direction as exemplified by Super Target and Wal-Mart Supercenter.

## ◆ GIVING THE ILLUSION OF QUANTITY

Quantity is often more illusion than reality in a fast-food restaurant. For example, the big, fluffy (and inexpensive) bun that surrounds the meat patty makes the burger seem bigger than it is. To further the illusion, the burger and various fixings are sized to stick out of the bun, as if the bun, as large as it is, cannot contain the "tremendous" portion within. Similarly, special scoops arrange fries in such a way that a portion looks enormous. The bags and boxes seem to bulge at the top, overflowing with french fries. The insides of the boxes for McDonald's large fries are striped to further the illusion. In fact, each package contains only a few pennies worth of potato. Indeed, there is a huge profit margin in the fries and other menu items. Burger King fries are sold at 400% of their cost! Drinks at Burger King involve a 600% markup.[41] Thus, the consumers' calculus is wrong: They are not getting a lot for a little.

To be fair, fast-food restaurants probably give more food for less money than is the case in a traditional restaurant. However, fast-food restaurants do much more business than a traditional restaurant. They may earn less profit on each meal, but they sell many more meals.

Many other McDonaldized systems offer illusory images of great quantity. For example, malls seem to offer a great variety of novel shopping opportunities, but one mall is much the same as virtually every other mall. Television appears to offer a wide variety of shows, but in fact, many are copies of already successful programs. *USA TODAY* appears to be a full-service newspaper, but most of it is snippets of news and fluff. Diet centers and diet programs promise great weight loss, but the vast majority of the clients who do lose the weight end up gaining it back very quickly. Professors who want to create the illusion of quantity in their list of publications include items such as self-published reports or books published by "vanity presses," which require payment from the author. Such books, often produced in very limited numbers, may reach few but the author's immediate family. Thus, what appears to be a lengthy list of publications may, on closer scrutiny, turn out to represent very modest productivity.

## ◆ REDUCING PRODUCTION
##   AND SERVICE TO NUMBERS

The emphasis on the number of sales made and the size of the products offered are not the only manifestations of calculability in fast-food restaurants. Another example is the great emphasis on the speed with which a meal can be served. In fact, Ray Kroc's first outlet was named McDonald's Speedee Service Drive-In. At one time, McDonald's sought to serve a hamburger, shake, and french fries in 50 seconds. The restaurant made a great breakthrough in 1959 when it served a record thirty-six hamburgers in 110 seconds.

### The Fast-Food Industry: A Precooked
### Hamburger Measures Exactly 3.875 Inches

Many other fast-food restaurants have adopted McDonald's zeal for measuring performance. Burger King, for example, seeks to serve a customer within three minutes of entering the restaurant.[42] The drive-through window drastically reduces the time required to process a customer through a fast-food restaurant. Speed is obviously a quantifiable factor of monumental importance in a fast-food restaurant.

Speed is even more important to the pizza-delivery business. At Domino's, the mantra is "Hustle! Do It! Hustle! Do It! Hustle! Do It!" and the "Domino's goal is eight minutes out the door."[43] Not only does the number sold depend on how quickly the pizzas can be delivered, but also a fresh pizza must be transported quickly to arrive hot. Special insulated containers now help to keep the pizzas hot longer. However, this emphasis on rapid delivery has caused several scandals. Pressure to make fast deliveries has led young delivery people to become involved in serious and sometimes fatal automobile accidents.

Still another aspect of the emphasis on quantity lies in the precision with which every element in the production of fast food is measured. At frozen yogurt franchises, containers are often weighed to be sure they include the correct quantity of frozen yogurt. In old-fashioned ice cream parlors, the attendants simply filled a container to the brim. McDonald's itself takes great care in being sure that each raw McDonald's hamburger weighs exactly 1.6 ounces—ten hamburgers to a pound of meat. The precooked hamburger measures precisely 3.875 inches in diameter, the bun exactly 3.5 inches. McDonald's invented the "fatilyzer" to ensure that its regular hamburger meat had no more than 19% fat.[44] Greater fat content would lead to greater shrinkage during cooking and prevent the hamburger from appearing too large for the bun. The french fry scoop helps make sure that each package has about the same number of fries. The automatic drink dispensers ensure that each cup gets the correct amount of soft drink with nothing lost to spillage.

Arby's has reduced the cooking and serving of roast beef to a series of exact measures.[45] All roasts weigh ten pounds at the start. They are roasted at 200 degrees Fahrenheit for 3.5 hours until the internal temperature is 135 degrees. Then they are allowed to cook in their own heat for twenty minutes more until the internal temperature is 140 degrees. By following these steps and making these measurements, Arby's doesn't need a skilled chef; virtually anyone who can read and count can cook an Arby's roast beef. When the roasts are done, each weighs between nine pounds, four ounces, and nine pounds, seven ounces. Every roast beef sandwich has three ounces of meat, allowing Arby's to get forty-seven sandwiches (give or take one) from each roast.

Burger King has also quantified quality control. Hamburgers must be served within ten minutes of being cooked. French fries may stand under the heat lamp for no more than seven minutes. A manager is allowed to throw away 0.3% of all food.[46]

The performance of fast-food restaurants is also assessed quantitatively, not qualitatively. At McDonald's, for example, central management judges the performance of each restaurant "by 'the numbers': by sales per crew person, profits, turnover, and QSC [Quality, Service, Cleanliness] ratings."[47]

While the fast-food restaurant has greatly increased the emphasis on calculability, it had many precursors, including the original *The Boston Cooking School Cook Book* (1896), in which Fannie Farmer emphasized precise measurement and in the process helped to rationalize home cooking:

Before her death she had changed American kitchen terminology from "a pinch" and "a dash" and "a heaping spoonful"—all vague terms which she detested—to her own precise, standardized, scientific terms, presenting a model of cooking that was easy, reliable, and could be followed even by inexperienced cooks. To Fannie Farmer, "the mother of level measurement," we can attribute the popularity of such precise everyday kitchen terms as level teaspoon, teaspoon, measuring cup, oven thermometer, and "bake at 350 degrees for 40 minutes."[48]

### The Workplace: A Penny the Size of a Cartwheel

With scientific management, Taylor intended to transform everything work related into quantifiable dimensions. Instead of relying on the worker's "rule of thumb," scientific management sought to develop precise measurements of how much work was to be done by each and every motion of the worker. Everything that could be reduced to numbers was then analyzed using mathematical formulas.

Calculability was clearly an aim when Taylor sought to increase the amount of pig iron a worker could load in a day: "We found that this gang were loading on the average about 12½ long tons per man per day. We were surprised to find, after studying the matter, that a first-class pig iron handler ought to handle between 47 and 48 long tons per day, instead of 12½ tons."[49] To try to nearly quadruple the workload, Taylor studied the way the most productive workers, the "first-class men," operated. He divided their work into its basic elements and timed each step with a stopwatch down to hundredths of a minute.

On the basis of this careful study, Taylor and his associates developed the one best way to carry pig iron. They then found a worker they could motivate to work this way—Schmidt, who was able and ambitious and to whom a penny looked "about the size of a cart-wheel," as one coworker said. Schmidt indicated that he wanted to be a "high-priced man." Taylor used a precise economic incentive: $1.85 per day, rather than the usual $1.15, if Schmidt agreed to work exactly the way Taylor told him to. After careful training and supervision, Schmidt successfully worked at the faster pace (and earned the higher pay); Taylor then selected and trained other employees to work the same way.

Schmidt and his successors were being asked to do about 3.6 times the normal amount of work for an approximately 60% increase in pay. Taylor defended this exploitation in various ways. For example, he argued that it would be unfair to workers in other areas who were working up to their capabilities to have pig iron handlers earn 3.6 times as much as they did. For another, Taylor argued that he and his associates had decided (without, of course, consulting the workers themselves) that a greater share of the profits would not be in the workers' interests. For Taylor, "the pig iron handler with his 60-percent increase in wages is not an object for pity but rather a subject for congratulations."[50]

Also illustrative of the impact of calculability on industry is the famous case of the Ford Pinto.[51] Because of competition from the manufacturers of small foreign cars, Ford rushed the Pinto into production, even though preproduction tests had indicated its fuel system would rupture easily in a rear-end collision. The expensive assembly line machinery for the Pinto was already in place, so Ford decided to go ahead with the production of the car without any changes. Ford based its decision on a quantitative comparison. The company estimated that the defects would lead to 180 deaths and about the same number of injuries. Placing a value, or rather a cost, on them of $200,000 per person, Ford decided that the total cost from these deaths and injuries would be less than the $11 per car it would cost to repair the defect. Although this calculation may have made sense from the point of view of profits, it was an unreasonable decision in that human lives were sacrificed and people maimed in the name of lower costs and higher profits. This is only one of the most extreme of a number of such decisions made daily in a society undergoing McDonaldization.

## ◆ CONCLUSION

Calculability, the second dimension of McDonaldization, involves an emphasis on quantification. This emphasis shows up in various ways but especially in the focus on the quantity rather than the quality of products, the widespread efforts to create the illusion of quantity, and the tendency to reduce production and service processes to numbers.

This emphasis on calculability brings with it many advantages, especially the ability to obtain large numbers and sizes of things at relatively little cost. However, it also brings with it a powerful downside, especially the fact that in a society that emphasizes quantity, goods and services tend to be increasingly mediocre.

# 5

# Predictability

◆

## It Never Rains on Those
## Little Houses on the Hillside

The third dimension of McDonaldization is predictability. In a rationalized society, people prefer to know what to expect in most settings and at most times. They neither desire nor expect surprises. They want to know that when they order their Big Mac today it will be identical to the one they ate yesterday and the one they will eat tomorrow. People would be upset if the special sauce was used one day, but not the next or if it tasted differently from one day to the next. They want to know that the McDonald's franchise they visit in Des Moines, Los Angeles, or Paris will appear and operate much the same as their local McDonald's. To achieve predictability, a rationalized society emphasizes discipline, order, systematization, formalization, routine, consistency, and methodical operation.

From the consumer's point of view, predictability makes for much peace of mind in day-to-day dealings. For workers, predictability makes tasks easier. In fact, some workers prefer effortless, mindless, repetitive work because, if nothing else, it allows them to think of other things, even daydream, while they are doing their tasks.[1] For managers and owners, too, predictability makes life easier: It helps them in managing both workers and customers and aids in anticipating needs for supplies and materials, personnel requirements, income, and profits.

However, predictability has a downside. It has a tendency to turn everything—consumption, work, management—into mind-numbing routine.

The major aspects of predictability to be covered in this chapter are creating predictable settings, scripting interaction with customers, making employee behavior predictable, creating predictable products and processes, and minimizing danger and unpleasantness.

## ♦ CREATING PREDICTABLE SETTINGS

A good place to begin a discussion of predictability is not with McDonald's but with another pioneer of rationalization: the motel chains. Most notable are Best Western, founded in 1946 (and which claims to be the world's largest hotel chain with over 4,000 hotels in eighty countries),[2] and Holiday Inn, which started in 1952 (and is now part of the Inter-Continental Hotels Group with more than 3,300 hotels in over 100 countries).[3] By the late 1950s, about five hundred Howard Johnson's restaurants were scattered around the United States, many with standardized motels attached to them. (Unlike other motel chains, Howard Johnson's has stagnated, and there are about the same number of its motels today as there were in 1952.)[4] These three motel chains had opened in anticipation of the massive expansion of highways and highway travel. Their success in bringing consistency to the motel and hotel industry has been widely emulated.

### Motel Chains: "Magic Fingers" but No Norman Bates

Before the development of such chains, motels were highly unpredictable and diverse. Run by local owners, every motel was different from every other. Because the owners and employees varied from one locale to another, guests could not always feel fully safe and sleep soundly. One motel might be quite comfortable, even luxurious, but another might well be a hovel. People could never be sure which amenities would be present—soap, shampoo, telephones, radio (and later television), air conditioning, and please don't forget the much-loved "Magic Fingers" massage system. Checking into a motel was an adventure; a traveler never knew what to expect.

In his classic thriller, *Psycho* (1960), Alfred Hitchcock beautifully exploited the anxieties about old-fashioned, unpredictable motels. The motel in the movie was creepy but not as creepy as its owner, Norman Bates. Although it offered few amenities, the Bates Motel room did come equipped with a peephole (something most travelers could do without) so that Norman could spy on his victims. Of course, the Bates Motel offered the ultimate in unpredictability: a homicidal maniac and a horrible death to unsuspecting guests.

Although very few motels in 1960 actually housed crazed killers, all sorts of unpredictabilities confronted travelers at that time. The motel chains took pains to make their guests' experience predictable. They developed tight hiring practices to keep "unpredictable" people from managing or working in them. Travelers could anticipate that a motel equipped with the familiar orange and green Holiday Inn sign (now gone the way of McDonald's oversized golden arches) would have most, if not all, the amenities they could reasonably expect in a moderately priced motel. Faced with the choice between a local, no-name motel and a Holiday Inn, many travelers preferred the predictable—even if it had liabilities (the absence of a personal touch, for example). The success of the early motel chains has led to many imitators, such as Ramada Inn and Rodeway Inn (now part of Choice Hotels International).

The more price-conscious chains—Super 8 (2,088 sites), Days Inn (1,944 locations) and Motel 6 (814 locations)—are, if anything, even more predictable.[5] The budget motel chains are predictably barren; guests find only the minimal requirements. But they expect the minimum, and that's what they get. They also expect, and receive, bargain-basement prices for the rooms.

### The Fast-Food Industry: Thank God for Those Golden Arches

The fast-food industry quickly adopted and perfected practices pioneered by, among other precursors, the motel chains. In fact, Robin Leidner argues that "the heart of McDonald's success is its uniformity and predictability . . . [its] relentless standardization." She argues that "there is a McDonald's way to handle virtually every detail of the business, and that doing things differently means doing things wrong."[6] Although McDonald's allows its franchisees and managers to innovate, "The object is to look for new innovative ways to create an experience that is exactly the same no matter what McDonald's you walk into, no matter where it is in the world."[7]

Like the motel chains, McDonald's (and many other franchises) devised a large and garish sign that soon became familiar to customers. McDonald's "golden arches" evokes a sense of predictability: "Replicated color and symbol, mile after mile, city after city, act as a tacit promise of *predictability* and stability between McDonald's and its millions of customers, year after year, meal after meal [italics added]."[8] Furthermore, each McDonald's presents a series of predictable elements—counter, menu marquee above it, "kitchen" visible in the background, tables and uncomfortable seats, prominent trash bins, drive-through windows, and so on.

This predictable setting appears not only throughout the United States but also in many other parts of the world. Thus, homesick American tourists can take comfort in the knowledge that nearly anywhere they go they will likely run into those familiar golden arches and the restaurant to which they have become so accustomed. Interestingly, even many non-Americans now take comfort in the appearance of a familiar McDonald's restaurant when they journey to other countries, including the United States itself.

### Other Settings: E.T. Can't Find His Home

As work settings, bureaucracies are far more predictable than other kinds of organizations. They engender predictability in at least three important ways:

1. *Offices.* People occupy "offices," or positions, each defined by a set of responsibilities and expected behaviors. Those who occupy an office are expected to live up to those expectations. Thus, coworkers or clients can expect the same performance from an office no matter who happens to occupy it. Although there is some leeway, occupants of given offices cannot refuse to perform their functions or do them very differently without being punished or fired.

2. *Hierarchies.* A bureaucracy also has a clear hierarchy of offices so that people know whom to take orders from and whom they may give orders to.

3. *Documentation.* Virtually everything in a bureaucracy exists in written form. Thus, those who read the organization's rules and regulations know what can be expected. Handling an issue often involves little more than filling out a particular form.

Modern suburban housing also demonstrates the predictability of settings in a McDonaldized society. A famous folk song characterizes the suburbs as

> Little boxes on the hillside,
> Little boxes made of ticky-tacky,

Little boxes, little boxes, little boxes
Little boxes all the same[9]

In many suburban communities, interiors and exteriors are little different from one house to another. Although some diversity exists in the more expensive developments, many suburbanites could easily wander into someone else's house and not realize immediately that they were not in their own home.

Furthermore, the communities themselves look very much alike. To replace mature trees bulldozed to allow for the more efficient building of houses, rows of saplings held up by posts and wire are planted. Similarly, hills are often bulldozed to flatten the terrain. Streets are laid out in familiar patterns. With such predictable landmarks, suburbanites may well enter the wrong suburban community or get lost in their own community.

Several of Steven Spielberg's movies take place in these rationalized suburbs. Spielberg's strategy is to lure viewers into this highly predictable world and then hit them with a highly unpredictable event. For example, in *E.T.* (1982) an extraterrestrial wanders into a suburban development of tract houses and is discovered by a child there who, up to that point, has lived a highly predictable suburban existence. The unpredictable E.T. eventually disrupts not only the lives of the child and his family but also the entire community. Similarly, *Poltergeist* (1982) takes place in a suburban household with evil spirits disrupting its predictable tranquility. (The spirits first manifest themselves through another key element of a McDonaldized society: the television set.) The great success of several of Spielberg's movies may be traceable to people's longing for some unpredictability, even if it is frightening and menacing, in their increasingly predictable suburban lives.

*The Truman Show* (1998) takes place in a community completely controlled by the director of a television show. The movie can be seen as a spoof of, and attack on, the Disneyesque "planned communities" springing up throughout the United States. These are often more upscale than the typical suburban community. The leading example of a planned community is, not surprisingly, Disney's town of Celebration, Florida. Potential homeowners must choose among approved options and are strictly limited in what they can do with their homes and property.[10] These communities go farther than traditional suburban developments in seeking to remove all unpredictability from peoples' lives.

Then there is another 1998 movie, *Pleasantville*, which depicts a 1950ish community that is tightly controlled and characterized by a high degree of conformity and uniformity. This is reflected in the fact that everything is depicted in black and white. However, as the story unfolds, things grow less and less predictable and color is gradually introduced into the movie. In the end, a far more unpredictable Pleasantville is depicted in full color.

Although they strive hard to be as predictable as possible, some of the more recent chains are finding a high degree of predictability an elusive goal. For example, haircutting franchises such as Hair Cuttery cannot offer a uniform haircut because every head is slightly different and every barber or hairdresser operates in a slightly idiosyncratic fashion. To reassure the anxious customer longing for predictability, MasterCuts, Great Clips, and Hair Cuttery and other haircutting franchises offer a common logo and signs, similar shop setup, and perhaps a few familiar products.

## ♦ SCRIPTING INTERACTION WITH CUSTOMERS

Even more reminiscent of *The Truman Show* are the scripts that McDonaldized organizations prepare for employees. In the movie, every character's interaction with Truman followed a script provided by the director to make Truman's actions more predictable. Similarly, fast-food restaurants tell employees what to say in various circumstances to make what they say, and what is said back to them, more predictable.

### The Fast-Food Industry: "Howdy Pardner" and "Happy Trails"

Much of what is said in fast-food restaurants by both employees and customers is ritualized,[11] routinized, even scripted.[12] For example, the Roy Rogers chain used to have its employees, dressed in cowboy and cowgirl uniforms, say, "Howdy Pardner" to every customer about to order food. After paying for the food, people were sent on their way with "Happy trails." The repetition of these familiar salutations visit after visit was a source of great satisfaction to regulars at Roy Rogers. Many people (including me) felt a deep personal loss when Roy Rogers ceased this practice. However, in a McDonaldized society, other types of pseudo interactions are increasingly the norm. Consumers have come to expect and maybe even like them and they might even look back on them longingly when interactions with their favorite robot are all they can expect on their visits to fast-food restaurants.

Not only are general scripts given to employees but also a series of subscripts that can be followed in the case of unusual requests or behaviors. There might be a subscript for customers who object to being subjected to the same scripted interaction as everyone else. In fact, the subscript might be written to appear as if it reflects the "real" feelings of the employee and is not scripted. For example, a subscript might direct employees to say they will bend the rules "just this once." Recalcitrant customers are satisfied because they feel as if they are getting individualized treatment and an authentic response, and managers are happy because their employees are following the subscripts.

Like all other aspects of McDonaldization, scripts can have positive functions. For example, scripts can be a source of power to employees, enabling them to control interaction with customers. Employees can fend off unwanted or extraordinary demands merely by refusing to deviate from the script. Employees can also use their routines and scripts to protect themselves from the insults and indignities that are frequently heaped on them by the public. Employees can adopt the view that the public's hostility is aimed not at them personally but at the scripts and those who created them. Overall, rather than being hostile toward scripts and routines, McDonald's workers often find them useful and even satisfying.[13]

However, employees and customers sometimes resist scripts (and other routines). As a result, what those who give and receive services actually say "is never entirely predictable."[14] People do not yet live in an iron cage of McDonaldization. In fact, they are unlikely ever to live in a totally predictable, completely McDonaldized world.

Nonetheless, the things McDonald's workers could do to exert some independence in their work are hardly overwhelming:

♦ They could say all sorts of things that are not in the script.
♦ They could go a "bit" beyond the routine by providing extra services or exchanging pleasantries.
♦ They could withhold smiles, act a bit impatient or irritated, or refuse to encourage the customer to return.
♦ They could focus on offering even speedier service to avoid demeaning behavior such as faking seeming friendliness.[15]

These all seem like very small deviations from an otherwise highly routinized workday.

As in the case of workers, customers also gain from scripts and routines: "Routinization can provide service-recipients with more reliable, less expensive, or speedier service, can protect them from incompetence, can minimize the interactive demands on them, and can clarify what their rights are." Such routines help guarantee equal treatment of all customers. Finally, routinization can help "establish a floor of civility and competence for which many customers have reason to be grateful."[16] Some customers appreciate the polite ritualized greetings they encounter at McDonaldized businesses.

However, there are exceptions. Some customers may react negatively to employees mindlessly following scripts, who may seem "unresponsive," or "robot-like."[17] Arguments may ensue, and angry customers may even leave without being served. In a classic scene from *Five Easy Pieces* (1970), Jack Nicholson's character stops at a diner and encounters a traditional greasy-spoon waitress, who is following a script: He cannot get an order of toast even though he could order a sandwich made *with* toast. Nicholson's character reacts even more strongly and negatively to the unresponsive script than he does to the surly waitress.

The fake friendliness of scripted interaction reflects the insincere camaraderie ("have a nice day") that characterizes not only fast-food restaurants but also all other elements of McDonaldized society, a camaraderie used to lure customers and keep them coming back. For example, before his death in 2002, TV screens were saturated with scenes of Wendy's owner and founder, Dave Thomas, extending a "personal invitation" to join him for a burger at his restaurant.[18]

### Other Settings: Even the Jokes Are Scripted

The fast-food industry is far from the only place we are likely to encounter scripted interaction. Telemarketing is another setting that usually provides scripts that workers must follow unerringly. The scripts are designed to handle most foreseeable contingencies. Supervisors often listen in on solicitations to make sure employees follow the correct procedures. Employees who fail to follow the scripts, or who do not meet the quotas for the number of calls made and sales completed in a given time, may be fired summarily.

Robin Leidner details how Combined Insurance tried to make life insurance sales predictable: "The most striking thing about Combined Insurance's training for its life insurance agents was the amazing degree of standardization for which the company was striving. The agents were told, in almost hilarious detail, what to say and do." In fact, a large portion of the agents' sales pitch was "supposed to be memorized and recited precisely as possible." One of the trainers told of a foreign salesman whose English was poor: "He learned the script phonetically and didn't even know what the words meant. . . . He sold twenty applications on his first day and is now a top executive."[19] The insurance agents were even taught the company's standard joke, as well as "the Combined shuffle"— the standardized movements, body carriage, and intonation.

McDonald's relies on external constraints on its workers, but Combined Insurance attempts to transform its workers. Combined workers are supposed to embrace a new self (a "McIdentity"[20]); in contrast, McDonald's employees are expected to suppress their selves. This dissimilarity is traceable to differences in the nature of the work in the two settings. Because McDonald's workers perform their tasks within the work setting, they can be controlled by external constraints. In contrast, Combined Insurance salespeople work door-to-door, with most of their work done inside customers' homes. Because external constraints do not work, Combined tries to change the agents into the kind of people the company wants. In spite of the efforts to control their personalities, however, the insurance agents retain some discretion as well as a sense of autonomy. Thus, although control over Combined workers goes deeper, McDonald's workers are still more controlled because virtually all decision making is removed from their jobs.

Leidner concludes, "No detail is too trivial, no relationship too personal, no experience too individual, no manipulation too cynical for some organization or person, in a spirit of helpfulness or efficiency, to try to provide a standard, replicable routine for it."[21]

Somewhat like Combined Insurance's sales force, politicians are increasingly constrained by scripts composed by their advisers. There was a time when U.S. presidents composed their own speeches, but with the presidency of Ronald Reagan, it became the norm to rely on words written by professional speechwriters (Bill Clinton was sometimes an exception to this norm[22]). Among many other scripted phrases was the first George Bush's famous "Read my lips: no new taxes,"[23] and his son is well-known for his reluctance to speak extemporaneously and his need to rely heavily on scripts written by his advisers and speechwriters. Bush Jr. was recently accused by many in the media of controlling who asked what questions during press conferences. During a March 6, 2003, last-minute prime-time conference, it was reported that "White House reporter Larry McQuillan, seated in the front row, stopped raising his hand after he realized that Bush—who himself used the word 'scripted' during the news conference to describe what was going on—was calling on names from a list and not deviating from it."[24]

## ♦ MAKING EMPLOYEE BEHAVIOR PREDICTABLE

The assembly line enhanced the likelihood of predictable work and products. The problem with the alternative is that the steps a craftsperson takes are somewhat unpredictable, varying from person to person and over time. Small but significant differences in the finished products crop up, which lead to unpredictabilities in the functioning and quality of the products. For instance, one car produced by a craftsperson would run far better or be much less prone to breakdowns than a car produced by another; cars produced on an assembly line are far more uniform. Realizing the benefits to be gained from predictable worker performance, many nonmanufacturing industries now have highly developed systems for making employee behavior more routine.

### The Fast-Food Industry: Even Hamburger University's Professors Behave Predictably

Because interaction between customer and counter person in the fast-food restaurant is limited in length and scope, it can be largely routinized. Thus, McDonald's has a series of regulations that employees must follow in their dealings with customers. There are, for example, seven steps to window service: greet the customer, take the order, assemble the order, present the order, receive payment, thank the customer, and ask for repeat business.[25] Fast-food restaurants also seek to make other work as predictable as possible. For example, all employees are expected to cook hamburgers in the same, one-best way. In other words, "Frederick Taylor's principles can be applied to assembling hamburgers as easily as to other kinds of tasks."[26]

Fast-food restaurants try in many ways to make workers look, act, and think more predictably.[27] Thus, all employees must wear uniforms and follow dress codes for things such as makeup, hair length, and jewelry. Training programs are designed to indoctrinate the worker into a "corporate culture,"[28] such as the McDonald's attitude and way of doing things. Highly detailed manuals spell out, among other things, "how often the bathroom must be cleaned to the temperature of grease used to fry potatoes . . . and what color nail polish to wear."[29] Finally, incentives (awards, for example) are used to reward employees who behave properly, and disincentives, ultimately firing, to deal with those who do not.

To help ensure predictable thinking and behavior among restaurant managers, McDonald's has them attend its central Hamburger University or one of its branches throughout the United States and the world.[30] Even the "professors" at Hamburger University behave predictably because "they work from scripts prepared by the curriculum development department."[31] Trained by such teachers, managers internalize McDonald's ethos and its way of doing things. As a result, in demeanor and behavior, McDonald's managers are hard to distinguish from one another. More important, because the managers train and oversee workers to help make them behave more predictably, managers use elaborate corporate guidelines that detail how virtually everything is to be done in all restaurants. McDonald's central headquarters periodically sends forth "undercover" inspectors to be sure that these guidelines are being enforced. These inspectors also check to see that the food meets quality control guidelines.

## Other Settings: That Disney Look

Amusement parks have adopted many similar techniques. For example, to overcome the problem of unpredictable appearance and behavior among employees, Disney has developed detailed guidelines about what Disney employees should look like (the "Disney look") and how they should act. Disney has assembled a long list of "do's" and "don'ts" for different kinds of employees. Female "cast members" (a Disney euphemism for its park employees) who are not in costume must not wear jeans, clinging fabrics, athletic shoes, socks of any kind, hoop earrings, bracelets, or more than two necklaces. Female hosts may not use eyeliner or frost their hair; they must use a deodorant or antiperspirant. Mustaches and beards are unacceptable for male hosts. The list goes on and on.[32]

Disney is not alone among amusement parks in the effort to make employee behavior predictable. At Busch Gardens, Virginia, "a certain amount of energy is devoted to making sure that smiles are kept in place. There are rules about short hair (for the boys) and no eating, drinking, smoking, or straw chewing on duty (for everyone). 'We're just supposed to be perfect, see,' one employee . . . said cheerfully."[33]

Not only do the employees at Busch Gardens all look alike, but they are also supposed to act alike:

Controlled environments hinge on the maintenance of the right kind of attitude among the lower echelons.

"It is kind of a rah-rah thing. We emphasize cleanliness, being helpful, being polite."

Consequently, there is a lot of talk at Busch Gardens about All-American images and keeping people up and motivated. At the giant, *somewhat* German restaurant, the Festhaus, there are contests to determine who has the most enthusiasm and best attitude. One of the prizes is free trips to King's Dominion, Busch Garden's arch rival up the road [italics added].[34]

Such techniques ensure that visitors to Busch Gardens and parks like it can expect to see and deal with highly predictable employees throughout their visit.

## ◆ CREATING PREDICTABLE PRODUCTS AND PROCESSES

The drive for increased predictability extends, not surprisingly, to the goods and services being sold and the methods used to produce and deliver them. Consider the uniformity that characterizes the chain stores dominating virtually all malls. Few of the products are unique—indeed many are globally available brand names—and procedures for displaying merchandise, greeting customers, ringing up purchases, and so on are amazingly similar.

The superstores that compete with smaller chain stores and local shops take predictability of product a giant step further. Take Barnes & Noble's superstores. Such superstores stock far more titles, perhaps as many as 150,000 per store, than small local bookstores. Although they focus on a few best-sellers, it is also true that the book superstores do stock large numbers of books that might not find their way into smaller, independent bookstores. Nevertheless, there is a downside to the increasing dominance of book superstores:

The problem . . . is . . . that they are all the same. They are formula stores, with centralized buying . . . with no links to . . . communities. . . . Independent stores are quirky and heterogeneous. Their stock may be broad or narrow, their service may be impeccable or surly, the temperaments of the owners are as varied as humanity itself. But every independent store is different. It is this diversity that gives strength to bookselling as a whole.[35]

Diversity is on the wane in a McDonaldizing world.

## The Fast-Food Industry: Even the Pickles Are Standardized

This brings us to the predictability of the food purveyed in fast-food restaurants. A short menu of simple foods helps ensure predictability. Hamburgers, fried chicken, pizza, tacos, french fries, soft drinks, shakes, and the like are all relatively easy to prepare and serve in a uniform fashion. Predictability in such products is made possible by the use of uniform raw ingredients, identical technologies for food preparation and cooking, similarity in the way the food is served, and identical packaging. As a trainer at Hamburger University puts it, "McDonald's has standards for everything down to the width of the pickle slices."[36]

Packaging is another important component of predictability in the fast-food restaurant. In spite of the fast-food restaurants' best efforts, unpredictabilities can creep in because of the nature of the materials—the food might not be hot enough, the chicken might be gristly or tough, or there may be too few pieces of pepperoni on a particular slice of pizza. Whatever the (slight) unpredictabilities in the food, the packaging—containers for the burgers, bags for the small fries, cardboard boxes for the pizzas—can always be the same and imply that the food will be too.

Predictable food also requires predictable ingredients. McDonald's has stringent guidelines on the nature (quality, size, shape, and so on) of the meat, chicken, fish, potatoes, and other ingredients purchased by each franchisee. The buns, for example, must be made of ordinary white bread from which all the chewy and nutritious elements of wheat, such as bran and germ, have been milled out. (One wit said of Wonder Bread, "I thought they just blew up library paste with gas and sent it to the oven."[37]) Because buns otherwise might grow stale or moldy, preservatives are added to retard spoilage. Precut, uniform frozen french fries rather than fresh potatoes are used.

The increasing use of frozen (or freeze-dried) foods addresses unpredictabilities related to the supply of raw materials. One of the reasons Ray Kroc eventually substituted frozen for fresh potatoes was that for several months a year it was difficult to obtain the desired variety of potato. Freezing potatoes made them readily available year-round. In addition, the potato peelings at each McDonald's outlet often created a stench that was anathema to Kroc and the sanitized (sterile?) world he sought to create. Frozen, peeled, and precut french fries solved this problem as well.

The predictability of foods in a McDonaldized society has led to a disturbing fact:

Regional and ethnic distinctions are disappearing from American cooking. Food in one neighborhood, city, or state looks and tastes pretty much like food anywhere else. Americans are sitting down to meals largely composed of such items as instant macaroni and cheese, soft white bread, oleomargarine, frozen doughnuts, and Jell-O. Today it is possible to travel from coast to coast, at any time of year, without feeling any need to change your eating habits. . . . Sophisticated processing and storage techniques, fast transport, and a creative variety of formulated convenience-food products have made it possible to ignore regional and seasonal differences in food production.[38]

### Entertainment: Welcome to McMovieworld

The earlier discussion of *Psycho* brings to mind the fact that the movie industry, too, values predictability. *Psycho* was followed by several sequels (as well as a recent [1998] shot-by-shot remake of the original). Many other horror films—such as *Halloween* (1978), *Nightmare on Elm Street* (1984), and *Scream* (1996)—also have had sequels. *The Ring* (2002) has not yet had a sequel, but it is a remake of hit the Japanese movie *Ringu* (1998). Outside the horror genre, movies that have been succeeded by one or more sequels (and prequels) include *The Godfather* (1972), *Star Wars* (1977), *Raiders of the Lost Ark* (1981), *Back to the Future* (1985), *Jurassic Park* (1993), *Mission Impossible* (1996), *X-Men* (1998), and *The Matrix* (1999). In a series of *Vacation* movies, Chevy Chase plays the same character; the only thing that varies very much is the vacation setting in which he practices his very familiar antics. These predictable products generally attract a large audience, but they often succeed at the expense of movies based on new concepts, ideas, and characters.

The studios like sequels ("Welcome to McMovieworld"[39]) because the same characters, actors, and basic plot lines can be used again and again. Furthermore, sequels seem more likely to succeed at the box office than completely original movies; profits are therefore more predictable. Presumably, viewers like sequels because they enjoy the comfort of encountering favorite characters played by familiar actors who find themselves in accustomed settings. Like a McDonald's meal, many sequels are not very good, but at least consumers know what they are getting.

Movies themselves seem to include increasingly predictable sequences and highly predictable endings. Dustin Hoffman contends that today's movie audiences would not accept the many flashbacks, fantasies, and dream sequences of his classic 1969 movie, *Midnight Cowboy*. Hoffman believes that this may be "emblematic of the whole culture":

My friend [director Barry Levinson] says we live in a McDonald's culture . . . because you aren't going to stop [at a restaurant] until you get what you already know . . . and in our culture now people want to know what they're getting when they go to the movies.[40]

The movie rating system allows people to predict the amount of violence, nudity, and potentially objectionable language they will see and hear. For example, a "G" rating means that the movie contains no nudity and objectionable language and only mild forms of violence; an "NC-17" rating means that all three will appear in the movie.[41]

On television, the parallel to sequels is "copycatting," or the producing of sitcoms and comedies "that are so similar as to be indistinct."[42] For example, "They all gather in apartments and offices that tend to have heightened, overly colorful, casual-by-design look, and they exchange jokes that frequently depend on body parts or functions for their punch."[43] Among recent or current TV fare, *Seinfeld, Drew Carey, Friends, Will and Grace,* and *Everybody Loves Raymond* come to mind. "Like McDonald's, prime time wants you to know exactly what you'll get no matter where you are, emphasizing the comforts of predictability over nutrition."[44]

The absence of that which is expected can spell trouble for a McDonaldized system. For example, Blockbuster experienced a slump several years ago largely stemming from the fact that hit movies were rarely in stock. To make the availability of movies more predictable, Blockbuster developed a new way of doing business with its suppliers. Instead of paying them a great deal up front for movies, Blockbuster now pays a small up front fee and then pays the supplier half the revenues from the rentals. Blockbuster can now stock as many as seven times as many new releases as it did previously. Thus, those who venture to Blockbuster these days are much more likely to find what they are looking for: "'When you walk into a Taco Bell, you expect to walk out with a taco. . . . It should be the same for a video store.'"[45]

Another form of entertainment that aims to provide no surprises is the package tour, which is as oriented to predictability as it is to efficiency. Tour operators have turned travel into a highly predictable product by creating trips that allow minimal contact with the people, culture, and institutions of visited countries. This creates a paradox: People go to considerable expense and effort to go to foreign countries where they have as little contact as possible with native culture.[46] A tour group from the United States will likely be made up of like-minded Americans.

Agencies use American carriers wherever possible or else local transports that offer the amenities expected by American tourists (perhaps even air-conditioning, stereo, bathroom). Tour guides are usually Americans or people who have spent time in America—at the very least, natives fluent in English who know all about the needs and interests of Americans. Restaurants visited on the tour either are American (perhaps associated with an American fast-food chain) or cater to the American palate. Hotels are also likely to be either American chains, such as the Sheraton and Hilton, or European hotels that have structured themselves to suit American tastes.[47] Each day offers a firm, often tight schedule, with little time for spontaneous activities. Tourists can take comfort from knowing exactly what they are going to do on a daily, even hourly, basis.

However, John Urry argues that the package tour has declined in popularity in recent years.[48] How do we reconcile this contention with the idea that McDonaldization is increasing? The answer lies in the fact that most societies have grown increasingly McDonaldized, with the result that there may be *less* need for McDonaldized tours. After all, since people traveling practically anywhere are likely to find McDonald's, Holiday Inn, Hard Rock Cafe, *USA TODAY*, and CNN, they may feel less need to be protected from unpredictabilities: Many of them have already been eliminated.

### Sports: There's Even a McStables

In tennis, the tiebreaker has made tennis matches more predictable. Prior to tiebreakers, to win a set, a player needed to win six games with a two-game margin over his or her opponent. But if the opponent was never more than one game behind, the set could go on and on. Some memorable, interminable tennis matches produced scores on the order of twelve to ten. With limitations imposed by television and other mass media, the tennis establishment decided to institute the tiebreaker in many tournaments. If a set is deadlocked at six games each, a twelve-point tiebreaker is played. The first player to get seven points with a two-point margin wins. A tie breaker might go beyond twelve points (if the players are tied at six points each), but it rarely goes on nearly as long as close matches occasionally used to.

An interesting example of predictability in a previously highly unpredictable area is the rationalization of racehorse training. Trainer Wayne Lukas has set up a string of stables around the United States that some have labeled "McStables." In the past, training stables were independent operations specific to a given track. Thus, training procedures varied greatly from one racetrack to another and from one stable to another. However,

> Lukas has thrived by establishing and supervising far-flung divisions of his stable. "I think the absolute key to doing this is quality control," he said. "You cannot ever see a deviation of quality from one division to the other. The barns are the same. The feeding program is the same. . . ."
> "This is what makes it easy to ship horses around the country. Most horses, when they ship, have to adjust. There's never an adjustment necessary in our divisions. *It's the McDonald's principle.* We'll give you a franchise, and that franchise is going to be the same wherever you go [italics added].[49]

Even horses now seem to thrive on predictability.

## ♦ MINIMIZING DANGER AND UNPLEASANTNESS

The attraction of the shopping mall can be credited, at least in part, to its ability to make shopping more predictable. For example, "One kid who works here [at a mall] told me why he likes the mall. . . . It's because no matter what the weather is outside, it's always the same in here. He likes that. He doesn't want to know it's raining—it would depress him."[50] Those who wander through malls are also relatively free from the crime that might beset them in city streets. The lack of bad weather and the relative absence of crime point to another predictable aspect of shopping malls—they are always upbeat.

Avoiding crime is a key factor in the rise of so-called family fun or pay-to-play centers. (Often, children pay an entrance fee, although, in a cute gimmick, parents may be "free.") These centers offer ropes, padded "mountains," tubes, tunnels, giant blocks, trapezes, and so on. They have proven popular in urban areas because they provide a safe haven in the crime-ridden cities.[51] Children are also seen as less likely to injure themselves in fun centers than in community playgrounds because of the nature of the equipment and the presence of staff supervisors. And there are safety checks to be sure that children do not leave with anyone but their parents. However, although fun centers are undoubtedly safer and less unpredictable, they have also been described as "antiseptic, climate-controlled, plastic world[s]."[52]

Modern amusement parks are in many ways much safer and more pleasant than their honky-tonk ancestors. The Disney organization quite clearly knew that to succeed it had to overcome the unpredictability of old amusement parks. Disneyland and Walt Disney World take great pains to be sure that the visitor is not subject to any disorder. You have already seen how the garbage is whisked away so that people do not have to be disturbed by the sight of trash. Vendors do not sell peanuts, gum, and cotton candy because they would make a mess underfoot. Visitors will not likely have their day disrupted by the sight of public drunkenness. Crime in the parks is virtually nonexistent. Disney offers a world of predictable, almost surreal, orderliness.

Few unanticipated things happen on any of the rides or in any of the attractions in contemporary theme parks. Of the Jungle Cruise ride at Disney World, a company publication says, "The *Jungle Cruise* is a favorite of armchair explorers, because it compresses weeks of safari travel into ten minutes [efficiency!] of fun, *without mosquitoes, monsoons, or misadventures* [italics added]."[53]

At one time, people went camping to escape the predictable routines of their daily lives. City dwellers fled their homes in search of nature, with little more than a tent and a sleeping bag. Little or nothing lay between the camper and the natural environment, leading to some unpredictable events. But that was the whole point. Campers might see a deer wander close to their campsite, perhaps even venture into it. Of course, they might also encounter the unexpected thunderstorm, tick bite, or snake, but these were accepted as an integral part of escaping one's routine activities. Here is the way one person describes the ups and downs of this kind of camping:

> Of course it began to pour. We had neglected to pack the main tent pole, which is like forgetting the mast on a sailboat. There is no tent without the tent pole. At first we failed to grasp this, so we kept trying to get the tent to stand. The whole structure kept collapsing like some big green bear that had been shot. Just when we were exasperated and began to dream of Holiday Inns, a deer appeared not two feet from our son.
> "Look!" our child said, enraptured. "Look, my first deer!"[54]

Some people still camp this way; however, many others have sought to eliminate unpredictability from camping. Said the owner of one campground, "All they wanted [in the past] was a space in the woods and an outhouse. . . . But nowadays people aren't exactly roughing it."[55] Instead of simple tents, modern campers might venture forth in a recreational vehicle (RV) such as a Winnebago or take a trailer with an elaborate pop-up tent, to protect them from the unexpected. Of course, "camping" in an RV also tends to reduce the likelihood of catching sight of wandering wildlife. Furthermore, the motorized camper carries within it all the elements that one has at home—refrigerator, stove, television, VCR, and stereo.

Camping technology has made for not only great predictability but also changes in the modern campgrounds. Relatively few people now pitch their tents in the unpredictable wilderness; most find their way into rationalized campgrounds, even "country-club campgrounds," spearheaded by franchises such as Kampgrounds of America (KOA), the latter with over 500 sites.[56] Said one camper relaxing in his air-conditioned thirty-two-foot trailer, "We've got everything right here. . . . It doesn't matter how hard it rains or how the wind blows."[57] Modern campgrounds are likely to be divided into sections—one for tents, another for RVs, each section broken into neat rows of usually tiny campsites. Hookups allow those with RVs to operate the various technologies encased within them. After campers have parked and hooked up their RVs or popped up their tents, they can gaze out and enjoy the sights—other cars, antennas, teenagers on motorbikes—in other words, many of the sights they tried to leave behind in the cities or suburbs. Campsite owners might also provide campers who are "roughing it" with such amenities as a well-stocked delicatessen, bathrooms and showers, heated swimming pools, a game room loaded with video games, a Laundromat, a TV room, a movie theater, and even entertainment such as bands or comedians.

There is certainly nothing wrong with wanting to be safe from harm. However, society as a whole has surrendered responsibility for providing safe environments to commercial interests. Because our city streets are unsafe, people shop in malls. Because our playgrounds are unsafe (and greatly limited), children play in commercial "fun" centers. The problem is that people are therefore spending large amounts of leisure time in commercial environments that are eager to lead them into a life of consumption. If the larger society provided safe and attractive recreation centers for both adults and children, we would not be forced to spend so much of our lives, and do so many things, in commercial venues.

The irony is that, in spite of their claim to safety, McDonaldized locations, especially fast-food restaurants, seem particularly prone to crime and violence. Said the owner of a fast-food outlet, "'Fast food for some reason is a target.'"[58] It may be that the iron cage sometimes forces people to lash out in the setting that is its leading example.

## ◆ CONCLUSION

Predictability is the third dimension of McDonaldization. It involves an emphasis on, for example, discipline, systematization, and routine so that things are the same from one time or place to another. Predictability is achieved in various ways, including the replication of settings, the use of scripts to control what employees say, the routinization of employee behavior, the offering of uniform products and processes, and the minimization of danger and unpleasantness.

As a result, we all live in an increasingly predictable world. This is reassuring to most of us, and we have come to expect, even demand, predictability. However, a predictable world can easily become a boring world. And if we seek to escape the boredom, we may well find that even the areas that people usually associate with escape have, themselves, become highly predictable. Tedium may now be a far greater threat than a bit of unpredictability.

# 6

# Control

◆

## Human and Nonhuman Robots

This chapter presents the fourth dimension of McDonaldization: increased control through the replacement of human with nonhuman technology. *Technology* includes not only machines and tools but also materials, skills, knowledge, rules, regulations, procedures, and techniques. Thus, technologies include not only the obvious, such as robots and computers, but also the less obvious, such as the assembly line, bureaucratic rules, and manuals prescribing accepted procedures and techniques. A *human technology* (a screwdriver, for example) is controlled by people; *a nonhuman technology* (the order window at the drive-through, for instance) controls people.

The great source of uncertainty, unpredictability, and inefficiency in any rationalizing system is people—either those who work within it or those served by it. Hence, efforts to increase control are usually aimed at both employees and customers, although processes and products may also be the targets.

Historically, organizations gained control over people gradually through increasingly effective technologies.[1] Eventually, they began reducing people's behavior to a series of machinelike actions. And once people were behaving like machines, they could be replaced with actual machines. The replacement of humans by machines is the ultimate stage in control over people; people can cause no more uncertainty and unpredictability because they are no longer involved, at least directly, in the process.

Control is not the only goal associated with nonhuman technologies. These technologies are created and implemented for many reasons, such as increased productivity, greater quality control, and lower cost. However, this chapter is mainly concerned with the ways nonhuman technologies have increased control over employees and consumers in a McDonaldizing society.

## ◆ CONTROLLING EMPLOYEES

Before the age of sophisticated nonhuman technologies, people were largely controlled by other people. In the workplace, owners and supervisors controlled subordinates directly, face-to-face. But such direct, personal control is difficult, costly, and likely to engender personal hostility. Subordinates will likely strike out at an immediate supervisor or an owner who exercises excessively tight control over their activities. Control through a technology is easier, less costly in the long run, and less likely to engender hostility toward supervisors and owners. Thus, over time, control by people has shifted toward control by technologies.[2]

### The Fast-Food Industry: From Human to Mechanical Robots

Fast-food restaurants have coped with problems of uncertainty by creating and instituting many nonhuman technologies. Among other things, they have done away with a cook, at least in the conventional sense. Grilling a hamburger is so simple that anyone can do it with a bit of training. Furthermore, even when more skill is required (as in the case of cooking an Arby's roast beef), the fast-food restaurant develops a routine involving a few simple procedures that almost anyone can follow. Cooking fast food is like a game of connect-the-dots or painting-by-numbers. Following prescribed steps eliminates most of the uncertainties of cooking.

Much of the food prepared at McDonaldized restaurants arrives preformed, precut, presliced, and "preprepared." All employees need to do, when necessary, is cook or often merely heat the food and pass it on to the customer. At Taco Bell, workers used to spend hours cooking meat and shredding vegetables. Now, the workers simply drop bags of frozen ready-cooked beef into boiling water. They have used preshredded lettuce for some time, and more recently preshredded cheese and prediced tomatoes have appeared.[3] The more that is done by nonhuman technologies before the food arrives at the restaurant, the less workers need to do and the less room they have to exercise their own judgment and skill.

McDonald's has developed a variety of machines to control its employees. The soft drink dispenser has a sensor that automatically shuts off the flow when the cup is full. Ray Kroc's dissatisfaction with the vagaries of human judgment led to the elimination of french fry machines controlled by humans and to the development of machines that ring or buzz when the fries are done or that automatically lift the french fry baskets out of the hot oil. When an employee controls the french fry machine, misjudgment may lead to undercooked, overcooked, or even burned fries. Kroc fretted over this problem: "It was amazing that we got them as uniform as we did, because each kid working the fry vats would have his own interpretation of the proper color and so forth."[4]

At the cash register, workers once had to look at a price list and then punch the prices in by hand—so that the wrong (even lower) amount could be rung up. Computer screens and computerized cash registers forestall that possibility.[5] All the employees need do is press the image on the register that matches the item purchased; the machine then produces the correct price.

If the objective in a fast-food restaurant is to reduce employees to human robots, we should not be surprised by the spread of robots that prepare food. For example, a robot cooks hamburgers at one campus restaurant:

> The robot looks like a flat oven with conveyor belts running through and an arm attached at the end. A red light indicates when a worker should slide in a patty and bun, which bob along in the heat for 1 minute 52 seconds. When they reach the other side of the machine, photo-optic sensors indicate when they can be assembled.
>
> The computer functioning as the robot's brain determines when the buns and patty are where they should be. If the bun is delayed, it slows the patty belt. If the patty is delayed, it slows bun production. It also keeps track of the number of buns and patties in the oven and determines how fast they need to be fed in to keep up speed.[6]

Robots offer a number of advantages—lower cost, increased efficiency, fewer workers, no absenteeism, and a solution to the decreasing supply of teenagers needed to work at fast-food restaurants. The professor who came up with the idea for the robot that cooks hamburgers said, "Kitchens have not been looked at as factories, which they are. . . . Fast-food restaurants were the first to do that."[7]

Taco Bell developed "a computer-driven machine the size of a coffee table that . . . can make and seal in a plastic bag a perfect hot taco."[8] Another company worked on an automated drink dispenser that produced a soft drink in fifteen seconds: "Orders are punched in at the cash register by a clerk. A computer sends the order to the dispenser to drop a cup, fill it with ice and appropriate soda, and place a lid on top. The cup is then moved by conveyor to the customer."[9] When such technologies are refined and prove to be less expensive and more reliable than humans, fast-food restaurants will employ them widely.

McDonald's experimented with a limited program called ARCH, or Automated Robotic Crew Helper. A french fry robot fills the fry basket, cooks the fries, empties the basket when sensors tell it the fries are done, and even shakes the fries while they are being cooked. In the case of drinks, an employee pushes a button on the cash register to place an order. The robot then puts the proper amount of ice in the cup, moves the cup under the correct spigot, and allows the cup to fill. It then places the cup on a conveyor, which moves it to the employee, who passes it on to the customer.[10]

Like the military, fast-food restaurants have generally recruited teenagers because they surrender their autonomy to machines, rules, and procedures more easily than adults.[11] Fast-food restaurants also seek to maximize control over the work behavior of adults. Even managers are not immune from such efforts. Another aspect of McDonald's experimental ARCH program is a computerized system that, among other things, tells managers how many hamburgers or orders of french fries they will require at a given time (the lunch hour, for example). The computerized system takes away the need to make such judgments and decisions from managers.[12] Thus, "Burger production has become an exact science in which everything is regimented, every distance calculated and every dollop of ketchup monitored and tracked."[13]

### Education: McChild Care Centers

Universities have developed a variety of nonhuman technologies to exert control over professors. For instance, class periods are set by the university. Students leave at the assigned time no matter where the professor happens to be in the lecture. Because the university requires grading, the professor must test students. In some universities, final grades must be submitted within forty-eight hours of the final exam, which may force professors to employ computer-graded, multiple-choice exams. Required evaluations by students may force professors to teach in a way that will lead to high ratings. The publishing demands of the tenure and promotion system may force professors to devote far less time to their teaching than they, and their students, would like.

An even more extreme version of this emphasis appears in the child care equivalent of the fast-food restaurant, KinderCare, which was founded in 1969, and now operates over 1,250 learning centers in the United States. Over 120,000 children between the ages of 6 weeks and 12 years attend the centers.[14] KinderCare tends to hire short-term employees with little or no training in child care. What these employees do in the "classroom" is largely determined by an instruction book with a ready-made curriculum. Staff members open the manual to find activities spelled out in detail for each day. Clearly, a skilled, experienced, creative teacher is not the kind of person that such "McChild" care centers seek to hire. Rather, relatively untrained employees are more easily controlled by the nonhuman technology of the omnipresent "instruction book."

Another example of organizational control over teachers is the franchised Sylvan Learning Center, often thought of as the "McDonald's of Education."[15] (There are over nine hundred Sylvan Learning Centers in the United States, Canada, and Asia.[16]) Sylvan Learning Centers are after-school centers for remedial education. The corporation "trains staff and tailors a McDonald's type uniformity, down to the U-shaped tables at which instructors work with their charges."[17] Through their training methods, rules, and technologies, for-profit systems such as the Sylvan Learning Center exert great control over their "teachers."

### Health Care: Who's Deciding Our Fate?

As is the case with all rationalized systems, medicine has moved away from human toward nonhuman technologies. The two most important examples are the growing importance of bureaucratic rules and controls and the growth of modern medical machinery. For example, the prospective payment and DRG (diagnostic related groups) systems—not physicians and their medical judgment—tend to determine how long a patient must be hospitalized. Similarly, the doctor operating alone out of a black bag with a few simple tools has virtually become a thing of the past. Instead, doctors serve as dispatchers, sending patients on to the appropriate machines and specialists. Computer programs can diagnose illnesses.[18] Although it is unlikely that they will ever replace the physician, computers may one day be the initial, if not the prime, diagnostic agents. It is now even possible for people to get diagnoses, treatment, and prescriptions over the Internet with no face-to-face contact with a physician.

These and other developments in modern medicine demonstrate increasing external control over the medical profession by third-party payers, employing organizations, for-profit hospitals, health maintenance organizations (HMOs), the federal government, and "McDoctors"-like organizations. Even in its heyday the medical profession was not free of external control, but now the nature and extent of the control is changing and its degree and extent is increasing greatly. Instead of decisions being made by the mostly autonomous doctor in private practice, doctors are more likely to conform to bureaucratic rules and regulations. In bureaucracies, employees are controlled by their superiors. Physicians' superiors are increasingly likely to be professional managers and not other doctors. Also, the existence of hugely expensive medical technologies often mandates that they be used. As the machines themselves grow more sophisticated, physicians come to understand them less and are therefore less able to control them. Instead, control shifts to the technologies as well as to the experts who create and handle them.

An excellent recent example of increasing external control over physicians (and other medical personnel) is called "pathways."[19] A pathway is a standardized series of steps prescribed for dealing with an array of medical problems. Involved are a series of "if-then" decision points—if a certain circumstance exists, the action to follow is prescribed. What physicians do in a variety of situations is determined by the pathway and *not* the individual physician. To put it in terms of this chapter, the pathway— a nonhuman technology—exerts external control over physicians.

Various terms have been used to describe pathways—standardization, "cookbook" medicine, a series of recipes, a neat package tied together with a bow, and so on—and all describe the rationalization of medical practice. The point is that there are prescribed courses of action under a wide range of circumstances. While doctors need not, indeed should not, follow a pathway at all times, they do so most of the time. A physician who spearheads the protocol movement says he grows concerned when physicians follow a pathway more than 92% of the time. While this leaves some leeway for physicians, it is clear that what they are supposed to do is predetermined in the vast majority of instances.

Let us take, for example, an asthma patient. In this case, the pathway says that if the patient's temperature rises above 101 degrees, then a complete blood count is to be ordered. A chest X ray is to be ordered under certain circumstances—if it's the patient's initial wheezing episode or if there is chest pain, respiratory distress, or a fever of over 101 degrees. And so it goes—a series of if-then steps prescribed for and controlling what physicians and other medical personnel do. While there are undoubted advantages associated with such pathways (e.g., lower likelihood of using procedures or medicines that have been shown not to work), they do tend to take decision making away from physicians. Continued reliance on such pathways is likely to adversely affect the ability of physicians to make independent decisions.

### The Workplace: Do as I Say, Not as I Do

Most workplaces are bureaucracies that can be seen as large-scale nonhuman technologies. Their innumerable rules, regulations, guidelines, positions, lines of command, and hierarchies dictate what people do within the system and how they do it. The consummate bureaucrat thinks little about what is to be done: He or she simply follows the rules, deals with incoming work, and passes it on to its next stop in the system. Employees need do little more than fill out the required forms, these days most likely right on the computer screen.

At the lowest levels in the bureaucratic hierarchy ("blue-collar work"), scientific management clearly strove to limit or replace human technology. For instance, the "one best way" required workers to follow a series of predefined steps in a mindless fashion. More generally, Frederick Taylor believed that the most important part of the work world was not the employees but, rather, the organization that would plan, oversee, and control their work.

Although Taylor wanted all employees to be controlled by the organization, he accorded managers much more leeway than manual workers. It was the task of management to study the knowledge and skills of workers and to record and tabulate them and ultimately to reduce them to laws, rules, and even mathematical formulas. In other words, managers were to take a body of human skills, abilities, and knowledge and transform them into a set of nonhuman rules, regulations, and formulas. Once human skills were codified, the organization no longer needed skilled workers. Management would hire, train, and employ unskilled workers in accord with a set of strict guidelines.

In effect, then, Taylor separated "head" work from "hand" work. Prior to Taylor's day, the skilled worker had performed both. Taylor and his followers studied what was in the heads of those skilled workers, then translated that knowledge into simple, mindless routines that virtually anyone could learn and follow. Workers were thus left with little more than repetitive "hand" work. This principle remains at the base of the movement throughout our McDonaldizing society to replace human with nonhuman technology.

Behind Taylor's scientific management, and all other efforts at replacing human with nonhuman technology, lies the goal of being able to employ human beings with minimal intelligence and ability. In fact, Taylor sought to hire people who resembled animals:

> Now one of the very first requirements for a man who is fit to handle pig iron as a regular occupation is that he shall be so stupid and so phlegmatic that he more nearly resembles in his mental make-up the ox than any other type. The man who is mentally alert and intelligent is for this very reason entirely unsuited to what would, for him, be the grinding monotony of work of this character. Therefore the workman who is best suited to han-dling pig iron is unable to understand the real science of doing this class of work. He is so stupid that the word "percentage" has no meaning to him, and he must consequently be trained by a man more intelligent than himself into the habit of working in accordance with the laws of this science before he can be successful.[20]

Not coincidentally, Henry Ford had a similar view of the kinds of people who were to work on his assembly lines:

> Repetitive labour—the doing of one thing over and over again and always in the same way—is a terrifying prospect to a certain kind of mind. It is terrifying to me. I could not possibly do the same thing day in and day out, but to other minds, perhaps I might say to the majority of minds, repetitive operations hold no terrors. In fact, to some types of mind thought is absolutely appalling. To them the ideal job is one where creative instinct need not be expressed. The jobs where it is necessary to put in mind as well as muscle have very few takers—we always need men who like a job because it is difficult. The average worker, I am sorry to say, wants a job in which he does not have to think. Those who have what might be called the creative type of mind and who thoroughly abhor monotony are apt to imagine that all other minds are similarly restless and therefore to extend quite unwanted sympathy to the labouring man who day in and day out performs almost exactly the same operation.[21]

The kind of person sought out by Taylor was the same kind of person Ford thought would work well on the assembly line. In their view, such people would more likely submit to external technological control over their work and perhaps even crave such control.

Not surprisingly, a perspective similar to that held by Taylor and Ford can be attributed to other entrepreneurs: "The obvious irony is that the organizations built by W. Clement Stone [the founder of Combined Insurance] and Ray Kroc, both highly creative and innovative entrepreneurs, depend on the willingness of employees to follow detailed routines precisely."[22]

Many workplaces have come under the control of nonhuman technologies. In the supermarket, for example, the checker once had to read the prices marked on food products and enter them into the cash register. As with all human activities, however, the process was slow, with a chance of human error. To counter these problems, many supermarkets installed optical scanners, which "read" a code preprinted on each item. Each code number calls up a price already entered into the computer that controls the cash register. This nonhuman technology has thus reduced the number and sophistication of the tasks performed by the checker. Only the less-skilled tasks remain, such as physically scanning the food and bagging it. And even those tasks are being eliminated with the development of self-scanning and having consumers bag their groceries, especially in discount supermarkets. In other words, the work performed by the supermarket checker, when it hasn't been totally eliminated, has been "de-skilled"; that is, a decline has occurred in the amount of skill required for the job.

The nonhuman technologies in telemarketing "factories" can be even more restrictive. Telemarketers usually have scripts they must follow unerringly. The scripts are designed to handle most foreseeable contingencies. Supervisors often listen in on solicitations to make sure employees follow the correct procedures. Employees who fail to meet the quotas for the number of calls made and sales completed in a given time may be fired summarily.

Similar control is exerted over the "phoneheads," or customer service representatives, who work for many companies. Those who handle reservations for the airlines (for example, United Airlines) must log every minute spent on the job and justify each moment away from the phone. Employees have to punch a "potty button" on the phone to let management know of their intentions. Supervisors sit in an elevated "tower" in the middle of the reservations floor, "observing like [prison] guards the movements of every operator in the room." They also monitor phone calls to make sure that employees say and do what they are supposed to. This control is part of a larger process of "omnipresent supervision increasingly taking hold in so many workplaces—not just airline reservations centers but customer service departments and data-processing businesses where computers make possible an exacting level of employee scrutiny."[23] No wonder customers often deal with representatives who behave like automatons. Said one employee of United Airlines, "My body became an extension of the computer terminal that I typed the reservations into. I came to feel emptied of self."[24]

Sometimes telephone service representatives are literally prisoners. Prison inmates are now used in at least 17 states in this way, and the idea is currently on the legislative table in several more states. The attractions of prisoners are obvious—they work for very little pay and they can be controlled to a far higher degree than even the "phoneheads" discussed above. Furthermore, they can be relied on to show up for work. As one manager put it, "I need people who are there every day."[25]

Many telemarketing firms are outsourcing much of their labor overseas, especially to India, where people who are desperate for well-paying jobs are willing to accept levels of control that would be found unacceptable by many in the United States. Indian call centers afford a number of advantages, including lower wage costs than in the United States; the availability of an English-speaking, computer-literate, and college-educated workforce with a strong work ethic; and significant experience and familiarity with business processes.[26]

Following the logical progression, some companies now use computer calls instead of having people solicit us over the phone.[27] Computer voices are far more predictable and controllable than even the most rigidly controlled human operator, including prisoners and those who work in Indian call centers. Indeed, in our increasingly McDonaldized society, I have had some of my most "interesting" conversations with such computer voices.

Of course, lower-level employees are not the only ones whose problem-solving skills are lost in the transition to more nonhuman technology. I have already mentioned the controls on professors and doctors. In addition, pilots flying the modern, computerized airplane (such as the Boeing 757, 767, and 777) are being controlled and, in the process, de-skilled. Instead of flying "by the seat of their pants" or using old-fashioned autopilots for simple maneuvers, modern pilots can "push a few buttons and lean back while the plane flies to its destination and lands on a predetermined runway." Said one FAA official, "We're taking more and more of these functions out of human control and giving them to machines." These airplanes are in many ways safer and more reliable than older, less technologically advanced models. However, pilots, dependent on these technologies, may lose the ability to handle emergency situations creatively. The problem, said one airline manager, is that "I don't have computers that will do that [be creative]; I just don't."[28]

## ◆ CONTROLLING CUSTOMERS

Employees are relatively easy to control, because they rely on employers for their livelihood. Customers have much more freedom to bend the rules and go elsewhere if they don't like the situations in which they find themselves. Still, McDonaldized systems have developed and honed a number of methods for controlling customers.

### The Fast-Food Industry: Get the Hell Out of There

Whether they go into a fast-food restaurant or use the drive-through window, customers enter a kind of conveyor system that moves them through the restaurant in the manner desired by the management. It is clearest in the case of the drive-through window (the energy for this conveyor comes from one's own automobile), but it is also true for those who enter the restaurant. Consumers know that they are supposed to line up, move to the counter, order their food, pay, carry the food to an available table, eat, gather up their debris, deposit it in the trash receptacle, and return to their cars.

Three mechanisms help to control customers:[29]

1. Customers receive cues (for example, the presence of lots of trash receptacles, especially at the exits) that indicate what is expected of them.

2. A variety of structural constraints lead customers to behave in certain ways. For example, the drive-through window, as well as the written instructions on the menu marquee at the counter (and elsewhere), gives customers few, if any, alternatives.

3. Customers have internalized taken-for-granted norms and follow them when they enter a fast-food restaurant.

When my children were young, they admonished me after we finished our meal at McDonald's (I ate in fast-food restaurants in those days before I "saw the light") for not cleaning up the debris and carting it to the trash can.

My children were, in effect, serving as agents for McDonald's, teaching me the norms of behavior in such settings. I (and most others) have long-since internalized these norms, and I still dutifully follow them these days on the rare occasions that a lack of any other alternative (or the need for a clean restroom) forces me into a fast-food restaurant.

One goal of control in fast-food restaurants is to influence customers to spend their money and leave quickly. The restaurants need tables to be vacated rapidly so other diners will have a place to eat their food. A famous old chain of cafeterias, the Automat,[30] was partly undermined by people who occupied tables for hours on end. The Automat became a kind of social center, leaving less and less room for people to eat the meals they had purchased. The deathblow was struck when street people began to monopolize the Automat's tables.

Some fast-food restaurants employ security personnel to keep street people on the move or, in the suburbs, to prevent potentially rowdy teenagers from monopolizing tables or parking lots. 7-Eleven has sought to deal with loitering teenagers outside some of its stores by playing saccharine tunes such as "Some Enchanted Evening." Said a 7-Eleven spokesperson, "They won't hang around and tap their feet to Mantovani."[31]

In some cases, fast-food restaurants have put up signs limiting a customer's stay in the restaurant (and even its parking lot), say, to twenty minutes.[32] More generally, fast-food restaurants have structured themselves so that people do not need or want to linger over meals. Easily consumed finger foods make the meal itself a quick one. Some fast-food restaurants use chairs that make customers uncomfortable after about twenty minutes.[33] Much the same effect is produced by the colors used in the decor: "Relaxation isn't the point. Getting the Hell out of there is the point. The interior colours have been chosen carefully with this end in mind. From the scarlet and yellow of the logo to the maroon of the uniform; everything clashes. It's designed to stop people from feeling so comfortable they might want to stay."[34]

## Other Settings: It's Like Boot Camp

In the university, students (the "consumers" of university services) are obviously even more controlled than professors. For example, universities often give students little leeway in the courses they may take. The courses themselves, often highly structured, force the students to perform in specific ways.

Control over students actually begins long before they enter the university. Grade schools in particular have developed many ways to control students. Kindergarten has been described as an educational "boot camp."[35] Students are taught not only to obey authority but also to embrace the rationalized procedures of rote learning and objective testing. More important, spontaneity and creativity tend not to be rewarded and may even be discouraged, leading to what one expert calls "education for docility."[36] Those who conform to the rules are thought of as good students; those who don't are labeled bad students. As a general rule, the students who end up in college are the ones who have successfully submitted to the control mechanisms. Creative, independent students are often, from the educational system's point of view, "messy, expensive, and time-consuming."[37]

The clock and the lesson plan also exert control over students, especially in grade school and high school. Because of the "tyranny of the clock," a class must end at the sound of the bell, even if students are just about to comprehend something important. Because of the "tyranny of the lesson plan," a class must focus on what the plan requires for the day, no matter what the class (and perhaps the teacher) may find interesting. Imagine "a cluster of excited children examining a turtle with enormous fascination and intensity. Now children, put away the turtle, the teacher insists. We're going to have our science lesson. The lesson is on crabs."[38]

In the health care industry, the patient (along with the physician) is increasingly under the control of large, impersonal systems. For example, in many medical insurance programs, patients can no longer decide on their own to see a specialist. Rather, the patient must first see a primary-care physician who must decide whether a specialist is necessary. Because of the system's great pressure on the primary physician to keep costs down, fewer patients visit specialists and primary-care physicians perform more functions formerly handled by specialists.

The supermarket scanners that control checkers also control customers. When prices were marked on all the products, customers could calculate roughly how much they were spending as they shopped. They could also check the price on each item to be sure that they were not being overcharged at the cash register. But with scanners, it is almost impossible for consumers to keep tabs on prices and on the checkers.

Supermarkets also control shoppers with food placement. For example, supermarkets take pains to put the foods that children find attractive in places where youngsters can readily grab them (for example, low on the shelves). Also, what a market chooses to feature through sale prices and strategic placement in the store profoundly affects what is purchased. Manufacturers and wholesalers battle one another for coveted display positions, such as at the front of the market or at the "endcaps" of aisles. Foods placed in these positions will likely sell far more than they would if they were relegated to their usual positions.

Malls also exert control over customers, especially children and young adults, who are programmed by the mass media to be avid consumers. Going to the mall can become a deeply ingrained habit. Some people are reduced to what Kowinski calls "zombies," shopping the malls hour after hour, weekend after weekend.[39] More specifically, the placement of food courts, escalators, and stairs force customers to traverse corridors and pass attractive shop windows. Benches are situated so that consumers might be attracted to certain sites even though they are seeking a brief respite from the labors of consumption. The strategic placement of shops, as well as goods within shops, leads people to be attracted to products in which they might not otherwise have been interested.

Computers that respond to the human voice via voice recognition systems exert great control over people. A person receiving a collect call might be asked by the computer voice whether she will accept the charges. The computer voice requests, "Please say yes or no." Although efficient and cost-saving, such a system has its drawbacks:

> The person senses that he cannot use free-flowing speech. He's being constrained. The computer is controlling him. It can be simply frustrating. ... People adapt to it, but only by filing it away subconsciously as another annoyance of living in our technological world.[40]

Even religion and politics are being marketed today, and like all McDonaldizing systems, they are adopting technologies that help them control the behavior of their "customers." For example, the Roman Catholic Church has its Vatican Television (which conducts about 130 televised broadcasts each year of events inside the Vatican).[41] More generally, instead of worshiping with a human preacher, millions of worshipers now "interact" with a televised image.[42] Television permits preachers to reach far more people than they could in a conventional church, so they can exert (or so they hope) greater control over what people believe and do and, in the process, extract higher contributions. TV preachers use the full panoply of techniques developed by media experts to control their viewers. Some use a format much like that of the talk shows hosted by Jay Leno or David Letterman, complete with jokes, orchestras, singers, and guests. Here is how one observer describes Vatican television: "The big advantage to the Vatican of having its own television operation . . . is that they can put their own spin on anything they produce. If you give them the cameras and give them access, they are in control."[43]

A similar point can be made about politics. The most obvious example is the use of television to market politicians and manipulate voters. Indeed, most people never see a politician except on TV, most likely in a firmly controlled format designed to communicate the exact message and image desired by the politicians and their media advisers. President Ronald Reagan raised such political marketing to an art form in the 1980s. On many occasions, visits were set up and TV images arranged (the president in front of a flag or with a military cemetery behind him) so that the viewers and potential voters received precisely the visual message intended by Reagan's media advisers. Tightly controlled TV images are similarly important to President George W. Bush, as reflected, for example, in his landing as "co-pilot" of a jet plane on an aircraft carrier in order to announce (erroneously) the end of hostilities with Iraq in 2003. Conversely, as we saw earlier, President Reagan and especially President George W. Bush tended to avoid freewheeling press conferences where they were not in control.

## ◆ CONTROLLING THE PROCESS AND THE PRODUCT

In a society undergoing McDonaldization, people are the greatest threat to predictability. Control over people can be enhanced by controlling processes and products, but control over processes and products also becomes valued in itself.

### Food Production, Cooking, and Vending: It Cooks Itself

Technologies designed to reduce uncertainties are found throughout the manufacture of food. For example, the mass manufacturing of bread is not controlled by skilled bakers who lavish love and attention on a few loaves of bread at a time. Such skilled bakers cannot produce enough bread to supply the needs of our society. Furthermore, the bread they do produce can suffer from the uncertainties involved in having humans do the work. The bread may, for example, turn out to be too brown or too doughy. To increase productivity and eliminate these unpredictabilities, mass producers of bread have developed an automated system in which, as in all automated systems, humans play a minimal role rigidly controlled by the technology:

> The most advanced bakeries now resemble oil refineries. Flour, water, a score of additives, and huge amounts of yeast, sugar, and water are mixed into a broth that ferments for an hour. More flour is then added, and the dough is extruded into pans, allowed to rise for an hour, then moved through a tunnel oven. The loaves emerge after eighteen minutes, to be cooled, sliced, and wrapped.[44]

In one food industry after another, production processes in which humans play little more than planning and maintenance roles have replaced those dominated by skilled craftspeople. The warehousing and shipping of food has been similarly automated.

Further along in the food production process, other nonhuman technologies have affected how food is cooked. Technologies such as ovens with temperature probes "decide" for the cook when food is done. Many ovens, coffeemakers, and other appliances can turn themselves on and off. The instructions on all kinds of packaged foods dictate precisely how to prepare and cook the food. Premixed products, such as Mrs. Dash, eliminate the need for the cook to come up with creative combinations of seasonings. Nissin Foods' Super Boil soup—"the soup that cooks itself!"—has a special compartment in the bottom of the can. A turn of a key starts a chemical reaction that eventually boils the soup.[45] Even the cookbook was designed to take creativity away from the cook and control the process of cooking.

Some rather startling technological developments have occurred in the ways in which animals are raised for food. For instance, "aquaculture," a $57-billion-a-year business in 2000,[46] is growing dramatically because of the spiraling desire for seafood in an increasingly cholesterol-conscious population.[47] Instead of the old inefficient, unpredictable methods of harvesting fish—a lone angler casting a line or even boats catching tons of fish at a time in huge nets—we now have the much more predictable and efficient "farming" of seafood. More than 50% of the fresh salmon found in restaurants is now raised in huge sea cages off the coast of Norway.

Sea farms offer several advantages. Most generally, aquaculture allows humans to exert far greater control over the vagaries that beset fish in their natural habitat, thus producing a more predictable supply. Various drugs and chemicals increase predictability in the amount and quality of seafood. Aquaculture also permits a more predictable and efficient harvest because the creatures are confined to a limited space. In addition, geneticists can manipulate them to produce seafood more efficiently. For example, it takes a standard halibut about ten years to reach market size, but a new dwarf variety can reach the required size in only three years. Sea farms also allow for greater calculability—the greatest number of fish for the least expenditure of time, money, and energy.

Relatively small, family-run farms for raising other animals are being rapidly replaced by "factory farms."[48] The first animal to find its way into the factory farm was the chicken. Here is the way one observer describes a chicken "factory":

> A broiler producer today gets a load of 10,000, 50,000, or even more day-old chicks from the hatcheries, and puts them straight into a long, windowless shed. . . . Inside the shed, every aspect of the birds' environment is controlled to make them grow faster on less feed. Food and water are fed automatically from hoppers suspended from the roof. The lighting is adjusted. . . . For instance, there may be bright light twenty-four hours a day for the first week or two, to encourage the chicks to gain [weight] quickly. . . .
> Toward the end of the eight- or nine-week life of the chicken, there may be as little as half a square foot of space per chicken—or less than the area of a sheet of quarto paper for a three-and-one-half-pound bird.[49]

Among its other advantages, such chicken farms allow one person to raise over fifty thousand chickens.

Raising chickens this way ensures control over all aspects of the business. For instance, the chickens' size and weight is more predictable than that of free-ranging chickens. "Harvesting" chickens confined in this way is also more efficient than is catching chickens that roam over large areas.

However, confining chickens in such crowded quarters creates unpredictabilities, such as violence and even cannibalism. Farmers deal with these irrational "vices" in a variety of ways, such as dimming the lights as chickens approach full size and "debeaking" chickens so they cannot harm each other.

Some chickens are allowed to mature so they can be used for egg production. However, they receive much the same treatment as chickens raised for food. Hens are viewed as little more than "converting machines" that transform raw material (feed) into a finished product (eggs). Peter Singer describes the technology employed to control egg production:

> The cages are stacked in tiers, with food and water troughs running along the rows, filled automatically from a central supply. They have sloping

wire floors. The slope . . . makes it more difficult for the birds to stand comfortably, but it causes the eggs to roll to the front of the cage where they can easily be collected . . . [and] in the more modern plants, carried by conveyor belt to a packing plant. . . . The excrement drops through [the wire floor] and can be allowed to pile up for many months until it is all removed in a single operation.[50]

This system obviously imposes great control over the production of eggs, leading to greater efficiency, to a more predictable supply, and more uniform quality than the old chicken coop.

Other animals—pigs, lambs, steers, and calves especially—are raised similarly. To prevent calves' muscles from developing, which toughens the veal, they are immediately confined to tiny stalls where they cannot exercise. As they grow, they may not even be able to turn around. Being kept in stalls also prevents the calves from eating grass, which would cause their meat to lose its pale color; the stalls are also kept free of straw, which, if eaten by the calves, would also darken the meat. "They are fed a totally liquid diet, based on nonfat milk powder with added vitamins, minerals, and growth-promoting drugs," says Peter Singer in his book, *Animal Liberation*.[51] To make sure the calves take in the maximum amount of food, they are given no water, which forces them to keep drinking their liquid food. By rigidly controlling the size of the stall and the diet, veal producers can maximize two quantifiable objectives: the production of the largest amount of meat in the shortest possible time and the creation of the tenderest, whitest, and therefore most desirable veal.

Employment of a variety of technologies obviously leads to greater control over the process by which animals produce meat, thereby increasing the efficiency, calculability, and predictability of meat production. In addition, they exert control over farm workers. Left to their own devices, ranchers might feed young steers too little or the wrong food or permit them too much exercise. In fact, in the rigidly controlled factory ranch, human ranch hands (and their unpredictabilities) are virtually eliminated.

## ◆ THE ULTIMATE EXAMPLES OF CONTROL? BIRTH AND DEATH

Not just fish, chickens, and calves are the being McDonaldized, but also people, especially the processes of birth and death.

### Controlling Conception: Even Granny Can Conceive

Conception is rapidly becoming McDonaldized, and increasing control is being exercised over the process. For example, the problem of male impotence[52] has been attacked by the burgeoning impotence clinics, some of which have already expanded into chains,[53] and an increasingly wide array of technologies, including medicine (especially Viagra) and mechanical devices. Many males are now better able to engage in intercourse and to play a role in pregnancies that otherwise might not have occurred.

Similarly, female infertility has been ameliorated by advances in the technologies associated with artificial (more precisely, "donor"[54]) insemination, in vitro fertilization,[55] intracytoplasmic sperm injection,[56] various surgical and nonsurgical procedures associated with the Wurn technique,[57] and so on. Some fertility clinics have grown so confident that they offer a money-back guarantee if there is no live baby after three attempts.[58] For those women who still cannot become pregnant or carry to term, surrogate mothers can do the job.[59] Even postmenopausal women now have the chance of becoming pregnant ("granny pregnancies");[60] the oldest, thus far, is a sixty-five-year-old Indian woman who gave birth to a boy in April 2003.[61] These developments and many others, such as ovulation predictor home tests,[62] have made having a child far more predictable. Efficient, easy-to-use home pregnancy tests are also available to take the ambiguity out of determining whether or not a woman has become pregnant.

One of the great unpredictabilities tormenting some prospective parents is whether the baby will turn out to be a girl or a boy. Sex selection[63] clinics have opened in England, India, and Hong Kong as the first of what may eventually become a chain of "gender choice centers." The technology, developed in the early 1970s, is actually rather simple: Semen is filtered through albumen to separate sperm with male chromosomes from sperm with female chromosomes. The woman is then artificially inseminated with the desired sperm. The chances of creating a boy are 75%; a girl, 70%.[64] A new technique uses staining of sperm cells to determine which cells carry X (male) and Y (female) chromosomes. Artificial insemination or in vitro fertilization then mates the selected sperm with an egg. The U.S. lab that developed this technique is able to offer a couple an 85% chance of creating a girl; the probabilities of creating a boy are still unclear but are expected to be lower.[65] The goal is to achieve 100% accuracy in using "male" or "female" sperm to tailor the sex of the offspring to the needs and demands of the parents.

The increasing control over the process of conception delights some but horrifies others: "Being able to specify your child's sex in advance leads to nightmare visions of ordering babies with detailed specifications, like cars with automatic transmission or leather upholstery."[66] Said a medical ethicist, "Choosing a child like we choose a car is part of a consumerist mentality, the child becomes a 'product' rather than a full human being."[67] By turning a baby into just another "product" to be McDonaldized—engineered, manufactured, and commodified—people are in danger of dehumanizing the birth process.

Of course, we are just on the frontier of the McDonaldization of conception (and just about everything else). For example, the first cloned sheep, Dolly (now deceased), was created in Scotland in 1996, and other animals have since been cloned. This opened the door to the possibility of the cloning of humans. In fact, Clonaid, a Raelian sect that believes aliens populated the earth through cloning and that the destiny of humankind is to clone, recently claimed (thus far unsubstantiated) to have cloned its fifth human being.[68] Cloning involves the creation of identical copies of molecules, cells, or even entire organisms.[69] This conjures up the image of the engineering and mass production of a "cookie-cutter" race of people, all good-looking, athletic, intelligent, free of genetic defects, and so on. If everyone were to be conceived through cloning, we would be close to the ultimate in the control of this process. And a world in which everyone was the same would be a world in which they would be ready to accept a similar sameness in everything around them. Of course, this is a science fiction scenario, but the technology needed to take us down this road is already here!

### Controlling Pregnancy: Choosing the Ideal Baby

Some parents wait until pregnancy is confirmed before worrying about the sex of their child. But then, amniocentesis can be used to determine whether a fetus is male or female. First used in 1968 for prenatal diagnosis, amniocentesis is a process whereby fluid is drawn from the amniotic sac, usually between the fourteenth and eighteenth weeks of pregnancy.[70] With amniocentesis, parents might choose to exert greater control over the process by aborting a pregnancy if the fetus is of the "wrong" sex. This is clearly a far less efficient technique than prepregnancy sex selection, because it occurs after conception. In fact, very few Americans (only about 5% in one study) say that they might use abortion as a method of sex selection.[71] However, amniocentesis does allow parents to know well in advance what the sex of their child will be.

Concern about a baby's sex pales in comparison to concern about the possibility of genetic defects. In addition to amniocentesis, a variety of recently developed tests can be used to determine whether a fetus carries genetic defects such as cystic fibrosis, Down syndrome, Huntington's disease, hemophilia, Tay-Sachs disease, and sickle-cell disease.[72] These newer tests include the following:

- *Chorionic villus sampling (CVS):* Generally done earlier than amniocentesis, between the tenth and twelfth weeks of pregnancy, CVS involves taking a sample from the fingerlike structures projecting from the sac that later becomes the placenta. These structures have the same genetic makeup as the fetus.[73]
- *Maternal serum alpha-fetoprotein (MSAFP) testing:* A simple blood test done in the sixteenth to eighteenth weeks of pregnancy. A high level of alpha-fetoprotein might indicate spina bifida; a low level might indicate Down syndrome.
- *Ultrasound:* A technology derived from sonar that provides an image of the fetus by bouncing high-frequency energy off it. Ultrasound can reveal various genetic defects, as well as many other things (sex, gestational age, and so on).

The use of all these nonhuman technologies has increased dramatically in recent years, with some (ultrasound, MSAFP) already routine practices.[74] Many other technologies for testing fetuses are also available, and others will undoubtedly be created.

If one or more of these tests indicate the existence of a genetic defect, then abortion becomes an option. Parents who choose abortion are unwilling to inflict the pain and suffering of genetic abnormality or illness on the child and on the family. Eugenicists feel that it is not rational for a society to allow genetically disabled children to be born and to create whatever irrationalities will accompany their birth. From a cost-benefit point of view (calculability), abortion is less costly than supporting a child with serious physical or mental abnormalities or problems, sometimes for a number of years. Given such logic, it makes sense for society to use the nonhuman technologies now available to discover which fetuses are to be permitted to survive and which are not. The ultimate step would be a societal ban on certain marriages and births, something that China has considered, with the goal of such a law being the reduction of the number of sick or retarded children that burden the state.[75]

Efforts to predict and repair genetic anomalies are proceeding at a rapid rate. The Human Genome Project constructed a map of 99% of the human genome's gene-containing regions.[76] When the project began, only about 100 human disease genes were known; today we know of over 140 such genes.[77] Such knowledge will allow scientists to develop new diagnostic tests and therapeutic methods. Knowledge of where each gene is and what each does will also extend the ability to test fetuses, children, and prospective mates for genetic diseases. Prospective parents who carry problematic genes may choose not to marry or not to procreate. Another possibility (and fear) is that as the technology gets cheaper and becomes more widely available, people may be able to do the testing themselves (we already have home pregnancy tests) and then make a decision to try a risky home abortion.[78] Overall, human mating and procreation will come to be increasingly affected and controlled by these new nonhuman technologies.

## Controlling Childbirth: Birth as Pathology

McDonaldization and increasing control is also manifest in the process of giving birth. One measure is the decline of midwifery, a very human and personal practice. In 1900, midwives attended about half of American births, but by 1986, they attended only 4%.[79] Today, however, midwifery has enjoyed a slight renaissance because of the dehumanization and rationalization of modern childbirth practices,[80] and 6.5% of babies in the United States are now delivered by midwives.[81] When asked why they sought out midwives, women complain about things such as the "callous and neglectful treatment by the hospital staff," "labor unnecessarily induced for the convenience of the doctor," and "unnecessary cesareans for the same reason."[82]

The flip side of the decline of midwives is the increase in the control of the birth process by professional medicine,[83] especially obstetricians. It is they who are most likely to rationalize and dehumanize the birth process. Dr. Michelle Harrison, who served as a resident in obstetrics and gynecology, is but one physician willing to admit that hospital birth can be a "dehumanized process."[84]

The increasing control over childbirth is also manifest in the degree to which it has been bureaucratized. "Social childbirth," the traditional approach, once took place largely in the home, with female relatives and friends in attendance. Now, childbirth takes place almost totally in hospitals, "alone among strangers."[85] In 1900, less than 5% of U.S. births took place in hospitals; by 1940, it was 55%; and by 1960, the process was all but complete, with nearly 100% of births occurring in hospitals.[86] In more recent years, hospital chains and birthing centers have emerged, modeled after my paradigm for the rationalization process—the fast-food restaurant.

Over the years, hospitals and the medical profession have developed many standard, routinized (McDonaldized) procedures for handling and controlling childbirth. One of the best known, created by Dr. Joseph De Lee, was widely followed through the first half of the twentieth century. De Lee viewed childbirth as a disease (a "pathologic process"), and his procedures were to be followed even in the case of low-risk births:[87]

1. The patient was placed in the lithotomy position, "lying supine with legs in air, bent and wide apart, supported by stirrups."[88]

2. The mother-to-be was sedated from the first stage of labor on.

3. An episiotomy[89] was performed to enlarge the area through which the baby must pass.

4. Forceps were used to make the delivery more efficient.

5. Describing this type of procedure, one woman wrote, "Women are herded like sheep through an obstetrical assembly line, are drugged and strapped on tables where their babies are forceps delivered."[90]

De Lee's standard practice includes not only control through nonhuman technology (the procedure itself, forceps, drugs, an assembly line approach) but most of the other elements of McDonaldization—efficiency, predictability, and the irrationality of turning the human delivery room into an inhuman baby factory. The calculability that it lacked was added later in the form of Emanuel Friedman's "Friedman Curve." This curve prescribed three rigid stages of labor. For example, the first stage was allocated exactly 8.6 hours, during which cervical dilation was to proceed from two to four centimeters.[91]

The moment that babies come into the world, they, too, are greeted by a calculable scoring system, the Apgar test. The babies receive scores of zero to two on each of five factors (for example, heart rate, color), with ten being the healthiest total score. Most babies have scores between seven and nine a minute after birth and scores of eight to ten after five minutes. Babies with scores of zero to three are considered to be in very serious trouble. Dr. Harrison wonders why medical personnel don't ask about more subjective things, such as the infant's curiosity and mood:

A baby doesn't have to be crying for us to know it is healthy. Hold a new baby. It makes eye contact. It breathes. It sighs. The baby has color. Lift it in your arms and feel whether it has good tone or poor, strong limbs or limp ones. The baby does not have to be on a cold table to have its condition measured.[92]

The use of various nonhuman technologies in the delivery of babies has tended to ebb and flow. The use of forceps, invented in 1588, reached a peak in the United States in the 1950s, when as many as 50% of all births involved their use. However, forceps fell out of vogue, and in the 1980s, only about 15% of all births employed forceps. Many methods of drugging mothers-to-be have also been widely used. The electronic fetal monitor became popular in the 1970s. Today, ultrasound is a popular technology.

Another worrisome technology associated with childbirth is the scalpel. Many doctors routinely perform episiotomies during delivery so that the opening of the vagina does not tear or stretch unduly during pregnancy. Often done to enhance the pleasure of future sex partners and to ease the passage of the infant, episiotomies are quite debilitating and painful for the woman. Dr. Harrison expresses considerable doubt about episiotomies. "I want those obstetricians to stop cutting open women's vaginas. Childbirth is not a surgical procedure."[93]

The scalpel is also a key tool in cesarean sections. Birth, a perfectly human process, has come to be controlled by this technology (and those who wield it) in many cases.[94] The first modern "C-section" took place in 1882, but as late as 1970, only 5% of all births involved cesarean. Its use skyrocketed in the 1970s and 1980s, reaching 25% of all births in 1987 in what has been described as a "national epidemic."[95] By the mid-1990s, the practice had declined slightly, to 21%.[96] However, as of August 2002, 25% of births were once again by cesarean, first-time C-sections were at an all-time high of almost 17%, and the rate of vaginal births after a previous cesarean was down to 16.5%.[97] This latter occurred even though the American College of Obstetricians formally abandoned the time-honored idea, "once a cesarean, always a cesarean." That is, it no longer supports the view that once a mother has a cesarean section, all succeeding births must be cesarean.

In addition, many people believe that cesareans are often performed unnecessarily. The first clue is historical data: Why do we see a sudden need for so many more cesareans? Weren't cesareans just as necessary a few decades ago? The second clue is data indicating that private patients who can pay are more likely to get cesareans than those on Medicaid (which reimburses far less) and are twice as likely as indigent patients to get cesareans.[98] Are those in higher social classes and with more income really more likely to need cesareans than those with less income and from the lower social classes?[99]

One explanation for the dramatic increase in cesareans is that they fit well with the idea of the substitution of nonhuman for human technology, but they also mesh with the other elements of the increasing McDonaldization of society:

- . ◆ They are more *predictable* than the normal birth process that can occur a few weeks (or even months) early or late. It is frequently noted that cesareans generally seem to be performed before 5:30 P.M. so that physicians can be home for dinner. Similarly, well-heeled women may choose a cesarean so that the unpredictabilities of natural childbirth do not interfere with careers or social demands.
- ◆ As a comparatively simple operation, the cesarean is more *efficient* than natural childbirth, which may involve many more unforeseen circumstances.
- ◆ Cesareans births are more *calculable,* normally involving no less than twenty minutes and no more than forty-five minutes. The time required for a normal birth, especially a first birth, may be far more variable.
- ◆ Irrationalities exist (see Chapter 7 for more on the irrationality of rationality), including the risks associated with surgery—anesthesia, hemorrhage, blood replacement. Compared with those who undergo a normal childbirth, women who have cesareans seem to experience more physical problems and a longer period of recuperation, and the mortality rate can be as much as twice as high. Then there are the higher costs associated with cesareans. One study indicated that physicians' costs were 68% higher and hospital costs 92% higher for cesareans compared with natural childbirth.[100]
- ◆ Cesareans are dehumanizing because a natural human process is transformed, often unnecessarily, into a nonhuman or even inhuman process in which women endure a surgical procedure. At the minimum, many of those who have cesareans are denied unnecessarily the very human experience of vaginal birth. The wonders of childbirth are reduced to the routines of a minor surgical procedure.

## Controlling the Process of Dying: Designer Deaths

The months or years of decline preceding most deaths involve a series of challenges irresistible to the forces of McDonaldization. In the natural order of things, the final phase of the body's breakdown can be hugely inefficient, incalculable, and unpredictable. Why can't all systems quit at once instead of, say, the kidneys going and then the intellect and then the heart? Many a dying person has confounded physicians and loved ones by rallying and persisting longer than expected or, conversely, giving out sooner than anticipated. Our seeming lack of control in face of the dying process is pointed up in the existence of powerful death figures in myth, literature, and film.

But now we have found ways to rationalize the dying process, giving us at least the illusion of control. Consider the increasing array of nonhuman technologies designed to keep people alive long after they would have expired had they lived at an earlier time in history. In fact, some beneficiaries of these technologies would not want to stay alive under those conditions that allow them to survive (a clear irrationality). Unless the physicians are following an advance directive (a living will) that explicitly states "do not resuscitate," or "no heroic measures," people lose control over their own dying process. Family members, too, in the absence of such directives, must bow to the medical mandate to keep people alive as long as possible.

At issue is who should be in control of the process of dying. It seems increasingly likely that the decision about who dies and when will be left to the medical bureaucracy. Of course, we can expect bureaucrats to focus on rational concerns. For instance, the medical establishment is making considerable progress in maximizing the number of days, weeks, or years a patient remains alive. However, it has been slower to work on improving the quality of life during the extra time. This focus on calculability is akin to the fast-food restaurant telling people how large its sandwiches are but saying nothing about their quality.

We can also expect an increasing reliance on nonhuman technologies. For example, computer systems may be used to assess a patient's chances of survival at any given point in the dying process—90%, 50%, 10%, and so on. The actions of medical personnel are likely to be influenced by such assessments. Thus, whether a person lives or dies may come to depend increasingly on a computer program.

As you can see, death has followed much the same path as birth. That is, the dying process has been moved out of the home and beyond the control of the dying and their families and into the hands of medical personnel and hospitals.[101] Physicians have gained a large measure of control over death just as they won control over birth, and death, like birth, is increasingly likely to take place in the hospital. In 1900, only 20% of deaths took place in hospitals; by 1977, it had reached 70%. By 1993, the number of hospital deaths was down slightly to 65%, but to that percentage must be added the increasing number of people who die in nursing homes (11%) and residences such as hospices (22%).[102] The growth of hospital chains and chains of hospices, using principles derived from the fast-food restaurant, signals death's bureaucratization, rationalization, even McDonaldization.

The McDonaldization of the dying process, as well as of birth, has spawned a series of counterreactions, efforts to cope with the excesses of rationalization. For example, as a way to humanize birth, interest in midwives has grown. However, the greatest counterreaction has been the search for ways to regain control over our own deaths. Advance directives and living wills tell hospitals and medical personnel what they may or may not do during the dying process. Suicide societies and books such as Derek Humphry's *Final Exit*[103] give people instructions on how to kill themselves. Finally, there is the growing interest in and acceptance of euthanasia,[104] most notably the work of "Dr. Death," Jack Kevorkian, whose goal is to give back to people control over their own deaths.

However, these counterreactions themselves have elements of McDonaldization. For example, Dr. Kevorkian (now serving a ten- to twenty-five-year prison term for second-degree murder) uses a nonhuman technology, a "machine," to help people kill themselves. More generally, and strikingly, he is an advocate of a "rational policy" for the planning of death.[105] Thus, the rationalization of death is found even in the efforts to counter it. Dr. Kervorkian's opponents have noted the limitations of his rational policy:

> It is not so difficult . . . to envision a society of brave new benignity and rationality, in which a sort of humane disposal system would tidy up and whisk away to dreamland the worst-case geezers and crones. They are, after all, incredibly expensive and non-productive. . . . And they are a terrible inconvenience to that strain of the American character that has sought to impose rational control on all aspects of life. . . .
>
> Would it be so farfetched to envision a society that in the name of efficiency and convenience . . . practiced Kevorkianism as a matter of routine in every community.[106]

## ♦ CONCLUSION

The fourth dimension of McDonaldization is control, primarily through the replacement of human with nonhuman technology. Among the many objectives guiding the development of nonhuman technologies, the most important here is increased control over the uncertainties created by people—especially employees and consumers. The ultimate in control is reached when employees are replaced by nonhuman technologies such as robots. Nonhuman technologies are also employed to control the uncertainties created by customers. The objective is to make them more pliant participants in McDonaldized processes. In controlling employees and consumers, nonhuman technologies also lead to greater control over work-related processes and finished products. However, the ultimate examples of the efforts at obtaining greater control through the use of nonhuman technologies are found in the realms of birth and death.

Clearly, the future will bring with it an increasing number of nonhuman technologies with greater ability to control people and processes. Even today, listening to audiotapes rather than reading books, for example, shifts control to those who do the reading on the tape: "The mood, pace and intonation of the words are decided for you. You can't linger or rush headlong into them anymore."[107] Military hardware such as "smart bombs" (for example, the "jdams"—joint direct attack munitions—used so frequently and with such great effect in the 2003 war with Iraq) adjust their trajectories without human intervention, but in the future, smart bombs may be developed that scan an array of targets and "decide" which one to hit. Perhaps the next great step will be the refinement of artificial intelligence, which gives machines the apparent ability to think and to make decisions as humans do.[108] Artificial intelligence promises many benefits in a wide range of areas (medicine, for example). However, it also constitutes an enormous step in de-skilling. In effect, more and more people will lose the opportunity, and perhaps the ability, to think for themselves.

# 7

# The Irrationality of Rationality

◆ ────────────────────────────────

## Traffic Jams on Those "Happy Trails"

**M** cDonaldization has swept across the social landscape because it offers increased efficiency, predictability, calculability, and control. Despite these assets, as the preceding chapters have shown, McDonaldization has some serious drawbacks. Rational systems inevitably spawn irrationalities that limit, eventually compromise, and perhaps even undermine their rationality.

At the most general level, the *irrationality of rationality* is simply a label for many of the negative aspects of McDonaldization. More specifically, irrationality can be seen as the opposite of rationality. That is, McDonaldization can be viewed as leading to inefficiency, unpredictability, incalculability, and loss of control.[1] Irrationality also means that rational systems are disenchanted; they have lost their magic and mystery. Most important, rational systems are unreasonable systems that deny the humanity, the human reason, of the people who work within them or are served by them. In other words, rational systems are dehumanizing. Please note, therefore, that although the terms *rationality* and *reason* are often used interchangeably, in this discussion they are antithetical phenomena: Rational systems are often unreasonable.

This chapter presents the costs of McDonaldization more systematically than previous chapters have done. As you will see, these costs include inefficiency, illusions of various types, disenchantment, homogenization, and dehumanization.

# ♦ INEFFICIENCY: LONG LINES AT THE CHECKOUT

Rational systems, contrary to their promise, often end up being quite inefficient. For instance, in fast-food restaurants, long lines of people often form at the counters, or parades of cars idle in the drive-through lanes. What is purported to be an efficient way to obtain a meal often turns out to be quite inefficient.

The fast-food restaurant is far from the only aspect of a McDonaldized society that exhibits inefficiency. Even the vaunted Japanese industry of the 1980s and early 1990s had its inefficiencies. Take the "just-in-time" system discussed in Chapter 2. Because this system often requires that parts be delivered several times a day, the streets and highways around a factory often became cluttered with trucks. Because of the heavy traffic, people were often late for work or for business appointments, resulting in lost productivity. But the irrationalities go beyond traffic jams and missed appointments. All these trucks used a great deal of fuel, very expensive in Japan, and contributed greatly to air pollution. The situation grew even worse when Japanese convenience stores, supermarkets, and department stores also began to use a just-in-time system, bringing even greater numbers of delivery trucks onto the streets.[2]

Here is the way columnist Richard Cohen describes another example of inefficiency in the McDonaldized world:

> Oh Lord, with each advance of the computer age, I was told I would benefit. But with each "benefit," I wind up doing more work. This is the ATM [automated teller machine] rule of life. . . . I was told—nay promised—that I could avoid lines at the bank and make deposits or withdrawals any time of the day. Now, there are lines at the ATMs, the bank seems to take a percentage of whatever I withdraw or deposit, and, of course, I'm doing what tellers (remember them?) used to do. Probably, with the new phone, I'll have to climb telephone poles in the suburbs during ice storms.[3]

Cohen underscores at least three different irrationalities: (1) Rational systems are not less expensive, (2) they force people to do unpaid work, and (3) most important here, they are often inefficient. It might be more efficient to deal with a human teller, either in the bank or at a drive-through window, than to wait in line at an ATM.

Similarly, preparing a meal might be more efficient at home than packing the family in the car, driving to McDonald's, loading up on food, and then driving home again. Meals cooked at home from scratch might not be more efficient, but certainly TV dinners and microwave meals are—maybe even full-course meals brought from the supermarket, Boston Market, or eatZi's. Yet many people persist in the belief, fueled by propaganda from the fast-food restaurants, that eating there is more efficient than eating at home.

Although the forces of McDonaldization trumpet greater efficiency, they never tell us for whom the system is more efficient. Is it efficient for consumers who need only a loaf of bread and a carton of milk to wend their way past thousands of items they don't need? Is it efficient for consumers to push their own food over the supermarket scanner, swipe their own credit or debit cards, and then bag their groceries themselves? Is it efficient for people to pump their own gasoline? Is it efficient for them to push numerous combinations of telephone numbers before they hear a human voice? Most often, consumers find that such systems are not efficient for them. Most of the gains in efficiency go to those who are pushing rationalization.

Those at the top of an organization impose efficiencies on those who work at or near the bottom of the system: the assembly line workers, the counter persons, the call center staff. The owners, franchisees, and top managers want to control subordinates, but they want their own positions to be as free of rational constraints—as inefficient—as possible. Subordinates are to follow blindly the rules, regulations, and other structures of the rational system while those in charge remain free to be creative.

## ◆ HIGH COST: BETTER OFF AT HOME

The efficiency of McDonaldization does not ordinarily save consumers money. For example, a small soda was shown to cost one franchise owner eleven cents, but it was sold for eighty-five cents.[4] A fast-food meal for a family of four might easily cost twenty or twenty-five dollars these days. Such a sum would go further spent on ingredients for a home-cooked meal.

As Cohen demonstrated in the case of ATMs, people must often pay extra to deal with the inhumanity and inefficiency of rationalized systems. The great success of McDonaldized systems, the rush to extend them to ever-new sectors of society, and the fact that so many people want to get into such businesses indicate that these systems generate huge profits.

Bob Garfield noted the expense of McDonaldized activities in his article "How I Spent (and Spent and Spent) My Disney Vacation."[5] Garfield took his family of four to Walt Disney World, which he found might be more aptly named "Expense World." The five-day vacation cost $1,700 in 1991; admission to Disney World alone cost $551.30. (And the prices keep going up. By 1998, the cost of admission for five days cost a family of four over $800,[6] and now [2003] $1,000, or more.) He calculates that in the five days, they had less than seven hours of "fun, fun, fun. That amounts to $261 c.p.f.h. (cost per fun hour)." Because most of his time in the Magic Kingdom was spent riding buses, "queuing up and shlepping from place to place, the 17 attractions we saw thrilled us for a grand total of 44 minutes."[7] Thus, what is thought to be an inexpensive family vacation turns out be quite costly.

## ◆ THE ILLUSION OF FUN: HA, HA, THE STOCK MARKET JUST CRASHED

If it really isn't so efficient and it really isn't so cheap, then what does McDonaldization—more specifically, the fast-food restaurant—offer people? Why has it been such a worldwide success? One answer: an illusion of efficiency and frugality. As long as people believe in the illusion, the actual situation matters little.

Perhaps more important, fast-food restaurants seem to offer, as Stan Luxenberg[8] has pointed out, fun. McDonald's uses a ubiquitous clown, Ronald McDonald, an array of cartoon characters, and a colorful decor to remind people that fun awaits them on their next visit. Some restaurants even offer playgrounds and children's rides, and such things are becoming progressively bigger and more "high tech."[9] It is not unusual to see a restaurant dwarfed by its playground. In essence, many fast-food restaurants are really amusement parks for food.

At one time, McDonald's actually went into the playground business. A wholly owned subsidiary, Leaps & Bounds, eventually opened forty-nine playgrounds before it was sold to the now-defunct Discovery Zone in 1994.[10] The playground equipment at Leaps & Bounds was derived from the sort of equipment found in the playgrounds at many McDonald's restaurants. A McDonald's spokesperson said that the idea grew out of the advertising theme of "food, folks and fun. . . . We just turned it around and put the fun first."[11] More than a few cynics would say that McDonald's has always put fun before food.

Not to be outdone, McDonald's in Japan joined forces with Toys "R" Us. A number of Toys "R" Us outlets include McDonald's restaurants. In aligning itself ever more closely with playgrounds and toys, McDonald's is making it increasingly clear that it is in the business of providing "fun."[12]

If you don't believe that fun has become the guiding principle, consider the food. Fast-food restaurants serve the kinds of finger foods bought at the stands in an amusement park. In what may be termed the "cotton candy principle," people pay a lot for a few pennies worth of food as long as it has a strong, pleasant, and familiar flavor. Indeed, what fast-food restaurants often sell is "salty candy."[13] One of the secrets of the McDonald's french fry is that it is coated with *both* salt and sugar.[14] People taste the salt and the sugar but rarely if ever the potato slice, little more than an excuse for the rest.

Today's diner often looks for theater more than food. Instead of a private, folded menu, McDonald's offers a marquee that, like the movie options at the local cineplex, presents the diner's alternatives.[15] Even at upscale restaurants, diners seek out the theatrical: "I would rather eat mediocre food in a fabulous room than sit somewhere dull and boring and eat fabulous food. . . . I'm looking for decor, scale, theatrics, a lot going on."[16] Hence, the growth of "entertainment" chains such as Hard Rock Cafe, Planet Hollywood,[17] Rainforest Cafe, and ESPN Zone with its walls of television sets and its game rooms.

Supermarkets are also increasingly entertainment centers, selling more and more "fun foods"—for example, breakfast cereals such as Count Chocula and Disney Mickey's Magix ("WOW! it turns the milk BLUE!"), and Snausages in a Blanket (dog treats). As one observer said,

> When The Shopper was young, Americans used to sing, "There's no business like show business," but they don't sing it much anymore, probably because just about every business is like show business now. Supermarkets are certainly no exception. These days, supermarkets are like theme parks.[18]

One supermarket chain (Stew Leonard's) in Connecticut and New York offers costumed characters (Daphne the Duck, Wow the Cow), singing and dancing mechanical bananas and celery sticks, and a cash register that moos when bills exceed $100. To entertain children, other supermarkets offer them their own minicarts to push through the store or attach plastic race cars to the front of full-size carts pushed by parents. Said the manager of one supermarket, "If your shopping experience with your kids is calm and relaxed, you're probably going to be interested in spending more."[19]

All this is part of the obsession with amusement. Neil Postman, in an aptly titled book, *Amusing Ourselves to Death,* argues that Las Vegas has become the symbol of this obsession because it "is a city entirely devoted to the idea of entertainment, and as such proclaims the spirit of a culture in which all public discourse increasingly takes the form of entertainment."[20] If Las Vegas, with its McDonaldized gambling, symbolizes the obsession with entertainment, then McDonald's symbolizes the emphasis on entertainment in the fast-food industry.

In another realm, journalism has also become more geared to entertainment. For example, *Business Week,* a rationalized magazine, is designed to be not only more efficient to read than the *Wall Street Journal* but also more enjoyable. An ad for *Business Week* claims, "We don't just inform you but we entertain you." Two critics say of this advertisement, "Is *Business Week* really serious? Are we to expect the following: Ha Ha Ha, Ha! The stock market just crashed! What a laugh! . . . Your company is going down the tubes. What fun!"[21] Similarly, television news is often described as "infotainment" because it combines news and show business. Chains of educational enterprises such as Sylvan Learning Center have been called "edutainment."

Entertainment is also central to the shopping mall which is, after all, the site of many Americans' favorite form of entertainment: shopping. Malls are designed to be fantasy worlds, theatrical settings for what Kowinski calls "the Retail Drama."[22] Both consumers and mall employees play important roles in this drama. The mall has a backdrop of ever-present Muzak to soothe the savage shopper and is loaded with props. Some of the props remain all year; others (for example, Christmas decorations) are brought in for special occasions and promotions. Restaurants, bars, movie theaters, and exercise centers add to the fun. On weekends, clowns, balloons, magicians, bands, and the like further entertain those on their way from one shop to another. Advising malls on ways to deal with the threat of shop-at-home alternatives, one marketing expert said, "You've got to make your centers more fun."[23]

The Mall of America in Bloomington, Minnesota, offers state-of-the-art shopping fun.[24] At the center of the Mall of America is a huge amusement park, Knott's Camp Snoopy, including a full-size roller coaster, an arcade, and shooting galleries. A system of acrylic tubes allows visitors to walk through an aquarium. Golf Mountain provides an eighteen-hole miniature-golf course on several levels. The mall also houses an enormous

LEGO structure, as well as a huge sports bar, a Hooters, and a Rainforest Cafe. And of course, it has a movie theater—with fourteen screens! Said one critic, "Mall of America is not a mall, it's a circus."[25]

Many retail chains contribute to the obsession with entertainment, earning the label "retailtainment." For example, at REI in Seattle one can climb a 65-foot rock. Niketown displays sports videos on three-story high screens. Abercrombie & Fitch plays videos of its models, and Gadzooks offers music videos.

## ♦ THE ILLUSION OF REALITY: EVEN THE "SINGERS" AREN'T REAL

Many aspects of a McDonaldized society involve deceptive settings and events (what Daniel Boorstin calls "pseudo-events"[26]), including the package tour; the modern campground; the international villages at amusement parks such as Busch Gardens; Las Vegas casino hotels like New York, New York; the computer-automated phone call; and false fraternization at chains such as Roy Rogers and NutriSystem. All may be viewed as part of Ian Mitroff and Warren Bennis's "unreality industry."[27] They have pointed out that whole industries attempt to produce and market unreality. McDonald's, for example, creates the illusion that people are having fun, that they are getting lots of french fries, and that they are getting a bargain when they purchase their meal. One infamous example of such unreality was the pop group Milli Vanilli. The two "singers" did not actually sing on their record album.[28]

From the wide range of unrealities, here are a few examples from the supermarket, where fewer and fewer things are what they appear to be:

- ♦ Sizzlean (fake "bacon") is made of beef and turkey, and kosher bacon has no pork.
- ♦ Molly McButter and Butter Buds have no butter.
- ♦ The turkey flavor in the frozen turkey TV dinner may well be artificial, because the natural flavor was removed during processing.
- ♦ The lemon smell in the laundry detergent usually does not come from lemons.

Such unreality, along with various pseudo-events, has become integral to McDonaldized society.

## ◆  FALSE FRIENDLINESS: "HI, GEORGE"

Because fast-food restaurants greatly restrict or even eliminate genuine fraternization, what workers and customers have left is either no human relationships or "false fraternization." Rule Number 17 for Burger King workers is "Smile at all times."[29] The Roy Rogers employees who used to say, "Happy trails" to me when I paid for my food really had no interest in what happened "on the trail." (In fact, come to think of it, they were really saying, in a polite way, "Get lost!") This phenomenon has been generalized to the many workers who say "Have a nice day" as customers depart. In fact, of course, they usually have no real interest in, or concern for, how the rest of a customer's day goes. Instead, in a polite and ritualized way, they are really saying, "Get lost," or move on so someone else can be served.

At NutriSystem, counselors receive a list of things to do to keep dieters coming back. The counselors are urged to "greet client by name with enthusiasm." Knowing the client's name creates a false sense of friendliness, as does the "enthusiastic" greeting. Counselors are also urged to "converse with client in a sensitive manner." The counselors are provided with a small, glossy card titled, "Personalized Approach at a Glance." The card rationalizes the personal greeting with pseudo-personalized responses to problematic situations. For example, if clients indicate that they feel they are receiving little support for the diet, the script urges the counselor to say, "I'm so glad to see you. I was thinking about you. How is the program going for you?" Is the counselor really glad to see the client? Really thinking about the client? Really concerned about how things are working out for the client? The answers to such questions are clear in a McDonaldized society.

In the mountain of computerized letters, or "junk mail," with which people are daily bombarded, great pains are sometimes taken to make a letter seem personal.[30] (Similarly, I now often get calls from telemarketers who start out by saying, "Hi, George.") In most cases, it is fairly obvious that a computer has generated the letter from a database of names. These letters are full of the kind of false fraternization practiced by Roy Rogers workers. For example, the letters often adopt a friendly, personal tone designed to lead people to believe that the head of some business has fretted over the fact that they haven't, for example, shopped in his or her department store or used his or her credit card in the past few months. For example, a friend of mine received a letter from a franchise, The Lube Center, a few days after he had his car lubricated (note the use of the first name and the "deep" personal concern):

> Dear Ken:
>
> We want to THANK YOU for choosing The Lube Center for all of your car's fluid needs. . . .
>
> We strongly recommend that you change your oil on a regular basis. . . . We will send you a little reminder card. . . . This will help *remind* you when your car is next due to be serviced. . . .
>
> We spend the time and energy to make sure that our employees are trained properly to give you the service that you deserve. . . .
>
> Holly O'Neill/Shane Williams
>
> The Lube Center Management [Italics added]

Several years ago, I received the following letter from a congressman from Long Island, even though I live in Maryland. The fact that I had never met Congressman Downey and knew nothing about him didn't prevent him from writing me a "personal" letter:

> Dear George:
>
> It is hard to believe, but I am running for my NINTH term in Congress! . . .
>
> When I think back over the 8,660 votes I've cast . . . I realize how many battles *we've shared.*
>
> Please let me know that I can count on you.
>
> Sincerely,
>
> Tom Downey [Italics added]

A *Washington Post* correspondent offers the following critique of false friendliness in junk mail:

By dropping in peoples' names and little tidbits gleaned from databases hither and yon in their direct mail pitches, these marketing organizations are trying to create the illusion of intimacy. In reality, these technologies conspire to *corrupt and degrade intimacy.* They cheat, substituting the insertable fact for the genuine insight. These pitches end up with their own synthetic substitutes for the real thing.[31]

However false it may be, such junk mail is designed to exert control over customers by getting them to take desired courses of action.

Mention might also be in this context of greeting cards as well as the cards now available on the Internet. False friendliness defines both.

## ♦ DISENCHANTMENT: WHERE'S THE MAGIC?

One of Max Weber's most general theses is that as a result of rationalization, the Western world has grown increasingly disenchanted.[32] The "magical elements of thought" that characterized less rationalized societies have been disappearing.[33] Thus, instead of a world dominated by enchantment, magic, and mystery, we have one in which everything seems clear, cut-and-dried, logical, and routine. As Schneider puts it, "Max Weber saw history as having departed a deeply enchanted past en route to a disenchanted future—a journey that would gradually strip the natural world both of its magical properties and of its capacity for meaning."[34] The process of rationalization leads, by definition, to the loss of a quality—enchantment—that was at one time very important to people. Although we undoubtedly have gained much from the rationalization of society in general, and from the rationalization of consumption settings in particular, we also have lost something of great, if hard to define, value. Consider how the dimensions of McDonaldization work against enchantment.

Efficient systems have no room for anything smacking of enchantment and systematically seek to root it out. Anything that is magical, mysterious, fantastic, dreamy, and so on is considered inefficient. Enchanted systems typically involve highly convoluted means to ends, and they may well have no obvious goals at all. Efficient systems do not permit such meanderings, and their designers and implementers will do whatever is necessary to eliminate them. The elimination of meanderings and aimlessness is one of the reasons that Weber saw rationalized systems as disenchanted systems.

Enchantment has far more to do with quality than with quantity. Magic, fantasies, dreams, and the like relate more to the inherent nature of an experience, and the qualitative aspects of that experience, than, for example, to the number of such experiences one has or the size of the setting in which they occur. An emphasis on producing and participating in a large number of experiences tends to diminish the magical quality of each of them. Put another way, it is difficult to imagine the mass production of magic, fantasy, and dreams. Such mass production may be common in the movies, but "true" enchantment is difficult, if not impossible, to produce in settings designed to deliver large quantities of goods and services frequently and over great geographic spaces. The mass production of such things is virtually guaranteed to undermine their enchanted qualities.

No characteristic of rationalization is more inimical to enchantment than predictability. Magical, fantastic, dreamlike experiences are almost by definition unpredictable. Nothing would destroy an enchanted experience more easily than having it become predictable or having it recur in the same way time after time.

Both control and the nonhuman technologies that produce it tend to be inimical to enchantment. As a general rule, fantasy, magic, and dreams cannot be subjected to external controls; indeed, autonomy is much of what gives them their enchanted quality. Fantastic experiences can go anywhere; anything can happen. Such unpredictability clearly is not possible in a tightly controlled environment. For some people, tight and total control could be a fantasy, but for many, it would be more a nightmare. Much the same can be said of nonhuman technologies. Cold, mechanical systems are usually the antithesis of the dream worlds associated with enchantment. Again, some people have fantasies associated with nonhuman technologies, but they, too, tend to be more nightmarish than dreamlike.

As you can see, McDonaldization is related to, if not inextricably intertwined with, disenchantment. A world without magic and mystery is another irrational consequence of increasing rationalization.

## ♦ HEALTH AND ENVIRONMENTAL HAZARDS: EVEN YOUR PETS ARE AT RISK

Progressive rationalization has threatened not only the fantasies but also the health, and perhaps the lives, of people. One example is the danger posed by the content of most fast food: a lot of fat, cholesterol, salt, and sugar. Such meals are the last things many Americans need, suffering as many of them do from obesity, high cholesterol levels, high blood pressure, and perhaps diabetes. In fact, there is much talk these days of an obesity epidemic (including children), and many observers place a lot of the blame on the fast-food industry, its foods, and its emphasis on "super-sizing" everything.[35]

Fast-food restaurants contribute to the development of these, and other, health problems later in life by helping to create poor eating habits in children. In targeting children, fast-food restaurants are creating not only lifelong devotees of fast food but also people who are addicted to diets high in salt, sugar, and fat.[36] An interesting study discovered that the health of immigrant children deteriorates the longer they are in the United States, in large part because their diet comes to more closely resemble the junk food diet of most American children.[37] Said a sociologist associated with the study, "'The McDonaldization of the world is not necessarily progress when it comes to nutritious diets.'"[38]

Attacks against the fast-food industry's harmful effects on health have mounted over the years. Many of the franchises have been forced to respond by offering salads, although the dressings for them are often loaded with salt and fat. Some fast-food restaurants have ceased cooking french fries in beef tallow and instead use vegetable oil.

Still, the typical McDonald's meal of a Big Mac, large fries, and a shake has more than 1,000 calories, few of them of great nutritional value. The trend toward larger and larger portions has only increased the problem. The substitution of a chocolate triple shake for a regular shake in that McDonald's meal raises the total to 1,690 calories. Burger King's Double Whopper with cheese alone has 960 calories (and 63 grams of fat).[39]

McDonaldization poses even more immediate health threats. Regina Schrambling links outbreaks of diseases such as salmonella to the rationalization of food production:

> Salmonella proliferated in the poultry industry only after beef became a four-letter word and Americans decided they wanted a chicken in every pot every night. But birds aren't like cars: you can't just speed up the factory line to meet demand. Something has got to give—and in this case it's been safety. Birds that are rushed to fryer size, then killed, gutted, and plucked at high speed in vast quantities are not going to be the cleanest food in the supermarket.[40]

Schrambling also associates salmonella with the rationalized production of eggs, fruit, and vegetables.[41] Food producers would do well to take note of the fact that Hudson Foods, a meatpacking company that supplied meat to McDonald's and Burger King, among others, was forced out of business because an outbreak of E. coli was traced to its frozen hamburgers.[42]

The fast-food industry has run afoul not only of nutritionists and epidemiologists but also of environmentalists. It produces an enormous amount of trash, some of which is nonbiodegradable. The litter from fast-food meals is a public eyesore across the countryside. Innumerable square miles of forest are sacrificed to provide the paper needed each year by McDonald's alone.[43] Whole forests are being devoured by the fast-food industry, even though some paper containers have been replaced by Styrofoam and other products. In fact, the current trend is back to paper (and other biodegradable) products; Styrofoam, virtually indestructible, piles up in landfills, creating mountains of waste that simply endure there for years, if not forever. Overall, despite various efforts to deal with its worst abuses, the fast-food industry contributes to global warming, destruction of the ozone layer, depletion of natural resources, and destruction of natural habitats.

Factory farms and aquaculture create additional environmental degradation and health hazards. For example, large-scale hog farms produce a huge amount of manure that ultimately finds its way into our waterways and then our drinking water; people have been made ill and women have had miscarriages as a result of drinking contaminated water.[44] The dosing of factory-farmed animals with antibiotics may lead to bacteria that are resistant to antibiotics, thereby putting at risk people who are infected with the bacteria.[45] Aquaculture creates a similar set of environmental problems and health risks to humans.[46]

McDonaldized systems pose a health hazard to pets, as well. Pets are affected by many of the health and environmental problems that affect humans and face distinctive threats of their own. Chains of pet superstores (examples include PETCO and PETsMART), employed automatic hair dryers to groom dogs. Unfortunately, some dogs were locked in cages and under the dryers for too long. Several died or were injured. Said the founder of a watchdog group, Grooming Accidents, Supervision and Prevention (GASP): "The whole notion of leaving a dog unsupervised with an electrical heater blowing makes no sense. They are treating animals like cars in an assembly line."[47]

Speaking of the automobile assembly line: It has experienced extraordinary success in churning out millions of cars a year. But all those cars have wreaked havoc on the environment. Their emissions pollute the air, soil, and water. An ever-expanding system of highways and roads has scarred the countryside. And we must not forget the thousands of people killed and the far greater number injured each year in traffic accidents.

## ◆ HOMOGENIZATION: IT'S NO DIFFERENT IN PARIS

Another irrational effect of McDonaldization is increased homogenization. Anywhere you go in the United States and, increasingly, throughout the world you are likely to find the same products offered in the same way.

The expansion of franchising across the United States means that people find little difference between regions and between cities.[48] On a global scale, travelers are finding more familiarity and less diversity. Exotic settings are increasingly likely sites for American fast-food chains. The McDonald's and Kentucky Fried Chicken in Beijing are but two examples.

Furthermore, in many nations, restaurant owners are applying the McDonald's model to native cuisine. In Paris, tourists may be shocked by the number of American fast-food restaurants, but even more shocked by the incredible spread of indigenous forms, such as the fast-food croissanterie. One would have thought that the French, who seem to consider the croissant a sacred object, would resist rationalizing its manufacture and sale, but that is just what has happened.[49] The spread of such outlets throughout Paris indicates that many Parisians are willing to sacrifice quality for speed and efficiency. And, you may ask, if the Parisian croissant can be tamed and transformed into a fast-food success, what food is safe?

The spread of American and indigenous fast food causes less and less diversity from one setting to another. In the process, the human craving for new and diverse experiences is being limited, if not progressively destroyed. It is being supplanted by the desire for uniformity and predictability.

In general, McDonaldized institutions have not been notably successful in creating new and different products. Please recall Ray Kroc's failures in this realm, notably the Hulaburger. Such systems excel instead at selling familiar products and services in shiny new settings or packages that can easily be replicated. For instance, the fast-food restaurant wraps that prosaic hamburger in bright packages and sells it in a carnival-like atmosphere that differs little from one locale to another. This point extends to many other manifestations of McDonaldization. For example, Jiffy Lube and its imitators sell people nothing more than the same old oil change and lube job.

Just as the franchises are leveling differences among goods and services, mail order catalogs are eliminating seasonal differences. When columnist Ellen Goodman received her Christmas catalog just as fall was beginning, she offered this critique: "The creation of one national mail-order market has produced catalogues without the slightest respect for any season or region. Their holidays are now harvested, transported and chemically ripened on the way to your home. . . . I refuse to fast forward through the fall."[50]

## ♦ DEHUMANIZATION: GETTING HOSED AT "TROUGH AND BREW"

The main reason to think of McDonaldization as irrational, and ultimately unreasonable, is that it tends to be dehumanizing. For example, the fast-food industry offers its employees what I have called "McJobs."[51] As a Burger King worker has noted, "A moron could learn this job, it's so easy" and "Any trained monkey could do this job."[52] Workers can use only a small portion of their skills and abilities. The minimal skill demands of the fast-food restaurant are irrational.

From the employee's perspective, McJobs are irrational because they don't offer much in the way of either satisfaction or stability. Employees are seldom allowed to use anything approaching all their skills and are not allowed to be creative on the job. The result is a high level of resentment, job dissatisfaction, alienation, absenteeism, and turnover.[53] In fact, the fast-food industry has the highest turnover rate—approximately 300% a year—of any industry in the United States. That means that the average fast-food worker lasts only about four months; the entire workforce of the fast-food industry turns over approximately three times a year.

Although the simple and repetitive nature of the jobs makes it relatively easy to replace workers who leave, such a high turnover rate is undesirable from the organization's perspective, as well as the employee's. It would clearly be better to keep employees longer. The costs involved in turnover, such as hiring and training, greatly increase with extraordinarily high turnover rates. In addition, failure to use employee's skills is irrational for the organization, because it could obtain much more from its employees for the money (however negligible) it pays them.

In the meatpacking industry, the demands of the fast-food industry are responsible, at least in part, for increasing dehumanization—inhuman work in inhumane conditions. Workers are reduced to fast-moving cogs in the assembly line killing and butchering of animals. They are forced to perform repetitive and physically demanding tasks on animals that may, at least initially, not even be dead. They are often covered in blood and forced to stand in pools of blood. They wield very sharp knives at great speed in close proximity to other workers. The result is an extraordinarily high injury (and even death) rate, although many injuries go unreported out of a fear of being fired for being injured and unable to perform at peak levels. Because they are often illegal immigrants, the workers are almost totally at the whim of a management that is free to hire and fire them at will. Management is also able to ignore the horrid working conditions confronted by these powerless employees or to make those conditions even more horrific.[54]

The fast-food restaurant also dehumanizes consumers. By eating on a sort of assembly line, diners are reduced to automatons rushing through a meal with little gratification derived from the dining experience or from the food itself. The best that can usually be said is that the meal is efficient and is over quickly.

Some customers might even feel as if they are being fed like livestock. This point was made on TV a number of years ago in a *Saturday Night Live* parody of a small fast-food chain called "Burger and Brew." In the skit, some young executives learn that a new fast-food restaurant called "Trough and Brew" has opened, and they decide to try it for lunch. When they enter the restaurant, bibs are tied around their necks. Then they discover what resembles a pig trough filled with chili and periodically refilled by a waitress scooping new supplies from a bucket. The customers bend over, stick their heads into the trough, and lap up the chili as they move along the trough, presumably making "high-level business decisions" en route. Every so often they come up for air and lap some beer from the communal "brew basin." After they have finished their "meal," they pay their bills "by the head." Since their faces are smeared with chili, they are literally "hosed off" before they leave the restaurant. The young executives are last seen being herded out of the restaurant, which is closing for a half-hour so that it can be "hosed down." *Saturday Night Live* was clearly ridiculing the fact that fast-food restaurants tend to treat their customers like lower animals.

Customers are also dehumanized by scripted interactions and other efforts to make interactions uniform. "Uniformity is incompatible when human interactions are involved. Human interactions that are mass-produced may strike consumers as dehumanizing if the routinization is obvious or manipulative if it is not."[55] Dehumanization occurs when prefabricated interactions take the place of authentic human relationships.

Bob Garfield's critique of Walt Disney World provides another example of dehumanized customers:

> I actually believed there was real fun and real imagination in store only to be confronted with an extruded, injection-molded, civil-engineered brand of fantasy, which is to say: no fantasy at all.
>
> From the network of chutes and corrals channeling people into attractions, to the chillingly programmed Stepford Wives demeanor of the employees, to the compulsively litter-free grounds, to the generalized North Korean model Socialist Society sense of totalitarian order, to the utterly passive nature of the entertainment itself, Disney turns out to be the very antithesis of fantasy, a remarkable technospectacle. . . .
>
> Far from liberating the imagination, Disney succeeds mainly in confining it. Like the conveyor "cars" and "boats" that pull you along steel tracks through "Snow White" and "World of Motion" and the "Speedway" rides, Disney is a plodding, precise, computer-controlled mechanism pulling an estimated 30 million visitors along the same calculated, unvarying, meticulously engineered entertainment experience. It occupies its customers without engaging them. It appeals to everybody while challenging nobody. . . .
>
> Imagine, for example, a fake submergence in a fake submarine for a fake voyage past fake coral and fake seafood, knowing full well that there are two magnificent aquariums within a 70-minute drive of your house.[56]

Thus, instead of being a creative and imaginative human experience, Disney World turns out to be an uncreative, unimaginative, and ultimately inhuman experience.

The automobile assembly line is well-known for the way it dehumanizes life on a day-to-day basis for those who work on it. Although Henry Ford felt, as we saw earlier, that he personally could not do the kind of repetitive work required on the assembly line, he believed that most people, with their limited mental abilities and aspirations, could adjust to it quite well. Ford said, "I have not been able to discover that repetitive labour injures a man in any way. . . . The most thorough research has not brought out a single case of a man's mind being twisted or deadened by the work."[57] However, objective evidence of the destructiveness of the assembly line is found in the high rates of absenteeism, tardiness, and turnover among employees. More generally, most people seem to find assembly line work highly alienating. Here is the way one worker describes it:

I stand in one spot, about a two- or three-feet area, all night. The only time a person stops is when the line stops. We do about thirty-two jobs per car, per unit, forty-eight units an hour, eight hours a day. Thirty-two times forty-eight times eight. Figure it out, that's how many times I push that button.[58]

Another worker offers a similar view: "What's there to say? A car comes, I weld it; a car comes, I weld it; a car comes, I weld it. One hundred and one times an hour." Others get quite sarcastic about the nature of the work: "There's a lot of variety in the paint shop. . . . You clip on the color hose, bleed out the color and squirt. Clip, bleed, squirt; clip, bleed, squirt, yawn; clip, bleed, squirt, scratch your nose."[59] Another assembly line worker sums up the dehumanization he feels: "Sometimes I felt just like a robot. You push a button and you go this way. You become a mechanical nut."[60]

Alienation affects not only those who work on the automobile assembly line but also people in the wide range of settings built, at least in part, on the principles of the assembly line.[61] In our McDonaldizing society, the assembly line has implications for many of us and for many different settings.

## Fast-Food Industry: Gone Is the "Greasy Spoon"

I have already mentioned several dehumanizing aspects of fast-food restaurants. Another is that they minimize contact among human beings. For example, the relationships between employees and customers are fleeting at best. Because employees typically work part-time and stay only a few months, even regular customers can rarely develop personal relationships with them. All but gone are the days when one got to know well a waitress at a diner or the short-order cook at a local "greasy spoon." There are fewer and fewer places where an employee knows who you are and knows what you are likely to order. Fast being overwhelmed are what Ray Oldenburg calls "great good places," such as local cafes and taverns.[62]

Contact between workers and customers at the fast-food restaurant is also very short. It takes little time at the counter to order, receive the food, and pay for it. Both employees and customers are likely to feel rushed and to want to move on, customers to their meal and employees to the next order.[63] There is virtually no time for customer and counter person to interact. This is even truer of the drive-through window, where thanks to the speedy service and the physical barriers, the server is even more distant.

These highly impersonal and anonymous relationships are heightened by the training of employees to interact in a staged, scripted, and limited manner with customers. Thus, the customers may feel that they are dealing with automatons rather than with fellow human beings. For their part, the customers are supposed to be, and often are, in a hurry, so they also have little to say to the McDonald's employee. Indeed, it could be argued that one of the reasons fast-food restaurants succeed is that they are in tune with our fast-paced and impersonal society. People in the modern world want to get on with their business without unnecessary personal relationships. The fast-food restaurant gives them precisely what they want.

Other potential relationships in fast-food restaurants are also limited greatly. Because employees remain on the job for only a few months, satisfying personal relationships among employees are unlikely to develop. In contrast, more permanent employment helps foster long-term relationships on the job. Furthermore, workers with more job stability are likely to get together after work hours and on weekends. The temporary and part-time character of jobs in fast-food restaurants, and other McDonaldized settings, largely eliminates the possibility of such personal relationships among employees.

Relationships among fast-food customers are largely curtailed as well. Although some McDonald's ads would have people believe otherwise, gone for the most part are the days when people met in the diner or cafeteria for coffee or a meal and lingered to socialize. Fast-food restaurants clearly do not encourage such socializing.

### Family: The Kitchen as Filling Station

Fast-food restaurants also tend to have negative effects on the family, especially the so-called family meal.[64] The fast-food restaurant is not conducive to a long, leisurely, conversation-filled dinnertime. Furthermore, because of the fast-food restaurant, teens are better able to go out and eat with their friends, leaving the rest of the family to eat somewhere else or at another time. Of course, the drive-through window only serves to reduce further the possibility of a family meal. The family that gobbles its food while driving on to its next stop can hardly enjoy "quality time."

Here is the way one journalist describes what is happening to the family meal:

> Do families who eat their suppers at the Colonel's, swinging on plastic seats, or however the restaurant is arranged, say grace before picking up a crispy brown chicken leg? Does dad ask junior what he did today as he remembers

he forgot the piccalilli and trots through the crowds over to the counter to get some? Does mom find the atmosphere conducive to asking little Mildred about the problems she was having with third conjugation French verbs, or would it matter since otherwise the family might have been at home chomping down precooked frozen food, warmed in the microwave oven and watching "Hollywood Squares"?[65]

There is much talk these days about the disintegration of the family, and the fast-food restaurant may well be a crucial contributor to that disintegration. Conversely, the decline of the family creates ready-made customers for fast-food restaurants.

In fact, dinners at home may now be not much different from meals at the fast-food restaurant. Families tended to stop having lunch together by the 1940s and breakfast together by the 1950s. Today, the family dinner is following the same route. Even at home, the meal is probably not what it once was. Following the fast-food model, people have ever more options to "graze," "refuel," nibble on this, or snack on that rather than sit down at a formal meal. Also, because it may seem inefficient to do nothing but just eat, families are likely to watch television or play computer games while they are eating. The din, to say nothing of the lure, of dinnertime TV programs such as *Wheel of Fortune* and of the "bings" and "whines" associated with computer games is likely to make it difficult for family members to interact with one another. We need to decide whether we can afford the loss:

> The communal meal is our primary ritual for encouraging the family to gather together every day. If it is lost to us, we shall have to invent new ways to be a family. It is worth considering whether the shared joy that food can provide is worth giving up.[66]

A key technology in the destruction of the family meal is the microwave oven and the vast array of microwavable foods it helped generate.[67] A *Wall Street Journal* poll indicated that Americans consider the microwave their favorite household product. Said one consumer researcher, "It has made even fast-food restaurants not seem fast because at home you don't have to wait in line." As a general rule, consumers demand meals that take no more than ten minutes to microwave, whereas in the past people were more often willing to spend a half hour or even an hour cooking dinner. This emphasis on speed has, of course, brought with it lower quality, but people do not seem to mind this loss: "We're just not as critical of food as we used to be."[68]

The speed of microwave cooking and the wide variety of microwavable foods make it possible for family members to eat at different times and places. With products such as "Kid's Kitchen," "Kid Cuisine," "Fun Feast," and "My Own Meals" (there are similar products in frozen food), even children can "zap" their own meals. As a result, "Those qualities of the family meal, the ones that imparted feelings of security and well-being, might be lost forever when food is 'zapped' or 'nuked' instead of cooked."[69]

The advances in microwave cooking continue. On some foods, plastic strips turn blue when the food is done. The industry has even promised strips that communicate cooking information directly to the microwave oven. "With cooking reduced to pushing a button, the kitchen may wind up as a sort of filling station. Family members will pull in, push a few buttons, fill up and leave. To clean up, all we need do is throw away plastic plates."[70]

The family meal is not the only aspect of family life threatened by McDonaldization. For example, busy and exhausted parents are being advised that instead of reading to their children at night, they should have them listen to audiotapes.[71]

Then there is Viagra. Although it can revive men's sex lives and enhance relationships, it can also cause problems between men and their mates. For example, there is, as yet, no corresponding medication for female partners. The result may be tension between an aging but eager man and his less than eager mate.[72] Newly reinvigorated men may also be motivated to seek younger, more vigorous partners, with the resulting threat to established relationships.

### Higher Education: Like Processing Meat

The modern university has, in various ways, become a highly irrational place. Many students and faculty members are put off by its factorylike atmosphere. They may feel like automatons processed by the bureaucracy and computers or feel like cattle run through a meat-processing plant. In other words, education in such settings can be a dehumanizing experience.

The masses of students; large, impersonal dorms; and huge lecture classes make getting to know other students difficult. The large lecture classes, constrained tightly by the clock, make it virtually impossible to know professors personally. At best, students might get to know a gradu- ate assistant teaching a discussion section. Grades may be derived from a series of machine-graded, multiple-choice exams and posted imperson- ally, often by Social Security number rather than name. In sum, students may feel like little more than objects into which knowledge is poured as they move along an information-providing and degree-granting educational assembly line.

Of course, technological advances are leading to even greater irrationalities in education. The minimal contact between teacher and student is being further limited by advances such as Internet education, educational television, closed-circuit television,[73] distance learning, computerized instruction, and teaching machines. At least in the case of Internet education, we have seen the ultimate step in the dehumanization of education: the elimination of a human teacher and of human interaction between teacher and student.

### Health Care: You're Just a Number

For the physician, the process of rationalization carries with it a series of dehumanizing consequences. At or near the top of the list is the shift in control away from the physician and toward rationalized structures and institutions. In the past, private practitioners had a large degree of control over their work, with the major constraints being peer control as well as the needs and demands of patients. In rationalized medicine, external control increases and shifts to social structures and institutions. Not only is the physician more likely to be controlled by these structures and institutions but also by managers and bureaucrats who are not themselves physicians. The ability of physicians to control their own work lives is declining. As a result, many physicians are experiencing increased job dissatisfaction and alienation. They are even turning toward unionization, as reflected in the dramatic 1999 decision by the highly conservative American Medical Association to form a labor union for doctors.[74]

From the patients' viewpoint, the rationalization of medicine causes a number of irrationalities. The drive for efficiency can make them feel like products on a medical assembly line. The effort to increase predictability will likely lead patients to lose personal relationships with physicians and other health professionals, because rules and regulations lead physicians to treat all patients in essentially the same way. This is also true in hospitals, where instead of seeing the same nurse regularly, a patient may see many different nurses. The result, of course, is that nurses never come to know their patients as individuals. Another dehumanizing development is the advent (at least in the United States) of "hospitalists," doctors who practice exclusively in hospitals. Now instead of seeing their personal physician (if they still have such a doctor), hospitalized patients are more likely to be seen by physicians whom they probably have never seen and with whom they have no personal relationship.[75]

As a result of the emphasis on calculability, the patient is more likely to feel like a number in the system rather than a person. Minimizing time and maximizing profits may lead to a decline in the quality of health care provided to patients.

Like physicians, patients are apt to be controlled increasingly by large-scale structures and institutions, which will probably appear to them as distant, uncaring, and impenetrable. Finally, patients are increasingly likely to interact with technicians and impersonal technologies. In fact, because more and more technologies may be purchased at the drug store, patients can test themselves and thereby cut out human contact with both physicians and technicians.

The ultimate irrationality of this rationalization would be the unanticipated consequences of a decline in the quality of medical practice and a deterioration in the health of patients. Increasingly rational medical systems, with their focus on lowering costs and increasing profits, may reduce the quality of health care, especially for the poorest members of society. At least some people may become sicker, and perhaps even die, because of the rationalization of medicine. Health in general may even decline. These possibilities can be assessed only in the future as the health care system continues to rationalize. Since the health care system will continue to rationalize, health professionals and their patients may need to learn how to control rational structures and institutions to ameliorate their irrational consequences.

### Dehumanized Death

Then there is the dehumanization of the very human process of death. People are increasingly likely to die (as they are likely to be born) impersonally, in the presence of total strangers:

> A patient is every day less a human being and more a complicated challenge in intensive care. To most of the nurses and a few of the doctors who knew him [a patient] before his slide into sepsis, there remains some of the person he was (or may have been), but to the consulting superspecialists . . . he is a case. . . . Doctors thirty years his junior call him by his first name. Better that, than to be called by the name of the disease or the number of the bed.[76]

This dehumanization is part of the process, according to Philippe Aries, by which the modern world has "banished death."[77] Here is the way Dr. Sherman Nuland describes our need to rationalize death:

We seek ways to deny the power of death and the icy hold in which it grips human thought. Its constant closeness has always inspired traditional methods by which we consciously and unconsciously disguise its reality, such as folk tales, allegories, dreams, and even jokes. In recent generations, we have added something new: We have created the *method of modern dying*. Modern dying takes place in modern hospitals, where it can be hidden, cleansed of its organic blight, and finally packaged for modern burial. We can now deny the power not only of death but of nature itself [italics added].[78]

Similarly, Jean Baudrillard has written of "designer deaths," paralleling "designer births":

To streamline death at all costs, to varnish it, cryogenically freeze it, or condition it, put make-up on it, "design" it, to pursue it with the same relentlessness as grime, sex, bacteriological or radioactive waste. The make-up of death . . . "designed" according to the purest laws of . . . international marketing.[79]

Closely related to the growing power of physicians and hospitals over death, nonhuman technologies play an increasing role in the dying process. Technology has blurred the line between life and death by, for example, keeping people's hearts going even though their brains are dead. Medical personnel have also come to rely on technology to help them decide when it is acceptable to declare death. What could be more dehumanizing than dying alone amid machines rather than with loved ones?

When people are asked how they wish to die, most respond something like this: quickly, painlessly, at home, surrounded by family and friends. Ask them how they expect to die, and the fear emerges: in the hospital, all alone, on a machine, in pain.[80]

Here is the way Nuland describes dehumanized death amid a sea of nonhuman technologies:

The beeping and squealing monitors, the hissings of respirators and pistoned mattresses, the flashing multicolored electronic signals—the whole techno-logical panoply is background for the tactics by which we are deprived of the tranquility we have every right to hope for, and separated from those few who would not let us die alone. By such means, biotechnology created to provide hope serves actually to take it away, and to leave our survivors bereft of the unshattered final memories that rightly belong to those who sit nearby as our days draw to a close.[81]

## ◆ CONCLUSION

Contrary to McDonald's propaganda and the widespread belief in it, fast-food restaurants and their clones in other areas of society are not reasonable, or even truly rational, systems. They spawn many problems for customers, including inefficiency rather than increased efficiency, relatively high costs, illusory fun and reality, false friendliness, disenchantment, threats to health and the environment, homogenization, and dehumanization. McDonaldization does have advantages, but these irrationalities clearly counterbalance and even overwhelm them. Recognizing these irrationalities is essential, because most of us have been exposed to little more than widely disseminated superlatives created by McDonaldized systems to describe themselves and further their interests.

# 8

# Globalization and McDonaldization

◆─────────────────────────

## Does It All Amount to ... Nothing?

The preceding five chapters have dealt with the basic characteristics of McDonaldization, as well as the irrationalities of rationality that seemingly inevitably accompany it. In the next two chapters, the focus shifts to McDonaldization as a type of *social change*.

While McDonaldization is, in itself, an important type of social change, in this chapter I consider its relationship to what many observers consider to be *the* most important and far-reaching change of our time—globalization. The following chapter (9) deals with a variety of other issues relating to McDonaldization as a type of social change, including the forces that drive it; its relationship to other recent social changes such as postindustrialism, post-Fordism, and postmodernism; whether there are any limits to it; and the future of the continuing process of McDonaldization. Whatever the specifics of that future, McDonaldization has certainly already embedded itself deeply into the social world, and it is likely to be with us for the foreseeable future. While many welcome this fact, many others worry about it. Thus, the final chapter offers a range of ideas on what those who are concerned about McDonaldization and its continuing spread can do to cope with, if not stem the tide toward, its increasing proliferation not only in the United States but throughout much of the world.

McDonaldization has many aspects and implications, but one thing that is abundantly clear is that it has global implications in terms of the exportation of McDonald's, as well as many other McDonaldized systems, from their largely American base to many other parts of the world. It is also clear that a wide range of indigenous McDonaldized forms have developed in those regions, and they are now increasingly being exported to various parts of the world, including back into the American market, the original source of much McDonaldization. Such global implications scream out for the need to analyze the relationship between McDonaldization and the larger process of globalization. This chapter will deal not only with that broad topic but also with how McDonaldization relates to my recent work on what I have called the "globalization of nothing."[1] To discuss the latter issue, I need to introduce the reader to what I mean by both globalization and nothing (and the related idea of something).

## ♦ GLOBALIZATION

Most generally, *globalization* can be defined as "the worldwide diffusion of practices, expansion of relations across continents, organization of social life on a global scale, and growth of a shared global consciousness."[2] It is clear that the world has been affected increasingly by globalization in general, as well as by the subdimensions of that process enumerated in this definition.

McDonaldization can be seen, at least in part, as one of a number of globalization processes.[3] While it is important to remember that McDonaldization is *not* only a globalization process (for example, it is also revolutionizing life *within* the United States), it is clear that in at least some of its aspects, it can be considered under that heading. Let us look at the relationship between McDonaldization and each of the four aspects of globalization that make up the definition of that term as it was employed above.

First, the *practices* (for example, putting customers to work, routinely eating meals quickly and on the run, using drive-through windows) developed by McDonald's (and other leaders of the fast-food industry) in the United States have been diffused to fast-food restaurants in many other countries around the world. More generally, a wide range of practices that define many different McDonaldized settings (for example, education, law enforcement) have similarly been disseminated globally. Thus, for example, universities in many parts of the world have been drawn toward the increasing use of large lecture-style classes, and police forces in many countries employ many of the efficient techniques for law enforcement and crowd control pioneered in the United States.

Second, many intercontinental *relationships* that did not exist before came into being as a result of the proliferation of McDonaldized systems. That is, the deep linkages among and between McDonaldized systems have necessitated a large number of such global relationships. For example, there are strong ties among the various restaurants around the world that are part of Yum! Brands, Inc. (for example, Kentucky Fried Chicken outlets in various geographic locales). Less formal, but no less important, are the relationships between law enforcement agencies or universities as they share knowledge of, and experiences with, the latest advances in the McDonaldization of their respective domains.

Third, the ensemble of these relationships has led to *new ways of organizing social life* throughout the world and across the globe. To put it most generally, the ways in which the social world is organized, even across great distances, have been McDonaldized. Thus, not only has the way people eat been restructured (for example, less in the home and more in fast-food restaurants) but so has the way higher education (fewer personal tutorials, more large lectures) and law enforcement (the increased use of "assembly line" justice) are structured. In innumerable ways, the organization of everyday life has been altered, sometimes dramatically, by the spread of McDonaldization across the globe.

Finally, McDonald's, to say nothing of the many other McDonaldized systems, has led to a new *global consciousness*. There are those who are well aware that they are part of an increasingly McDonaldized world and who revel in that knowledge. Thus, some people are more willing to travel to far-off locales because they know that their ability to adjust to those settings will be made easier by the existence of familiar McDonaldized settings. However, there are others with a similar (if not greater) level of awareness who abhor the process and what it is doing to their lives and the lives of many throughout the world. Such people may be disinclined to travel to at least some places because they know they have become so highly McDonaldized. Most generally, McDonald's and other McDonaldized businesses are such active and aggressive marketers that people can hardly avoid being conscious of them and the way they are changing their lives and the lives of many others throughout the world.

Thus, while it is many other things, McDonaldization is an aspect of globalization. This is reflected in the ease with which the basic elements of the definition of globalization can be applied to it.

## Globalization: Glocalization and Grobalization

One of today's leading globalization theorists, Roland Robertson, has recently outlined what he considers to be *the* key issues in globalization theory.[4] While all are important, three lie at the center of this chapter (and the issue of the relationship between globalization and McDonaldization), and two are closely related to one another. The two interrelated issues are these:

*"Does global change involve increasing homogeneity or increasing heterogeneity or a mixture of both?"*

*"What is the relationship between the local and the global?"*[5]

These two issues are tightly linked. Global heterogeneity predominates when local (or indigenous) practices are dominant in different geographic locations throughout the world. That is, the way various things are done differs from one locality to another, leading to a high level of heterogeneity. It is highly unlikely that any given locality, left on its own, would do anything exactly like the way it is done in any other locality. In contrast, the predominance of the global in different locales throughout the world would be associated with greater homogenization. That is, similar global inputs and pressures would lead many localities to do various things in much the same way. Whatever the mix (and today there is always a mix) of the local and the global, heterogeneity and homogeneity, the third issue raised by Robertson remains of great importance:

*"What drives the globalization process? What is its motor force?"*[6]

The answer to this last question(s) is highly complex since there is certainly no single driving force, nor is there a single process of globalization. However, later in this chapter, after the approach to the globalization process being used here is specified, I will discuss McDonaldization as one of the major motor forces—others are capitalism and Americanization—in globalization.

Whatever the answers to the above questions, to say nothing of the other central questions that he raises,[7] it is clear that to Robertson, and many other students of globalization, the central issue is the relationship between the highly interrelated topics of homogeneity-heterogeneity and the global-local. Indeed, Robertson is known not only for his interest in these issues but for his effort to deal with this relationship through the articulation of a now-famous concept—"glocalization"—that emphasizes the integration of the global and the local and involves far more heterogeneity than homogeneity.[8] While glocalization is an integrative concept, and Robertson is certainly interested in both sides of the glocal-global, homogenization-heterogenization continua, he is inclined to emphasize the importance of the glocal and the existence of heterogeneity that tends to be associated with it.[9]

The concept of glocalization gets to the heart of not only Robertson's views, but also what many other contemporary theorists interested in globalization think about the nature of transnational processes.[10] *Glocalization* can be defined as *the interpenetration of the global and the local, resulting in unique outcomes in different geographic areas.* That is, global forces, often associated with a tendency toward homogenization, run headlong into the local in any geographic location. Rather than either one overwhelming the other, the global and the local interpenetrate, producing unique outcomes in each location.

This emphasis on glocalization has a variety of implications for thinking about globalization in general. First, it leads to the view that the world is growing increasingly pluralistic. Glocalization theory is exceptionally sensitive to differences within and between areas of the world. Thus, the glocal realities in one part of the world are likely to be quite different from such realities in other parts of the world. Such a view of the world leads one to downplay many of the fears associated with globalization in general (and McDonaldization more specifically), especially the fear of increasing homogeneity throughout the world.

This absence of fear of the negative aspects of globalization is associated with a tendency on the part of those who emphasize glocalization to argue that individuals and local groups have great power to adapt, innovate, and maneuver within a glocalized world. Glocalization theory sees individuals and groups as important and creative agents. Thus, while they may be subject to globalizing processes, these powerful individuals and groups are not likely to be overwhelmed by, and subjugated to, them. Rather, they are likely to modify and adapt them to their own needs and interests. In other words, they are able to glocalize them.

Thus, social processes, especially those that relate to globalization, are seen as relational and contingent. That is, forces pushing globalization emanate from many sources, but they generally face counterforces in any given area of the world. Consequently, what develops in any area is a result of the relationship between these forces and counterforces. This also means that whether or not the forces of globalization overwhelm the local is contingent on the specific relationship between the forces and counterforces in any given locale. Where the counterforces are weak, globalizing forces may successfully impose themselves, but where they are strong (and to glocalization theorists, they appear strong in most areas), a glocal form is likely to emerge that uniquely integrates the global and the local. Thus, to fully understand globalization, we must deal with the specific and contingent relationships that exist in any given locale.

From the point of view of glocalization, the forces impelling globalization are *not* seen as (totally) coercive but, rather, as providing material to be used, in concert with the local, in individual and group creation of distinctive glocal realities. Thus, for example, the global mass media (say, CNN or Al-Jazeera) are not seen as defining and controlling what people think and believe in a given locale but, rather, as providing them with additional inputs that are integrated with many other media inputs (especially those that are local) to create unique sets of ideas and viewpoints.

There is no question that glocalization is an important part of globalization, but it is far from the entire story. Furthermore, while, as we will see, some degree of glocalization occurs under the heading of McDonaldization, another side of globalization relates better to McDonaldization. That aspect of globalization is well described by the concept of grobalization, coined in my book *The Globalization of Nothing*, for the first time as a much-needed companion to the notion of glocalization.[11] *Grobalization* focuses on *the imperialistic ambitions of nations, corporations, organizations, and the like and their desire, indeed need, to impose themselves on various geographic areas.*[12] Their main interest is in seeing their power, influence, and in some cases profits *grow* (hence the term *gro*balization) throughout the world. Grobalization involves a variety of subprocesses, three of which—capitalism, Americanization, and McDonaldization[13]—are not only central driving forces in grobalization but also of particular interest to the author. While all three were dealt with in *The Globalization of Nothing*, the focus below will naturally be on McDonaldization. That is, McDonaldization is both a major example of, and a key driving force in, grobalization.

*Grobalization* leads to a variety of ideas that are largely antithetical to the basic ideas associated with glocalization. Rather than emphasizing the great diversity among various glocalized locales, grobalization leads to the view that the world is growing increasingly similar. While it is recognized that there are differences within and between areas of the world, what is emphasized is their increasing similarity. Thus, grobalization theory is especially sensitive to the increasing number of similarities that characterize many areas of the world. This, of course, tends to heighten the fears of those who are concerned about the increasing homogenization associated with globalization.

In contrast to the view associated with glocalization, individuals and groups throughout the world are seen as having relatively little ability to adapt, innovate, and maneuver within a grobalized world. Grobalization theory sees larger structures and forces tending to overwhelm the ability of individuals and groups to create themselves and their worlds.

In yet another stark contrast, grobalization tends to see social processes as largely unidirectional and deterministic. That is, the forces flow from the global to the local, and there is little or no possibility of the local having any significant impact on the global. As a result, the global is generally seen as largely determining what transpires at the local level; the impact of the global is not seen as contingent on what transpires at the local level or on how the local reacts to the global. Thus, grobalization tends to overpower the local. It also limits the ability of the local to act and react, let alone to act back on the grobal.

Thus, from the perspective of grobalization, global forces *are* seen as largely determining what individual(s) and groups think and do throughout the world. For example, this view accords far more power to grobal media powers such as CNN and Al-Jazeera to influence people in any given geographic area than does the viewpoint that emphasizes glocalization.

### ◆ MCDONALDIZATION AND GROBALIZATION

In terms of globalization, the McDonaldization thesis contends that highly McDonaldized systems—and more important, the principles that lie at their base—have been exported from the United States to much of the rest of the world. Many nations throughout the world, and innumerable subsystems within each, are undergoing the process of McDonaldization. To put it another way, the influence of McDonaldization has been *growing* throughout much of the world, and this clearly places it under the heading of *grobalization*. The major driving force is economics—the ability of McDonaldized systems to increase profits continually is based on the need to steadily expand markets throughout the world. However, other factors help account for the growing global presence of McDonaldization, including a deep belief in the system by those who push it and a strong desire on the part of those who do not have it to obtain it.

It is interesting to note that when they have addressed the McDonaldization thesis and related ideas, globalization theorists, especially those committed to the ideas of heterogeneity and glocalization, have tended to be critical of it for its emphasis on grobalization and the resulting focus on its homogenizing impact on much of the rest of the world. For example, Robertson, the person who, as we have seen, is most associated with the idea of glocalization, says that "the frequent talk about the McDonaldization of the world . . . has been strongly tempered by what is increasingly known about the ways in which such products or services are actually *the basis for localization.*"[14]

McDonaldization is obviously a global perspective, especially a grobal one, but it is both less and more than a theory of globalization. On the one hand, McDonaldization does not involve anything approaching the full range of global processes. For example, many economic, cultural, political, and institutional aspects of globalization are largely unrelated to McDonaldization. On the other hand, McDonaldization involves much more than an analysis of its global impact. For example, much of it involves the manifold transformations taking place *within* the United States, the source and still the center of this process. Furthermore, one can analyze the spread of McDonaldization (once it has arrived) *within* many other nations and even subareas of those nations. In addition, one can, as we have seen, look at the McDonaldization of various aspects of the social world—religion, higher education, politics, and so on—without considering the global implications for each. Thus, McDonaldization is not coterminous with globalization, nor is it solely a global process. Nonetheless, McDonaldization has global implications and can thus be a useful lens through which to examine changes taking place around the globe.

What is clear is that McDonaldization deserves a place in any thoroughgoing account of globalization, especially grobalization. There can be little doubt that the logic of McDonaldization generates a set of values and practices that have a competitive advantage over other models. It not only promises many specific advantages, it also reproduces itself more easily than other models of consumption (and in many other areas of society, as well). The success of McDonaldization in the United States over the past half century, coupled with the international ambitions of McDonald's and its ilk, as well as those of indigenous clones throughout the world, strongly suggests that McDonaldization will continue to make inroads into the global marketplace, not only through the efforts of existing corporations but also via the diffusion of the paradigm.

It should be noted, however, that the continued advance of McDonaldization, at least in its present form, is far from assured. In fact, there are even signs in the United States, as well as in other parts of the world, of what I have previously called *deMcDonaldization*.[15] I have already touched on this issue in Chapter 1 in discussing McDonald's "troubles," and I will have more to say about it in Chapter 9. Nonetheless, at the moment and for the foreseeable future, McDonaldization will continue to be an important force, and it is clearly and unequivocally not only a grobal process but also one that contributes mightily to the spread of "nothingness."

## ◆ NOTHING-SOMETHING AND MCDONALDIZATION

I have now discussed the ideas of glocalization-grobalization as they relate to McDonaldization, but a second set of ideas—nothing-something, also derived from *The Globalization of Nothing*—needs to be discussed here. As we will see, these ideas relate not only directly to McDonaldization but also to its relationship to globalization in general and grobalization-glocalization in particular.

Nothing can be defined as a *"social form that is generally[16] centrally[17] conceived, controlled and comparatively devoid of distinctive substantive content."*[18] It should be abundantly clear that any McDonaldized system, with the fast-food restaurant being a prime example, would be a major form of nothing. However, it is important to point out that there are many other examples of nothing that have little or no direct relationship to McDonaldization.

Let us look at the example of a chain of fast-food restaurants from the point of view of the basic components of our definition of nothing. First, as parts of chains, fast-food restaurants are, virtually by definition, centrally conceived. That is, those who created the chain and are associated with its central offices conceived of the chain originally and are continually involved in its reconceptualization. For their part, owners and managers of local chain restaurants do little or no conceptualizing on their own. Indeed, they have bought the rights to the franchise, and continue to pay a percentage of their profits for it, because they want those with the demonstrated knowledge and expertise to do the conceptualizing.

This relative absence of independent conceptualization at the level of the local franchise is one of the reasons we can think of the franchise as nothing.

We are led to a similar view when we turn to the second aspect of our definition of nothing—control.[19] Just as those in the central office do the conceptualization for the local franchises, they also exert great control over them. Indeed, to some degree, such control is derived from the fact that conceptualization is in the hands of the central office; the act of conceptualizing and reconceptualizing the franchise yields a significant amount of control. However, control is exercised by the central office over the franchises in more direct ways as well. For example, it may get a percentage of a local franchise's profits, and if its cut is down because profits are down, the central office may put pressure on the local franchise to alter its procedures to increase profitability. The central office may also deploy inspectors to make periodic and unannounced visits to local franchises. Those franchises found not to be operating the way they are supposed to will come under pressure to bring their operations in line with company standards. Those that do not are likely to suffer adverse consequences, including the ultimate punishment of the loss of the franchise. Thus, local franchises can also be seen as nothing because they do not control their own destinies.

The third aspect of our definition of nothing is that it involves social forms largely lacking in distinctive content. This is essentially true by definition of chains of franchised fast-food restaurants. That is, the whole idea is to turn out restaurants that are virtual clones of one another. To put it another way, the goal is to produce restaurants that are as alike one another as possible—they generally look much the same from outside, they are structured similarly within, the same foods are served, workers act and interact in much the same way, and so on. There is little that distinguishes one outlet of a chain of fast-food restaurants from all the others.

Thus, there is a near perfect fit between the definition of nothing offered above and a chain of fast-food restaurants. However, this is a rather extreme view since, in a sense, "nothing is nothing." In other words, all social forms (including fast-food restaurants) have characteristics that deviate from the extreme form of nothing. That is, they involve some local conceptualization and control, and each one has at least some distinctive elements. To put this another way, all social forms have some elements of somethingness. Consequently, we need to think not only in terms of nothing but also in terms of something as well as a something-nothing continuum.

This leads us to a definition of *something* as *"a social form that is generally*[20] *indigenously conceived, controlled, and comparatively rich in distinctive substantive content."*[21] This makes it clear that neither nothing nor something exists independently of the other; *each makes sense only when paired with, and contrasted to, the other.*

If a fast-food restaurant is an example of nothing, then a meal cooked at home from scratch would be an example of something. The meal is conceived by the individual cook and not by a central office. Control rests in the hands of that cook. Finally, that which the cook prepares is rich in distinctive content and different from that prepared by other cooks, even those who prepare the same meals.

While nothing and something are presented as if they were a dichotomy,[22] we really need to think in terms of a *continuum* from something to nothing, and that is precisely the way the concepts will be employed here—as the two poles of that continuum. Thus, while a fast-food restaurant falls toward the nothing end of the continuum, every fast-food restaurant has at least some elements that are different from all others; each has some elements of somethingess associated with it. Conversely, while every home-cooked meal is distinctive, they are likely to have at least some elements in common (for example, they may rely on a common cookbook or recipe) and therefore have some elements of nothingness. Therefore, no social form exists at the extreme nothing or something pole of the continuum; they *all* fall somewhere between the two. However, it remains the case that some lie closer to the nothing end of the continuum, whereas others lie more toward the something end. In terms of our interests here, fast-food restaurants, and more generally all McDonaldized systems, fall toward the nothing end of the something-nothing continuum.

## ◆ NOTHING-SOMETHING AND GROBALIZATION-GLOCALIZATION

I turn now to a discussion of the relationship between grobalization-glocalization and something-nothing and its implications for our understanding of McDonaldization. Figure 8.1 offers the four basic possibilities that emerge when we crosscut the grobalization-glocalization and something-nothing continua. It should be noted that while this yields four "ideal types," there are no hard-and-fast lines between them. This is reflected in the use of both dotted lines and multidirectional arrows in Figure 8.1.

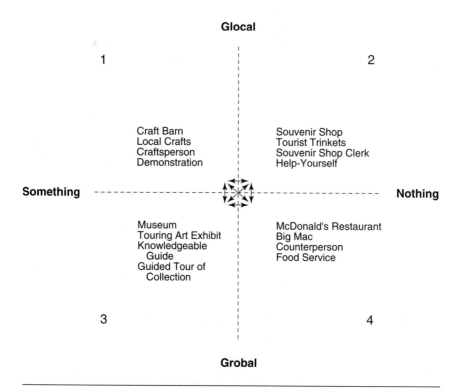

**Figure 8.1**    The Relationship Between Glocal–Grobal and Something–Nothing
With Examples

Source: Adapted from George Ritzer. *The Globalization of Nothing.* Thousand Oaks, CA: Pine
Forge Press, 2004, p. 98.

Quadrants 1 and 4 in Figure 8.1 are of greatest importance, at least for
the purposes of this analysis. They represent a key point of tension and
conflict in the world today. Clearly, there is great pressure to grobalize
nothing, and often all that stands in its way in terms of achieving global
hegemony is the glocalization of something. We will return to this conflict
and its implications below.

While the other two quadrants (2 and 3) are clearly residual in nature
and of secondary importance, it is necessary to recognize that there is, at
least to some degree, a glocalization of nothing (quadrant 2) and a grobalization of something (quadrant 3). However, whatever tensions may exist
between them are of far less significance than those between the grobalization of nothing and the glocalization of something. A discussion of the

glocalization of nothing and the grobalization of something makes it clear that grobalization is not an unmitigated source of nothing (it can involve something) and glocalization is not to be seen solely as a source of something (it can involve nothing).

## The Grobalization of Something

Some types of something have been grobalized to a considerable degree. For example, gourmet foods, handmade crafts, custom-made clothes, and Rolling Stones concerts are now much more available throughout the world, and more likely to move transnationally, than ever before in history. In a very specific example in the arts, a touring series of Silk Road concerts recently brought together Persian artists and music, an American symphony orchestra, and Rimsky-Korsakov's (Russian) *Scheherazade*.[23]

Returning to Figure 8.1, we can use as an example of the grobalization of something touring art exhibitions of the works of Vincent Van Gogh, the museums throughout the world in which such exhibitions occur, the knowledgeable guides who show visitors the highlights of the exhibition,[24] and the detailed information and insights they are able to impart in response to questions from gallery visitors.

In spite of the existence of examples like these, why is there comparatively little affinity between grobalization and something? That is, why is grobalization more likely to be associated with nothing than something? Among the most important reasons are the following:

1. There is simply far less demand throughout the world for most forms of something, at least in comparison with the demand for nothing. One reason for this is that the distinctiveness of something tends to appeal to a far more limited audience than does nothing, be it gourmet foods, handmade crafts, or Rolling Stones or Silk Road concerts.

2. The complexity of something, especially the fact that it is likely to have many different elements, means that it is more likely to have at least some characteristics that will be off-putting, or even offend, large numbers of people in many different cultures. For example, a Russian audience at a Silk Road concert might be bothered by the juxtaposition of Persian music with that of Rimsky-Korsakov.

3. The various forms of something are usually more expensive, frequently much more expensive, than competing forms of nothing (gourmet food is much more costly than fast food, although as we saw earlier, fast food can

be expensive for what you get). Higher cost means, of course, that far fewer people can afford something. As a result, the global demand for expensive forms of something is minuscule in comparison with that for the inexpensive varieties of nothing.

4. Because the prices are high and the demand is comparatively low, far less can be spent on the advertising and marketing of something, and this serves to keep demand low (and in some cases, tends to prevent demand from getting too high.)

5. Something is far more difficult to mass manufacture and, in some cases (Silk Road concerts, Van Gogh exhibitions), impossible to produce in this way.

6. Since the demand for something is less price sensitive than nothing (the relatively small number of people who can afford it are willing, and often able, to pay almost any price), there is less need to mass manufacture it (assuming it could be produced in this way) in order to lower prices.

7. The costs of shipping (insurance, careful packing and packaging, special transports) of something are usually very high, adding to the price and thereby reducing the demand.

8. It could also be argued that the fact that the grobalization of something (compared with nothing) occurs to a lesser degree helps to distinguish something from nothing. Because it is relatively scarce, something retains its status and its distinction from nothing. If something came to be mass produced and grobalized, it is likely that it would move toward the nothing end of the continuum.

## The Grobalization of Nothing

The example of the grobalization of nothing in Figure 8.1 is a meal at McDonald's. There is little or nothing distinctive about any given McDonald's restaurant, the food served there, the people who work in these settings, and the "services" they offer. And, of course, there has been a very aggressive effort to expand the presence of McDonald's throughout much of the world. Thus, the global expansion of McDonald's (and other fast-food chains) is a near-perfect example of the grobalization of nothing.

The main reasons for the strong affinity between grobalization and nothing are basically the inverse of the reasons for the lack of such affinity between grobalization and something. For example:

1. Above all, there is a far greater demand throughout the world for nothing than something. This is the case because nothing tends (although not always[25]) to be less expensive than something, with the result that more people can afford the former than the latter (As we know, McDonald's places great emphasis on its low prices and "value meals").

2. Large numbers of people are also far more likely to want the various forms of nothing because their comparative simplicity and lack of distinctiveness appeals to a wider range of tastes (the food at McDonald's is famous for its simple and familiar—salty and sweet—taste).

3. In addition, as pointed out earlier, that which is nothing, largely devoid of distinctive content, is far less likely to bother or offend those in other cultures (although it has aroused outrage in some cultures, McDonald's simple and basic foods have shown the ability to fit into many different cultures).

4. Finally, because of the far greater potential sales, much more money can be, and is, devoted to the advertising and marketing of nothing, thereby creating a still greater demand for it than for something (McDonald's spends huge sums on advertising and has been very successful at generating great demand for its fare).

Given the great demand, it is far easier to mass-produce and -distribute the empty forms of nothing than the substantively rich forms of something. Indeed, many forms of something lend themselves best to limited, if not one-of-a-kind, production. A skilled potter may produce a few dozen pieces of pottery and an artist a painting or two in, perhaps, a week, a month, or even a year(s). While these craft and art works may, over time, move from owner to owner in various parts of the world, this traffic barely registers in the total of all global trade and commerce. Of course, there are the rare masterpieces that may bring millions of dollars, but in the main, these one-of-a-kind works are small-ticket items. In contrast, thousands, even many millions, and sometimes billions of varieties of nothing are mass-produced and sold throughout the globe. Thus, the global sale of fast food like Big Macs, Whoppers, Kentucky Fried Chicken, as well as the myriad other forms of nothing, is a far greater factor in grobalization than the international sale of pieces of high art (for example, the art of Van Gogh) or of tickets to the Rolling Stones' most recent world tour.

Furthermore, the economics of the marketplace demands that the massive amount of nothing that is produced be marketed and sold on a grobal basis. For one thing, the economies of scale mean that the more that is produced and sold, the lower the price. This means that, almost inevitably, American producers of nothing (and they are, by far, the world leaders in this) must become dissatisfied with the American market, no matter how vast it is, and aggressively pursue a world market for their products. The greater the grobal market, the lower the price that can be charged (McDonald's can buy hamburger meat on the global market at rock-bottom prices because of the huge number of burgers it sells), and this, in turn, means that even greater numbers of nothing can be sold to far reaches of the globe in less-developed countries.

Another economic factor stems from the demand of the stock market that corporations that produce and sell nothing (indeed, all corporations) increase sales and profits from one year to the next. The stocks of those corporations (and McDonald's has recently been one of them) that simply meet the previous year's profitability, or experience a decline, are likely to be punished in the stock market and see their stock prices fall, sometimes precipitously. To increase profits continually, the corporation is forced, as Karl Marx understood long ago, to continue to search out new markets. One way of doing that is to constantly expand globally. In contrast, since something is less likely to be produced by corporations, certainly the large corporations listed in the stock market, there is far less pressure to expand the market for it. In any case, given the limited number of these things that can be produced by artisans, skilled chefs, artists, and so on, there are profound limits on such expansion. This, in turn, brings us back to the pricing issue and relates to the price advantage that nothing ordinarily has over something. As a general rule, the various types of nothing cost far less than something. The result, obviously, is that nothing can be marketed globally far more aggressively than something.

Also, nothing has an advantage in terms of transportation around the world. These are things that generally can be easily and efficiently packaged and moved, often over vast areas. The frozen hamburgers and french fries that are the basis of McDonald's business are prime examples of this. Clearly, it would be much harder to package and move fresh hamburgers and freshly sliced potatoes, especially over large distances. Furthermore, because the unit cost of such items is low, it is of comparatively little consequence if they go awry, are lost, or are stolen. In contrast, it is more difficult and expensive to package something—say, a piece of handmade pottery or an antique vase—and losing such things, having them stolen, or their being broken is a disaster. As a result, it is far more expensive to insure something than nothing, and this difference is another reason for the cost advantage that nothing has over something. These sorts of things serve to greatly limit the global trade in items that can be included under the heading of something.

## The Glocalization of Nothing

Historically there has been a tendency to romanticize and glorify the local, and in recent years, globalization theorists have tended to overestimate the glocal. It is seen by many as not only the alternative to the evils of grobalization but also as a key source of much that is worthwhile in the world today. Globalization theorists often privilege the glocal something over the grobal nothing[26] (as well as over the glocal nothing which rarely appears in their analyses).

While most globalization theorists are not postmodernists (Mike Featherstone is one exception;[27] see Chapter 9 for more on postmodernism), the wide-scale acceptance of various postmodern ideas (and the rejection of many modern positions) has helped lead to positive attitudes toward glocalization among many globalization theorists. Friedman is one who explicitly links "cultural pluralism" and the "postmodernization of the world."[28] The postmodern perspective is linked to glocalization theory in a number of ways. For example, the work of Michel de Certeau and others on the power of the agent in the face of larger powers (like grobalization) fits with the view that indigenous actors can create unique phenomena out of the interaction of the global and the local. De Certeau, for one, talks of actors as "unrecognized producers, poets of their own affairs, trailblazers in the jungles of functionalist rationality."[29] A similar focus on the local community gives it the power to create unique glocal realities.[30] More generally, a postmodern perspective is tied to hybridity, which, in turn, is "subversive" of modern perspectives such as "essentialism and homogeneity."

While there are good reasons for the interest in, and preference for, glocalization among globalization theorists,[31] it is clearly overdone. For one thing, grobalization (especially of nothing) is far more prevalent and powerful than glocalization (especially of something). For another, glocalization itself is a significant source of nothing.

One of the best examples of the glocalization of nothing is to be found in the realm of tourism,[32] especially where the grobal tourist meets the local manufacturer and retailer (where they still exist) in the production and sale of glocal goods and services (this is illustrated in quadrant 2 of Figure 8.1). There are certainly instances, perhaps even many of them, where tourism stimulates the production of something—well-made, high-quality craft products made for discerning tourists or meals lovingly prepared by local chefs using traditional recipes and the best of local ingredients. However, far more often, and increasingly as time goes by, grobal tourism leads to the glocalization of nothing. Souvenir shops are likely to be bursting at the seams with trinkets reflecting a bit of the local culture. Such souvenirs are increasingly likely to be mass-manufactured, perhaps using components from other parts of the world, in local factories. If demand grows great enough and the possibilities of profitability high enough, low-priced souvenirs may be manufactured by the thousands or millions elsewhere in the world and then shipped back to the local area to be sold to tourists (who may not notice, or care about, the "made in China" label embossed on their souvenir replicas of the Eiffel Tower). The clerks in these souvenir shops are likely to offer little in the way of personalized service, and tourists are highly likely to serve themselves. Similarly, large numbers of meals slapped together by semiskilled chefs to vaguely suggest local cooking are far more likely than authentic meals that are true to the region or that truly integrate local elements. They are likely to be offered in "touristy" restaurants and to be served by waitpersons who offer little in the way of service.

Another major example involves the production of native shows—often involving traditional costumes, dances, and music—for grobal tourists. While these could be something, there is a very strong tendency for them to be transformed into nothing to satisfy grobal tour operators and their clientele. Hence, these shows are examples of the glocalization of nothing because they become centrally conceived and controlled empty forms. They are often watered down, if not eviscerated, with esoteric or possibly offensive elements removed. The performances are designed to please the throngs of tourists and to put off as few of them as possible. They take place with great frequency, and interchangeable performers often seem as if they are going through the motions in a desultory fashion. This is about all the grobal tourists want in their rush (and that of the tour operator) to see a performance, eat an ersatz local meal, and then move on to the next stop on the tour. Thus, in the area of mass tourism—in souvenirs, performances, and meals—we are far more likely to see the glocalization of nothing than of something.

## The Glocalization of Something

The example of the glocalization of something in Figure 8.1 (quadrant 1) is in the realm of indigenous crafts like pottery or weaving. Such craft products are quite distinctive, and they are likely to be displayed and sold in unique places like craft barns. A craftsperson is likely to make and demonstrate his or her wares, and customers are apt to be offered a great deal of service by such craftspeople.

Such glocal products are likely to remain something, although there are certainly innumerable examples of glocal forms of something (for example, Russian matryoshka [stacking] dolls) that have been transformed into glocal, and in some cases grobal, forms of nothing. In fact, there is often a kind of progression here from glocal something to glocal nothing as demand grows and then to grobal nothing[33] if some entrepreneur believes that there might be a global market for such products. However, some glocal forms of something (indigenous cooking and art) are able to resist this process.

Glocal forms of something tend to remain as such for various reasons:

1.  For one thing, they tend to be costly, at least in comparison with mass-manufactured competitors. High price tends to keep demand down locally, let alone globally.

2.  Glocal forms of something are loaded with distinctive content. Among other things, this means that they are harder and more expensive to produce, and consumers, especially in other cultures, find them harder to understand and appreciate. Furthermore, their idiosyncratic and complex character makes it more likely that those in other cultures will find something about them they do not like or even find offensive.

3.  Those who create glocal forms of something are not, unlike larger manufacturers of nothing, pushed to expand their business and increase profits to satisfy stockholders and the stock market. While craftspeople are not immune to the desire to earn more money, the pressure to do so is more internal than external, and it is not nearly as great or inexorable. In any case, the desire to earn more money is tempered by the fact that the production of each craft product is time-consuming and there are just so many of them that can be produced in a given time. Furthermore, craft products are even less likely to lend themselves to mass marketing and advertising than they are to mass manufacture.

This discussion of the four types of globalization serves to put that which is McDonaldized in a larger category (the grobalization of nothing) and that, in turn, in the larger context of other major types of globalization. More important, what is being argued here is that *the* most important form of globalization today is the grobalization of nothing, especially the grobalization of McDonaldized forms of nothing.

While the grobalization of nothing is at odds with the glocalization of something, it is clear that much of the power today lies with the grobalization of nothing, which threatens to overwhelm and undermine the glocalization of something (through, for example, McDonaldizing these forms of something).

The grobalization of nothing is also at odds with the grobalization of something, but these two processes seem able to exist rather comfortably side by side. One reason is that the two processes tend to serve very different audiences and rarely confront one another in the global marketplace. Another is that the grobalization of something is minuscule in comparison with the grobalization of nothing, and the latter has little difficulty simply ignoring it.

Finally, there is no conflict between the grobalization and the glocalization of nothing. Not only are both involved in the sale of nothing, but both are subject to the process of McDonaldization. While grobalization is the natural home of McDonaldization, it is increasingly likely that the glocal is subjected to McDonaldization and is offering McDonaldized products that manage to continue to reflect something of the local.

Given this overview of globalization theory, especially my recent work on the globalization of nothing (and related ideas), let us turn now to a more specific discussion of McDonaldization in this context. There are two polar positions on the global implications of McDonaldization, and they parallel the two central quadrants in Figure 8.1—the glocalization of something and the grobalization of nothing—and the fundamental conflict between them. On the one side are those who see McDonald's (as the prime representative of McDonaldization) as a force that integrates with the local to produce new glocal phenomena. This leads to the view that McDonaldization is, at worst, a benign or, at best, a positive force in the world, producing new and welcome social forms. On the other side are the critics of McDonaldization who see it as a grobalizing force that overwhelms the local. Here, McDonaldization is seen as a largely negative force, destroying local differences and leading to more global homogeneity.

## ◆ THE CASE FOR MCDONALDIZATION AS AN EXAMPLE OF THE GLOCALIZATION OF SOMETHING

There is no question that McDonald's (and other McDonaldized systems) adapt to local conditions, realities, and tastes. In fact, the president of McDonald's International says that the goal of the company is to "become as much a part of the local culture as possible."[34] Although its basic menu remains intact around the globe, McDonald's has added these local foods (among many others):

- Norway: McLaks—a grilled salmon sandwich with dill sauce on a whole-grain bread
- Netherlands: Groenteburger—a vegetarian burger
- Uruguay: McHuevos—hamburgers with poached egg—and McQuesos—toasted cheese sandwiches
- Japan: Chicken Tatsuta sandwich—fried chicken spiced with soy sauce and ginger, with cabbage and mustard mayonnaise
- Philippines: McSpaghetti—with tomato sauce or a meat sauce with frankfurter bits[35]
- Russia: Pirozhok—potato, mushroom, and cheese pies[36]

In England, McDonald's has adapted to the country's growing love affair with Indian food by offering "McChicken Korma Naan" and "Lamb McSpicy."[37]

And, of course, McDonald's is not alone in this effort to adapt by offering food suited to local tastes and preferences. For example, in Israel during Passover, Pizza Hut sells pizza with unleavened bread and KFC's fried chicken has barbecue sauce rather than breading. Not to be outdone, McDonald's makes its Chicken McNuggets with matzo meal.[38]

McDonald's also adapts to the local environment in the way it operates its outlets.

- In Beijing, the menu is identical to that in America, but the food is eaten more as a snack than a meal. In spite of perceiving the food as a snack, Beijing customers (and those in other nations, as well) often linger for hours rather than eating quickly and leaving or taking their food with them as they depart the drive-through window. Perhaps the biggest difference, however, is that in Beijing, McDonald's presents itself as a local company and as a place to "hang out" and have ceremonies (for example, children's birthday parties) rather than someplace to get in and out of as quickly as possible. Each outlet employs five to ten female receptionists; these "Aunt McDonalds"[39] (Ronald McDonald is known as "Uncle McDonald" in Taiwan) primarily deal with children and talk to parents.[40]

- As in Beijing, McDonald's in Hong Kong is a more human setting, with customers taking about twice as much time as Americans to eat their food. It is a teenage hangout from three to six in the afternoon, and McDonald's makes no effort to limit table time; it feels more like "home."[41] Employees rarely smile at customers. Instead, they display the traits valued in that culture—"competence, directness, and unflappability."[42] Those who eat in Hong Kong McDonald's do not bus their own debris. In addition, napkins are dispensed one at a time, because if they were placed in a public dispenser, they would disappear very quickly.

• In Taipei, McDonald's is also a hangout for teenagers. Generally, it is treated as a home away from home; it is "familiar and indigenous."[43] The same customers return over and over and come to know one another quite well.

As a way of summarizing the preceding examples, James L. Watson contends that "East Asian consumers have quietly, and in some cases stubbornly, transformed their neighborhood McDonald's into [g]local institutions."[44] Or even more on target from the perspective of the argument being made in this section, Watson argues that in Hong Kong it "is no longer possible to distinguish what is local and what is not."[45] In China, McDonald's is seen as much a Chinese phenomenon as it is an American phenomenon. In Japan, McDonald's is perceived by some as "*Americana as constructed* by the Japanese."[46] In James L. Watson's terms, it is a "transnational" phenomenon. To Watson, rather than being monolithic, McDonald's is a "federation of semi-autonomous enterprises."[47]

All these examples point to McDonald's (and more generally McDonaldization) as a glocal phenomenon, and in making this case, the implication is that what is produced is—in the terms of this analysis—something. While what is produced is sometimes described as local, it is clearly not local since it is affected, often profoundly, by the global; it is an integration of the global and the local—it is glocal! It cannot be thought of as grobal since the local is not being overwhelmed but, rather, integrated with the global. And much of what is produced at the glocal level can be thought of as something, or at least as lying closer to that end of the something-nothing continuum than clearly grobal phenomena such as Big Macs or Chicken McNuggets. While they may be the same throughout Uruguay, McHuevos or McQuesos are unique in content, if for no other reason than they are not sold in many, if any, other countries. In contrast, of course, the Big Mac sold in Uruguay is just about the same as one sold anywhere else. Similarly, because people are encouraged to hang out in some McDonald's in East Asia, they are more likely to create a unique social environment there than they are in most other places where they rarely stay long enough to create anything unique.

There is no question that McDonald's (and other McDonaldized systems) adapts in various ways to local realities throughout the world. The ability to adapt has helped McDonald's to succeed overseas. However, if McDonald's adapts too much—if it abandons its standard foods and methods of operation[48] and thus loses its identity and uniformity—it will undermine the source of much of its worldwide success. If local McDonald's around the world go their own way, will they eventually cease to be identifiable as McDonald's? Will the company itself (or at least its international operations) eventually be undermined, and perhaps destroyed, by such local adaptation?

♦ **THE CASE FOR MCDONALDIZATION AS AN EXAMPLE OF THE GROBALIZATION OF NOTHING**

As is made clear at the close of the preceding section, McDonaldized systems must be standardized. Thus, they cannot help but impose themselves (and their standardized products and systems), at least to some degree, on local markets throughout the world. Although McDonald's may adapt to local realities in various ways, its basic menu and the fundamental operating procedures remain essentially the same everywhere in the world. In this sense, McDonald's can be seen as the epitome of the grobalization of nothing. Thus, the "nothingness" of its standard fare and its basic operating principles tend to threaten, and in many cases replace, local fare and principles of operation.

The enormous expansion in the international arena of the giant fast-food chains that originated in the United States is one manifestation of the grobalization of nothing. In many ways, however, the mere existence of standard American chains in other countries is *not* the most important indicator of the grobalization of nothing in the form of the spread of McDonaldization; rather, it is the existence of indigenous clones of those McDonaldized enterprises in an increasing number of countries throughout the world. After all, the presence of American imports could simply be a manifestation of an invasion of isolated and superficial elements that represent no fundamental threat to, or change in, a local culture. But the emergence of native versions does reflect an underlying change in those societies, a genuine McDonaldization, and powerful evidence of the grobalization of nothing.

The following examples reflect the power of McDonald's to transform local restaurants. They are also manifestations of nothing in the sense that they are largely lacking in distinctive content and aping many standards developed by McDonald's and others of its ilk.

- The success of the many McDonald's in Russia[49] led to the development of indigenous enterprises such as Russkoye Bistro. Said Russkoye Bistro's deputy director, "If McDonald's had not come to our country, then we probably wouldn't be here."[50] Furthermore, "We need to create fast food here that fits our lifestyle and traditions. . . . We see McDonald's like an older brother . . . We have a lot to learn from them."[51]

- In China, Ronghua Chicken and Xiangfei Roast Chicken emulate Kentucky Fried Chicken. The Beijing Fast Food Company has almost a thousand local restaurants and street stalls that sell local fare. Several of the company's executives are former employees of KFC or McDonald's, where they learned basic management techniques. Even "the most famous restaurant in Beijing—Quanjude Roast Duck Restaurant—sent its management staff to McDonald's in 1993 and then introduced its own 'roast duck fast food' in early 1994."[52]

- In Japan, the strongest competitor to McDonald's is Mos Burger (with over 1,500 outlets), which serves "a sloppy-joe-style concoction of meat and chile sauce on a bun."[53] The corporate parent also operates chains under other names such as Chirimentei, a chain of 161 Chinese noodle shops in Japan (and 2 more in the People's Republic of China), Nakau (rice and Japanese noodles) with 82 outlets, and Mikoshi, 4 Japanese noodle houses in California.[54]

- In Seoul, competitors to McDonald's include Uncle Joe's Hamburger (the inventor of the *kimchi* burger, featuring an important local condiment made from spicy pickled cabbage[55]) and Americana.[56]

Beyond providing a model for local restaurants (and many other local institutions), McDonaldization poses a threat to the customs of society as a whole. This involves the grobalization of nothing to the degree that distinctive local customs are dropped and replaced by those that have their origins elsewhere and are lacking in distinction. For example,

- While their parents still call them "chips," British children now routinely ask for "french fries."[57]
- In Korea (and Japan), the individualism of eating a meal at McDonald's threatens the commensality of eating rice, which is cooked in a common pot, and of sharing side dishes.
- As in the United States, McDonald's has helped to transform children into customers in Hong Kong (and in many other places).
- Immigrants to Hong Kong are given a tour that ends at McDonald's.[58] If all cities did this, there would, at least in this case, be nothing to distinguish one city from another.
- In Japan, McDonald's is described as a new "local" phenomenon. A Japanese Boy Scout was surprised to find a McDonald's in Chicago; he thought it was a Japanese firm.[59]

As local residents come to see McDonald's and McDonaldized systems as their own, the process of McDonaldization, and more generally the grobalization of nothing, will surely embed itself ever more deeply into the realities of cultures throughout the world.[60] For example, the traditional and quite distinctive Japanese taboo against eating while standing has been undermined by the fast-food restaurant. Also subverted to some degree is the cultural sanction against drinking directly from a can or bottle. The norm against eating with one's hands is holding up better (the Japanese typically eat their burgers in the wrappers so that their hands do not touch the food directly). Nevertheless, the fact that deeply held norms are being transformed by McDonald's is evidence of the profound impact of McDonaldization. It reflects the grobalization of nothing in the sense that norms common in the United States and elsewhere (for example, eating while standing and drinking from a can) are now replacing norms distinctive to Japan (and many other nations).

McDonaldization and the grobalization of nothing are powerful global realities, but they do not affect all nations, nor do they affect nations to the same degree. For example, Korea, unlike other East Asian locales, has a long history of anti-Americanism (coexisting with pro-American feelings) and of fearing that Americanism will destroy Korean self-identity. Thus, one would anticipate more opposition there to McDonaldization than in most other nations.

Despite the negative effects of McDonaldization on local customs, we must not forget that McDonaldized systems bring with them many advances. For example, in Hong Kong (and in Taipei), McDonald's served as a catalyst for improving sanitary conditions at many other restaurants in the city.

In addition, McDonaldization has at times helped resuscitate local traditions. For example, although fast-food restaurants have boomed in Taipei, they have encouraged a revival of indigenous food traditions, such as the eating of betel nuts. More generally, in his book, *Jihad vs. McWorld*, Benjamin Barber argues that the spread of "McWorld" brings with it the development of local fundamentalist movements ("Jihads") deeply opposed to McDonaldization.[61] However, in the end, Barber concludes that McWorld will win out over Jihad. To succeed on a large scale, he says, fundamentalist movements must begin to use McDonaldized systems (such as e-mail, the Internet, television).

## ◆ CONCLUSION

McDonaldization is clearly a global process—one aspect of the broader process of globalization. More specifically, it is a prime example of the grobalization of nothing. As such, it confronts the glocalization of something and threatens, like all other grobalizing forces, to overwhelm the glocalization of something. Thus, while there is an argument to be made on behalf of the idea of McDonald's becoming a glocal phenomenon, a much stronger case can be made for McDonaldization as a grobal force, especially one that furthers, and is an inherent part of, the grobalization of nothing.

# 9

# McDonaldization in a Changing World

◆————————————————

## Are There Any Limits?

As noted in the preceding chapter, McDonaldization can be seen as an important aspect of the most powerful process of social change of our time—globalization, especially the grobalization of nothing. However, there is much more to the relationship between McDonaldization and social change, and this chapter deals with several of the most relevant issues. First, while in the preceding chapter it was shown that McDonaldization is one of the key driving forces in the grobalization of nothing, in this chapter we look at some of the forces driving McDonaldization. Second, the chapter will cover the relationship between McDonaldization and three more of the most important social changes of our time—the rise of postindustrial, post-Fordist, and postmodern society. Third, the discussion will shift to a much more specific issue, the ascent of Mt. Everest, because it seems to indicate that there are no limits to the expansion of McDonaldization. However, in the final section of this chapter, we will deal with several developments, especially McDonald's current problems (touched on in Chapter 1), that seem to indicate that there *are* limits to this process. In this context, I offer some thoughts on the likely future of both McDonald's and McDonaldization. As we will see, those futures are not necessarily tightly linked to one another. That is, the decline of McDonald's does *not* necessarily auger a slowdown, let alone reversal, in the McDonaldization of society.

## ◆ THE FORCES DRIVING MCDONALDIZATION: IT PAYS, WE VALUE IT, IT FITS

The attractiveness of the principles that lie at the base of McDonaldization help to account for its spread, but three other factors are also important in understanding its increasing prevalence: (1) material interests, especially economic goals and aspirations; (2) the culture of the United States, which values McDonaldization as an end in itself; and (3) McDonaldization's attunement to important changes taking place within society.

### Higher Profits and Lower Costs

Max Weber argued that, ultimately, material or, more specifically, economic interests drive the increasing rationalization of capitalist societies. Profit-making enterprises pursue McDonaldization because it leads to lower costs and higher profits. Clearly, greater efficiency and increased use of nonhuman technology are often implemented to increase profitability. Greater predictability provides, at the minimum, the climate needed for an organization to be profitable and for its profits to increase steadily from year to year. An emphasis on calculability, on things that can be quantified, helps lead to decisions that can produce and increase profits and makes possible measurements of profitability. In short, people and organizations profit greatly from McDonaldization, and as a result, they aggressively seek to extend its reach.

Although not oriented to profits, nonprofit organizations also press McDonaldization for material reasons. Specifically, it leads to lower costs, which permit nonprofit agencies, often in tight economic circumstances, to remain in operation and perhaps even to expand.

Interestingly, the dramatic changes that took place in the former Soviet Union and Eastern Europe in the late 20th century can be explained in these terms. These formerly communist societies tended to be character-ized by inefficiency, incalculability, and unpredictability and tended to be relatively slow to introduce advanced technologies (except in the mili-tary). These societies therefore suffered grave economic (and social) problems that forced them to abandon communism and move toward a more rational, marketlike economy. Russia, the other former Soviet states, and Eastern Europe are now moving, fitfully and differentially, toward greater rationalization, driven largely by a desire to improve their economic situation.

## McDonaldization for Its Own Sake

Although economic factors lie at the root of McDonaldization, it has become such a desirable process that many people and enterprises pursue it as an end in itself. Many have come to value efficiency, calculability, predictability, and control and seek them out whether or not economic gains will result. For example, eating in a fast-food restaurant or having a microwave dinner at home may be efficient, but it is more costly than preparing the meal "from scratch." Because they value efficiency, people are willing to pay the extra cost.

However, at a more macroscopic level, one may well question the rationality of McDonaldization. It may make economic sense for yet another entrepreneur to open still another McDonaldized institution, but does it make economic sense at the societal level to have so many of them concentrated in given locales? After all, the Wendy's burger is about the same as the McDonald's burger. Thus, McDonaldization does not always make economic sense. This means that McDonaldization cannot be explained solely in terms of material interests. It has become valued in and of itself.

Americans have long valued rationalization, efficiency, and so on, and McDonald's has simply built on that value system. Furthermore, since its proliferation in the late 1950s, McDonald's (to say nothing of the myriad other agents of rationalization) has invested enormous amounts of money and great effort in convincing people of its value and importance. Indeed, it now proclaims itself a part of a rich American tradition rather than, as many people believe, a threat to it. Many Americans have eaten at McDonald's in their younger years, gone out with teenage buddies for a burger, taken their children there at various times as they grew up, or gone there to have a cup of coffee with their parents. McDonald's has exploited such emotional baggage to create a large number of highly devoted customers. Even though McDonald's is built on rational principles, its customers' loyalty is as much emotional as it is rational. Thus, McDonaldization is likely to proceed apace for two reasons: It offers the advantages of rationality, and people are committed to it emotionally. This commitment is what leads people to ignore McDonald's disadvantages; this acceptance, in turn, helps open the world to even further advances in McDonaldization.

While adults may have an emotional commitment to McDonald's, this is even more true of children.[1] In fact, children care little about the rational aspects of McDonald's; they are drawn to it because of emotions created to a large extent by advertisements. Children value McDonald's for its own sake and not because it seems to offer material advantages.

Even new entrepreneurs may be attracted to opening a franchise because it has become such an attractive and popular method of operating a business. In so doing, they may ignore the fact that a given franchise market is saturated and there is little chance of making a profit in such a market.

## McDonaldization and the Changing Society

A third explanation of the rush toward McDonaldization is that it meshes well with other changes occurring in American society and around the world. For example, the number of single-parent families and the number of women working outside the home have increased greatly. There is less likely to be anyone with time to shop, prepare the ingredients, cook the food, and clean up afterward. There may not even be time (or money), at least during the workweek, for meals at traditional restaurants. The speed and efficiency of a fast-food meal fits in well with these realities. Many other McDonaldized institutions offer similar matches.

The fast-food model also thrives in a society that emphasizes mobility, especially by automobile. Teenagers and young adults in the United States (and elsewhere), the most likely devotees of the fast-food restaurant, now have ready access to automobiles. And they need automobiles to frequent most fast-food restaurants, except those found in the hearts of large cities.

More generally, the fast-food restaurant suits a society in which people prefer to be on the move.[2] Going out for a McDonaldized dinner, or any other rationalized activity, is in tune with the demands of such a society; even better is the use of the drive-through window so that people do not even have to stop to eat. Further serving McDonaldization is the increasing number of people who travel about, either on business or for vacations. People on the move seem to like the idea that even though they are in a different part of the country (or the world), they can still go to a familiar fast-food restaurant to eat the same foods they enjoy at home.

The increasing affluence of at least a portion of the population, accompanied by more discretionary funds, is another factor in the success of fast-food restaurants. People who have extra funds can support a fast-food "habit" and eat at such restaurants regularly. At the same time, the fast-food restaurant offers poor people the possibility of an occasional meal out.

The increasing influence of the mass media also contributes to the success of fast-food restaurants. Without saturation advertising and the ubiquitous influence of television and other mass media, fast-food restaurants would not have succeeded as well as they have. Similarly, the extensive advertising employed by McDonaldized systems such as H&R Block, Jenny Craig, and Pearle Vision centers has helped make them resounding successes.

Of course, technological change has probably played the greatest role in the success of McDonaldized systems. Initially, technologies such as bureaucracies, scientific management, the assembly line, and the major product of that production system, the automobile, all contributed to the birth of the fast-food society. Over the years, innumerable technological developments have both spurred, and been spurred by, McDonaldization: the "fatilyzer," automatic drink dispensers, supermarket scanners, foods that cook themselves, the microwave oven, aquaculture, factory farming, credit and debit cards, the StairMaster, DVDs, the twenty-four-second clock in professional basketball, recreation vehicles (RVs), ATMs, voice mail, health maintenance organizations (HMOs), CDs, OnStar navigation systems, and many others. Many technological marvels of the future will either arise from the expanding needs of a McDonaldizing society or help create new areas to be McDonaldized.

Today, the computer is the technology that contributes the most to the growth of McDonaldization.[3] In this light, mention should be made of the burgeoning importance of the Internet. One online service, America Online (AOL) grew from 3 million members in 1995 to 26.5 million in December, 2002.[4] Internet technology such as portals (for example, Internet Explorer) and search engines (for example, Yahoo! and Google), have greatly rationalized and simplified access to the Internet. Today, the Internet is user-friendly and accessible to millions of people who are largely ignorant of computer technology and computer programming.[5]

## ◆ OTHER MAJOR SOCIAL CHANGES: MCDONALDIZATION IN THE ERA OF THE "POSTS"

In this book, I present McDonaldization as a central social change in the modern world. However, a number of other contemporary social changes— especially the rise of postindustrial, post-Fordist, and postmodern society—need to be related to the McDonaldization of society. Those who focus on these changes tend to argue that we have already moved beyond the modern world and into a new, starkly different society. These views imply that a "modern" phenomenon such as McDonaldization is likely to soon disappear. I maintain, however, that McDonaldization and its modern (as well as industrial and Fordist) characteristics are not only here for the foreseeable future but are also influencing society at an accelerating rate. Although important postindustrial, post-Fordist, and postmodern trends are also occurring, some thinkers associated with these perspectives have been too quick to declare an end to modernity, at least in its McDonaldized form.

## Postindustrialism and McDonaldization: "Complexification" and Simplification

Daniel Bell (and many others) argues that we have moved beyond industrial society to a new, postindustrial society.[6] Among other things, this means that the focus in society has shifted from producing goods to providing services. Throughout most of the 20th century, the production of goods such as steel and automobiles dominated the economy of the United States. Today, however, the economy is dominated by services such as those related to education, computers, health care, and fast food. The rise of new technologies and the growth in knowledge and information processing is also characteristic of postindustrial society. Professionals, scientists, and technicians have increased in number and importance. The implication is that postindustrial society will be dominated by creative knowledge workers and not by routinized employees of McDonaldized systems.

However, the low-status service occupations that are so central to a McDonaldized society show no sign of disappearing. In fact, they have expanded. Above all, however, McDonaldization is built on many of the ideas and systems of industrial society, especially bureaucratization, the assembly line, and scientific management. Society is certainly postindustrial in many ways, and knowledge workers have grown more important, but the spread of McDonaldization indicates that some aspects of industrial society are still with us and will remain so for some time to come.

In *Post-Industrial Lives*, Jerald Hage and Charles Powers argue in favor of the postindustrial thesis.[7] Among other things, they contend that a new postindustrial organization has arisen and coexists with the classic industrial organization, as well as with other organizational forms. The postindustrial organization has a number of characteristics, including a leveling of hierarchical distinctions, a blurring of boundaries between organizations, a more integrated and less specialized organizational structure, an increase in behavior that is not bound by rules, and hiring policies that emphasize the creativity of potential employees. In contrast, McDonaldized organizations continue to be hierarchical, the behavior of employees and even managers is tightly bound by rules, and the last thing in the minds of those hiring for most jobs is creativity. Hage and Powers see jobs involving "tasks that are most clearly defined, technically simple, and most often repeated" being eliminated by automation.[8] While many such jobs have been eliminated in heavy industry, they are not only alive and well, but growing, in McDonaldized service organizations.[9] Postindustrial organizations are also characterized by customized work and products, while standardized work (everyone follows the same procedures, scripts) and uniform products are the norm in McDonaldized settings. Unquestionably, postindustrial organizations are on the ascent, but McDonaldized organizations are also spreading. Modern society sustains contradictory organizational developments.

Hage and Powers envision a broader change in society as a whole. The emphasis has come to be on creative minds, complex selves, and communication among people who have these characteristics. They argue that "complexification will be the prevailing pattern of social change in postindustrial society."[10] Although some aspects of modern society are congruent with that image, McDonaldization demands uncreative minds, simple selves, and minimal communication dominated by scripts and routines. McDonaldization emphasizes "simplification" not "complexification."

In sum, the postindustrial thesis is not wrong but is more limited than many of its adherents believe. Postindustrialization coexists with McDonaldization. The latter not only shows no sign of disappearing but is in fact dramatically increasing in importance. My view is that *both* complexification and simplification will prevail but in different sectors of the economy and the larger society.

## Fordism and Post-Fordism: Or Is It McDonaldism?

A similar issue concerns a number of thinkers, especially those associated with Marxism, who claim that industry has undergone a transition from Fordism to post-Fordism. Fordism, of course, refers to the ideas, principles, and systems spawned by the famous industrialist and founder of the Ford Motor Company, Henry Ford.

Fordism has a number of characteristics:

- *Mass production of homogeneous products.* While they offer infinitely more variation than Ford's original Model-T, today's automobiles remain largely homogeneous, at least by type of automobile. In fact, in the United States in 1995, Ford introduced a so-called world car (the most current example is the Focus), an automobile that is sold in much the same form in many global markets.

- *Inflexible technologies, such as the assembly line.* Despite the introduction of many robots to replace human workers and experiments with altering assembly lines, especially those undertaken by Volvo in Sweden, today's lines look much like they did in Henry Ford's day.

- *Standardized work routines, or Taylorism.* The person who puts hubcaps on cars does the same task over and over, more or less the same way each time.

- *Efforts to increase productivity.* Increases in productivity come from "economies of scale as well as the deskilling, intensification, and homogenization of labor."[11] *Economy of scale* means simply that larger factories producing larger numbers of products can manufacture each individual product more cheaply than small factories producing goods in small numbers. *De-skilling* means that productivity increases if many workers do jobs requiring little or no skill (for example, putting hubcaps on cars) rather than, as had been the case in the past, a few workers with great skill doing all the work. *Intensification* means the more demanding and faster the production process, the greater the productivity. *Homogenization of labor* means that workers do highly specialized work (putting on hubcaps, for example), making them easily replaceable.

- *Market for mass-produced items.* Such a market is related to the homogenization of consumption patterns. In the automobile industry, Fordism led to a national market for automobiles in which similarly situated people bought similar, if not identical, automobiles.

Although Fordism grew throughout the twentieth century, especially in the heavy industry of the United States, it reached its peak and began to decline in the 1970s. The oil crisis of 1973 and the subsequent downturn in the American automobile industry (and the rise of its Japanese counterpart) were primary factors in the decline of Fordism.

Some argue that the decline of Fordism has been accompanied by the rise of post-Fordism, which has a number of its own distinguishing characteristics:

- *Declining interest in mass products and growing interest in more customized and specialized products.* Style and quality are especially valued. Rather than drab and uniform products, people want flashier goods that are easily distinguishable.[12] Post-Fordist consumers are willing to pay more for distinctive, high quality products.

- *Shorter production runs.* The more specialized products demanded in post-Fordist society require smaller and more productive systems. Huge factories producing uniform products are replaced with smaller plants turning out a wide range of products.

- *Flexible production.* In the post-Fordist world, new technologies make flexible production profitable. For example, computerized equipment that can be reprogrammed to produce different products replaces the old, single-function technology. This new production process is controlled through more flexible systems—for example, a more flexible form of management.

- *More capable workers.* Post-Fordist systems require more from workers than was required from their predecessors. For example, workers need more diverse skills and better training to handle the more demanding, more sophisticated technologies. These new technologies require workers who can handle more responsibility and operate with greater autonomy.

- *Greater differentiation.* As post-Fordist workers become more differentiated, they come to want more differentiated commodities, lifestyles, and cultural outlets. In other words, greater differentiation in the workplace leads to greater differentiation in the society as a whole. The result is more diverse demands from consumers and thus still greater differentiation in the workplace.

Although these elements of post-Fordism have emerged in the modern world, elements of old-style Fordism persist and show no signs of disappearing; there has been no clear historical break with Fordism. In fact, "McDonaldism," a phenomenon that clearly has many things in common with Fordism, is growing at an astounding pace in contemporary society. Among the things McDonaldism shares with Fordism are the following:

- Homogeneous products dominate a McDonaldized world. The Big Mac, the Egg McMuffin, and Chicken McNuggets are identical from one time and place to another.
- Technologies such as Burger King's conveyor system, as well as the french fry and soft drink machines throughout the fast-food industry, are as rigid as many of the technologies in Henry Ford's assembly line system.
- The work routines in the fast-food restaurant are highly standardized. Even what the workers say to customers is routinized.

- ♦ The jobs in a fast-food restaurant are de-skilled; they take little or no skill.
- ♦ The workers are homogeneous and interchangeable.
- ♦ The demands and the actions of the customers are homogenized by the needs of the fast-food restaurant. Don't dare ask for a not so well-done burger; what is consumed and how it is consumed is homogenized by McDonaldization.

Thus, Fordism is alive and well in the modern world, although it has been transformed to a large extent into McDonaldism. Furthermore, classic Fordism—for example, in the form of the assembly line—remains a significant presence in American industry.

Post-Fordism and Fordism/McDonaldism coexist. However, post-Fordism's emphasis on the production and sale of quality products would seem inconsistent with one of the fundamental tenets of McDonaldization: the emphasis on quantity and the corresponding de-emphasis on quality. While this is generally the case, is it impossible to McDonaldize quality products? In some cases—for example, haute cuisine or outstanding cakes from skilled bakers—quality cannot be McDonaldized. But in others, quality and McDonaldization are not inimical. Take the boom in Starbucks coffee shops.[13] Starbucks sells, at high prices, high-quality coffee (at least compared with most American coffee, especially that sold in McDonald's and similar settings). Starbucks has been able to McDonaldize the coffee business without sacrificing quality. Regarding service, which is of similar complexity in McDonald's and Starbucks, the latter has self-consciously sought to counter the problems found in McDonaldized systems. Starbucks' founder states:

Service is a lost art in America. I think people want to do a good job, but if they are treated poorly they get beaten down. . . . It's not viewed as a professional job in America to work behind a counter. We don't believe that. We want to provide our people with dignity and self-esteem, and we can't do that with lip service. So we offer tangible benefits. The attrition rate in retail fast food is between 200 and 400 percent a year. At Starbucks, it's 60 percent.[14]

Since service is more complex than brewing coffee, it remains to be seen whether Starbucks can offer high-quality service on a widespread and continuing basis.

## Postmodernism: Are We Adrift in Hyperspace?

From the more general theoretical perspective known as "postmodernism,"[15] we have entered, or are entering, a new postmodern society that represents a radical break with modern society; postmodernity follows and supplants modernity. Modern society is thought of as highly rational and rigid, while postmodern society is seen as less rational, more irrational, and more flexible. To the degree that postmodernity is seen as a successor to modernity, postmodern social theory stands in opposition to the McDonaldization thesis: The idea that irrationality is increasing contradicts the view that there is an increase in rationality. If we have, in fact, entered a new postmodern era, then McDonaldization would be confronted with a powerful opposing force.

However, less radical postmodern orientations allow us to see phenomena such as McDonald's as having *both* modern and postmodern characteristics.[16] Thus, while McDonald's can be associated with postmodernism, it can also be linked to various phenomena that could be identified with modernism (as well as with industrialism and Fordism). For example, McDonald's has succeeded in automating the customer. That is, when customers enter the fast-food restaurant or wend their way along the drive-through, they enter a kind of automated system through which they are impelled and from which they are ultimately ejected when they have been "refueled." In this way, McDonald's looks more like a factory than a restaurant. However, it is not a "sweat shop for its customers, but a high tech factory."[17] Therefore, from this postmodernist perspective, McDonald's is as much a modern as a postmodern phenomenon.

David Harvey offers a different, but still moderate, postmodernist argument. Harvey sees great changes in society and argues that these changes lie at the base of postmodern thinking. But he also sees many continuities between modernity and postmodernity. His major conclusion is that, although "there has certainly been a sea change in the surface appearance of capitalism since 1973. . . . the underlying logic of capitalist accumulation and its crisis tendencies remain the same."[18]

Central to Harvey's argument is the idea of time-space compression. He believes that modernism compresses both time and space, speeding the pace of life and shrinking the globe (for example, computers allowing us to send e-mail messages almost instantly to anyplace in the world), and that the process has accelerated in the postmodern era. But earlier epochs in capitalism have undergone essentially the same process: "We have, in short, witnessed another fierce round in that process of annihilation of space through time that has always lain at the center of capitalism's dynamic."[19] Thus, to Harvey, postmodernity is *not* discontinuous with modernity; they both reflect the same underlying dynamic.

As an example of space compression within the McDonaldized world, consider that foods once available only in foreign countries or large cities are now quickly and widely available throughout the United States because of the spread of fast-food chains dispensing Italian, Mexican, or Cajun food. Similarly, in the realm of time compression, foods that formerly took hours to prepare can now take seconds in a microwave oven or be purchased in minutes at shops (such as an outlet of the eatZi's chain) offering pre-prepared foods.

Time-space compression is manifested in many other ways, as well. For example, in the 2003 war with Iraq, television (especially CNN and MSNBC) transported viewers instantaneously from one place to another—from air raids in Baghdad, to correspondents embedded in military units deep in Iraqi territory, to military briefings in Qatar. Viewers learned about many military developments at the same time, and perhaps even before, the generals and the president of the United States did.

The best-known argument linking modernity and postmodernity is made by Fredric Jameson in the essay (later, book), "Postmodernism, or the Cultural Logic of Late Capitalism."[20] This title clearly indicates Jameson's Marxist position that capitalism (certainly a "modern" phenomenon), now in its "late" phase, continues to dominate today's world. However, it has now spawned a new cultural logic—postmodernism. In other words, although the cultural logic may have changed, the underlying economic structure remains continuous with earlier forms of capitalism: That is, it is still "modern." Furthermore, capitalism continues to be up to its same old tricks of spawning a cultural system to help it maintain itself.

The late phase of capitalism involves "a prodigious expansion of capital into hitherto uncommodified areas."[21] Jameson sees this expansion as not only consistent with Marxist theory but as creating an even purer form of capitalism. For Jameson, the key to contemporary capitalism is its multinational character and the fact that multinational corporations (such as McDonald's) have greatly increased the range of products transformed into commodities. Even aesthetic elements that people usually associate with culture have been turned into commodities (art, for example) to be bought and sold in the capitalist marketplace. As a result, extremely diverse elements make up the new postmodern culture.

Jameson's image of postmodern society has five basic elements, each of which can be related to the McDonaldization of society.

*Association with late capitalism.* Unquestionably, McDonaldization can be associated with earlier forms of capitalism. For example, McDonaldization is often spurred on by the material interests of owners and investors. But

McDonaldization also exemplifies the multinationalism of late capitalism. Many McDonaldized businesses are international, with their major growth now taking place in the global marketplace.

*Superficiality.* The cultural products of postmodern society do not delve deeply into underlying meanings. A good example is Andy Warhol's famous painting of Campbell's soup cans, which appear to be nothing more than perfect representations of those cans. To use a key term associated with postmodern theory, the painting is a *simulation* (for more on this, see below), and it is difficult to distinguish between the original and the copy. A simulation is also a copy of a copy. In fact, Warhol reputedly painted his soup cans not from the cans themselves but from a photograph of them. Jameson describes a simulation as "the identical copy for which no original ever existed."[22] By definition, a simulation is superficial and inauthentic.

A McDonaldized world is characterized by such superficiality. People pass through McDonaldized systems without being touched by them; for example, customers maintain a fleeting and superficial relation with McDonald's, its employees, and its products. McDonald's products also provide wonderful examples of simulations. Each Chicken McNugget is a copy of a copy; no original Chicken McNugget ever existed. The original, the chicken, is hardly recognizable in the McNugget. The Chicken McNugget is "fake chicken."

*Waning of emotion or affect.* Jameson contrasts another of Warhol's paintings, a near-photographic representation of Marilyn Monroe, to a classic modernist piece—Edvard Munch's *The Scream.* Munch's surreal painting represents a person in the depth of despair, or in sociological terms, anomie or alienation. In contrast, Warhol's painting of Marilyn Monroe expresses no genuine emotion. Postmodernists would assert that the modern world caused the alienation depicted by Munch but that in the postmodern world depicted by Warhol, fragmentation has tended to replace alienation. Since the world, and the people in it, have become fragmented, the emotion that remains is "free-floating and impersonal."[23] However, a peculiar kind of euphoria is associated with these postmodern feelings, what Jameson calls "intensities." As an example, he presents a photorealist cityscape "where even automobile wrecks gleam with some new hallucinatory splendour."[24] Euphoria based on automobile disasters in the midst of urban squalor is, indeed, a peculiar kind of emotion.[25]

Clearly, the McDonaldized world is one in which the sincere expression of emotion and affect have been all but eliminated. At McDonald's, little or no emotional bond can develop among customers, employees, managers, and owners. The company strives to eliminate genuine emotion so things can operate as smoothly, as rationally, as possible. A McDonaldized world is also fragmented: People go to McDonald's today, Denny's tomorrow, and Pizza Hut the day after. Although alienation in the McDonaldized world, especially among employees, reflects the modern world, McDonaldization also offers the free-floating affect described by Jameson. People may feel angry about and hostile toward the McDonaldized world, but they do not ordinarily know where to direct their anger and hostility.[26] After all, so many different things seem to be undergoing McDonaldization. In spite of the lack of affect in a McDonaldized society, people often feel a kind of intensity, a euphoria when they enter one of its domains. The bright lights, gaudy colors, garish signs, children's playgrounds, and so on give visitors the impression that they have entered an amusement park and are in for an exciting time.

*Loss of historicity.* Postmodernists assert that historians can never find the truth about the past or even put together a coherent story about it. So they must be satisfied with creating pastiches, or hodgepodges, of ideas about the past, sometimes contradictory and confused—a "random cannibalization of all styles of the past."[27] Furthermore, there is no clear sense of historical development, of time passing, in the postmodern world. Past and present are inextricably intertwined. For example, historical novels such as E. L. Doctorow's *Ragtime* present the "disappearance of the historical referent. This historical novel can no longer set out to represent historical past; it can only 'represent' our ideas and stereotypes about that past."[28] Another example is the 1981 movie *Body Heat*, which while clearly about the present, creates an atmosphere reminiscent of the 1930s. To do this,

> The object world of the present-day—artifacts and appliances, even automobiles, whose styling would serve to date the image—is elaborately edited out. Everything in the film, therefore, conspires to blur its official contemporaneity and to make it possible for the viewer to see it as though it were set in some eternal Thirties, beyond historical time.[29]

Such a movie or novel is a "symptom of the waning of our historicity."[30] The inability to distinguish between past, present, and future shows up at the individual level in a kind of schizophrenia. For the postmodern individual, events are fragmented and discontinuous.

McDonaldized systems generally lack a sense of history as well. People find themselves in settings that either defy attempts to pinpoint them historically or that present a pastiche of many historical epochs. The best example of the latter is Disney World with its hodgepodge of past, present, and future worlds. Furthermore, visitors to McDonaldized settings tend to lack a sense of the passage of time. In many cases, the designers of the system intentionally remove references to time. The best examples are shopping malls and Las Vegas casinos, both of which usually lack visible clocks and windows. However, not all aspects of the McDonaldized world create such timelessness, indicating their continuing modernity. For those who choose to eat in a fast-food restaurant, time has been made important (for examples, by signs giving a 20-minute limit on the use of tables) to prevent them from lingering. On the other hand, the drive-through window seems part of a timeless web, one link in an unending chain of destinations.

*Reproductive technologies.* Jameson argues that in postmodern society, productive technologies such as the automobile assembly line have been replaced by reproductive technologies, especially electronic media such as the television set and the computer. That is, postmodern technologies reproduce over and over that which has been produced before. Unlike the "exciting" technologies of the industrial revolution, these new technologies flatten all images and make each indistinguishable from the others. These "implosive" technologies of the postmodern era give birth to very different cultural products than the explosive technologies of the modern era.

Although the McDonaldized systems do make use of some of the old-fashioned productive technologies (the assembly line, for example), they are dominated by reproductive technologies. In Chapter 2, I discussed how the fast-food restaurants have merely reproduced products, services, and technologies long in existence. What they produce are flattened, featureless products—the McDonald's hamburger and services (the scripted interaction with the counter person).

In sum, Jameson presents an image of postmodernity in which people are adrift and unable to comprehend the multinational capitalist system or the explosively growing culture and commodity market in which they live. As a paradigm of this world and of each person's place in it, Jameson offers the example of Los Angeles's Hotel Bonaventure, designed by a famous postmodern architect, John Portman. People are unable to get their bearings in the hotel's lobby, an example of what Jameson calls *hyperspace,* an area where modern conceptions of space are useless in helping people orient themselves. This lobby is surrounded by four absolutely symmetrical towers containing the rooms. In fact, the hotel had to add color coding and directional signals because people had such difficulty getting their bearings in the hotel lobby as it was originally designed.

The situation confronting visitors to the Bonaventure serves as a metaphor for people's inability to get their bearings in the multinational economy and cultural explosion of late capitalism. What they need are new kinds of maps. The need for such maps reflects Jameson's view that people have moved from a world defined temporally to one defined spatially. Indeed, the idea of hyperspace, and the example of the lobby of the Hotel Bonaventure, reflects the dominance of space in the postmodern world. Thus, for Jameson, the central problem today is that people have lost their ability to position themselves within postmodern space and to map that space.

Similarly, while the interior of any given setting is clearly marked and quite familiar, the McDonaldized world as a whole is disorienting and difficult to map. For instance, you can be in downtown Beijing and still eat at McDonald's and Kentucky Fried Chicken. Because space and the things associated with particular places are changing dramatically, people no longer know quite where they are and are in need of new guides. Excellent examples of hyperspace include the shopping mall, the large Las Vegas casino, and Disney World—all highly McDonaldized.

McDonaldization fits Jameson's five characteristics of postmodern society but perhaps only because he sees postmodernity as simply a late stage of modernity. In part, because of this inability to draw a clear line, some scholars reject the idea of a new, postmodern society. Says one, "I do not believe that we live in 'New Times,' in a 'post-industrial and postmodern age' fundamentally different from the capitalist mode of production globally dominant for the past two centuries."[31]

In *Enchanting a Disenchanted World: Revolutionizing the Means of Consumption,* I come to a similar conclusion.[32] McDonald's and other fast-food restaurants, shopping malls, cybermalls, Disney World, cruise ships, and so on are all examples of the "new means of consumption." These are all post-World War II phenomena that have revolutionized the way we consume by rationalizing the structures in which we consume. As discussed in Chapter 7, McDonaldization tends to bring with it disenchantment, or a loss of magic and mystery. Disenchanted structures are unlikely to attract consumers. In response to this problem, the new means of consumption have, at least to some degree, been reenchanted, incorporating ever-more spectacular features to draw in consumers seeking euphoria in a world lacking in emotion. This is the characteristic that associates the new means of consumption with postmodernism.

One of the central issues in *Enchanting a Disenchanted World* is how enchantment can be created in such rationalized structures so that consumers are lured to them and into spending money. There are several answers:

- Paradoxically, rationalization itself can be enchanting. We are drawn, for example, by the "magic" of McDonald's ability to serve our food almost instantaneously (at least most of the time), the ability of Amazon.com to deliver one of its million-plus books in a day or two, and all the sights and sounds available in settings such as Disney World or the Las Vegas Strip.

- The simulated character of these settings helps to make them magical. Thus, Disney and Las Vegas can juxtapose a wide range of fake worlds within a single geographic area (the various countries represented in Epcot Center and the New York, New York, Bellagio, and Paris casino hotels). Visiting so many "real" worlds would require far more expensive and time-consuming around-the-world journeys. Instead, one can magically visit their simulations in a single locale.

- The new means of consumption are made magical by the implosion, or collapse, of what were once multiple, separate locales into a single site. For example, the Mall of America is an enormous lure because it combines under one roof a shopping mall and an amusement park. Some Las Vegas casino hotels now also house amusement parks and shopping malls. McDonald's has imploded into many settings, including Wal-Mart and Disney World. Imagine the excitement of a child finding McDonald's in Disney World.

In a variety of other ways, modernity (rationalization) and postmodernity (reenchantment through postmodern processes of simulation and implosion) coexist within the McDonaldized means of consumption.

Clearly, McDonaldization shows no signs of disappearing and being replaced by new, postmodern structures. However, McDonaldized systems do exhibit many postmodern characteristics side-by-side with modern elements. Thus, we are safe in saying that the McDonaldizing world demonstrates aspects of *both* modernity and postmodernity. And this clearly indicates that postmodernity does not represent a barrier to continued McDonaldization.

# ◆ ARE THERE ANY LIMITS TO THE EXPANSION OF MCDONALDIZATION?

The discussion in the preceding sections, as well as in the last chapter, implies that McDonaldization is inexorable—globalization, postindustrialism, post-Fordism, and postmodernism create no insurmountable barriers to its continued expansion and may even contribute to it. While, as we will see, there are contraindications to such inexorability, we turn first to another, this time more specific, example of the forward march of McDonaldization.

## A "Yellow Brick Road" to the Summit of Everest?

The issue of the limits of McDonaldization is raised, at least implicitly, in Jon Krakauer's *Into Thin Air*, which describes several death-defying efforts to climb Mt. Everest in 1996. It is clear that there have been efforts to McDonaldize death-defying acts such as mountain climbing in general,[33] and Everest in particular, but it is also clear from the death of twelve people in the 1996 ascent that this "intrinsically irrational act"[34] cannot, at least as yet, be totally rationalized. Krakauer describes the variety of steps that have been taken over the years to McDonaldize the ascent.

At the top of the list are technological advances such as sophisticated climbing gear; canisters to supply supplemental oxygen at higher altitudes; helicopters for transport to the take-off point for the climb (a trip that used to take more than a month) and for the rescue of ill or injured climbers; medical technologies (and personnel) to deal with problems associated with falls, acute altitude sickness, and the like; and computers, the Internet, and fax machines to keep in touch with climbers as they ascend. Krakauer also cites organizational arrangements designed to prevent people from going it alone and to make the climbing team operate like a well-oiled machine. One group leader was lauded for his "impressive organizational skills" and his "elaborate systems."[35]

The best example of the effort to rationalize the climbing of Everest in 1996 was one team's system for "fast-track acclimatization" to the debilitating altitudes.[36] It involved fewer trips from base camp and each successive excursion involved trekking a standard number of feet up the mountain. Overall, the "fast-track" method involved spending four weeks above 17,000 feet, eight nights at 21,300 or higher, and only one night at 24,000 feet before climbers began the ascent to the 29,028 foot summit of Everest. The standard, less rationalized procedure involves climbers spending more time at 21,300 feet and higher, and there is at least one climb to 26,000 feet before attempting to reach the summit. On the basis of his observations, Krakauer cautiously concludes: "There is little question that extending the current eight- or nine-night acclimatization period at 21,000 to 24,000 feet would provide a greater margin of safety."[37]

Those who sought to McDonaldize the climbing of Everest can be described as trying to turn the route up the mountain into a nice, smooth, safe "toll road."[38] They stood to earn higher fees and to recruit more well-heeled climbers in the future if they could demonstrate that the dangers associated with climbing Everest were under control. Said one group leader: "We've got the big E figured out, we've got it totally wired. These days, I'm telling you, we've built a yellow brick road to the summit."[39]

However, the limitations of such efforts are reflected in the argument that an expedition up Everest "can't be run like a Swiss train."[40] Several irrationalities of rationality are associated with such a McDonaldized effort. Traffic jams were created on the mountain because so many groups with so many people were attempting the climb. Paying climbers tended to be ill trained, ill prepared, and dependent on the guides. Most were strangers without much knowledge of one another's strengths and limitations as climbers. Because the climbers were paying large fees, leaders found it hard to say no to them even in situations where the climbers should have been refused.

But the best example of the irrationality of rationality relates to acclimatization. The fast-track method of acclimatization was efficient and allowed people to climb higher and faster and to get to the top quicker, but it depended on the use of bottled oxygen at higher levels. The lack of adequate time for acclimatization at each level made it harder for those involved in the 1996 climb to survive when oxygen proved unavailable at the higher levels.

The 1996 ascent exhibited other irrationalities, including inexperienced climbers, a guide who was climbing Everest for the first time, the apparent selfishness of another guide, the "damn-the-torpedoes" approach of one group leader, the competitive rivalry between group leaders, and the violation of one group's own deadline to begin descending from the summit. Such irrationalities are not inherent in the effort to climb Everest or in the rationalization of mountain climbing, but similar things are likely to occur and contribute to problems on any given climb.

Beyond the irrationalities of rationality and the irrationalities of this particular climb, there is the inherent irrationality of seeking to ascend

Mt. Everest. Since organized climbs began in 1921, more than 130 people have died on Everest, one death for every four people who have reached the summit. As climbers ascend ever higher, physiological problems mount. Crevasses can shift, causing climbers to hurtle to their death. Rocks careening down the mountain take their toll. The wind chill can reach minus-100 degrees. But the biggest irrationality is the weather: In 1996, a completely unexpected storm killed those twelve climbers who were attempting to reach the peak, the largest single death toll in the history of Everest ascents.

The 1996 Everest disaster would seem to indicate that, despite people's best efforts, McDonaldization has limits. We certainly will never fully rationalize such death-defying activities as the climbing of Everest. But McDonaldization is not an all-or-nothing process; there are degrees of McDonaldization. Thus, we will continue to try to minimize the irrationalities associated with mountain climbing. In the case of Mount Everest, future climbers can learn from the 1996 disaster (and others) and develop methods to minimize or eliminate the risks. The biggest danger is the unexpected storm, but improved weather-forecasting and -sensing devices can be developed and deployed.

Apparently many of those lessons have been learned. Preliminary 2003 spring season numbers indicated new records for the most summits in one day (on May 22, 2003, over 109 people were atop Everest) and the most in one year (over 238, with the fall season yet to come). No one perished in the course of these ascents.[41] Furthermore, two of the successful climbers were part of a "reality TV" program sponsored by Toyota for the Outdoor Life Network (OLN).[42]

While further accidents and deaths will mark future ascents of Everest (surprise storms will occur again), we may well be closer to something approximating a "yellow brick road to the summit" of Everest (perhaps operated by Disney). But long before then, it is likely that those daredevils who have found Everest so alluring will seek out some less McDonaldized adventure.

As we have seen earlier in this book in the cases of birth and death, and now in the case of death-defying activities such as the climbing of Mt. Everest, there is great momentum to the process of McDonaldization, but there are also natural limits that present some powerful barriers to it. While there may still be barriers in the natural world, are there any to be found in the social and economic world? That is, is there anything to stop McDonaldization from altering everything about social and economic life not only in the United States but around the world?

### ◆ LOOKING TO THE FUTURE: DE-MCDONALDIZATION?

In Chapter 1, I discussed the issue of McDonald's current (21st century) problems and made it clear that while McDonald's may be under siege, that represents no threat to the continued existence and further proliferation of McDonaldization. Here, I offer some more general thoughts on the future of both McDonald's and McDonaldization.

### The Future of McDonald's and Franchises: A Model of All That Is Bad?

A variety of developments threaten the future of McDonald's. The company will not be filing for bankruptcy any time soon, but the various storm clouds are worth noting.[43]

The first is the difficulties McDonald's has been having in the United States. Its growth overseas has been nothing short of meteoric, and its overseas business is highly profitable; however, the fast-food industry in the United States is saturated, and growth has flattened. What's worse, McDonald's share of that flat market has been declining. McDonald's faces stiff competition from Mexican fast-food and pizza franchises. In addition, upscale franchises such as Red Lobster are exhibiting greater profitability. McDonald's has tried, and continues to try, to do a number of things (such as introducing new menu items) to reinvigorate its American sales, but in the main, they have been notable failures. Continued failure to improve its position in the American market is a huge problem on its own, and it could eventually carry over into the international arena and ultimately threaten the company as a whole. McDonald's has not been helped by the problems discovered recently in beef and hamburger meat. Examples include the "mad cow disease" scare in England (and in 2003 in Canada) and several outbreaks of E. coli.[44]

The second worrisome trend from McDonald's point of view is the expansion of worldwide efforts, like those to be discussed in Chapter 10, to oppose its operation and its practices. Especially threatening is the coalition of groups convinced that McDonald's is a symbol of problems such as environmental degradation, dietary dangers, the evils of capitalism, poor working conditions, faltering unionization, neglected children, and the threat of Americanization. As an international operation with thousands of local outposts, McDonald's (although not McDonaldization) is vulnerable to both international campaigns and local opposition. Once, and perhaps still, the model corporation (in a positive sense) in the eyes of many, McDonald's is now in danger of becoming the paradigm for all that is bad in the world. While the media in 1999 were filled with pictures of Serbs smashing windows at two McDonald's restaurants in Belgrade, nearby shops featuring other American products (Levi's, Harley Davidson) were untouched and operating normally.[45] Similarly, an American decision to add a 100% tariff on Roquefort cheese led to protests that included the dumping of rotten vegetables and piles of manure at, and the trashing of, local McDonald's restaurants in France.[46] More recently, in the wake of the 2003 war with Iraq, the opening of fast-food restaurants that closely copied McDonald's coexisted with anti-Americanism and running battles with American troops occupying the country.[47]

Yet another threat to McDonald's stems from the difficulty any corporation has in staying on top indefinitely. Sooner or later, internal problems (such as declining profits or stock prices or lack of managerial creativity), external competition, or some combination of the two will, if they have not already, set McDonald's on a downward course. In the end, it could become a pale imitation of what is still a corporate powerhouse. These factors might even lead eventually to its complete disappearance.

More generally, the franchise system of which McDonald's is a part is not an unqualified success. A surprising number of franchise systems have experienced serious difficulties, and many fail. For example, Wrap&Roll, which sold stuffed tortillas, closed its outlets because diners found the menu too limited.[48] Club Med, one of the pioneers of inclusive, rationalized vacations, is losing money and seeking a new niche and identity.[49] The Body Shop is having difficulty, especially in its money-losing American chain.[50] The huge Boston Market (formerly Boston Chicken) chain, pioneer in the "home meal replacement" business, went bankrupt, the victim of overexpansion, a questionable financing system, steep competition in the roast chicken market, and a failed effort to expand beyond its base in the chicken business. A regional developer of Boston Markets moaned, "'We thought we had a concept that was the next McDonald's.'"[51] Ironically, Boston Market was purchased by McDonald's and is now one of its subdivisions. Even Starbucks has had its financial problems[52] and was the subject of several protests.[53] Although McDonald's is a great success in France, Burger King was forced to close its restaurants there, including the one on the Champs-Elysées.[54] Holiday Inn is experiencing problems, in part because it is perceived as "old and tired."[55] Another problem within franchising is the conflict between franchisers and franchisees over expansion, which threatens existing franchisees.[56] McDonald's works hard to maintain its franchises but could suffer in a general retreat from that business model.

Nor is the potential for failure restricted to franchises and chains; it extends to innovations designed to further McDonaldize already ratio-nalized systems. The Checkout Channel was created for consumers wait-ing in fast-food restaurant and supermarket checkout lines: People would be able to wait in line and watch television at the same time. Thus, an executive of the firm that developed the television network says, "One of the biggest customer concerns is the problem of queuing. . . . Anything a retailer can do to lessen the perceived wait is going to be a benefit."[57] Note the tacit admission that people are waiting in line for their fast food (and groceries)—that fast food isn't so fast, that these efficient systems aren't so efficient. In the end, Checkout Channel failed—in part because the programs tended to repeat every few minutes. This irritated counter and checkout personnel who, as a result, often turned off the TV monitor.

### The Future of McDonaldization: "Miss Hap's" and "Miss Steak's"

As was made clear in Chapter 1, we must not confuse threats to McDonald's and related enterprises with the threats to the process of McDonaldization. McDonald's will almost undoubtedly disappear at some point in the future, but at that point, the McDonaldization process will likely be even more deeply entrenched in American society and throughout much of the world. In the eventuality that McDonald's should some day be down or even out, we may need to find a new model and even a new name for the process, but that process (generically, the ratio-nalization process) will continue, almost certainly at an accelerating rate.

But aren't there countertrends that seem to add up to more than a threat to McDonald's? That add up to a threat to the process of McDonaldization itself? Indeed, there are, and several are worth discussing.

One is the apparent rise of small, non-McDonaldized businesses. The major example in my area, the suburbs of Washington, D.C., is the open-ing of a large number of small, high-quality bakeries (we will discuss a specific example in detail in Chapter 10). Of course, bakeries are not the only example; many different types of such non-McDonaldized small businesses are to be found.

Such enterprises were far more commonplace before the explosive growth of McDonaldized systems. Under pressure from McDonaldized competitors, they seemed to have all but disappeared. But lately, they have begun to reappear, at least in part as a counterreaction against McDonaldization. However, as discussed in the next chapter, these alternatives are probably not a serious threat to McDonaldization.

Another countertrend to McDonaldization has popped up in the sports world. Until recently, promoters have tried to make sporting events, as products, more predictable. The modern, symmetrical baseball stadium makes the balls that hit the walls carom more predictably. Greater consistency from one park to another also standardizes the distance and height a baseball must be hit to be a home run. Modern stadiums were designed to replace nonrationalized and unpredictable baseball stadiums such as Boston's Fenway Park, with its grass playing field and asymmetrical dimensions. Fenway's famous "Green Monster," a close but high wall in left field, makes home runs of relatively short high flies (routine outs in other stadiums), and well-hit but low line drives hit the wall for base hits. At Wrigley Field in Chicago, balls sometimes get lost in the ivy that covers the fences. But stadiums like these have been the exception in major league baseball. Interestingly, nostalgia for the halcyon days of the game seems to be working against symmetrical baseball parks. Some of the newest baseball parks, such as Oriole Park at Camden Yards, are quite asymmetrical. Such parks exploit nostalgia by bringing back many features associated with the older ballparks. For example, Oriole Park retained and rebuilt an old warehouse, which serves as an old-fashioned backdrop for the stadium. Still, although these new "retro" stadiums are throwbacks to some extent, we must remember that they retain many highly rationalized elements.

Yet another countertrend worth noting is the rise of McDonaldized systems that are able to produce high-quality products. I have already discussed on several occasions one major example of this: the large and fast-growing chain of Starbucks coffee shops. Starbucks has shown that it is possible to create a McDonaldized system that dispenses quality products. On the surface, its success challenges McDonaldization as we have known it (especially the mediocrity associated with it) and the McDonaldization thesis. However, Starbucks is in many ways an atypical chain:

- ♦ It sells variations on what is essentially one simple product—coffee.[58]
- ♦ Consistently producing a good cup of coffee is relatively easy, especially with advanced technologies.
- ♦ The patrons of Starbucks are willing to pay a relatively large sum for a good cup of coffee. In fact, getting a cup of coffee at Starbucks may at times cost as much as having lunch at McDonald's.

Most chains are not able to meet these conditions with the result that they are likely to remain both McDonaldized and mediocre. Also, despite its high quality, Starbucks continues to be McDonaldized in many ways (for example, the different types of cups of coffee are predictable from one time or place to another). However, more chains may be inspired to follow the Starbucks' model.

In this context, it is useful to discuss an analogy between Ford/Fordism and McDonald's/McDonaldism. In the early days of the mass production of cars, people had little or no choice; there was little or no variation in the quality of their options. Over the years, of course, and especially today in the era of post-Fordism, people have a great deal of choice in automobiles. Among other things, they can choose high-quality cars (Mercedes Benz or BMW) versus standard-quality cars (Ford Focus or Plymouth Neon). However, cars are all made using standardized parts and assembly line techniques. That is, high-quality cars can be produced using Fordist techniques.

A parallel point can be made about McDonald's and McDonaldization. In its early years, the focus of fast-food restaurants was on the most mundane, low-quality, standardized products. Today, however, people are demanding more choices in foods, including higher-quality foods that do not cause them to sacrifice the advantages of McDonaldization. Just as we can produce a Mercedes Benz using Fordist principles, we can, for example, offer high-quality quiche using the tenets of McDonaldization. The only thing that stands in the way of a chain of restaurants offering a range of high-quality quiches is the likelihood that demand for such a product would be rather low.

Does this mean that, just as some say we have moved into a post-Fordist era, we will soon be entering an epoch of post-McDonaldization? To some degree it does. But just as I think that the argument in favor of post-Fordism is overblown, I would not push the post-McDonaldization thesis too far. Just as today's post-Fordist systems are heavily affected by Fordism, tomorrow's post-McDonaldized systems will continue to be powerfully affected by McDonaldism.

It is possible to McDonaldize any product, even the highest-quality products, at least to some degree. What seems to defy McDonaldization is the kind of thing that is the essence of a fine restaurant ("something," to use a term introduced in Chapter 8): skilled preparation of complex dishes changing from day to day with the availability of ingredients or the whim of the chef.

Starbucks (and high-quality restaurant chains such as Morton's) deviates from other McDonaldized systems largely on one dimension: calculability.

It tends to emphasis quality more and quantity less. But what of the other dimensions? For example, could one build a chain on the basis of inefficiency? Or unpredictability? Or on the use of human rather than nonhuman technology? All these seem highly unlikely. However, a time might come when most systems are so highly McDonaldized that a large market emerges among those who crave a respite from McDonaldization. A chain of inefficient, labor-intensive outlets offering unpredictable goods and services might be able to carve out a niche for itself under such circumstances. However, if such a chain were successful, it would quickly come under pressure to McDonaldize. The paradoxical challenge would be to McDonaldize things such as inefficiency and unpredictability. Ironically, it undoubtedly could be done—a chain that efficiently manifests inefficiency, one that is predictably unpredictable, and so on.

Imagine, for example, a chain of restaurants that rationalizes unpredictability; in postmodern terms it produces a "simulated" unpredictability. (I have dubbed this imaginary burger and fries chain "Miss Hap's"; it would have a steakhouse companion, "Miss Steak's."[59]) Procedures to handle unpredictability would need to be created, procedures designed to attract customers fed up with predictable systems. Then these procedures would be broken down into a series of routine steps, which are then codified and made part of the company manual. New employees would be taught the steps needed to perform unpredictably. In the end, we would have a restaurant chain that had rationalized unpredictability. On cue, for example, the busperson would effortlessly drop a plate of spaghetti into the lap of an occasional customer. Leaving aside the whimsical example, it is clearly possible to rationalize the seemingly irrational and in the process to produce a system that might well have a ready-made market in a highly McDonaldized society. In fact, Seuss Landing at the Universal Studios Florida theme park is "curvy and lumpy" following Dr. Seuss's style rather than characterized by straight lines. It has crooked windows, curled lightning rods, and bent palm trees.[60]

Another potential threat to McDonaldization is "sneakerization." There is considerable evidence that we have entered a postindustrial era that disdains the kinds of standardized, "one-size-fits-all" products at the heart of McDonaldized systems. Instead, what we see is much more customization. Certainly, true customization (for example, made-to-measure suits) is not easily amenable to McDonaldization. However, customization in this context is more akin to niche marketing. With "sneakerization," for example, we now have hundreds, or even thousands, of different styles of sneakers produced for various niches in the market (runners, walkers, aerobic exercisers, and so on). This, of course, is not true customization; sneakers are not being made-to-measure for a specific user. Similar developments are everywhere. Over one hundred types of Walkman are manufactured, three thousand kinds of Seiko watches, and eight hundred models of Phillips color televisions.[61]

The central point to be made here is that in fact sneakerization does not reflect a trend toward de-McDonaldization. Large companies such as Nike produce hundreds of thousands or even millions of pairs of each type of sneaker, with the result that each is amenable to McDonaldized production (as well as marketing, distribution and sales). In fact, one future direction for McDonaldization involves its application to products and services sold in smaller and smaller quantities. Undoubtedly, some absolute lower limit exists below which it is not profitable to McDonaldize (at least to a high degree), but that limit is likely to become lower and lower with further technological advances. That is, we will be able to apply economies of scale to increasingly small production runs. More and different sneakers, more sneakerization, do not represent significant threats to McDonaldization.

A similar argument can be made about what has been termed "mass customization."[62] Examples include Dell building a computer to customer specifications, fine hotels offering in their restaurants napkins and matchboxes with an individual customer's name on them, and Planters offering different size packages of mixed nuts to diverse retailers such as Wal-Mart and 7-Eleven.[63] Logosoftwear.com offers customized caps, shirts, team uniforms, signs, and banners.[64] They will print or embroider your name, address, or logo anywhere you want on, say, a T-shirt and for an additional charge will place them elsewhere on the shirt. This process is less McDonaldized than the mass production of thousands or even millions of the same T-shirt with, say, a Nike logo on it. Mass production is more efficient, it permits greater predictability, more of it is amenable to quantification, and it relies more on nonhuman technologies than the customized production of T-shirts, even the way Logosoftwear.com does it. However, the procedures at Logosoftwear.com are clearly far more McDonaldized than the traditional methods of producing customized clothing. Thus, we are talking here, as is usually the case, about degrees of McDonaldization.

The same kind of thing occurs in the production of intangible products too. CNN pioneered McDonaldized television news (CNN Headline News with its thirty-minute pattern of news, business, sports, and entertainment) not only in the United States but throughout much of the world. However, in recent years, CNN has moved in the direction of regionalizing its news—that is, offering somewhat different news programs to different regions of the world.[65] In addition to such "sneakerized" news, CNN, in collaboration with Oracle, is also offering CNN Custom News through the Internet.[66] The fact is, however, that to a large degree it remains the same homogenous product "sliced and diced" in many different ways.

The production and sale of goods and services in increasingly small quantities and of higher-quality products represent new directions for McDonaldization. But they do not represent de-McDonaldization. Thus, although it is possible to conceive of the decline, even demise of McDonald's, there is little to support the notion that McDonaldization is decelerating, let alone disappearing.[67]

## ♦ CONCLUSION

This chapter has explored various forces impelling McDonaldization, as well as a number of the social and economic barriers to that process. We find not only much that is fostering the process but also a number of barriers to it. However, while such barriers exist, none are likely in the near future to stem the tide in the direction of McDonaldization or reverse it and lead to de-McDonaldization.

Yet no social institution lasts forever. McDonaldization, too, will some-day pass from the scene. McDonaldized systems will remain powerful until the nature of society has changed so dramatically that they can no longer adapt to it. In Chapter 2, I discussed bureaucracies, scientific management, and the assembly line as predecessors of McDonaldization. When McDonald's has, like its predecessors, receded in importance (or even passed from the scene), it will be remembered for the dramatic impact it had, both positive and negative. Sometime in the future, some author will cite McDonald's as a precursor—to what is likely to be a still more rational world. The term *McDonaldization* may no longer be appropriate, but we will need a similar concept to get at the essence of the latest phase and manifestations of rationalization.

# 10

## Dealing with McDonaldization

◆

### A Practical Guide

What can people do to deal with an increasingly McDonaldized world? The answer to that question depends, at least in part, on their attitudes toward McDonaldization. Many people view a McDonaldized world as a "velvet cage." To them, McDonaldization represents not a threat, but nirvana. Weber's metaphor of an iron cage of rationalization communicates a sense of coldness, hardness, and great discomfort. But many people like, even crave, McDonaldization and welcome its proliferation. This is certainly a viable position and one especially likely to be adopted by those who have lived only in McDonaldized societies and who have been reared since the advent of the McDonaldized world. McDonaldized society, the only world they know, represents their standard of good taste and high quality. They can think of nothing better than a world uncluttered with too many choices and options. They like the predictability of many aspects of their lives. They relish an impersonal world in which they interact with human and nonhuman automatons. They seek to avoid, at least in the McDonaldized portions of their world, close human contact. Such people probably represent an increasingly large portion of the population.

For many other people, McDonaldization is a "rubber cage," the bars of which can be stretched to allow adequate means for escape. Such people dislike many aspects of McDonaldization but find others quite appealing. Like those who see themselves in a velvet cage, these people may well like the efficiency, speed, predictability, and impersonality of McDonaldized systems and services. Such people may be busy and therefore appreciate obtaining a meal (or some other McDonaldized service) efficiently. However, they also realize the costs of McDonaldization and therefore seek to escape it when they can. Its efficiencies may even enhance their ability to escape from it. That is, getting a fast meal may allow them the time to luxuriate in other, nonrationalized activities. These are the types of people who on weekends and vacations go into the wilderness to camp the old-fashioned way; go mountain climbing, spelunking, fishing, hunting (without elaborate equipment), antique hunting, and museum browsing; and search out traditional restaurants, inns, and bed and breakfasts. Such people try to humanize their telephone answering machines with creative messages such as, "Sorry, ain't home, don't break my heart when you hear the tone."[1] These are also the people who continue to bake and prepare elaborate home-cooked meals from scratch. Said one devotee of baking from scratch, "The hands-on hobby of bread baking clings to life for reasons that go beyond food. It's an experience and a process. . . . It's the getting there that's the payoff for me. I need to knead." Said another, "There's a magic to it, isn't there?"[2]

However, while the bars may seem like rubber, they are still there. For example, a company that sells prerecorded, humorous messages has come into existence to rationalize the escape route for those who prefer creative answering machine messages. Thus, people can now buy a tape of an impressionist imitating Humphrey Bogart to answer their phone: "Of all the answering machines in the world, you had to call this one."[3] Similarly, for many, home baking has been reduced to the use of bread-baking machines, which do not produce a very good loaf, but "do everything but butter the bread."[4]

The third type of person believes that the McDonaldized cage is made of iron. If the impregnability of the cage has not led such a person to surrender completely, he or she is likely to be deeply offended by the process but to see few, if any, ways out. Unlike the second type of person, these people see escape routes (if they see them at all) providing only temporary respites that will soon fall under the sway of McDonaldization. They share the dark and pessimistic outlook of Max Weber and myself, viewing the future as a "polar night of icy darkness and hardness."[5] These are the severest critics of McDonaldization and the ones who see less and less place for themselves in modern society.[6]

This chapter suggests actions open to each of these three types of people in a McDonaldized world. Those who think of McDonaldization as a velvet cage will do nothing but continue to frequent fast-food restaurants and their clones within other sectors of society and even actively seek to McDonaldize new, as yet unrationalized venues. At the other extreme, those who think of it as an iron cage may want to work for the radical transformation of McDonaldized society, which might involve efforts to return to a pre-McDonaldized world or to create a new non-McDonaldized world out of the rubble created by the fall of the golden arches.

Primarily, however, this chapter is directed at those who think in terms of a rubber or iron cage who are interested in ameliorating some of the problems associated with McDonaldization. In the main, the focus here is on more moderate ways of dealing with McDonaldization.

I begin by discussing some attempts at the creation of non-McDonaldized institutions. Second, I provide an overview of collective efforts to modify McDonaldized systems and limit their negative effects. Finally, I discuss a few examples of other, more individual ways people deal with a McDonaldized society.

## ◆ CREATING "REASONABLE" ALTERNATIVES: SOMETIMES YOU REALLY DO HAVE TO BREAK THE RULES

The excesses of McDonaldization have led to the development of less rationalized alternatives. They do not put a premium on the efficient production of goods and services or the efficient processing of customers. They focus on high-quality products instead of large quantities. They revel in the unpredictabilities of their products and services. Instead of nonhuman technologies, they tend to employ skilled human beings who practice their crafts relatively unconstrained by external controls. Hence, these are not McDonaldized settings for workers or customers.

Alternatives to rationalized settings exist in businesses and other social institutions. For example, food co-ops specializing in vegetarian and health foods offer an alternative to the supermarket.[7] The food is healthier than that in supermarkets, the shoppers are often members of the co-op and therefore actively involved in its management, and the employees are frequently more involved in and committed to their work.

In education, alternatives to highly rational state universities are small schools such as Hampshire College[8] of Amherst, Massachusetts, which has the motto, "Where It's Okay to Go Outside the Lines." (The fast-food restaurants are not above using similar mottoes; for example, Burger King uses "Sometimes You Gotta Break the Rules," even though that's the last thing it wants people to do.) At such colleges, there are no specialized majors or grade point averages.

As nonrationalized institutions become successful, pressures mount to McDonaldize them. Then the issue becomes how to avoid rationalization. One thing to avoid is too much expansion. At some point, any institution will grow so large that it requires increasingly rational principles to function. With larger size comes another danger—franchising, which almost by definition brings with it rationalization. Because greater size and franchising hold out the almost overpowering lure of greater profits, the entrepreneurs behind a nonrationalized business must always keep the reasons for creating such a business in the forefront of their thinking. They must also keep in mind their obligations to the customers who frequent them because they are not McDonaldized. However, as creatures of a capitalist society, they might well succumb to greater profitability and allow their businesses to expand or to be franchised. If they did, I would hope they would use their profits to begin new nonrationalized enterprises.

Three specific examples of entrepreneurs' efforts to resist McDonaldization are discussed below. They show successful resistance as well as its pitfalls. That is, as they became successful, these enterprises were drawn into McDonaldizing their products and operations, and thereby, that which made them successful was undermined. There will also be a discussion of the automobile industry and efforts, especially in Sweden, to change in order to alleviate some of the problems associated with McDonaldization.

## Marvelous Market: "Crunchy Crusts and Full Taste"

Washington, D.C.'s Marvelous Market was a good example of a relatively nonrational, reasonable business.[9] I hasten to add that from its inception it did not eschew all aspects of the rational model. It was a take-out market, emphasizing that its foods could be picked up "quickly" and used to prepare an "effortless" dinner. Thus, even a business developed in reaction to McDonaldization cannot totally ignore the demands of a society grown accustomed to the fast-food system.

However, Marvelous Market was primarily oriented toward reason rather than rationality, most notably in its emphasis on quality rather than quantity. Here is the way its newsletter talked about food: "Cuisine is not just a way of cooking; it is a way of life. Food is much more than the answer to hunger. Food triggers moods and memories, reveals needs and desires, releases tensions and stimulates creativity."[10] (Can you imagine a fast-food restaurant saying this?) The main product at Marvelous Market was bread:

> I [the owner] moved to Washington in 1961, and was told right away, "There is no good bread in Washington." I have heard that flat sentence over the years, thousands of times, probably. It is said commonly by people talking wistfully about the old days.
>
> I don't expect to hear it any longer. The old days have arrived.
>
> Marvelous Market's breads have crunchy crusts and full tastes. . . .
>
> Every day you will find round loaves of walnut bread and rye with currants, great batards of sourdough, chewy country loaves with big holes, bread with rosemary and black olives, baguettes baked once before lunch and, so that they will be perfectly fresh for dinner, again at 4pm.
>
> This bread may be a little startling to people accustomed to . . . soft presliced loaves wrapped in plastic bags. You have not tasted breads like this before; they are . . . addictive.

Marvelous Market's newsletter concluded, "We are most of all determined to sell foods with great taste."

Marvelous Market was not an efficient operation. Its foods were unpredictable. Customers dealt with people rather than automatons or robots. Says Marvelous Market, "You will find a friendly store where the bakers and cooks talk and explain, and work on new recipes for breads and foods."

Stores and shops like this have existed all along, although fast-food outlets have forced many out of business. What is new is the birth of shops specifically created to provide an alternative for people fed up with the excesses of McDonaldization. But for a variety of reasons, I think that places like Marvelous Market are doomed to be restricted to isolated pockets of the McDonaldized society:

- ◆ The growth of such places is restricted by their very nature. With increasing size come ever-greater threats to quality.
- ◆ Not many people have the skills and inclinations needed to open places like Marvelous Market.
- ◆ A population reared from infancy on fast foods will likely regard fast-food products as the ultimate in quality. The McDonald's hamburger bun, not the "batard," is apt to be that generation's standard of quality. One mother of a four-year-old said, "One day I hope that Kevin will appreciate my cooking. . . . But for now, I can't even compete with a Big Mac and fries."[11]
- ◆ Most important, if such markets and shops really show signs of taking over a significant share of the market, the forces of McDonaldization will notice

and seek to transform them into rationalized systems that can be franchised around the world. For instance, Gulf and Western or some other large conglomerate could have bought out Marvelous Market, rationalized its products (much as Kentucky Fried Chicken did to poor old Colonel Sanders's recipes), and created a worldwide chain of Marvelous Markets.

Marvelous Market quickly became a phenomenal success in the Washington area. Because sales grew so dramatically, it could not handle the demand. The market soon had to limit bread purchases to two loaves per person and close for several hours during the day. The owner ordered new, larger ovens, opened another bakery devoted solely to production and not sales, bought a truck to dispense bread at various locations in the Washington area, and began selling his breads to supermarkets and restaurants. As this expansion took place, the owner claimed that his market continued to emphasize quality: "And certainly we're trying to attend to quality, refusing to increase our output faster than we can, refusing to give up our hand-shaping, pulling off our shelves each week hundreds of pounds of bread that don't meet our standards." However, in my view, and the view of many other customers, the quality of the bread did suffer; for example, the store sold more burned loaves. The demand for quantity seemed to cause the quality to deteriorate.

In light of these problems, the owner published an open letter to his customers on November 9, 1991, on the opening of his new bakery. On the one hand, the letter recognized that in various ways growth had created irrationalities:

We are in transition . . .

In the process we have offended some of you because the *quality of our bread* has been erratic, and we haven't adhered to our schedule of breads. . . .

On some days of the week, like Saturday, *we run out of products* before you can come. Many of you who might wish to be on the courts playing tennis or at the firm billing clients, now stand in line Saturday mornings. . . .

Moreover, although you have been fairly tolerant over the months in *quality variations*, we have been offended by them consistently [italics added].

On the other hand, the owner promised that expansion would not mean a decline in quality (and other irrationalities):

So we built a large new bakery, putting into it the best equipment capable of producing our kinds of breads. It is *not automated* equipment; we make breads in the other bakery just as we make them here, *slowly, by hand* . . . we'll be able to get *far more quality and consistency* in our breads.

In addition, we managed to attract as leader of the new bakery . . . one of the premier bakers of the country. . . .

For those who think that we are going to follow the course of other Washington bakeries which began with promise and then compromised, it's not going to happen here.

Clearly aware of the dangers of rationalizing his operation, the owner of Marvelous Market tried to avoid them while he greatly expanded the market's business. However, he failed. The original Marvelous Market went bankrupt, and in 1996 the business was sold. (Undeterred, the owner started a new business, the Bread Line, which specializes in non-McDonaldized "fast food" such as "freshly baked hand-held food"—sandwiches, pizzas, roast pork buns, and so on.[12]) The rapid rise and descent of Marvelous Market represents *both* the attractiveness of offering an alternative to McDonaldization and the almost irresistible pressures to McDonaldize such an operation once it has become successful.

Small businesses like Marvelous Market have grave difficulty today remaining in business. There are generally a number of things they can do, such as developing their own distinctive personality (versus the sameness of the chains), finding a niche not served by the chains, offering different products, and meeting the competition from the chains by extending to customers some of the things the chains do such as accepting returns and offering free gift wrap.[13]

## Ben & Jerry's: "Caring Capitalism"

A far more established and well-known alternative to the highly rationalized business model is the Ben & Jerry's ice cream company, with headquarters in Waterbury, Vermont.[14] With a $12,000 initial investment, Ben & Jerry's began selling ice cream on May 5, 1978, in a refurbished gas station. Neither Ben Cohen nor Jerry Greenfield had any real experience in the business. They set out to sell a high-quality product at a low price. That quality is characterized by the high fat content of the ice cream and the large chunks of add-ins. (In fact, Ben had a "fanatical commitment to producing a high-quality product."[15] However, the use of large chunks did not arise from some rational decision-making process but rather from Ben's inability to distinguish subtle flavors.) The commitment to high quality is reflected in the way Super Fudge Chunk ice cream was created in 1985:

[Ben] came up with a formula that called for liquid chocolate syrup to be pumped into our regular chocolate mix. The result was an ice cream that was incredibly rich, fudgy, and intensely flavorful. For add-ins, Ben settled on white and dark chocolate chunks, chocolate-covered almonds, pecans and walnuts. . . . He set the specs so that the total amount of chunks, by weight and volume, would be 40 percent more than we used in any other flavor. It was by far the most expensive product we'd ever made, but that was of absolutely no consequence to Ben, who never let concerns about cost of goods distract him during the creative process. If it tasted great, Ben figured we'd make money on it.[16]

The first shop was anything but rational. The frequently long lines at the counters reflected its inefficiency. Unpredictability arose in variations in the scoop size and inconsistent service. Calculability was almost nonexistent. Two months after opening, the shop was closed and a sign posted: "'We're closed today so we can figure out if we're making any money.'"[17] From the beginning, and to some degree even now, the technology was primitive and exerted minimal control over employees. In contrast to rationalized, McDonaldized businesses,

Ben and Jerry came to describe their business as being "funky," which to them meant honest, no frills, handmade, and homemade. It was on the opposite end of the spectrum from slick, refined, polished, or packaged.[18]

In a conscious effort to differentiate itself from the cold impersonality of rationalized businesses, Ben & Jerry's has sought to be known as the "company that cares." It seeks to integrate its "progressive" values—for example, addressing the problem of poverty—into its day-to-day business.[19] Unlike most of its rationalized alternatives, Ben & Jerry's cares not only about quality but also about its workers and the environment. The company policy until 1995 was that executives could earn no more than five times the earnings of the lowest-paid worker. Practicing "caring capitalism," the company commits 7.5% of its pretax earnings to its foundation, which makes grants to organizations "committed to imaginative social change"; pays premiums for milk to assist Vermont's ailing family farms; and purchases blueberries from local Indians, peaches from black Georgia farmers, and nuts from the natives of the Amazonian rain forest. Its corporate shareholder meetings involve not only the usual election of directors but also nontraditional activities such as videotaping messages to Congress promoting shareholders' favorite causes.

Ben & Jerry's avoids and limits environmental damage caused by corporate activities. The company recycles plastic and cardboard, uses recycled paper in its offices, and conserves energy. In their stores, they also now use the "eco-pint" container made out of an unbleached brown kraft paperboard as "a critical first step toward a totally biodegradable pint made without added chlorine." In addition, in 2002, they partnered with the Dave Matthews Band and SaveOurEnvironment.org in a campaign to fight global warming.[20] Ben & Jerry's even acknowledges that its main product, its super premium ice cream, endangers the health of at least some people. Its 1990 annual report stated that "ice cream has nutritional value, despite its high fat and sugar content. People who should not eat it for health reasons are free to choose not to eat it."[21] More concretely, in recent years the company has begun to market actively both light ice milk and low-fat frozen yogurt. These products reflect Ben & Jerry's concern for health (although it actively markets its super premium ice cream and gives each of its employees three free pints of ice cream per day). They also reflect an increasingly health-conscious public growing resistant to high-fat ice cream.

The company also sought to avoid some of the effects of McDonaldization on its employees. Employees did not wear uniforms or follow scripts; in fact, Ben & Jerry's "embraced diverse lifestyles, people could dress the way they wanted, and you could personalize your work-place however you saw fit."[22] Ben and Jerry themselves customarily came to work in T-shirts and sneakers. At least until recently, employees seemed to adore their jobs. Workers could exercise at least some choice over the tasks they performed on any given day. The company had a "joy gang," which sought to take some of the drudgery out of work. One could watch "the employees cheerfully yuk it up during a public tour of the pastel-colored Waterbury facility"; an executive answering machine might have told a caller that the officer is unavailable because he or she is "off doing transcendental meditation";[23] and a letter I received from the Ben & Jerry's public relations officer was signed by the "P.R. Info Queen." Then there were the many employee benefits, such as free massages, free health club membership, profit sharing, and child care. Said one worker, "It's what a job should be." One journalist describes it as "the friendliest of employee-friendly firms."[24]

However, from the beginning, Ben & Jerry's showed signs of McDonaldization. For example, there was early concern with the inconsistent size of the scoops and periodic efforts to rationalize the process. In one effort, later abandoned because of its inefficiency, they used scales to weigh the cones. The first Ben & Jerry's franchised "scoop shop" opened in Vermont in 1981; the first out-of-state franchise opened in 1983. Today, there are 235 scoop shops in the United States, as well as a number of others in France, Israel, The Netherlands, and the United Kingdom.[25] To meet demand, others, under license to the company, began to produce some of Ben & Jerry's ice cream. Sales, profits, and the number of employees grew dramatically. As early as 1982, Jerry was conscious of the rationalization underway: "We'd started as this homemade ice cream parlor and evolved into a sort of a manufacturing plant. . . . Where it used to be that we made every batch of ice cream and scooped every cone, now there were people buying our ice cream who had never met Ben or Jerry."[26]

Jerry left the company but returned a few years later to seek to combine economic success with the values that had built the company in the first place. Having achieved international success, the company made a conscious policy to limit growth. In contrast to the growth-conscious leaders of virtually all McDonaldized businesses, "Ben never bought into the argument that a business that wasn't growing was dying."[27] The company limited franchise growth and focused on improving its ties to existing franchisees. Similarly, it slowed the growth in the number of employees. A consultant was hired to improve both job and product quality.[28]

Patricia Aburdene, coauthor (with John Naisbitt) of *Megatrends 2000*, saw Ben & Jerry's as "most certainly . . . the new model of the corporate form that we will see created in the 1990s and into the 21st century."[29] This view stands in contrast to my own, that the highly rationalized McDonald's and not the determinedly nonrationalized Ben & Jerry's will most likely continue to serve as the primary corporate model. At the minimum, to represent a viable alternative, Ben & Jerry's needed to be vigilant and demonstrate that it could both be successful and ward off McDonaldization over the long haul.

Recent developments offer little comfort to the opponents of McDonaldization. Most important, after a long series of problems, Ben & Jerry's was sold to a huge conglomerate, Unilever, in 2000. The company was allowed to operate independently of Unilever's other ice cream businesses, and it retains an independent board of directors. Nevertheless, it seems likely that many of Ben & Jerry's non-McDonaldized policies and procedures will come under pressure from such a necessarily highly rationalized conglomerate. In fact, by the end of 2000, a Unilever executive was appointed the new CEO of Ben & Jerry's. One indication of increasing McDonaldization is that today the company Web site does not list a "P.R. Info Queen," but rather a much more prosaic "Director of Public Relations."[30]

### B&Bs: Alternatives to "McBed, McBreakfasts"

Another example of a nonrationalized alternative to the McDonaldized enterprise is the bed-and-breakfast (B&B). In fact, one news report on B&Bs

was titled, "B&Bs Offer Travelers Break from McBed, McBreakfast."[31] B&Bs are private homes that rent out rooms to travelers and offer them home-style hospitality and a breakfast in the morning. Traditionally, the hosts live in the home while they operate it, taking a personal interest in the guests. Although B&Bs have existed for a long time, they began to boom at the beginning of the 1980s.[32] Some travelers had grown weary of the cold impersonality of rationalized motel rooms and sought out instead the types of nonrationalized accommodations offered by B&Bs. Said one visitor to a B&B, "It was marvelous. . . . The innkeepers treated us like family. It was so comfortable and friendly and charming and romantic."[33]

But success, once again, has brought with it signs of McDonaldization. The range of amenities offered at B&Bs is expanding, and the prices are rising. It is getting harder to distinguish B&Bs from inns or small hotels. Owners increasingly no longer live in the B&B but hire managers to run them. Said one observer, "Your best B & Bs are those where the owner is on the premises. . . . When the owner leaves and hires a manager, bad things start happening. Dust balls start accumulating under the beds, the coffee gets stale, and the toast is burnt."[34] In other words, quality suffers. With the expansion of B&Bs, the American Bed and Breakfast Association came into existence in 1981, and guidebooks about B&Bs proliferated. Now inspections are being undertaken, standards developed, and a rating system implemented. In other words, efforts are underway to rationalize the burgeoning B&B industry.

The pressure to McDonaldize is even greater in England. The British Tourist Authority is pressing B&Bs that want an officially approved crown rating to offer a set of uniform amenities, such as full-length mirrors, ironing boards, telephones, televisions, and trouser presses. Such pressures lead to the homogenization of B&Bs and to increasing difficulty in distinguishing them from motel and hotel accommodations. B&Bs are rated by how many amenities they have rather than more esthetic, subjective, and nonquantifiable factors, such as the warmth of the welcome, the friendliness of the atmosphere, the attractiveness of the setting, or the historical or architectural value of the building.[35]

### Swedish Auto Assembly Lines: Eliminating the Worst Excesses

McDonaldized systems can also modify themselves to eliminate the worst problems associated with the process. The best examples of this reversal are found in the automobile industry and its assembly line technology. The automobile companies have sought, often only after considerable external pressure, to reduce some of the worst irrationalities associated with the automobile and its production. Under pressure from environmentalists, the automobile companies have done a few things to help reduce air pollution from automobiles. When pressed by the government and by severe competition from abroad, the industry made automobiles smaller and more fuel efficient (although it has since moved on to selling huge, gas-guzzling, polluting recreational vehicles).

However, the greatest irrationality in the industry is associated with work on the automobile assembly line. The high speed of the traditional assembly line and the ultraspecialization of the jobs make the work alienating and dehumanizing. For many years, workers and their unions pressed the automobile companies to improve the nature of the work. However, the companies did very little except perhaps pay workers more. With plenty of people available and eager to replace disgruntled workers on the assembly line, companies faced little real pressure to humanize the work.

In the 1960s and 1970s, especially in Sweden, a number of factors helped lead to significant humanization of assembly line work.[36] Many Swedish workers did not like work on the automobile assembly line. Their distaste was even greater because they tended to be more highly educated and to have higher aspirations than their American counterparts. They showed their greater distaste through high levels of absenteeism, tardiness, sabotage, and turnover. Swedish industrialists could not, like their counterparts in the United States, ignore these problems, especially turnover. With little unemployment in Sweden in the 1960s, it was difficult, if not impossible, to replace workers who quit their jobs. Thus, the Swedes were forced to take steps to reduce the dehumanizing and alienating aspects of work on the assembly line.

The Swedish automobile companies (now owned, at least in part, by American automobile companies), Saab and especially Volvo, greatly modified the assembly line to eliminate its worst excesses. The single long line was divided into subsections, each handled by a relatively small work group of about twenty-five to thirty workers. A sense of community was engendered among the members of the work group. Instead of performing highly specialized tasks, each member of the group was allowed to perform a number of more complex tasks. Workers could also trade jobs. Instead of being told which tasks to do and how to do them, work groups and their members could decide for themselves, within limits. These changes met with considerable success, at least initially.

The U.S. automobile industry expressed considerable interest in these humanizing reforms. However, without the pressure of a low unemployment rate, as in Sweden, very few actual changes took place until many years later. And then, the changes came about not so much to humanize work but to compete better with the Japanese automobile industry.

## ♦ FIGHTING BACK COLLECTIVELY: SAVING HEARTS, MINDS, TASTE BUDS, AND THE PIAZZA DI SPAGNA

All the preceding examples can be seen as positive efforts to resist McDonaldization. However, more direct, often more negative, actions are available. If a number of people band together, they can form a movement against a specific component of the process (for example, McDonald's or Wal-Mart) or against the process in general. The three most important examples of such social movements are the national and sometimes international campaigns against McDonald's (the McLibel Support Campaign, National Heart Savers), against fast food (Slow Food), and against Wal-Mart and other chains and superstores (Sprawl-Busters). Let us look briefly at each, as well as a number of efforts by local communities to combat McDonaldization.

### McLibel Support Group: McDonald's Pyrrhic Victory

The origins of the McLibel Support Campaign are traceable to a libel suit brought by McDonald's (United Kingdom) against two unemployed associates of London Greenpeace, Helen Steel and David Morris.[37] They were involved in the distribution of a "fact sheet" that faulted McDonald's for many of the things that it stands accused of in this book (endangering people's health, damaging the environment, and offering poor working conditions and pay). The trial, which ended in January 1997, took more than thirty months to complete and became the longest running libel trial in England's history. The judge found for McDonald's on most counts but on several matters favored the position taken by the defendants. For example, the judge ruled that McDonald's exploits children, deceptively claims that its food is nutritious, and poses a risk to the health of its long-term customers. But this was a Pyrrhic victory for McDonald's, one that was widely seen as a public relations disaster.

McDonald's spent around $15 million on the trial, hiring the best lawyers, while the impecunious Steel and Morris defended themselves. Of further embarrassment to McDonald's is the fact that Steel and Morris continue to appeal the verdict. Says Helen Steel: "Although it's over 12 years since the writs were served on us, Dave and I are still working on McLibel. We've lodged a case with the European Court of Human Rights, arguing the U.K. libel system breaches the right to freedom of speech and the right to a fair trial. We're also both involved with a local group—Haringey Solidarity Group, working on a variety of local issues and campaigns."[38]

Several million copies of the original leaflet "What's Wrong with McDonald's: Everything They Didn't Want You to Know" have been distributed around the world, and it has been translated into a number of languages. More important, a site created on the World Wide Web (www.mcspotlight.org) reports an average of 1.5 million "hits" a month.[39] It has become the heart of a global movement in opposition to McDonald's as well as other aspects of McDonaldization.[40] It acts as the repository for information on actions taken against local McDonald's throughout the world and offers information on conducting such actions.[41] It is also the driving force in the annual Worldwide Anti-McDonald's Day.[42] Among "McSpotlight's" other targets is the Body Shop, which is accused of concealing behind its "green" image the fact that its products are detrimental to the environment, that it pays low wages, and that it encourages consumerism.

McLibel also supports the unionization of McDonald's workers, and there are occasional signs in the United States and elsewhere of efforts in this direction.[43] Although this initiative flies in the face of the general decline of labor unions, should it become successful, it would offer another base of opposition against McDonaldization. However, fast-food restaurants have shown little inclination to deal with dehumanizing working conditions. Burger King, for example, has fought hard against unionization.[44] McDonald's is also well-known for its hostility toward unions. For example, it destroyed a union in Moscow even after having signed a collective agreement with it and shut down a store in Germany to avoid dealing with a workers council.[45] As long as a steady supply of people is willing to work in such settings for even just a few months, fast-food chains will not do much about their working conditions.

In some locales, McDonald's has faced an inadequate supply of workers from its traditional labor pool—teenagers. Rather than improve the work to attract more workers and keep them on the job longer, McDonald's has responded by broadening its hiring net. It now seeks out teenagers who live in distant communities, hires disabled adults, and brings older employees, often retirees, into a program called "McMasters."[46]

In the past, McDonald's would not hire older people because management believed that they would find the low wages and nature of the work intolerable. However, many older workers, such as those permanently laid off from dying or declining "smokestack industries" like steel, are desperate enough for work that they will tolerate these conditions. KinderCare also hires older people to make up for the shortage in younger workers. In fact, one expert said, "For old people who need to be needed, it [KinderCare] sure beats working in McDonald's."[47]

### National Heart Savers Association: McClog the Artery

Numerous nutritionists have criticized fast food. Even comedian and talk-show host Johnny Carson got into the act, labeling the McDonald's burger "McClog the Artery."[48] By far the most notable critic of fast-food fare has been Phil Sokoloff and his nonprofit organization, National Heart Savers Association. In 1990, Sokoloff took out full-page advertisements in the *New York Times* and twenty-two other major newspapers with the headline "The Poisoning of America." The ads singled out McDonald's for serving food high in fat and cholesterol. In addition, Mr. Sokoloff is hailed by many as having done more than anyone else to educate people about cholesterol and heart health. He has indeed spent more than $15 million of his own money to help educate Americans about their potentially unhealthy eating habits.[49]

When Sokoloff first began running such ads in 1988, McDonald's responded to them by calling them "reckless, misleading, the worst kind of sensationalism."[50] But Sokoloff persisted, and in July 1990, he ran ads with the lead "McDonald's, Your Hamburgers *Still* Have Too Much Fat! And Your French Fries Still Are Cooked with Beef Tallow." With surveys showing that people were reducing their patronage of fast-food restaurants, McDonald's and other chains buckled. By mid-1991, Burger King, Wendy's, and McDonald's announced that they would use vegetable oils to cook french fries. Said Sokoloff, "I couldn't be happier. Millions of ounces of saturated fat won't be clogging the arteries of American people."[51] However, recent research has shown that french fries cooked in vegetable oil generally have as much artery-clogging fat as those cooked in beef tallow.[52]

McDonald's has also responded more broadly to these criticisms. In late 1990, McDonald's unveiled its Lean Deluxe burger. Instead of the

Quarter Pounder's twenty grams of fat and 410 calories, the Lean Deluxe burger offered ten grams of fat and 310 calories. (Cinnabon responded to a similar attack by offering a Minibon Delight, with 40% less fat than the Minibon.[53]) Although still far from a diet food, the Lean Deluxe reflected McDonald's responsiveness on this issue. In 1991, McDonald's went even further and introduced the McLean Deluxe hamburger with about 9% fat (still considered far too high by many nutritionists), less than half the fat in a typical McDonald's burger. To accomplish this feat, McDonald's added carrageen, a seaweed extract, to the McLean Deluxe. This additive binds water to the meat, preventing it from being too dry because of its lower fat content. To make up for the loss of flavor, McDonald's added natural beef flavoring to the mix.

Other chains, some of which sell hamburgers with as much as 25% fat, were not quick to jump on the low-fat bandwagon. Said one Hardee's spokesperson, "We're not going to sell a water-and-seaweed burger."[54] Burger King experimented with Weight Watchers products for awhile in the early 1990s but soon halted that effort. After having come under attack for the fat and calories in at least some of its food, in early 1995 Taco Bell announced a new line of products, "Border Lights." These have about half the fat and one-fifth fewer calories than regular menu items. To accomplish this goal, Taco Bell used leaner meat, low-fat cheese, and nonfat sour cream.[55] Subway advertises that its food is less fattening and uses "Jared" in its ads as an example of someone who lost a great deal of weight while eating Subway's low-fat subs.

Interestingly, most of these efforts failed. McDonald's dropped the McLean Deluxe in 1996 because of extremely slow sales.[56] Taco Bell was forced to cut back on its low-fat items.[57] The products tended to be tasteless, often took too long to prepare, and found little acceptance among denizens of fast-food restaurants, who are generally not there to diet. In 2003, McDonald's sought to appeal to those interested in low-fat meals with the introduction of several new salads.

### Slow Food: Creating a Place for Traditional, Regional, High-Quality Food

The Slow Food movement had its origins in a mid-1980s grassroots movement, organized by an Italian food critic,[58] against the opening of a McDonald's in Rome (see below). It is opposed to the homogenization of food styles and takes as its mission "'to give voice to local cooking styles and small-time food producers.'" It has also taken on the task of "fending off the homogenizing effects of European Union regulations on regional culinary treasures."[59] More positively, its objectives are "to provide members from all different countries with an identity."[60]

Slow Food (www.slowfood.com) has sought, quite successfully, to become a force throughout the world and now has about 70,000 members in over forty-five countries.[61] It has a number of specific objectives. First, it supports traditional ways of growing and raising food that is exceptional in quality and taste. Second, it favors the eating of such food as opposed to the alternatives produced by McDonaldized corporations. Third, it seeks to continue local traditions not only in how food is produced but in what is eaten and how it is prepared. Fourth, it favors food preparation that is traditional and as close to handmade as possible. Fifth, it favors raw ingredients that are as specific to the place in which the food is made as possible. Sixth, it fights against environmental degradations that threaten local methods of producing food. Seventh, it supports the local shopkeeper and restaurateur (it favors "local inns and cafes"[62]) in their efforts to survive in the face of the onslaught of powerful global competitors, especially those that are highly McDonaldized. Eighth, it creates local "convivia" throughout the world that meet and engage in actions to further the above causes. Ninth, it has created an "Ark of Taste," which lists hundreds of foods that are endangered and in need of protection. In what is clearly a direct assault on McDonaldized food, it is argued, "Ark foods must live in the modern world—must withstand the threats posed by bland, synthetic, mass-produced and menacingly cheap food."[63] Tenth, it seeks to involve restaurants, communities, cities, national governments, and intergovernmental agencies in the support of slow food. Eleventh, it offers annual Slow Food awards, especially to those "who preserve biodiversity as it relates to food—people who may in the process save whole villages and ecosystems."[64] Twelfth, it offers special prizes and support to Third World efforts, and it seeks to help organize local efforts there to help conserve "prizewinners' plants, animals, and foods."[65]

In these and many other ways, Slow Food is fighting to sustain the continued existence of non-McDonaldized alternatives within the realm of food. Such alternatives in all realms and of all types need organizations like Slow Food, and efforts such as these, if it, and we, are not to be inundated by a sea of McDonaldized phenomena. There is no reason why similar global organizations cannot be formed with the objective of sustaining non-McDonaldized alternatives, and warding off the onslaught of McDonaldization, in various realms.

While the maintenance and defense of non-McDonaldized alternatives are both important, it must be remembered that the Slow Food Movement does not want to be seen as creating a "museum." That is, it is not interested in simply maintaining the past and present, but it is also concerned with creating the future. This means that it is important for it, and all organizations like it, to be actively involved in encouraging the creation of *new*, non-McDonaldized forms. This may involve new combinations of that which already exists or the creation of that which is entirely new. The latter is no easy task, but it must not be lost sight of in the effort to maintain extant, non-McDonaldized forms.

This is clearly a movement of a very different order from either the McLibel group or National Heart Savers. The impoverished targets of the McDonald's libel suit are a far cry from the mainly well-heeled gourmets drawn to Slow Food, its convivia around the world, and its regular meetings—Salone del Gusto—oriented to the appreciation of gourmet food. Most of the supporters of McLibel would be shocked by the prices for a meal at the Salone del Gusto; the supporters of National Heart Savers would be appalled at the number of smokers at the Slow Food meetings and the fat content of many of the foods (the pasta dish tagliolini has 40 egg yolks per kilo). Slow Food is focusing mainly on the issue of the poor quality of food (and, implicitly, almost all other products) in McDonaldized restaurants and food emporia, while McLibel is focusing on threats to health (as is National Heart Savers), the environment, and the workers.

However, Slow Food does have a more populist side in which it seeks to support and reward small farmers, beekeepers, and other workers who continue to produce high-quality products in traditional ways. Slow Food is also very concerned about the environment. Whatever the differences in goals, methods, and social class of most of the participants, these groups all share a hostility to the McDonaldization of society and are seeking to ameliorate its worst excesses, if not support and create alternatives to it.

Mention should also be made of the related Slow Cities movement that seeks to bring many of these principles to bear on cities in Italy and beyond. It seeks to go beyond food, to protect art, architecture, a way of life—culture in general—from McDonaldization (and Americanization). Said the mayor of the Tuscan city of Greve, "The American urban model has invaded our cities and risks making Italian towns look the same. We want to stop this kind of globalization."[66] This mayor also links the Slow Cities movement to sustaining alternatives to McDonaldization: "We can't stop large, fast-food chains [from] coming here if they request it, but we hope that people who come to our towns will not want to eat exactly the same hamburger they can eat in Melbourne, London or Paris, but want something genuine and different."[67]

## Sprawl-Busters: A "Hit List" of McDonaldized Superstores

Sprawl-Busters (www.sprawl-busters.com), founded by Al Norman, grew out of his successful effort to keep Wal-Mart out of his hometown, Greenfield, Massachusetts. Now the organization offers consulting services to local communities that want to keep out McDonaldized superstores and chains. For his efforts, the TV program *60 Minutes* called Norman "the guru of the anti-Wal-Mart movement."[68]

Among the services offered by Sprawl-Busters to local communities is help with overseeing media operations, raising money, petitioning for referendums, conducting data searches, and the like. Beyond Wal-Mart, organizations on Sprawl-Buster's "hit list" include Super Kmart, Home Depot, CVS, and Rite-Aid. The main objective is to keep such superstores and chains out in order to protect local businesses and the integrity of the local community. As of April 2003, they claim to have prevented the entry of "big box" stores into almost 200 communities.[69] Al Norman has recently published *Slam-Dunking Wal-Mart: How You Can Stop Superstore Sprawl in Your Hometown.*[70]

## Local Protests: Not Wanting to Say "Bye-Bye to the Neighborhood"

Some local communities have fought hard on their own, at times successfully, against the invasion of fast-food restaurants[71]—against the garish signs and structures, traffic, noise, and rowdy nature of some of the clientele drawn to fast-food restaurants. Most generally, they have fought against the irrationalities and assaults on tradition that the fast-food restaurant represents. Thus, some of the communities highly attractive to fast-food chains (for example, Sanibel Island in Florida) have few, if any, fast-food restaurants.

The resort village of Saugatuck, Michigan, fought McDonald's attempt to take over the site of a quaint old cafe called Ida Red's. Said one local businessman, "People can see McDonald's anywhere—they don't come to Saugatuck for fast food." The owner of a local inn seemed to recognize that the town was really resisting the broader process of rationalization: "It's the Howard Johnson's, the McDonald's, the malls of the world that we're fighting against. . . . You can go to a mall and not know what state you're in. We're a relief from all that."[72]

Outside the United States, the resistance has often been even greater. The opening of the first McDonald's in Italy, for example, led to widespread protests involving several thousand people. The Italian McDonald's opened near the picturesque Piazza di Spagna in Rome adjacent to the headquarters of the famous fashion designer Valentino. One Roman politician claimed that McDonald's was "the principal cause of degradation of the ancient Roman streets."[73] More recently, protests against the opening of a McDonald's in the medieval main market square of Krakow, Poland, led one critic to say,

> The activities of this firm are symbolic of mass industrial civilization and a superficial cosmopolitan way of life. . . . Many historic events happened in this place, and McDonald's would be the beginning of the cultural degradation of this most precious urban area.[74]

The elegant resort city of Hove is the largest town (67,602 inhabitants) in Great Britain without a McDonald's or a Burger King.[75] Because of the resistance to the fast-food invasion, Hove has a thriving and diverse restaurant business, including on its main street "six Italian, five Indian and two French restaurants, two pizza parlours, two kebob shops, Japanese, Thai, American, Spanish, Turkish and English restaurants, a continental brasserie, a coffee shop and a fish-and-chip emporium."[76]

Other McDonaldized businesses have encountered similar opposition. For example, in San Francisco, local businesses blocked, at least for a time, the opening of a new Blockbuster outlet. Said the owner of a local video store, "Blockbuster is using predatory methods to kill off the smaller stores. If we get Blockbuster, then McDonald's, Boston Chicken and Sizzler are next, and you can say bye-bye neighborhood."[77]

Despite the passionate resistance to McDonaldized businesses in some locales, few communities have successfully kept franchises out completely. Similarly, small communities have usually been unsuccessful[78] in keeping out Wal-Mart stores, even though they usually devastate local businesses when they move in[79] and hurt the communities further on the rare occasions when they depart.[80]

In response to such protests and criticisms, and as an attempt to forestall them in the future, McDonald's is building outlets that fit better into the community in which they are placed. Thus, a McDonald's in Miami's

Little Havana has a Spanish-style roof and feels more like a hacienda. Another in Freeport, Maine, looks like a quaint New England inn.[81] The 12,000th McDonald's restaurant, opened in 1991, stands in a restored 1860s white colonial house on Long Island. The interior has a 1920s look.[82] McDonald's managing director of Polish operations said, "We took a 14th-century building that was devastated and restored it to its natural beauty."[83]

In Vienna, McDonald's opened "McCafe." However, the effort is being opposed by the Union of Vienna Coffee Houses, which fears the closing of the famed local coffee houses. Said the owner of one such cafe, "'You can never bring them back. . . . What we offer is an extension of the Viennese living room—a lifestyle.'"[84]

McDonald's has also shown signs of responding to environmental groups, creating packaging less harmful to the environment.[85] In 1990, McDonald's began eliminating its polystyrene "clamshell" hamburger box. The box had been attacked by environmentalists because the production of the boxes generated pollutants. More important, the boxes lingered for decades in landfills or on the sides of roads. A paper wrapping with a cellophane-like outer wrapper took their place. In addition, McDonald's has purchased more than $4 billion in recycled products and reduced packaging by over 200,000 tons. Following measures recommended by the EPA's Green Lights program, they have started designing their buildings to be more energy efficient and trained managers to reduce energy use in their restaurants. Furthermore, McDonald's corporation has entered into a partnership with Conservation International in an effort to focus on water and energy conservation and the protection and maintenance of animal and plant biodiversity.[86] Another fast-food franchise, Hardee's, announced in 1991 that it would use recycled polystyrene in its packages. Said one environmentalist, "I think that the public is pressuring these people into taking positive steps."[87]

Responses to complaints indicate that the fast-food restaurant is quite an adaptable institution, although all these adaptations remain within the broad confines of rationality. Some people have actually complained about the disappearance of the huge, old-fashioned golden arches, and at least one McDonald's franchise has responded by bringing them back. On the other hand, in response to complaints from upscale clientele about the dehumanizing dining environment, a McDonald's in Manhattan's financial district offers Chopin on a grand piano, chandeliers, marble walls, fresh flowers, a doorman, and hosts who show people to their tables. The golden arches are virtually invisible. However, besides a few classy additions to the menu (espresso, cappuccino, tarts), the menu is largely the same as in all other McDonald's (albeit with slightly higher prices). Said one visitor, underscoring the continuity between this franchise and all others, "A smashing place, and the best thing is you can still eat with your fingers."[88]

What keeps the fast-food business on its toes is the knowledge that food fashions change; even the giant franchises can find themselves on the brink of bankruptcy. By 1990, the Chock Full o' Nuts chain of coffee shops in New York City was left with only one outlet; at its peak in the 1960s, it comprised about eighty restaurants. Its nutty cheese sandwich, "cream cheese and chopped nuts on dark raisin bread wrapped in plain, waxed paper" has been described as "the original fast food."[89] Then there is Howard Johnson's (HoJo's), once a chain restaurant leader but now reduced to a motel chain. Said an expert on restaurant chains, "In the '60s, [Howard Johnson's] were the No. 1 chain. . . . They could have had the whole world at their fingertips, but they sat on it. . . . They were stuck in the 1950s and 1960s. Howard Johnson's just sat there with its ice cream and clams."[90]

## ♦ COPING INDIVIDUALLY: "SKUNK WORKS," BLINDFOLDED CHILDREN, AND FANTASY WORLDS

Individuals uncomfortable with or opposed to McDonaldization can challenge it in many ways. People who think of the bars of the rationalized cage as made of rubber may choose to extract the best of what the McDonaldized world has to offer without succumbing to its dangers and excesses. This is not easy to do, however, because the lure of McDonaldized institutions is great, and it is easy to become a devotee of, and enmeshed in, rationalized activities. Those who use rationalized systems for what they have to offer need to keep the dangers of McDonaldization always in the forefront of their thinking. But being able to get a bank balance in the middle of the night, to avoid hospital emergency rooms by having minor problems cared for at "McDoctors," and to lose weight quickly and safely at Jenny Craig, among many other conveniences, are all attractive possibilities for most people.

How can people take advantage of the best that the McDonaldized world has to offer without becoming imprisoned in that world? For one thing, they can use McDonaldized systems only when such use is unavoidable or when what they have to offer cannot be matched by nonrationalized systems. To help limit their use, perhaps we should put warning labels on the front doors of McDonaldized systems much like those found on cigarette packs:

WARNING!
Sociologists have found that habitual use of McDonaldized systems is hazardous to your physical and psychological well-being and to society as a whole.

Above all, people should avoid the routine and systematic use of McDonaldized systems. To avoid the iron cage, they must seek out nonrationalized alternatives whenever possible. Such a search for these niches is difficult and time-consuming. Using the various aspects of McDonaldized society is far easier than finding and using nonrationalized alternatives. Avoiding McDonaldization requires hard work and vigilance.

The most extreme step would be to pack up and leave the highly McDonaldized society of the United States. However, many, if not most, other societies have embarked on the rationalization process or are about to. Thus, a move to another society might buy people some time, but eventually, McDonaldization would have to be confronted, this time in a less familiar context.

## Nonrationalized Niches: Life in the Skunk Works

Far less extreme than seeking to exit a McDonaldized society are efforts to carve out nonrationalized niches in rationalized systems. I will focus here on the work world; however, similar niches can be carved in every other social institution.

The ability to carve out such a niche tends to be related to one's position in the occupational hierarchy. Those in higher-ranking occupations have a greater ability to create such niches than those in lower-status occupations. Physicians, lawyers, accountants, architects, and the like in private practice have the capacity to create such an environment for themselves. Within large organizations, the general (unwritten) rule for those at the top seems to be to impose rationality on others, especially those with little power, while keeping their own work as nonrational as possible. Rationalization is something to be imposed on others, especially those with little power.

Some people in lower-ranking occupations are also in a position to be largely free of rationalization. For example, taxi drivers, because they work primarily on their own, are free to construct a nonrationalized work life. They can go where they want, choose their passengers, and eat and take breaks when they wish. Similar possibilities exist for night guards and maintenance workers in automated factories. Those who work on their own or in relative isolation within an organization are in a better position to create a nonrationalized work environment.

Take the position of a tenured senior college professor at a large state university (no names, please) as an extreme example of a position that enables the creation of a nonrationalized work life in an otherwise highly rational university bureaucracy. This semester, for example, our professor teaches on Monday afternoons from 3:00 to 4:15 and evenings from 6:30 to 9:00 and on Wednesday afternoons from 3:00 to 4:15. In addition, office hours (about two hours a week), an occasional faculty meeting (one hour, once a month), and an occasional committee meeting are the only other work hours determined by the university. The professor will often be on campus at other times but for various appointments arranged at her convenience. Furthermore, the preset class hours run for only thirty weeks, or two full semesters, each year, leaving the other twenty-two weeks virtually free. Thus, for only a few hours a week and a little more than half the year does she have to be at any particular place doing any particular thing at any particular time. In other words, her work time is almost totally nonrationalized.

If she wanted, as a tenured full professor, she could idle her days away. However, she chooses to occupy herself with professional activities, such as writing books and articles. But how, when, and what she writes is totally nonrationalized: in the middle of the night or early in the morning; on a word processor, a yellow pad, or even a stone tablet; about McDonaldization or the latest demographic trends. She can write clad in a business suit or in her bathrobe. She can take a break when she likes, go for daily walks with her dog, or listen to her favorite book-on-tape whenever she pleases. In short, her work life is almost totally nonrationalized.

It is possible to find such nonrationalized work in other types of organizations, at least to some degree. For example, some high-tech organizations have created and encouraged the use of "skunk works," where people can be insulated from routine organizational demands and do their work as they see fit.[91] Skunk works emphasize creativity and innovation, not conformity. Thomas Peters and Robert Waterman describe them as singularly nonrational, even irrational, work settings:

They were creating almost radical *decentralization and autonomy,* with its attendant *overlap, messiness* around the edges, *lack of coordination, internal competition,* and somewhat *chaotic* conditions, in order to breed the entrepreneurial spirit. They had *forsworn* a measure of *tidiness* in order to achieve regular innovation [italics added].[92]

The italicized terms in the preceding quotation would all be considered nonrational or irrational from the point of view of a McDonaldized society.

Nonrationalized times and places tend to be conducive to creativity. It is difficult to be creative in the face of incessant, externally imposed, and repetitive demands. Thus, working in a nonrationalized setting serves not only the individual but many employers and society as well. All need a steady influx of creative new ideas and products, which are far less likely to emanate from rigidly controlled bureaucratic settings than they are from skunk works.

Even in highly rationalized organizations, people can carve out nonrationalized workspaces and times. For example, by finishing routine tasks quickly, a worker would leave himself or herself time to engage in nonrationalized, albeit work-related, activities. I am not suggesting that finding nonrationalized occupations or carving out nonrationalized spaces within McDonaldized organizations is easy. Nor am I suggesting that everyone can operate in a nonrationalized way all the time. But it is possible for some people, some of the time, to carve out nonrationalized niches for themselves.

I would not want to push this idea too far for several reasons:

♦ Rationalized organizations provide the resources and settings needed to do creative work and the outlets for that work. In other words, nonrationalized niches of creativity need the support of rationalized systems.

♦ No large-scale organization can exist if it is composed of nothing but such niches. The result would be organizational chaos.

♦ Not everyone wants to work, or is capable of working, in such nonrationalized niches; indeed, many people prefer their workdays to be highly routinized.

Thus, I am not arguing for a work world composed of nothing but creative occupational spaces. However, I do assert the need for more nonrationalized niches in an otherwise highly rationalized world.

People may also be able to create and operate nonrationalized niche businesses in an otherwise highly McDonaldized environment. Marvelous Market, Ben & Jerry's, and B&Bs are examples of such businesses. Some

independent video stores have been able to survive by focusing on foreign movies, classics in black-and-white, movies from independent filmmakers, movies aimed at specific ethnic or racial groups, and especially, the pornographic movies eschewed by chains like Blockbuster.[93] They also offer more personalized service (not charging for late returns if there is a good excuse, offering suggestions for good movies, taking special orders), a wider range of products, even pickup and delivery. Local, independent restaurants, too, have been able to find niches for themselves in an industry that is probably more McDonaldized than any other.[94] Said the owner of a small local chain (but a chain nonetheless) of restaurants: "'There are always going to be savvy restaurateurs who can beat the chains. . . . All is not lost.'"[95] Some embattled small local bookshops have survived by, for example, hosting discussion groups, having regular author appearances, specializing in particular kinds of books, and so on.[96]

## A Range of Individual Actions: If All Else Fails, Save the Children

The following list contains suggestions for individuals who want to combat McDonaldization.[97] Some of these suggestions are offered "tongue-in-cheek," although the reader should not lose sight of the fact that McDonaldization is an extremely serious problem.

- ♦ For those of you who can afford it, avoid living in apartments or tract houses. Try to live in an atypical environment, preferably one you have built yourself or have had built for you. If you must live in an apartment or a tract house, humanize and individualize it.
- ♦ Avoid daily routine as much as possible. Try to do as many things as possible in a different way from one day to the next.
- ♦ More generally, do as many things as you can for yourself. If you must use services, frequent nonrationalized, nonfranchised establishments. For example, lubricate your own car. If you are unwilling or unable to do so, have it done at your local, independent gasoline station. Do not, at all costs, frequent one of the franchised lube businesses.
- ♦ Instead of popping into H&R Block at income-tax time, hire a local accountant, preferably one who works out of an office in his or her home.
- ♦ Similarly, the next time a minor medical or dental emergency leads you to think of a "McDoctor" or a "McDentist," resist the temptation and go instead to your neighborhood doctor or dentist, preferably one in solo practice.
- ♦ The next time you need a pair of glasses, use the local storefront optometrist rather than Pearle Vision, for example.
- ♦ Avoid Hair Cuttery, Supercuts, and other haircutting chains; go instead to a local barber or hairdresser.

- At least once a week, pass up lunch at McDonald's and frequent a local cafe or deli. For dinner, again at least once a week, stay at home, unplug the microwave, avoid the freezer, and cook a meal from scratch.
- To really shake up the clerk at the department store, use cash rather than your credit card.
- Send back to the post office all junk mail, especially that addressed to "occupant" or "resident."
- The next time a computer phones you, gently place the phone on the floor, thereby allowing the disembodied voice to drone on, occupying the line so that others will not be bothered by such calls for awhile.
- When dialing a business, always choose the option that permits you to speak to a real person.
- Never buy artificial products such as Molly McButter and Butter Buds.
- Seek out restaurants that use real china and metal utensils; avoid those that use materials such as Styrofoam that adversely affect the environment.
- Organize groups to protest abuses by McDonaldized systems. As you have seen, these systems do adapt to such protests. If you work in such a system, organize your coworkers to create more humanized working conditions.
- If you must frequent a fast-food restaurant, dine at one, such as In-N-Out Burger (a chain—*not* franchised—of almost two hundred restaurants in California, Nevada, and Arizona) that has demonstrated sensitivity to the dangers of McDonaldization by, for example, making its hamburgers to order one at a time from fresh (not frozen) meat and by cutting its french fries in the restaurant from fresh potatoes.
- If you are a regular at McDonald's, try to get to know the counter people. Also, do whatever else you can to humanize and subvert the system. For example, instead of hastening through their meal, many breakfast customers, especially among the elderly, form informal "breakfast clubs" and "come every day of the week to read their papers, chat, drink coffee, and gobble down an Egg McMuffin."[98] If breakfasts can be de-McDonaldized, why not other meals? Why not other aspects of the fast-food experience?
- Read the *New York Times* rather than *USA TODAY* once a week. Similarly, watch PBS news once a week, with its three long stories, rather than the network news shows with their numerous snippets or, god forbid, CNN Headline News.
- More generally, watch as little television as possible. If you must watch TV, choose PBS. If you must watch one of the networks, turn off the sound and avert your eyes during commercials. After all, most commercials are sponsored by enterprises that tout the virtues of rationalization.
- Avoid most finger foods. If you must eat finger foods, make them homemade sandwiches and fresh fruits and vegetables.
- On your next vacation, go to only one locale and get to know it and its inhabitants well.

- ◆ Never enter a domed stadium or one with artificial grass; make periodic pilgrimages to Fenway Park in Boston and Wrigley Field in Chicago.
- ◆ Avoid classes with short-answer tests graded by computer. If a computer-graded exam is unavoidable, make extraneous marks and curl the edges of the exam so that the computer cannot deal with it.
- ◆ Seek out small classes; get to know your professors.
- ◆ Go to no movies that have roman numerals after their names.

Regina Schrambling has developed a variety of strategies similar to those in the previous list for dealing with the health threats (especially Salmonella) posed by the rationalization of food production.[99] Interestingly, Schrambling recognizes that returning to the prerationalized raising of chickens is not the answer. She argues that the "lifestyles" of such chickens, including "worm-grubbing," led to the possibility of Salmonella even in the prerationalized days of chicken production. Nevertheless, she prefers to shop at farmers' markets and buy chickens raised the older way. She buys her eggs "in hand-packed boxes from the same New York State farmer." In her view, such eggs are fresher and cleaner than mass-produced eggs. She also purchases cantaloupes from farmers' markets and refuses to buy them in supermarkets because they have been in transit so long that there is an increased risk of spoilage and disease. Although rationalization has allowed people to eat fruits and vegetables year-round, it creates costs and dangers. As she puts it, they have been raised "in countries where we would never dare drink the water, where pesticides banned here are used freely." Thus, of course, she buys fruits and vegetables only during their local seasons.

More generally, Schrambling argues that people need to understand the limited seasons for fruits and vegetables:

We would remember that the strawberry crop is really as fleeting as fireflies, that sweet corn waits for no one; it's best when eaten within hours of leaving the stalk. There's nothing like the farmers' market in January, with only potatoes and squash and apples for sale, to give a deep new appreciation of nature's cycles.

People need to understand that "we can't have all of the food all of the time."[100]

Schrambling's position seems reasonable, even laudable, but the forces of McDonaldization continue to press forward. For example, science has recently discovered that genetically altered tomatoes can be prevented from producing the gas that causes them to ripen.[101] Thus, the tomatoes, and potentially many other fruits and vegetables, can be left on the vine until maturity instead of being picked early, shipped great distances without refrigeration, stored for weeks, and then ripened through exposure to ethylene gas when the retailer wishes to put them up for sale. If this technique proves viable commercially, people will, contrary to Schrambling, have many fruits and vegetables and cut flowers "all the time."

Similarly, the strawberry crop may now not be as "fleeting" as Schrambling says. The Driscoll strawberry, grown in Watsonville, California ("the strawberry capital of the world"), is big, glossy, and, most important, available all year round because of the favorable climate. Surprisingly, Driscoll strawberries "actually have some flavor, too."[102]

Given the attention that McDonaldized systems devote to marketing to children, it is particularly important that steps be taken to prevent children from becoming mindless supporters. Fast-food restaurants sponsor cartoon programs, have tie-ins with movies aimed at children, and offer numerous promotions involving toys. In fact, McDonald's has become the "the world's biggest toymaker on a unit basis," commissioning about 1.5 billion toys per year, more than Hasbro or Mattel.[103] According to the president of a sales promotion agency, "'In research, we've seen the kids are clearly motivated by the toy, not the meal.'"[104]

To protect children, try the following:

♦ Instead of using a "McChild" care center, leave your child with a responsible neighbor interested in earning some extra money.
♦ Keep your children away from television as much as possible and encourage them to participate in creative games. It is especially important that they not be exposed to the steady barrage of commercials from rationalized institutions, especially on Saturday morning cartoon shows.
♦ Lead efforts to keep McDonaldization out of the school system.
♦ If you can afford it, send your child to a small, non-McDonaldized educational institution.
♦ Above all, when possible, avoid taking your children to fast-food restaurants or their clones in other domains. If no alternatives are present (for example, you're on a highway and the only options are various fast-food chains), consider blindfolding your child until the ordeal is over. (Remember, some of these suggestions are only half serious.)

### Freedom: If You Can't Cope, Can You Escape?

What if, as likely, all your collective and individual efforts at coping with McDonaldization fail? What else can you do? Suicide is one possibility, but that does seem too extreme, even to me. However, some less radical but still effective ways of escaping rationalized society may exist.

One possibility is to flee to an area that has been designed as an escape area. In his book *Ways of Escape,* Chris Rojek discusses such obvious examples as theme parks (for example, Disney World) and heritage sites (for example, Gettysburg battlefields), as well as less obvious sites such as "black spots" (for example, John F. Kennedy's grave site in Arlington Cemetery or Auschwitz) and "literary landscapes" (for example, Ernest Hemingway's haunts in Key West, Florida).[105] To the degree that such sites are not McDonaldized, they could serve as escape areas. However, the problem is the strong pressure to McDonaldize them, especially when they are designed for or come to attract hordes of people. Disney World was McDonaldized from the beginning, and the others tend to grow more McDonaldized over time as they attract more people.

More generically, Rojek analyzes tourist sites such as the beach and the wilderness as places that offer people "loopholes of freedom."[106] Again, to the degree that such sites remain largely or totally free of McDonaldization, they can serve as regions of escape. However, they too are under powerful pressure to McDonaldize as soon as a significant number of people discover them as escape zones.

In *Escape Attempts: The Theory and Practice of Resistance to Everyday Life,* Stanley Cohen and Laurie Taylor outline a number of highly diverse ways of escaping the routines of everyday life.[107] Although not all routines are the result of McDonaldization (sometimes, for example, people develop their own routines), an increasing number are part of this process. Many of the alternatives discussed by Cohen and Taylor are subject to McDonaldization, but two deserve some attention. The first is escaping within oneself, especially through fantasy. No matter how McDonaldized the setting, one can escape into an internal fantasy world of one's own making. Thus, while wandering through the highly McDonaldized fantasies created by Disney World, people can dwell on fantasies of their own creation, perhaps even inspired by the prefabricated fantasies around them. There is a tendency to buy into, and internalize, those prefabricated, McDonaldized fantasies, but they can be evaded within the depths of one's own fantasy world. Escape into one's own fantasy world does nothing about challenging or changing McDonaldized systems, but it does offer those who want it a viable way out.

Another possibility is what Cohen and Taylor call "trips to the edge" or what Michel Foucault calls "limit experiences."[108] These are defined by "excess" and "outrage" involving things like hard drugs. But one need not buy into these precise methods in an effort to act in an excessive and outrageous manner. One can, for example, "leave everything behind, travel light."[109] Walk across the United States (avoiding highways, motel chains, and fast-food restaurants, among many other places), camp (with nothing that has labels like REI, L.L. Bean, Coleman, and Winnebago) on a mountain in Tibet, take a year off and write that book or song or symphony you've always wanted to write (preferably using pad and pencil). Oh, you can use drugs or sex to excess if you like, but they are not the only ways to go to the limit or the edge not yet reached by McDonaldization. Just remember, although you might fall off (there may be no McDonaldized nets to save you), the journey should be exhilarating. But hurry, McDonaldization is NEVER far behind.

#### ◆ CONCLUSION

A wide range of steps can be taken to cope with or escape from McDonaldization. However, I hold little hope that such actions would reverse the trend toward McDonaldization, even if most of us were to employ them. But despite this fatalistic view, I think the struggle is worthwhile:

- ◆ Making the effort will mitigate the worst excesses of McDonaldized systems.
- ◆ It will lead to the discovery, creation, and use of more niches where individuals and groups who are so inclined can escape McDonaldization for at least a part of their day or even a larger portion of their lives.
- ◆ Perhaps most important, the struggle itself is ennobling. In nonrationalized, individual, and collective struggles, people can express genuinely human reason in a world that in nearly all other ways has set up rationalized systems to deny people this expression.

Although I have emphasized the irresistibility of McDonaldization throughout this book, my fondest hope is that I am wrong. Indeed, a major motivation behind this book is to alert readers to the dangers of McDonaldization and to motivate them to act to stem its tide. I hope that people can resist McDonaldization and create instead a more reasonable, more human world.

Some years ago, McDonald's was sued by the famous French chef, Paul Bocuse, for using his picture on a poster without his permission. Enraged, Bocuse said, "How can I be seen promoting this tasteless, boneless food in which everything is soft." Nevertheless, Bocuse seemed to acknowledge the inevitability of McDonaldization: "There's a need for this kind of thing . . . and trying to get rid of it seems to me to be as futile as trying to get rid of the prostitutes in the Bois de Bologne."[110] Lo and behold, two weeks later, it was announced that the Paris police had cracked down on prostitution in the Bois de Bologne. Said a police spokesperson, "There are none left." Thus, just as Chef Bocuse was wrong about the prostitutes, perhaps I am wrong about the irresistibility of McDonaldization. Yet before I grow overly optimistic, it should be noted that "everyone knows that the prostitutes will be back as soon as the operation is over. In the spring, police predict, there will be even more than before."[111] Similarly, it remains likely that no matter how intense the opposition, the future will bring with it more rather than less McDonaldization.

Even if McDonaldization grows more prevalent, I hope that you will follow some of the advice outlined in this chapter for protesting and mitigating its worst effects. Faced with Max Weber's iron cage and the image of a future dominated by the polar night of icy darkness and hardness, I hope that if nothing else you will consider the words of the poet Dylan Thomas: "Do not go gentle into that good night . . . Rage, rage against the dying of the light."[112]

# Bibliography

Rather than repeating the citations listed in the endnotes, I would like to use this section to cite some of the major academic works that served as resources for this book. There are three categories of such resources. The first is the work of Max Weber, especially that dealing with rationalization. The second is the work of various neo-Weberians who have modified and expanded on Weber's original ideas. Finally, there is a series of works that focus on specific aspects of our McDonaldizing society.

## ◆ WORKS BY MAX WEBER

Max Weber. *The Protestant Ethic and the Spirit of Capitalism*. New introduction and translation by Stephen Kalberg, 3rd Roxbury ed. Los Angeles, CA: Roxbury 2002.

Max Weber. "Religious Rejections of the World and Their Directions." In H. H. Gerth and C. W. Mills, eds., *From Max Weber: Essays in Sociology*. New York: Oxford University Press, 1915/1958, pp. 323–359.

Max Weber. "The Social Psychology of the World Religions." In H. H. Gerth and C. W. Mills, eds., *From Max Weber: Essays in Sociology*. New York: Oxford University Press, 1915/1958, pp. 267–301.

Max Weber. *The Religion of China: Confucianism and Taoism*. New York: Macmillan, 1916/1964.

Max Weber. *The Religion of India: The Sociology of Hinduism and Buddhism*. Glencoe, IL: Free Press, 1916–1917/1958.

Max Weber. *The Rational and Social Foundations of Music*. Carbondale: Southern Illinois University Press, 1921/1958.

Max Weber. *Economy and Society: An Outline of Interpretive Sociology*. Edited by Guenther Roth and Claus Wittich; translated by Ephraim Fischoff et al. Berkeley: University of California Press, 1978.

Max Weber. *General Economic History*. Translated by Frank H. Knight. Mineola, NY: Dover, 1927/2003.

## ◆ WORKS BY NEO-WEBERIANS

Rogers Brubaker. *The Limits of Rationality: An Essay on the Social and Moral Thought of Max Weber.* London: Allen & Unwin, 1984.

Randall Collins. "Weber's Last Theory of Capitalism: A Systematization." *American Sociological Review* 45(1980):925–942.

Randall Collins. *Weberian Sociological Theory.* Cambridge, UK: Cambridge University Press, 1985.

Arnold Eisen. "The Meanings and Confusions of Weberian 'Rationality.'" *British Journal of Sociology* 29(1978):57–70.

Harvey Greisman. "Disenchantment of the World." *British Journal of Sociology* 27(1976):497–506.

Harvey Greisman and George Ritzer. "Max Weber, Critical Theory and the Administered World." *Qualitative Sociology* 4(1981):34–55.

Jurgen Habermas. *The Theory of Communicative Action.* Vol. 1, *Reason and the Rationalization of Society.* Boston: Beacon, 1984.

Stephen Kalberg. "Max Weber's Types of Rationality: Cornerstones for the Analysis of Rationalization Processes in History." *American Journal of Sociology* 85(1980):1145–1179.

Stephen Kalberg. "The Rationalization of Action in Max Weber's Sociology of Religion." *Sociological Theory* 8(1990):58–84.

Stephen Kalberg. *Max Weber's Comparative Historical Sociology.* Chicago: University of Chicago Press, 1994.

Stephen Kalberg. "Max Weber." In George Ritzer, ed., *The Blackwell Companion to Major Social Theorists.* Oxford, UK: Blackwell, 2000, pp. 144–204.

Donald Levine. "Rationality and Freedom: Weber and Beyond." *Sociological Inquiry* 51(1981):5–25.

Arthur Mitzman. *The Iron Cage: An Historical Interpretation of Max Weber.* With a new introduction by the author; preface by Lewis A. Coser. New Brunswick, NJ: Transaction Books, 1985.

Wolfgang Mommsen. *The Age of Bureaucracy.* New York: Harper & Row, 1974.

George Ritzer. "Professionalization, Bureaucratization and Rationalization: The Views of Max Weber." *Social Forces* 53(1975):627–634.

George Ritzer and Terri LeMoyne. "Hyperrationality." In George Ritzer, ed., *Metatheorizing in Sociology.* Lexington, MA: Lexington Books, 1991, pp. 93–115.

George Ritzer and David Walczak. "Rationalization and the Deprofessionalization of Physicians." *Social Forces* 67(1988):1–22.

Guenther Roth and Reinhard Bendix, eds. *Scholarship and Partisanship: Essays on Max Weber.* Berkeley: University of California Press, 1971.

Lawrence Scaff. *Fleeing the Iron Cage: Culture, Politics, and Modernity in the Thought of Max Weber.* Berkeley: University of California Press, 1989.

Wolfgang Schluchter. *The Rise of Western Rationalism: Max Weber's Developmental History.* Translated, with an introduction, by Guenther Roth. Berkeley: University of California Press, 1981.

Mark A. Schneider. *Culture and Enchantment*. Chicago: University of Chicago Press, 1993.

Alan Sica. *Weber, Irrationality and Social Order*. Berkeley: University of California Press, 1988.

Ronald Takaki. *Iron Cages: Race and Culture in 19th-Century America*, Rev. ed. New York: Oxford University Press, 2000.

## ◆ WORKS ON VARIOUS ASPECTS OF A MCDONALDIZING SOCIETY

Mark Alfino, John Caputo, and Robin Wynyard, eds. *McDonaldization Revisited*. Westport, CT: Greenwood, 1998.

Benjamin Barber. *Jihad vs. McWorld*. New York: Times Books, 1995.

Zygmunt Bauman. *Modernity and the Holocaust*. Ithaca, NY: Cornell University Press, 2000.

Daniel Bell. *The Coming of Post-Industrial Society: A Venture in Social Forecasting*. Special anniversary ed., with a new foreword by the author. New York: Basic Books, 1999.

Max Boas and Steve Chain. *Big Mac: The Unauthorized Story of McDonald's*. New York: E. P. Dutton, 1976.

Daniel J. Boorstin. *The Image: A Guide to Pseudo-Events in America*. With a new foreword by the author and an afterword by George F. Will, 25th anniversary ed. New York: Atheneum, 1987.

Pierre Bourdieu. *Distinction: A Social Critique of the Judgment of Taste*. Cambridge, MA: Harvard University Press, 1984.

Alan Bryman. *Disney and His Worlds*. London: Routledge, 1995.

Alan Bryman. "The Disneyization of Society." *Sociological Review* 47(1999):25–47.

Alan Bryman. *The Disneyization of Society*. London: Sage, 2004.

Deborah Cameron. *Good to Talk? Living in a Communication Culture*. London: Sage, 2000.

Simon Clarke. "The Crisis of Fordism or the Crisis of Social Democracy?" *Telos* 83(1990):71–98.

Ben Cohen, Jerry Greenfield, and Meredith Mann. *Ben & Jerry's Double-Dip: How to Run a Values-Led Business and Make Money, Too*. New York: Fireside, 1998.

Stanley Cohen and Laurie Taylor. *Escape Attempts: The Theory and Practice of Everyday Life*, 2nd ed. London: Routledge, 1992.

Thomas S. Dicke. *Franchising in America: The Development of a Business Method, 1840–1980*. Chapel Hill: University of North Carolina Press, 1992.

John Drane. *The McDonaldization of the Church*. London: Darton, Longman and Todd, 2001.

Richard Edwards. *Contested Terrain: The Transformation of the Workplace in the Twentieth Century*. New York: Basic Books, 1979.

Marshall Fishwick, ed. *Ronald Revisited: The World of Ronald McDonald*. Bowling Green, OH: Bowling Green University Press, 1983.

Stephen M. Fjellman. *Vinyl Leaves: Walt Disney World and America*. Boulder, CO: Westview, 1992.

James T. Flink. *The Automobile Age*. Cambridge: MIT Press, 1988.

Henry Ford. *My Life and Work*. Garden City, NY: Doubleday, Page, 1922.

Thomas L. Friedman. *The Lexus and the Olive Tree*, Rev. ed. New York: Farrar, Straus, Giroux, 2000.

Herbert J. Gans. *The Levittowners: Ways of Life and Politics in a New Suburban Community*. With a new preface by the author. New York: Columbia University Press, 1967/1982.

Barbara Garson. *All the Livelong Day: The Meaning and Demeaning of Routine Work*, Rev. and updated ed. New York: Penguin Books, 1994.

Steven L. Goldman, Roger N. Nagel, and Kenneth Preiss. *Agile Competitors and Virtual Organizations: Strategies for Enriching the Customer*. New York: Van Nostrand Reinhold, 1995.

Richard E. Gordon, Katharine K. Gordon, and Max Gunther. *The Split Level Trap*. New York: Gilbert Geis, 1960.

Roger Gosden. *Designing Babies: The Brave New World of Reproductive Technology*. New York: W. H. Freeman, 1999.

Harold Gracey. "Learning the Student Role: Kindergarten as Academic Boot Camp." In Dennis Wrong and Harold Gracey, eds., *Readings in Introductory Sociology*. New York: Macmillan, 1967.

Harry L. Gracey. "Learning the Student Role: Kindergarten as Academic Boot Camp." In James M. Henslin, ed., *Down to Earth Sociology*. New York: Free Press, 2001.

Allen Guttmann. *From Ritual to Record: The Nature of Modern Sports*. New York: Cambridge University Press, 1978.

Jeffrey Hadden and Charles E. Swann. *Prime Time Preachers: The Rising Power of Televangelism*. Reading, MA: Addison-Wesley, 1981.

Jerald Hage and Charles H. Powers. *Post-Industrial Lives: Roles and Relationships in the 21st Century*. Newbury Park, CA: Sage, 1992.

David Harvey. *The Condition of Postmodernity: An Enquiry into the Origins of Cultural Change*. Oxford: Basil Blackwell, 1989.

Dennis Hayes and Robin Wynyard, eds. *The McDonaldization of Higher Education*. Westport, CT: Bergin and Garvey, 2002.

Kathleen Jamieson. *Eloquence in an Electronic Age: The Transformation of Political Speechmaking*. New York: Oxford University Press, 1988.

Robert Kanigel. *One Best Way: Frederick Winslow Taylor and the Enigma of Efficiency*. New York: Viking, 1997.

Kincheloe, Joe L. *The Sign of the Burger: McDonald's and the Culture of Power*. Philadelphia: Temple University Press, 2002.

Aliza Kolker and B. Meredith Burke. *Prenatal Testing: A Sociological Perspective*. Westport, CT: Bergin & Garvey, 1994.

William Severini Kowinski. *The Malling of America: An Inside Look at the Great Consumer Paradise*. New York: William Morrow, 1985.

Jon Krakauer. *Into Thin Air.* New York: Anchor, 1997.

Ray Kroc. *Grinding It Out.* New York: Berkeley Medallion Books, 1977.

Corby Kummer. *The Pleasures of Slow Food: Celebrating Authentic Traditions, Flavors, and Recipes.* San Francisco: Chronicle Books, 2002.

Raymond Kurzweil. *The Age of Intelligent Machines.* Cambridge: MIT Press, 1990.

Fred "Chico" Lager. *Ben & Jerry's: The Inside Scoop.* New York: Crown, 1994.

Frank Lechner and John Boli. *The Globalization Reader,* 2nd ed. Oxford, UK: Blackwell, 2004.

Robin Leidner. *Fast Food, Fast Talk: Service Work and the Routinization of Everyday Life.* Berkeley: University of California Press, 1993.

John F. Love. *McDonald's: Behind the Arches,* Rev. ed. New York: Bantam Books, 1995.

Stan Luxenberg. *Roadside Empires: How the Chains Franchised America.* New York: Viking, 1985.

Jean-Francois Lyotard. *The Postmodern Condition: A Report on Knowledge.* Minneapolis: University of Minnesota Press, 1984.

Frank Mankiewicz and Joel Swerdlow. *Remote Control: Television and the Manipulation of American Life.* New York: Time Books, 1978.

Jessica Mitford. *The American Way of Birth.* New York: Plume, 1993.

Ian I. Mitroff and Warren Bennis. *The Unreality Industry: The Deliberate Manufacturing of Falsehood and What It Is Doing to Our Lives.* New York: Oxford University Press, 1993.

Sherwin B. Nuland. *How We Die: Reflections on Life's Final Chapter.* New York: Knopf, 1994.

Martin Parker and David Jary. "The McUniversity: Organization, Management and Academic Subjectivity." *Organization* 2(1995):319–337.

Thomas J. Peters and Robert H. Waterman. *In Search of Excellence: Lessons from America's Best-Run Companies.* New York: Harper & Row, 1982.

Neil Postman. *Amusing Ourselves to Death: Public Discourse in the Age of Show Business.* New York: Viking, 1985.

Neil Postman. *Technopoly: The Surrender of Culture to Technology.* New York: Knopf, 1992.

Peter Prichard. *The Making of McPaper: The Inside Story of USA TODAY.* Kansas City, MO: Andrews, McMeel and Parker, 1987.

Stanley Joel Reiser. *Medicine and the Reign of Technology.* Cambridge, UK: Cambridge University Press, 1978.

Ester Reiter. *Making Fast Food: From the Frying Pan into the Fryer,* 2nd ed. Montreal and Buffalo: McGill-Queen's University Press, 1997.

George Ritzer. "The McDonaldization of Society." *Journal of American Culture* 6(1983):100–107.

George Ritzer. *Expressing America: A Critique of the Global Credit Card Society.* Newbury Park, CA: Pine Forge Press, 1995.

George Ritzer. *The McDonaldization Thesis.* London: Sage, 1998.

George Ritzer. *Enchanting a Disenchanted World: Revolutionizing the Means of Consumption.* Thousand Oaks, CA: Pine Forge Press, 1999.

George Ritzer. *The Globalization of Nothing*. Thousand Oaks, CA: Pine Forge, 2004.

George Ritzer, ed. *McDonaldization: The Reader*. Thousand Oaks, CA: Pine Forge, 2002.

George Ritzer, ed. "McDonaldization: Chicago, America, the World." Special issue. *American Behavioral Scientist* 47(October 2003).

George Ritzer and David Walczak. "The Changing Nature of American Medicine." *Journal of American Culture* 9(1987):43–51.

Roland Robertson. *Globalization: Social Theory and Global Culture*. London: Sage, 1992.

Chris Rojek. *Ways of Escape: Modern Transformations in Leisure and Travel*. London: Routledge, 1993.

Eric Schlosser. *Fast Food Nation*. Boston: Houghton Mifflin, 2001.

Charles E. Silberman. *Crisis in the Classroom: The Remaking of American Education*. New York: Random House, 1970.

Peter Singer. *Animal Liberation*, 2nd ed. New York: New York Review of Books, 1990.

Alfred P. Sloan, Jr. *My Years at General Motors*. Garden City, NY: Doubleday, 1964.

Barry Smart, ed. *Resisting McDonaldization*. London: Sage, 1999.

Frederick W. Taylor. *The Principles of Scientific Management*. New York: Harper & Row, 1947.

John Vidal. *McLibel: Burger Culture on Trial*. New York: New Press, 1997.

James L. Watson, ed. *Golden Arches East: McDonald's in East Asia*. Stanford, CA: Stanford University Press, 1997.

Shoshana Zuboff. *In the Age of the Smart Machine: The Future of Work and Power*. New York: Basic Books, 1988.

# Notes

## ◆ CHAPTER 1

1. For a similar but narrower viewpoint to the one expressed here, see Benjamin R. Barber. "Jihad vs. McWorld." *The Atlantic Monthly*, March 1992, pp. 53–63; *Jihad vs. McWorld*. New York: Times Books, 1995. For a more popular discussion of a similar conflict, see Thomas L. Friedman, *The Lexus and the Olive Tree: Understanding Globalization*. New York: Farrar, Straus, and Giroux, 1999.

2. This stands in contrast to Eric Schlosser's (2001) best-selling *Fast Food Nation* (Boston: Houghton Mifflin) which *is* about the fast-food industry and devotes much attention to McDonald's.

3. Since the publication of the first edition of this book in 1993, the term *McDonaldization* has, at least to some degree, become part of the academic and public lexicon. For example, among the academic works are Dennis Hayes and Robin Wynyard, Eds. *The McDonaldization of Higher Education*. Westport, CT: Bergin and Garvey, 2002; John Drane. *The McDonaldization of the Church*. London: Darton, Longman and Todd, 2001; Barry Smart, ed. *Resisting McDonaldization*. London: Sage, 1999; Mark Alfino, John Caputo, and Robin Wynyard, eds. *McDonaldization Revisited*. Westport, CT: Greenwood, 1998; a special issue of the Dutch journal *Sociale Wetenschappen* (vol. 4, 1996) devoted to McDonaldization; the essays in my *McDonaldization: The Reader*. Thousand Oaks, CA: Pine Forge Press, 2002; and a special issue (also edited by me) of the *American Behavioral Scientist* titled "McDonaldization: Chicago, America, the World" (October, 2003). One finds many mentions of McDonaldization in the popular media.

4. Alan Bryman has suggested the term *Disneyization*, which he defines in a parallel manner: "the process by which the *principles* of Disney theme parks are coming to dominate more and more sectors of American society as well as the rest of the world" (p. 26). See Alan Bryman. "The Disneyization of Society." *Sociological Review* 47(February, 1999):25–47, and Alan Bryman. *The Disneyization of Society*. London: Sage (2004).

5. See George Ritzer, ed. *McDonaldization: The Reader*. Thousand Oaks, CA: Pine Forge Press, 2002.

6. McDonald's. *2002 Summary Annual Report*. Oak Brook, IL, 2003.

7. McDonald's Web site: www.mcdonalds.com

8. Martin Plimmer. "This Demi-Paradise: Martin Plimmer Finds Food in the Fast Lane Is Not to His Taste." *Independent* (London), January 3, 1998, p. 46.

9. International Franchise Association: www.franchise.org/resourcectr/faq/q4.asp

10. The rest are either company owned (19%) or affiliates (14%); McDonald's. *2002 Summary Annual Report*. Oak Brook, IL, 2003.

11. Yum! Brands Web site: www.yum.com/investors/overview.htm

12. Yum! Brands Web site: www.yum.com/investors/overview.htm

13. Subway Web site: www.subway.com

14. Subway press release, "Subway Restaurants Named Number One Franchise." January, 2003.

15. Starbucks Web site: www.starbucks.com; Lorraine Mirabella. "Trouble Brews for Starbucks as Its Stock Slides 12 Percent." *Baltimore Sun,* August 1, 1998, p. 10c; Margaret Webb Pressler. "The Brain behind the Beans." *Washington Post,* October 5, 1997, pp. H01ff; Alex Witchell. "By Way of Canarsie, One Large Hot Cup of Business Strategy." *New York Times,* December 14, 1994, p. C8.

16. Glenn Collins. "A Big Mac Strategy at Porterhouse Prices." *New York Times,* August 13, 1996, p. D1.

17. Glenn Collins. "A Big Mac Strategy at Porterhouse Prices." *New York Times,* August 13, 1996, p. D1.

18. Glenn Collins. "A Big Mac Strategy at Porterhouse Prices." *New York Times,* August 13, 1996, p. D1.

19. A similar high-priced chain of steakhouses, Ruth's Chris, claims, perhaps a little too loudly and self-consciously, "Ours is not a McDonald's concept" (Glenn Collins. "A Big Mac Strategy at Porterhouse Prices." *New York Times,* August 13, 1996, p. D1). Even if it is true (and that's doubtful), it makes it clear that all restaurants of this type must attempt to define themselves, either positively or negatively, against the standard set by McDonald's.

20. Timothy Egan. "Big Chains Are Joining Manhattan's Toy Wars." *New York Times,* December 8, 1990, p. 29.

21. Stacey Burling. "Health Club . . . For Kids." *Washington Post,* November 21, 1991, p. D5.

22. Tamar Lewin. "Small Tots, Big Biz." *New York Times Magazine,* January 19, 1989, p. 89.

23. McDonald's Web site: www.mcdonalds.com/corporate/press/financial/2002/10222002

24. McDonald's Web site: www.mcdonalds.com/corporate

25. McDonald's Web site: www.mcdonalds.com/corporate/investor/financialinfo/annual/report/business/russia

26. Robin Young. "Britain Is Fast-Food Capital of Europe." *Times* (London), April 25, 1997.

27. Ilene R. Prusher. "McDonaldized Israel Debates Making Sabbath 'Less Holy.'" *Christian Science Monitor*, January 30, 1998, p. 8.

28. Blockbuster Web site: www.blockbuster.com

29. Wal-Mart Web site: www.walmartstores.com

30. Tim Hortons Web site: www.timhortons.com; Les Whittington. "Tim Hortons: Canada Success Story." *Gazette* (Montreal), October 17, 1997, pp. F4ff.

31. Eric Margolis. "Fast Food: France Fights Back." *Toronto Sun*, January 16, 1997, p. 12.

32. Valerie Reitman. "India Anticipates the Arrival of the Beefless Big Mac." *Wall Street Journal*, October 20, 1993, pp. B1, B3.

33. Mos Food Services Web site: www.mos.co.jp

34. Alison Leigh Cowan. "Unlikely Spot for Fast Food." *New York Times*, April 29, 1984, sec. 3, p. 5.

35. Peter S. Goodman. "Familiar Logo on Unfamiliar Eateries in Iraq." *Washington Post*, May 26, 2003, pp. A1, A14.

36. The Body Shop Web site: www.thebodyshop.com

37. Philip Elmer-Dewitt. "Anita the Agitator." *Time*, January 25, 1993, pp. 52ff; Eben Shapiro. "The Sincerest Form of Rivalry." *New York Times*, October 19, 1991, pp. 35, 46; Bath & Body Works Web site: www.bathandbodyworks.com

38. Pret a Manger Web site: www.pretamanger.co.uk/philosophy

39. "Stylish, Swedish, 60-ish; Ikea's a Global Phenomenon." *Western Mail*, May 20, 2003, p. 1.

40. H&M Web site: www.hm.com

41. Marshall Fishwick, ed. *Ronald Revisited: The World of Ronald McDonald*. Bowling Green, OH: Bowling Green University Press, 1983.

42. John F. Harris. "McMilestone Restaurant Opens Doors in Dale City." *Washington Post*, April 7, 1988, p. D1.

43. E. R. Shipp. "The McBurger Stand That Started It All." *New York Times*, February 27, 1985, sec. 3, p. 3.

44. McDonald's Web site: www.media.mcdonalds.com/secured/company/history/storemuseum/index.html

45. Bill Keller. "Of Famous Arches, Beeg Meks and Rubles." *New York Times*, January 28, 1990, sec. 1, pp. 1, 12.

46. "Wedge of Americana: In Moscow, Pizza Hut Opens 2 Restaurants." *Washington Post*, September 12, 1990, p. B10.

47. Jeb Blount. "Frying Down to Rio." *Washington Post/Business*, May 18, 1994, pp. F1, F5.

48. Thomas L. Friedman. *The Lexus and the Olive Tree: Understanding Globalization*. New York: Farrar, Straus and Giroux, 1999, p. 235.

49. Thomas Friedman. "A Manifesto for the Fast World." *New York Times Magazine*, March 28, 1999, pp. 43–44.

50. Economist Web site: www.economist.com/markets/bigmac/displayStory.cfm?story_id=1730909

51. Thomas Friedman. "A Manifesto for the Fast World." *New York Times Magazine,* March 28, 1999, p. 84.

52. Conrad Kottak. "Rituals at McDonald's." In Marshall Fishwick, ed., *Ronald Revisited: The World of Ronald McDonald.* Bowling Green, OH: Bowling Green University Press, 1983, pp. 52–58.

53. Bill Keller. "Of Famous Arches, Beeg Meks and Rubles." *New York Times,* January 28, 1990, sec. 1, pp. 1, 12.

54. William Severini Kowinski. *The Malling of America: An Inside Look at the Great Consumer Paradise.* New York: William Morrow, 1985, p. 218.

55. Stephen M. Fjellman. *Vinyl Leaves: Walt Disney World and America.* Boulder, CO: Westview Press, 1992. In another example of other countries creating their own McDonaldized systems and exporting them, Japan's Sega Enterprises opened the first SegaWorld indoor urban theme park in London in 1996; see "A Sega Theme Park for Piccadilly Circus." *New York Times,* February 14, 1995, p. D5.

56. Bob Garfield. "How I Spent (and Spent and Spent) My Disney Vacation." *Washington Post/Outlook,* July 7, 1991, p. B5. See also Margaret J. King. "Empires of Popular Culture: McDonald's and Disney." In Marshall Fishwick, ed., *Ronald Revisited: The World of Ronald McDonald.* Bowling Green, OH: Bowling Green University Press, 1983, pp. 106–119.

57. Steven Greenhouse. "The Rise and Rise of McDonald's." *New York Times,* June 8, 1986, sec. 3, p. 1.

58. Richard L. Papiernik. "Mac Attack?" *Financial World,* April 12, 1994, p. 30.

59. Laura Shapiro. "Ready for McCatfish?" *Newsweek,* October 15, 1990, pp. 76–77; N. R. Kleinfeld. "Fast Food's Changing Landscape." *New York Times,* April 14, 1985, sec. 3, pp. 1, 6.

60. Louis Uchitelle. "That's Funny, Those Pickles Don't Look Russian." *New York Times,* February 27, 1992, p. A4.

61. Center for Defense Information Web site: www.cdi.org/russia/246-16.cfm

62. Nicholas D. Kristof. "Billions Served (and That Was Without China)." *New York Times,* April 24, 1992. p. A4.

63. Gilbert Chan. "Fast Food Chains Pump Profits at Gas Stations." *Fresno Bee,* October 10, 1994, p. F4.

64. Cynthia Rigg. "McDonald's Lean Units Beef up NY Presence." *Crain's New York Business,* October 31, 1994, p. 1.

65. Anthony Flint. "City Official Balks at Placement of McDonald's at New Courthouse." *Boston Globe,* March 9, 1999, p. B3.

66. Anita Kumar. "A New Food Revolution on Campus." *St. Petersburg Times,* May 11, 2003, p. 1A.

67. Carole Sugarman. "Dining Out on Campus." *Washington Post/Health,* February 14, 1995, p. 20.

68. Edwin McDowell. "Fast Food Fills Menu for Many Hotel Chains." *New York Times,* January 9, 1992, pp. D1, D6.

69. Dan Freedman. "Low Fat? The Kids Aren't Buying; Districts Struggle to Balance Mandates for Good Nutrition with Reality in the Cafeteria." *The Times Union*, September 22, 2002, p. A1.

70. "Back to School: School Lunches." *Consumer Reports*, September 1998, p. 49.

71. Mike Berry. "Redoing School Cafeterias to Favor Fast-Food Eateries." *Orlando Sentinel*, January 12, 1995, p. 11.

72. "Grade 'A' Burgers." *New York Times*, April 13, 1986, pp. 12, 15.

73. Gloria Pitzer. *Secret Fast Food Recipes: The Fast Food Cookbook*. Marysville, MI: Author.

74. This discussion is derived from George Ritzer. "Revolutionizing the World of Consumption." *Journal of Consumer Culture* 2 (2002):103–118.

75. George Anders. "McDonald's Methods Come to Medicine as Chains Acquire Physicians' Practices." *Wall Street Journal*, August 24, 1993, pp. B1, B6.

76. Peter Prichard. *The Making of McPaper: The Inside Story of USA TODAY*. Kansas City, MO: Andrews, McMeel and Parker, 1987.

77. I would like to thank Lee Martin for bringing this case (and menu) to my attention.

78. Peter Prichard. *The Making of McPaper: The Inside Story of USA TODAY*. Kansas City, MO: Andrews, McMeel and Parker, 1987, pp. 232–233.

79. Howard Kurtz. "Slicing, Dicing News to Attract the Young." *Washington Post*, January 6, 1991, p. A1.

80. Kathryn Hausbeck and Barbara G. Brents. "McDonaldization of the Sex Industries?" In George Ritzer, ed. *McDonaldization: The Reader*. Thousand Oaks, CA: Pine Forge Press, 2002, pp. 91–106.

81. Nicholas D. Kristof. "Court Test Is Likely on Dial-a-Porn Service Game." *New York Times*, October 15, 1986, sect. 1, p. 16.

82. Cited in Robin Leidner. *Fast Food, Fast Talk: Service Work and the Routinization of Everyday Life*. Berkeley: University of California Press, 1993, p. 9.

83. Jean Sonmor. "Can We Talk Sex: Phone Sex Is Hot-Wiring Metro's Lonely Hearts." *Toronto Sun*, January 29, 1995, pp. M11ff.

84. Jean Sonmor. "Can We Talk Sex: Phone Sex Is Hot-Wiring Metro's Lonely Hearts." *Toronto Sun*, January 29, 1995, pp. M11ff.

85. Martin Gottlieb. "Pornography's Plight Hits Times Square." *New York Times*, October 5, 1986, sec. 3, p. 6.

86. Arthur Asa Berger. *Signs in Contemporary Culture: An Introduction to Semiotics*, 2nd ed. Salem, WI: Sheffield, 1999.

87. Max Weber. *Economy and Society*. Totowa, NJ: Bedminster, 1921/1968; Stephen Kalberg. "Max Weber's Types of Rationality: Cornerstones for the Analysis of Rationalization Processes in History." *American Journal of Sociology* 85 (1980):1145–1179.

88. Ian Mitroff and Warren Bennis. *The Unreality Industry: The Deliberate Manufacturing of Falsehood and What It Is Doing to Our Lives*. New York: Birch Lane, 1989, p. 142.

89. Martin Plimmer. "This Demi-Paradise: Martin Plimmer Finds Food in the Fast Lane Is Not to His Taste." *Independent* (London), January 3, 1998, p. 46.

90. Robin Leidner has developed the idea of scripts in her book, *Fast Food, Fast Talk: Service Work and the Routinization of Everyday Life*. Berkeley: University of California Press, 1993.

91. The idea of recipes comes from the work of Alfred Schutz. See, for example, *The Phenomenology of the Social World*. Evanston, IL: Northwestern University Press, 1932/1967.

92. Robin Leidner. *Fast Food, Fast Talk: Service Work and the Routinization of Everyday Life*. Berkeley: University of California Press, 1993, p. 82.

93. As we will see in Chapter 6, this increased control often comes from the *substitution of nonhuman for human technology*.

94. Robert J. Samuelson. "In Praise of McDonald's." *Washington Post*, November 1, 1989, p. A25.

95. Edwin M. Reingold. "America's Hamburger Helper." *Time*, June 29, 1992, pp. 66–67.

96. I would like to thank my colleague, Stan Presser, for suggesting that I enumerate the kinds of advantages listed on these pages.

97. It should be pointed out that the words *rational, rationality,* and *rationalization* are being used differently here and throughout the book than they are ordinarily employed. For one thing, people usually think of these terms as being largely positive; something that is rational is usually considered to be good. However, they are used here in a generally negative way. The positive term in this analysis is genuinely human "reason" (for example, the ability to act and work creatively), which is seen as being denied by inhuman, rational systems such as the fast-food restaurant. For another, the term rationalization is usually associated with Freudian theory as a way of explaining away some behavior, but here it describes the increasing pervasiveness of rationality throughout society. Thus, in reading this book, you must be careful to interpret the terms in these ways rather than in the ways they are conventionally employed.

98. Timothy Egan. "In Land of French Fry, Study Finds Problems." *New York Times*, February 7, 1994, p. A10.

99. Alan Riding. "Only the French Elite Scorn Mickey's Debut." *New York Times*, April 13, 1992, p. A13.

100. George Stauth and Bryan S. Turner. "Nostalgia, Postmodernism and the Critique of Mass Culture." *Theory, Culture and Society* 5(1988):509–526; Bryan S. Turner. "A Note on Nostalgia." *Theory, Culture and Society* 4(1987):147–156.

101. Lee Hockstader. "No Service, No Smile, Little Sauce." *Washington Post*, August 5, 1991, p. A12.

102. Douglas Farah. "Cuban Fast Food Joints Are Quick Way for Government to Rally Economy." *Washington Post*, January 24, 1995, p. A14.

103. In this sense, this resembles Marx's critique of capitalism. Marx was not animated by a romanticization of precapitalist society but, rather, by the desire to produce a truly human (communist) society on the base provided by capitalism.

Despite this specific affinity to Marxist theory, this book is, as you will see, premised far more on the theories of Max Weber.

104. These concepts are associated with the work of the social theorist, Anthony Giddens. See, for example, *The Constitution of Society*. Berkeley: University of California Press, 1984.

105. What Ray Oldenburg calls "great good places." See Ray Oldenburg. *The Great Good Place*. New York: Marlowe, 1989/1997.

## ◆ CHAPTER 2

1. Although the precursors discussed throughout this chapter do not exhaust the rationalized institutions that predate McDonald's, they are the most important for understanding McDonald's and McDonaldization.

2. This discussion of Weber's ideas is based on Max Weber. *Economy and Society*. Totowa, NJ: Bedminster, 1921/1968.

3. The fast-food restaurant can also be seen as part of a bureaucratic system; in fact, huge conglomerates (for example, Yum! Brands, Inc.) now own many of the fast-food chains.

4. Weber called the latter *substantive rationality*, to distinguish it from formal rationality.

5. Ronald Takaki. *Iron Cages: Race and Culture in 19th-Century America*. New York: Oxford University Press, 1990, p. ix.

6. Harvey Greisman. "Disenchantment of the World." *British Journal of Sociology* 27(1976):497–506.

7. Although Club Med is currently restructuring its operations.

8. Zygmunt Bauman. *Modernity and the Holocaust*. Ithaca, NY: Cornell University Press, 1989, p. 149.

9. Zygmunt Bauman. *Modernity and the Holocaust*. Ithaca, NY: Cornell University Press, 1989, p. 8.

10. However, in contemporary Rwanda, an estimated 800,000 people were killed in 100 days (three times the rate of Jewish dead during the Holocaust) in warfare between the Hutus and Tutsis. The methods employed—largely by machete—were decidedly not rationalized. See Philip Gourevitch. *We Wish to Inform You That Tomorrow We Will Be Killed with Our Families: Stories from Rwanda*. New York: Farrar, Straus and Giroux, 1998.

11. As you will see in Chapter 3, the fast-food restaurants enhance their efficiency by getting customers to perform (without pay) a variety of their tasks.

12. Zygmunt Bauman. *Modernity and the Holocaust*. Ithaca, NY: Cornell University Press, 1989, p. 103.

13. Zygmunt Bauman. *Modernity and the Holocaust*. Ithaca, NY: Cornell University Press, 1989, p. 89.

14. Zygmunt Bauman. *Modernity and the Holocaust*. Ithaca, NY: Cornell University Press, 1989, p. 8.

15. Zygmunt Bauman. *Modernity and the Holocaust.* Ithaca, NY: Cornell University Press, 1989, p. 102.

16. Feingold, cited in Zygmunt Bauman. *Modernity and the Holocaust.* Ithaca, NY: Cornell University Press, 1989, p. 136.

17. Frederick W. Taylor. *The Principles of Scientific Management.* New York: Harper & Row, 1947; Robert Kanigel. *One Best Way: Frederick Winslow Taylor and the Enigma of Efficiency.* New York: Viking, 1997.

18. Frederick W. Taylor. *The Principles of Scientific Management.* New York: Harper & Row, 1947, pp. 6–7.

19. Frederick W. Taylor. *The Principles of Scientific Management.* New York: Harper & Row, 1947, p. 11.

20. George Ritzer and Terri LeMoyne. "Hyperrationality: An Extension of Weberian and NeoWeberian Theory." In George Ritzer, ed., *Metatheorizing in Sociology.* Lexington, MA: Lexington Books, 1991, pp. 93–115.

21. Ester Reiter. *Making Fast Food.* Montreal and Kingston: McGill-Queen's University Press, 1991, pp. 112–114.

22. Henry Ford. *My Life and Work.* Garden City, NY: Doubleday, 1922; James T. Flink. *The Automobile Age.* Cambridge: MIT Press, 1988.

23. Henry Ford. *My Life and Work.* Garden City, NY: Doubleday, 1922, p. 80.

24. Bruce A. Lohof. "Hamburger Stand Industrialization and the Fast-Food Phenomenon." In Marshall Fishwick, ed., *Ronald Revisited: The World of Ronald McDonald.* Bowling Green, OH: Bowling Green University Press, 1983, p. 30; see also Ester Reiter. *Making Fast Food.* Montreal and Kingston: McGill-Queen's University Press, 1991, p. 75.

25. Marshall Fishwick. "Cloning Clowns: Some Final Thoughts." In Marshall Fishwick, ed., *Ronald Revisited: The World of Ronald McDonald.* Bowling Green, OH: Bowling Green University Press, 1983, pp. 148–151. For more on the relationship described in the same paragraph between the automobile and the growth of the tourist industry, see James T. Flink. *The Automobile Age.* Cambridge: MIT Press, 1988.

26. General Motors, especially Alfred Sloan, further rationalized the automobile industry's bureaucratic structure. Sloan is famous for GM's multidivisional system, in which the central office handled long-range decisions while the divisions made the day-to-day decisions. This innovation proved so successful in its day that the other automobile companies as well as many other corporations adopted it. See James T. Flink. *The Automobile Age.* Cambridge: MIT Press, 1988; Alfred P. Sloan, Jr. *My Years at General Motors.* Garden City, NY: Doubleday, 1964.

27. "Levitt's Progress." *Fortune,* October 1952, pp. 155ff.

28. Richard Perez-Pena. "William Levitt, 86, Suburb Maker, Dies." *New York Times,* January 29, 1994, p. 26.

29. "The Most House for the Money." *Fortune,* October 1952, p. 152.

30. "The Most House for the Money." *Fortune,* October 1952, p. 153.

31. Herbert Gans. *The Levittowners: Ways of Life and Politics in a New Suburban Community.* New York: Pantheon, 1967, p. 13.

32.   Patricia Dane Rogers. "Building . . . " *Washington Post/Home,* February 2, 1995, pp. 12, 15; Rebecca Lowell. "Modular Homes Move Up." *Wall Street Journal,* October 23, 1998, p. W10.

33.   Richard E. Gordon, Katherine K. Gordon, and Max Gunther. *The Split Level Trap.* New York: Gilbert Geis Associates, 1960.

34.   Georgia Dullea. "The Tract House as Landmark." *New York Times,* October 17, 1991, pp. C1, C8.

35.   Herbert Gans. *The Levittowners: Ways of Life and Politics in a New Suburban Community.* New York: Pantheon, 1967, p. 432.

36.   William Severini Kowinski. *The Malling of America: An Inside Look at the Great Consumer Paradise.* New York: William Morrow, 1985.

37.   Kara Swisher. "A Mall for America?" *Washington Post/Business,* June 30, 1991, pp. H1, H4.

38.   "First Foreign-Funded Department Store Closes in China's Wuhan." *Asia Pulse,* November 7, 2001, Northern Territory Regional Section.

39.   Janice L. Kaplan. "The Mall Outlet for Cabin Fever." *Washington Post/Weekend,* February 10, 1995, p. 53.

40.   William Severini Kowinski. *The Malling of America: An Inside Look at the Great Consumer Paradise.* New York: William Morrow, 1985, p. 25. For a discussion of the significance of the mall in the history of consumption, see Lizabeth Cohen, *Consumer's Republic: The Politics of Mass Consumption in Postwar America.* New York: Alfred A. Knopf, 2003, especially Chapter 6.

41.   Ray Kroc. *Grinding It Out.* New York: Berkeley Medallion Books, 1977; Stan Luxenberg. *Roadside Empires: How the Chains Franchised America.* New York: Viking, 1985; and John F. Love. *McDonald's: Behind the Arches.* Toronto: Bantam, 1986.

42.   John F. Love. *McDonald's: Behind the Arches.* Toronto: Bantam, 1986, p. 18.

43.   John F. Love. *McDonald's: Behind the Arches.* Toronto: Bantam, 1986, p. 20.

44.   Thomas S. Dicke. *Franchising in America: The Development of a Business Method, 1840–1980.* Chapel Hill: University of North Carolina Press, 1992, pp. 2–3.

45.   Taco Bell Web site: www.tacobell.com

46.   John Vidal. *McLibel: Burger Culture on Trial.* New York: New Press, 1997, p. 34.

47.   Wayne Huizenga played a similar role in the video business in taking over a chain developed by a Dallas entrepreneur and turning it into the Blockbuster empire. See David Altaner. "Blockbuster Video: 10 Years Running Family-Oriented Concept Has Changed Little Since 1985, When Chain Was Founded by a Dallas Businessman." *Sun-Sentinel* (Fort Lauderdale), October 16, 1995, pp. 16ff.

48.   John F. Love. *McDonald's: Behind the Arches.* Toronto: Bantam, 1986, pp. 68–69.

49.   McDonald's Web site: www.mcdonalds.com/corporate/careers/hambuniv

50.   Like McDonald's Hamburger University, Burger King set up its own Burger King University in 1978; see Ester Reiter. *Making Fast Food.* Montreal and Kingston: McGill-Queen's University Press, 1991, p. 68.

51.   John F. Love. *McDonald's: Behind the Arches.* Toronto: Bantam, 1986, pp. 141–142.

## ◆ CHAPTER 3

1. Herbert Simon. *Administrative Behavior*, 2nd ed. New York: Free Press, 1957.

2. Ray Kroc. *Grinding It Out*. New York: Berkeley Medallion Books, 1977, p. 8.

3. Max Boas and Steve Chain. *Big Mac: The Unauthorized Story of McDonald's*. New York: E. P. Dutton, 1976, pp. 9–10.

4. Max Boas and Steve Chain. *Big Mac: The Unauthorized Story of McDonald's*. New York: E. P. Dutton, 1976, pp. 9–10.

5. Ray Kroc. *Grinding It Out*. New York: Berkeley Medallion Books, 1977, pp. 96–97.

6. Jill Lawrence. "80 Pizzas Per Hour." *Washington Post*, June 9, 1996, pp. W07ff.

7. Arthur Kroker, Marilouise Kroker, and David Cook. *Panic Encyclopedia: The Definitive Guide to the Postmodern Scene*. New York: St. Martin's, 1989, p. 119.

8. Michael Lev. "Raising Fast Food's Speed Limit." *Washington Post*, August 7, 1991, p. D1.

9. Jim Kershner. "Trays of Our Lives: Fifty Years after Swanson Unveiled the First TV Dinner, Meals-in-a-Box Have Never Been Bigger." *Spokesman Review*, March 19, 2003, p. D1.

10. "The Microwave Cooks Up a New Way of Life." *Wall Street Journal*, September 19, 1989, p. B1; "Microwavable Foods: Industry's Response to Consumer Demands for Convenience." *Food Technology* 41(1987):52–63.

11. "Microwavable Foods: Industry's Response to Consumer Demands for Convenience." *Food Technology* 41(1987):54.

12. Eben Shapiro. "A Page from Fast Food's Menu." *New York Times*, October 14, 1991, pp. D1, D3.

13. Boston Market Web site: www.bostonmarket.com/newsroom/index.jsp

14. Alan J. Wax. "Takeout Meals Take Off." *Newsday*, July 27, 1998, pp. C08ff.

15. Alan J. Wax. "Takeout Meals Take Off." *Newsday*, July 27, 1998, pp. C08ff.

16. I would like to thank Dora Giemza for the insights into NutriSystem. See also "Big People, Big Business: The Overweight Numbers Rising, Try NutriSystem." *Washington Post/Health*, October 10, 1989, p. 8.

17. Lisa Schnirring. "What's Behind the Women-Only Fitness Center Boom?" *Physician and Sportsmedicine* 30(November 2002):15.

18. William Severini Kowinski. *The Malling of America: An Inside Look at the Great Consumer Paradise*. New York: William Morrow, 1985, p. 61.

19. BrewThru Web site: www.brewthru.com

20. Wendy Tanaka. "Catalogs Deck Halls to Tune of Billions: Mail Order Called 'Necessity' for Consumers." *Arizona Republic*, December 9, 1997, p. A3.

21. Robin Herman. "Drugstore on the Net." *Washington Post/Health*, May 4, 1999, pp. 15ff.

22. Doris Hajewski. "Employees Save Time by Shopping Online at Work." *Milwaukee Journal Sentinel*, December 16, 1998, pp. B1ff.

23. Bruno Giussani. "This Development Is One for the Books." *Chicago Tribune*, September 22, 1998, pp. C3ff.

24. L. Walker. "Google Turns Its Gaze on Online Shopping." *Washington Post* December, 15, 2002, p. H7.

25. George Ritzer. *Expressing America: A Critique of the Global Credit Card Society.* Thousand Oaks, CA: Pine Forge Press, 1995.

26. Dennis Hayes and Robin Wynyard, eds. *The McDonaldization of Higher Education.* Westport, CT: Bergin and Garvey, 2002; Martin Parker and David Jary. "The McUniversity: Organization, Management and Academic Subjectivity." *Organization* 2(1995):1–19.

27. Linda Perlstein. "Software's Essay Test: Should It Be Grading?" *Washington Post,* October 13, 1998, pp. A1ff.

28. Michael Miller. "Professors Customize Textbooks, Blurring Roles of Publisher, Seller and Copy Shop." *Wall Street Journal,* August 16, 1990, pp. B1, B4.

29. See www.wisetermpapers.com or www.12000papers.com

30. See www.edutie.com

31. George Ritzer and David Walczak. "The Changing Nature of American Medicine." *Journal of American Culture* 9(1987):43–51.

32. Julia Wallace. "Dr. Denton Cooley: Star of 'The Heart Surgery Factory.'" *Washington Post,* July 19, 1980, p. A6.

33. "Moving Right Along." *Time,* July 1, 1985, p. 44.

34. Mark Potts. "Blockbuster Struggles with Merger Script." *Washington Post/Washington Business,* December 9, 1991, p. 24; Eben Shapiro. "Market Place: A Mixed Outlook for Blockbuster." *New York Times,* February 21, 1992, p. D6.

35. Blockbuster Web site: www.blockbuster.com

36. Susan Karlin. "Video on Demand Is Ready, but the Market Is Not." *New York Times,* October 10, 2002, p. G8.

37. Frank Ahrens. "Video Stores: Are They Headed to the Bottom?" *Washington Post,* September 2, 1998, pp. D1ff.

38. Steve Fainaru. "Endangered Species: Will the Corner Video Store Disappear in the Interactive Age?" *Boston Globe,* January 16, 1994, p. A1.

39. "Earful of Books." *Business Wire,* July 13, 2001.

40. "Nation's Largest Audiobook-Only Retailer Uniquely Positioned to Capitalize On Robust Industry Growth." *PR Newswire,* March 14, 2002.

41. Thom Weidlich. "Have Book, Will Travel: Audio Adventures." *Direct* 10(July 1, 1998):23.

42. Clint Williams. "Reads on the Road: Books on Tape Racking Up Miles While Easing Commuter Stress." *Atlanta Journal and Constitution,* February 7, 1998, pp. 01Jff.

43. Will Workman. "Digital Audio Enables 'Internet Walkman.'" *Computer Shopper,* May 1998, pp. 089ff.

44. Stephen Fjellman. *Vinyl Leaves: Walt Disney World and America.* Boulder, CO: Westview, 1992.

45. Michael Harrington. "To the Disney Station." *Harper's,* January 1979, pp. 35–39.

46. Lynn Darling. "On the Inside at Parks a la Disney." *Washington Post,* August 28, 1978, p. A10.

47. I would like to thank Steve Lankenau for suggesting to me some of the points about McDonaldization and health clubs made on this page.

48. On another dimension of McDonaldization, exercise machines also offer a high degree of calculability, with many of them registering miles run, level of difficulty, and calories burned.

49. Jeffrey Hadden and Charles E. Swann. *Primetime Preachers: The Rising Power of Televangelism.* Reading, MA: Addison Wesley, 1981.

50. John Tagliabue. "Indulgences by TV." *New York Times,* December 19, 1985, sec. 1, p. 8.

51. John Drane. *The McDonaldization of the Church.* London: Darton, Longman, and Todd, 2001, p. 36.

52. Don Slater. "'You Press the Button, We Do the Rest': Some Thoughts on the McDonaldization of the Internet." Paper presented at the Meetings of the Eastern Sociological Society, March 6, 1999.

53. JoAnna Daemmrich. "Candidates Increasingly Turn to Internet." *Baltimore Sun,* October, 21, 1998, pp. 1Bff.

54. Glenn Kessler and James Rowell. "Virtual Medical Symposia: Communicating Globally, Quickly, and Economically; Use Internet." *Medical Marketing and Media,* September 1998, pp. 60ff.

55. "Student Internet Research Made Efficient and Effective." *THE Journal (Technological Horizons in Education),* October 1998, pp. 88ff.

56. Noreen Seebacher. "Love at e-mail.com." *Detroit News,* December 18, 1998, pp. E1ff.

57. Russell Blinch. "Instant Message Programs Keep Millions Ecstatic." *Denver Rocky Mountain News,* May 11, 1998, p. 6B.

58. Jennifer Lenhart. "'Happy Holidays,' High-Tech Style." *Washington Post,* December 20, 1998, pp. B1ff.

59. They have already McDonaldized the process of breeding, raising, and slaughtering chickens (see Chapter 6).

60. Henry Ford. *My Life and Work.* Garden City, NY: Doubleday, 1922, p. 72.

61. However, in recent years, H&R Block has been buying up traditional accounting practices to offer a fuller range of accounting services to some clients. See Doug Sword. "H&R Block to Buy Local Accounting Practice." *Indianapolis Star,* September 10, 1998, p. C01.

62. Daniel Boorstin. *The Image: A Guide to Pseudo-Events in America.* New York: Harper Colophon, 1961, p. 135.

63. Ian Mitroff and Warren Bennis. *The Unreality Industry: The Deliberate Manufacturing of Falsehood and What It Is Doing to Our Lives.* New York: Birch Lane, 1989, p. 12.

64. Thomas R. Ide and Arthur J. Cordell. "Automating Work." *Society* 31(1994):68.

65. Steak n Shake Web site: www.steaknshake.com

66. This once-thriving chain of over 600 restaurants has been reduced to a small number of independent operations in the Northeast; see Sandra Evans. "Roy Rogers Owners Hope for Happy Trails." *Washington Post,* August 4, 1997, pp. F05ff.

67. See www.kioskcom.com/articles_detail.php?ident=1801 and www.trian-gletechjournal.com/news/article?item_id=4855

68. Eric Palmer. "Scan-do Attitude: Self-Service Technology Speeds Up Grocery Shopping." *Kansas City Star,* April 8, 1998, pp. B1ff.

69. Eben Shapiro. "Ready, Set, Scan That Melon." *New York Times,* June 14, 1990, pp. D1, D8.

70. Eben Shapiro. "Ready, Set, Scan That Melon." *New York Times,* June 14, 1990, pp. D1, D8.

71. Chris Woodyard. "Grocery Shoppers Can Be Own Cashiers." *USA TODAY,* March 9, 1998, p. 6B.

72. Robert Kisabeth, Anne C. Pontius, Bernard E. Statland, and Charlotte Galper. "Promises and Pitfalls of Home Test Devices." *Patient Care* 31(October 15, 1997):125ff.

73. Barry Meier. "Need a Teller? Chicago Bank Plans a Fee." *Washington Post,* April 27, 1995, pp. D1, D23.

74. Thomas R. Ide and Arthur J. Cordell. "Automating Work." *Society* 31(1994):65ff.

75. James Barron. "Please Press 2 for Service; Press ? for an Actual Human." *New York Times,* February 17, 1989, pp. A1, B2.

76. Michael Schrage. "Calling the Technology of Voice Mail into Question." *Washington Post,* October 19, 1990, p. F3.

77. Personal communication between Mike Ryan (my assistant) with Rose Cowan at the Bureau of the Census.

## ◆ CHAPTER 4

1. Just as quality is equated with quantity, quality is also equated with other aspects of McDonaldization, such as "standardization and predictability." See Ester Reiter. *Making Fast Food.* Montreal and Kingston: McGill-Queen's University Press, 1991, p. 107.

2. Shoshana Zuboff. *In the Age of the Smart Machine: The Future of Work and Power.* New York: Basic Books, 1988.

3. Bruce Horovitz. "Fast-Food Chains Bank on Bigger-Is-Better Mentality." *USA TODAY,* September 12, 1997, p. 1b.

4. In addition, as you will see in Chapter 10, protests against these garish signs helped lead to their virtual disappearance.

5. "Taco Bell Delivers Even Greater Value to Its Customers by Introducing Big Fill Menu." *Business Wire*, November 2, 1994.

6. Philip Elmer-DeWitt. "Fat Times." *Time*, January 16, 1995, pp. 60–65.

7. Barbara W. Tuchman. "The Decline of Quality." *New York Times Magazine*, November 2, 1980, p. 38. For example, United Airlines does not tell people anything about the quality of their numerous flights, such as the likelihood that their planes will be on time.

8. Marion Clark. "Arches of Triumph." *Washington Post/Book World*, June 5, 1977, p. G6.

9. A. A. Berger. "Berger vs. Burger: A Personal Encounter." In Marshall Fishwick, ed., *Ronald Revisited: The World of Ronald McDonald*. Bowling Green, OH: Bowling Green University Press, 1983, p. 126.

10. Max Boas and Steven Chain. *Big Mac: The Unauthorized Story of McDonald's*. New York: Dutton, 1976, p. 121.

11. Max Boas and Steven Chain. *Big Mac: The Unauthorized Story of McDonald's*. New York: Dutton, 1976, p. 117.

12. A. C. Stevens. "Family Meals: Olive Garden Defines Mediocrity." *Boston Herald*, March 2, 1997, p. 055.

13. "The Cheesecake Factory Restaurants Celebrate 25th Anniversary." *Business Wire*, February 25, 2003.

14. Susan Gervasi. "The Credentials Epidemic." *Washington Post*, August 30, 1990, p. D5.

15. Iver Peterson. "Let That Be a Lesson: Rutgers Bumps a Well-Liked but Little-Published Professor." *New York Times*, May 9, 1995, p. B1.

16. Kenneth Cooper. "Stanford President Sets Initiative on Teaching." *Washington Post*, March 3, 1991, p. A12.

17. Kenneth Cooper. "Stanford President Sets Initiative on Teaching." *Washington Post*, March 3, 1991, p. A12.

18. Dennis Hayes and Robin Wynyard. "Introduction." In Dennis Hayes and Robin Wynyard, eds., *The McDonaldization of Higher Education*. Westport, CT: Bergin and Garvey, 2002, p. 11.

19. An example of hundreds of DRGs is DRG 236. "Fractures of Hip and Pelvis." A set amount is reimbursed by Medicare for medical procedures included under that heading and all other DRGs.

20. Dan Colburn. "Unionizing Doctors: Physicians Begin Banding Together to Fight for Autonomy and Control over Medical Care." *Washington Post/Health*, June 19, 1985, p. 7.

21. Frank Mankiewicz and Joel Swerdlow. *Remote Control: Television and the Manipulation of American Life*. New York: Time Books, 1978, p. 219.

22. Erik Larson. "Watching Americans Watch TV." *Atlantic Monthly*, March 1992, p. 66; see also Peter J. Boyer. "TV Turning to People Meters to Find Who Watches What." *New York Times*, June 1, 1987, pp. A1, C16.

23. Jennifer L. Stevenson. "PBS Is a Roost for Canceled 'I'll Fly Away.'" *San Diego Union-Tribune*, August 11, 1993, p. E10.

24.  Nielsen Web site: www.nielsenmedia.com/FAQ/index.html

25.  Kristin Tillotson. "TV Sweeps: April 24–May 21." *Star Tribune* (Minneapolis), April 20, 1997, pp. 1Fff.

26.  Paul Farhi. "A Dim View of Ratings." *Washington Post,* April 11, 1996, p. D09.

27.  Sports are not alone in this; the political parties have shortened and streamlined their conventions to accommodate the needs and demands of television.

28.  Allen Guttman. *From Ritual to Record: The Nature of Modern Sports.* New York: Cambridge University Press, 1978, p. 47.

29.  Allen Guttman. *From Ritual to Record: The Nature of Modern Sports.* New York: Cambridge University Press, 1978, p. 51.

30.  For those unfamiliar with baseball, a designated hitter is one of a team's starting players and takes a regular turn at bat throughout a game. A pinch hitter comes in during a game and bats for one of the players in the game. Pinch hitters almost always get only that one turn at bat during the game.

31.  However, specialization in baseball has more than compensated for this, and it is undoubtedly the case that people now see more rather than less use of relief pitchers. Indeed, there are now very specialized relief roles—the "long reliever" who comes in early in the game, the "closer" who finishes off a game in which his team is ahead, and relievers who specialize in getting out left- or right-handed batters.

32.  Carl Schoettler. "Examining the Pull of the Poll." *Sun* (Baltimore), October 11, 1998, pp. 13Fff.

33.  Kathleen Jamieson. *Eloquence in an Electronic Age: The Transformation of Political Speechmaking.* New York: Oxford University Press, 1988, p. 11.

34.  Kathleen Jamieson. *Eloquence in an Electronic Age: The Transformation of Political Speechmaking.* New York: Oxford University Press, 1988; see also Marvin Kalb. "TV, Election Spoiler." *New York Times,* November 28, 1988. p. A25.

35.  Sam Marullo. *Ending the Cold War at Home: From Militarism to a More Peaceful World Order.* New York: Lexington Books, 1993.

36.  Peter Prichard. *The Making of McPaper: The Inside Story of USA TODAY.* Kansas City, MO: Andrews, McMeel and Parker, 1987, p. 8; although the paper has been improving somewhat, see Howard Kurtz. "Surprise! We Like McPaper." *Brill's Content,* September 1998, pp. 125ff.

37.  That the newspaper can be read in a single sitting at a fast-food restaurant reminds me of the line in the movie *The Big Chill,* spoken by Michael (played by Jeff Goldblum), who writes for a magazine resembling *People:* "Where I work we only have one editorial rule: You can't write anything longer than the average person can read during the average crap."

38.  Peter Prichard. *The Making of McPaper. The Inside Story of USA TODAY.* Kansas City, MO: Andrews, McMeel and Parker, 1987, pp. 113, 196.

39.  Interestingly, packaged tours may have declined from their peak, but that may be due to the fact that most societies have become so McDonaldized that there is less need for packaged tours.

40. Kmart Web site: www.kmart.com

41. Ester Reiter. *Making Fast Food*. Montreal and Kingston: McGill-Queen's University Press, 1991, p. 84.

42. Ester Reiter. *Making Fast Food*. Montreal and Kingston: McGill-Queen's University Press, 1991, p. 85.

43. Jill Lawrence. "80 Pizzas Per Hour." *Washington Post*, June 9, 1996, pp. W07ff.

44. Stan Luxenberg. *Roadside Empires: How the Chains Franchised America*. New York: Viking, 1985, pp. 73–74.

45. Stan Luxenberg. *Roadside Empires: How the Chains Franchised America*. New York: Viking, 1985, p. 80.

46. Stan Luxenberg. *Roadside Empires: How the Chains Franchised America*. New York: Viking, 1985, pp. 84–85.

47. Robin Leidner. *Fast Food, Fast Talk: Service Work and the Routinization of Everyday Life*. Berkeley: University of California Press, 1993, p. 60.

48. Stuart Flexner. *I Hear America Talking*. New York: Simon & Schuster, 1976, p. 142.

49. Frederick W. Taylor. *The Principles of Scientific Management*. New York: Harper & Row, 1947, p. 42.

50. Frederick W. Taylor. *The Principles of Scientific Management*. New York: Harper & Row, 1947, p. 138.

51. Mark Dowie. "Pinto Madness." *Mother Jones*, September/October 1977, pp. 24ff.

## ◆ CHAPTER 5

1. W. Baldamus. "Tedium and Traction in Industrial Work." In David Weir, ed., *Men and Work in Modern Britain*. London: Fontana, 1973, pp. 78–84.

2. Best Western Web site: www.bestwestern.com/aboutus/index.asp

3. InterContinental Hotels Group Web site: www.ichotelsgroup.com

4. Howard Johnson Hotel Web site: www.hojo.com/HowardJohnson/control/brand_history

5. Entrepreneur Web site: www.entrepreneur.com/franzone/cats/0,6587,12-12-1-HOTEL,00.html

6. Robin Leidner. *Fast Food, Fast Talk: Service Work and the Routinization of Everyday Life*. Berkeley: University of California Press, 1993, pp. 45–47, 54.

7. Cited in Robin Leidner. *Fast Food, Fast Talk: Service Work and the Routinization of Everyday Life*. Berkeley: University of California Press, 1993, p. 82.

8. Margaret King. "McDonald's and the New American Landscape." *USA TODAY*, January 1980, p. 46.

9. Malvina Reynolds' lyrics are reprinted by permission of Schroder Music Co., ASCAP, copyright 1962.

10.  Marcus Palliser. "For Suburbia Read Fantasia Disney Has Created the American Dream Town in Sunny Florida." *Daily Telegraph,* November 27, 1996, pp. 31ff.

11.  Conrad Kottak. "Rituals at McDonald's." In Marshall Fishwick, ed., *Ronald Revisited: The World of Ronald McDonald.* Bowling Green, OH: Bowling Green University Press, 1983, pp. 52–58.

12.  Robin Leidner. *Fast Food, Fast Talk: Service Work and the Routinization of Everyday Life.* Berkeley: University of California Press, 1993.

13.  Robin Leidner. *Fast Food, Fast Talk: Service Work and the Routinization of Everyday Life.* Berkeley: University of California Press, 1993.

14.  Robin Leidner. *Fast Food, Fast Talk: Service Work and the Routinization of Everyday Life.* Berkeley: University of California Press, 1993, p. 6.

15.  Robin Leidner. *Fast Food, Fast Talk: Service Work and the Routinization of Everyday Life.* Berkeley: University of California Press, 1993, p. 135.

16.  Robin Leidner. *Fast Food, Fast Talk: Service Work and the Routinization of Everyday Life.* Berkeley: University of California Press, 1993, pp. 220, 230.

17.  Robin Leidner. *Fast Food, Fast Talk: Service Work and the Routinization of Everyday Life.* Berkeley: University of California Press, 1993.

18.  I will have more to say about this aspect of McDonaldization in Chapter 7.

19.  Robin Leidner. *Fast Food, Fast Talk: Service Work and the Routinization of Everyday Life.* Berkeley: University of California Press, 1993, pp. 107, 108.

20.  Elspeth Probyn. "McIdentities: Food and the Familial Citizen." *Theory, Culture and Society* 15(1998):155–173.

21.  Robin Leidner. *Fast Food, Fast Talk: Service Work and the Routinization of Everyday Life.* Berkeley: University of California Press, 1993, p. 10.

22.  Julia Malone. "With Bob Dole Speaking in Marietta Saturday, Here's a Look at the Art of Writing and Delivering Political Speeches." *Atlanta Journal and Constitution,* June 6, 1996, p. 14A.

23.  Mark Lawson. "JFK Had It . . . Martin Luther King Had It . . . Bob Dole Doesn't." *Guardian* (London), September 18, 1996, pp. T2ff.

24.  Peter Johnson. "Bush Has Media Walking a Fine Line." *USA Today,* March 10, 2003, p. 3D.

25.  Leidner reports that employees are encouraged to vary the process in order to reduce the customers' feelings of depersonalization. But at the franchise in which she worked, limits were placed on even this.

26.  Robin Leidner. *Fast Food, Fast Talk: Service Work and the Routinization of Everyday Life.* Berkeley: University of California Press, 1993, p. 25.

27.  Robin Leidner. *Fast Food, Fast Talk: Service Work and the Routinization of Everyday Life.* Berkeley: University of California Press, 1993.

28.  Harrison M. Trice and Janice M. Beyer. *The Cultures of Work Organizations.* Englewood Cliffs, NJ: Prentice Hall, 1993.

29.  Mary-Angie Salva-Ramirez. "McDonald's: A Prime Example of Corporate Culture." *Public Relations Quarterly* 40(December 22, 1995):30ff.

30. Dick Schaaf. "Inside Hamburger University." *Training*, December 1994, pp. 18–24.

31. Robin Leidner. *Fast Food, Fast Talk: Service Work and the Routinization of Everyday Life*. Berkeley: University of California Press, 1993, p. 58.

32. The information in this section comes from an official Disney publication.

33. Lynn Darling. "On the Inside at Parks a la Disney." *Washington Post*, August 28, 1978, p. A10.

34. Lynn Darling. "On the Inside at Parks a la Disney." *Washington Post*, August 28, 1978, p. A10.

35. Alexander Cockburn. "Barnes & Noble Blunder." *The Nation*, July 15, 1996, 263, p. 7.

36. Robin Leidner. *Fast Food, Fast Talk: Service Work and the Routinization of Everyday Life*. Berkeley: University of California Press, 1993, p. 58.

37. Henry Mitchell. "Wonder Bread, Any Way You Slice It." *Washington Post*, March 22, 1991, p. F2.

38. William Serrin. "Let Them Eat Junk." *Saturday Review*, February 2, 1980, p. 18.

39. Matthew Gilbert. "In McMovieworld, Franchises Taste Sweetest." *Commercial Appeal* (Memphis), May 30, 1997, pp. E10ff.

40. John Powers. "Tales of Hoffman." *Washington Post Sunday Arts,* March 5, 1995, p. G6.

41. Relating this to calculability, the ratings are quantified by age: "PG" means that children under thirteen may attend; "PG-13" indicates that a movie may be inappropriate for children under thirteen; "R" means that children under seventeen need parental consent (supposedly); and "NC-17" is supposed to ban all children under seventeen from the movie.

42. Matthew Gilbert. "TV's Cookie-Cutter Comedies." *Boston Globe*, October 19, 1997, pp. N1ff.

43. Matthew Gilbert. "TV's Cookie-Cutter Comedies." *Boston Globe*, October 19, 1997, pp. N1ff.

44. Matthew Gilbert. "TV's Cookie-Cutter Comedies." *Boston Globe*, October 19, 1997, pp. N1ff.

45. Phyllis Furman. "At Blockbuster Video, A Fast Fix Moves Flicks." *Daily News* (New York), July 27, 1998, p. 23.

46. Similarly, Busch Gardens offers European attractions, such as a German-style beer hall, without having its clientele leave the predictable confines of the United States and the even more predictable surroundings of the modern amusement park.

47. At the opening of the Istanbul Hilton, Conrad Hilton said. "Each of our hotels . . . is a 'little America.'" This quotation is from Daniel J. Boorstin. *The Image: A Guide to PseudoEvents in America*. New York: Harper Colophon, 1961, p. 98.

48. John Urry. *The Tourist Gaze: Leisure and Travel in Contemporary Societies*. London: Sage, 1990.

49. Andrew Beyer. "Lukas Has the Franchise on Almighty McDollar." *Washington Post,* August 8, 1990, pp. F1, F8.

50. William Severini Kowinski. *The Malling of America: An Inside Look at the Great Consumer Paradise.* New York: William Morrow, 1985, p. 27.

51. Iver Peterson. "Urban Dangers Send Children Indoors to Play: A Chain of Commercial Playgrounds Is One Answer for Worried Parents." *New York Times,* January 1, 1995, sec. 1, p. 29.

52. Jan Vertefeuille. "Fun Factory: Kids Pay to Play at the Discovery Zone and While That's Just Fine with Many Parents, It Has Some Experts Worried." *Roanoke Times & World News,* December 8, 1994, Extra, pp. 1ff.

53. Cited in Stephen J. Fjellman. *Vinyl Leaves: Walt Disney World and America.* Boulder, CO: Westview, 1992, p. 226.

54. Beth Thames. "In the Mists of Memory, Sun Always Shines on Family Camping." *New York Times,* July 9, 1986, p. C7.

55. Dirk Johnson. "Vacationing at Campgrounds Is Now Hardly Roughing It." *New York Times,* August 28, 1986, p. B1.

56. "CountryClub Campgrounds." *Newsweek,* September 24, 1984, p. 90; KOA Web site: www.koa.com

57. Dirk Johnson. "Vacationing at Campgrounds Is Now Hardly Roughing It." *New York Times,* August 28, 1986, p. B1.

58. Kristin Downey Grimsley. "Risk of Homicide Is Higher in Retail Jobs: Half of Workplace Killings Sales-Related." *Washington Post,* July 13, 1997, pp. A14ff.

## ◆ CHAPTER 6

1. Richard Edwards. *Contested Terrain: The Transformation of the Workplace in the Twentieth Century.* New York: Basic Books, 1979.

2. Richard Edwards. *Contested Terrain: The Transformation of the Workplace in the Twentieth Century.* New York: Basic Books, 1979.

3. Michael Lev. "Raising Fast Food's Speed Limit." *Washington Post,* August 7, 1991, pp. D1, D4.

4. Ray Kroc. *Grinding It Out.* New York: Berkeley Medallion, 1977, pp. 131–132.

5. Eric A. Taub. "The Burger Industry Takes a Big Helping of Technology." *New York Times,* October 8, 1998, pp. 13Gff.

6. William R. Greer. "Robot Chef's New Dish: Hamburgers." *New York Times,* May 27, 1987, p. C3.

7. William R. Greer. "Robot Chef's New Dish: Hamburgers." *New York Times,* May 27, 1987, p. C3.

8. Michael Lev. "Taco Bell Finds Price of Success (59 cents)." *New York Times,* December 17, 1990, p. D9.

9. Calvin Sims. "Robots to Make Fast Food Chains Still Faster." *New York Times,* August 24, 1988, p. 5.

10. Chuck Murray. "Robots Roll from Plant to Kitchen." *Chicago Tribune–Business,* October 17, 1993, pp. 3ff; "New Robots Help McDonald's Make Fast Food Faster." Business Wire, August 18, 1992.

11. In recent years, the shortage of a sufficient number of teenagers to keep turnover-prone fast-food restaurants adequately stocked with employees has led to a widening of the traditional labor pool of fast-food restaurants.

12. Chuck Murray. "Robots Roll from Plant to Kitchen." *Chicago Tribune–Business,* October 17, 1993, pp. 3ff.

13. Eric A. Taub. "The Burger Industry Takes a Big Helping of Technology." *New York Times,* October 8, 1998, pp. 13Gff.

14. KinderCare Web site: www.kindercare.com/about_6.php3

15. "The McDonald's of Teaching." *Newsweek,* January 7, 1985, p. 61.

16. Sylvan Learning Center Web site: www.educate.com/about.html

17. "The McDonald's of Teaching." *Newsweek,* January 7, 1985, p. 61.

18. William Stockton. "Computers That Think." *New York Times Magazine,* December 14, 1980, p. 48.

19. Bernard Wysocki, Jr. "Follow the Recipe: Children's Hospital in San Diego Has Taken the Standardization of Medical Care to an Extreme." *Wall Street Journal* April 22, 2003, p. R4ff.

20. Frederick W. Taylor. *The Principles of Scientific Management.* New York: Harper & Row, 1947, p. 59.

21. Henry Ford. *My Life and Work.* Garden City, NY: Doubleday, 1922, p. 103.

22. Robin Leidner. *Fast Food, Fast Talk: Service Work and the Routinization of Everyday Life.* Berkeley: University of California Press, 1993, p. 105.

23. Virginia A. Welch. "Big Brother Flies United." *Washington Post–Outlook,* March 5, 1995, p. C5.

24. Virginia A. Welch. "Big Brother Flies United." *Washington Post–Outlook,* March 5, 1995, p. C5.

25. StopJunkCalls Web site: www.stopjunkcalls.com/convict.htm

26. Staff. "Call Centres Become Bigger." Global News Wire, *India Business Insight,* September 30, 2002.

27. Gary Langer. "Computers Reach Out, Respond to Human Voice." *Washington Post,* February 11, 1990, p. H3.

28. Carl H. Lavin. "Automated Planes Raising Concerns." *New York Times,* August 12, 1989, pp. 1, 6.

29. Robin Leidner. *Fast Food, Fast Talk: Service Work and the Routinization of Everyday Life.* Berkeley: University of California Press, 1993.

30. L. B. Diehl and M. Hardart. *The Automat: The History, Recipes, and Allure of Horn and Hardart's Masterpiece.* New York: Clarkson Potter, 2002.

31. "Disenchanted Evenings." *Time,* September 3, 1990, p. 53.

32. Ester Reiter. *Making Fast Food.* Montreal and Kingston: McGill-Queens University Press, p. 86.

33. Stan Luxenberg. *Roadside Empires: How the Chains Franchised America.* New York: Viking, 1985.

34. Martin Plimmer. "This Demi-Paradise: Martin Plimmer Finds Food in the Fast Lane Is Not to His Taste." *Independent* (London), January 3, 1998, p. 46.

35. Harold Gracey. "Learning the Student Role: Kindergarten as Academic Boot Camp." In Dennis Wrong and Harold Gracey, eds., *Readings in Introductory Sociology.* New York: Macmillan, 1967, pp. 243–254.

36. Charles E. Silberman. *Crisis in the Classroom: The Remaking of American Education.* New York: Random House, 1970, p. 122.

37. Charles E. Silberman. *Crisis in the Classroom: The Remaking of American Education.* New York: Random House, 1970, p. 137.

38. Charles E. Silberman. *Crisis in the Classroom: The Remaking of American Education.* New York: Random House, 1970, p. 125.

39. William Severini Kowinski. *The Malling of America: An Inside Look at the Great Consumer Paradise.* New York: William Morrow, 1985, p. 359.

40. Gary Langer. "Computers Reach Out, Respond to Human Voice." *Washington Post,* February 11, 1990, p. H3.

41. Vatican Web site: www.vatican.va/news_services/television

42. Jeffrey Hadden and Charles E. Swann. *Prime Time Preachers: The Rising Power of Televangelism.* Reading, MA: Addison-Wesley, 1981.

43. E. J. Dionne, Jr. "The Vatican Is Putting Video to Work." *New York Times,* August 11, 1985, sec. 2, p. 27.

44. William Serrin. "Let Them Eat Junk." *Saturday Review,* February 2, 1980, p. 23.

45. "Super Soup Cooks Itself." *Scholastic News,* January 4, 1991, p. 3.

46. AquaSol, Inc. Web site: www.fishfarming.com

47. Martha Duffy. "The Fish Tank on the Farm." *Time,* December 3, 1990, pp. 107–111.

48. Peter Singer. *Animal Liberation: A New Ethic for Our Treatment of Animals.* New York: Avon, 1975.

49. Peter Singer. *Animal Liberation: A New Ethic for Our Treatment of Animals.* New York: Avon, 1975, pp. 96–97.

50. Peter Singer. *Animal Liberation: A New Ethic for Our Treatment of Animals.* New York: Avon, 1975, pp. 105–106.

51. Peter Singer. *Animal Liberation: A New Ethic for Our Treatment of Animals.* New York: Avon, 1975, p. 123.

52. Lenore Tiefer. "The Medicalization of Impotence: Normalizing Phallocentrism." *Gender and Society* 8(1994):363–377.

53. Cheryl Jackson. "Impotence Clinic Grows into Chain." *Tampa Tribune–Business and Finance,* February 18, 1995, p. 1.

54. Annette Baran and Reuben Pannor. *Lethal Secrets: The Shocking Consequences and Unresolved Problems of Artificial Insemination.* New York: Warner, 1989.

55. Paula Mergenbagen DeWitt. "In Pursuit of Pregnancy." *American Demographics,* May 1993, pp. 48ff.

56. Eric Adler. "The Brave New World: It's Here Now, Where In Vitro Fertilization Is Routine and Infertility Technology Pushes Back All the Old Limitations." *Kansas City Star,* October 25, 1998, pp. G1ff.

57. Clear Passage Web site: www.clearpassage.com/about_infertility_therapy.htm

58. "No Price for Little Ones." *Financial Times*, September 28, 1998, pp. 17ff.

59. Diederika Pretorius. *Surrogate Motherhood: A Worldwide View of the Issues.* Springfield, IL: Charles C Thomas, 1994.

60. Korky Vann. "With In-Vitro Fertilization, Late-Life Motherhood Becoming More Common." *Hartford Courant*, July 7, 1997, pp. E5ff.

61. Ian MacKinnon. "Mother of Newborn Child Says She Is 65." *The Times* (London), April 10, 2003, Overseas News sec., p. 28.

62. Angela Cain. "Home Test Kits Fill an Expanding Health Niche." *Times Union-Life and Leisure* (Albany, NY), February 12, 1995, p. 11.

63. Neil Bennett, ed. *Sex Selection of Children.* New York: Academic Press, 1983.

64. "Selecting Sex of Child." *South China Morning Post*, March 20, 1994, p. 15.

65. Rick Weiss. "Va. Clinic Develops System for Choosing Sex of Babies." *Washington Post*, September 10, 1998, pp. A1ff; Randeep Ramesh. "Can You Trust That Little Glow When You Choose Sex?" *Guardian* (London), October 6, 1998, pp. 14ff; Abigail Trafford. "Is Sex Selection Wise?" *Washington Post*, September 22, 1998, pp. Z6ff.

66. Janet Daley. "Is Birth Ever Natural?" *The Times* (London), March 16, 1994, p. 18.

67. Matt Ridley. "A Boy or a Girl: Is It Possible to Load the Dice?" *Smithsonian* 24(June 1993):123.

68. Gina Kolata and Kenneth Chang. "For Clonaid, a Trail of Unproven Claims." *New York Times*, January 1, 2003, p. A13.

69. Roger Gosden. *Designing Babies: The Brave New World of Reproductive Technology.* New York: W. H. Freeman, 1999, p. 243.

70. Rayna Rapp. "The Power of 'Positive' Diagnosis: Medical and Maternal Discourses on Amniocentesis." In Donna Bassin, Margaret Honey, and Meryle Mahrer Kaplan, eds., *Representations of Motherhood.* New Haven, CT: Yale University Press, 1994, pp. 204–219.

71. Aliza Kolker and B. Meredith Burke. *Prenatal Testing: A Sociological Perspective.* Westport, CT: Bergin & Garvey, 1994, p. 158.

72. Jeffrey A. Kuller and Steven A. Laifer. "Contemporary Approaches to Prenatal Diagnosis." *American Family Physician* 52(December 1996):2277ff.

73. Aliza Kolker and B. Meredith Burke. *Prenatal Testing: A Sociological Perspective.* Westport, CT: Bergin & Garvey, 1994; Ellen Domke and Al Podgorski. "Testing the Unborn: Genetic Test Pinpoints Defects, But Are There Risks?" *Chicago Sun-Times*, April 17, 1994, p. C5.

74. However, some parents do resist the rationalization introduced by fetal testing. See Shirley A. Hill. "Motherhood and the Obfuscation of Medical Knowledge." *Gender and Society* 8(1994):29–47.

75. Mike Chinoy. *CNN News.* February 8, 1994.

76. Joan H. Marks. "The Human Genome Project: A Challenge in Biological Technology." In Gretchen Bender and Timothy Druckery, eds., *Culture on the Brink: Ideologies of Technology.* Seattle, WA: Bay Press, 1994, pp. 99–106; R. C. Lewontin.

"The Dream of the Human Genome." In Gretchen Bender and Timothy Druckery, eds., *Culture on the Brink: Ideologies of Technology.* Seattle, WA: Bay Press, 1994, pp. 107–127; Staff. "Genome Research: International Consortium Completes Human Genome Project." *Genomics & Genetics Weekly,* May 9, 2003, p.32.

77. Staff. "Genome Research: International Consortium Completes Human Genome Project." *Genomics & Genetics Weekly,* May 9, 2003, p.32.

78. Matt Ridley. "A Boy or a Girl: Is It Possible to Load the Dice?" *Smithsonian* 24(June 1993):123.

79. Jessica Mitford. *The American Way of Birth.* New York: Plume, 1993.

80. For a critique of midwifery from the perspective of rationalization, see Charles Krauthammer. "Pursuit of a Hallmark Moment Costs a Baby's Life." *Tampa Tribune,* May 27, 1996, p. 15.

81. Judy Foreman. "The Midwives' Time Has Come—Again." *Boston Globe,* November 2, 1998, pp. C1ff.

82. Jessica Mitford. *The American Way of Birth.* New York: Plume, 1993, p. 13.

83. Catherine Kohler Riessman. "Women and Medicalization: A New Perspective." In P. Brown, ed., *Perspectives in Medical Sociology.* Prospect Heights, IL: Waveland, 1989, pp. 190–220.

84. Michelle Harrison. *A Woman in Residence.* New York: Random House, 1982, p. 91.

85. Judith Walzer Leavitt. *Brought to Bed: Childbearing in America, 1750–1950.* New York: Oxford University Press, 1986, p. 190.

86. Judith Walzer Leavitt. *Brought to Bed: Childbearing in America, 1750–1950.* New York: Oxford University Press, 1986, p. 190.

87. Paula A. Treichler. "Feminism, Medicine, and the Meaning of Childbirth." In Mary Jacobus, Evelyn Fox Keller, and Sally Shuttleworth, eds., *Body Politics: Women and the Discourses of Science.* New York: Routledge, 1990, pp. 113–138.

88. Jessica Mitford. *The American Way of Birth.* New York: Plume, 1993, p. 59.

89. An episiotomy is an incision from the vagina toward the anus to enlarge the opening needed for a baby to pass.

90. Jessica Mitford. *The American Way of Birth.* New York: Plume, 1993, p. 61.

91. Jessica Mitford. *The American Way of Birth.* New York: Plume, 1993, p. 143.

92. Michelle Harrison. *A Woman in Residence.* New York: Random House, 1982, p. 86.

93. Michelle Harrison. *A Woman in Residence.* New York: Random House, 1982, p. 113.

94. Jeanne Guillemin. "Babies by Cesarean: Who Chooses, Who Controls?" In P. Brown, ed., *Perspectives in Medical Sociology.* Prospect Heights, IL: Waveland, 1989, pp. 549–558.

95. L. Silver and S. M. Wolfe. *Unnecessary Cesarean Sections: How to Cure a National Epidemic.* Washington, DC: Public Citizen Health Research Group, 1989.

96. Joane Kabak. "C Sections." *Newsday,* November 11, 1996, pp. B25ff.

97. Susan Brink. "Too Posh to Push?" *U.S. News & World Report,* August 5, 2002, Health and Medicine sec., p. 42.

98. Randall S. Stafford. "Alternative Strategies for Controlling Rising Cesarean Section Rates." *JAMA*, February 2, 1990, pp. 683–687.

99. Jeffrey B. Gould, Becky Davey, and Randall S. Stafford. "Socioeconomic Differences in Rates of Cesarean Sections." *New England Journal of Medicine*, 321(4)(July 27, 1989):233–239; F. C. Barros et al. "Epidemic of Caesarean Sections in Brazil." *The Lancet*, July 20, 1991, pp. 167–169.

100. Randall S. Stafford. "Alternative Strategies for Controlling Rising Cesarean Section Rates." *JAMA*, February 2, 1990, pp. 683–687.

101. Although, more recently, insurance and hospital practices have led to more deaths in nursing homes or even at home.

102. Sherwin B. Nuland. *How We Die: Reflections on Life's Final Chapter*. New York: Knopf, 1994, p. 255; National Center for Health Statistics. *Vital Statistics of the United States, 1992–1993, Volume II—Mortality, Part A*. Hyattsville, MD: Public Health Service, 1995.

103. Derek Humphry. *Final Exit: The Practicalities of Self-Deliverance and Assisted Suicide for the Dying*, 3rd ed. New York: Delta, 2002.

104. Richard A. Knox. "Doctors Accepting of Euthanasia, Poll Finds: Many Would Aid in Suicide Were It Legal." *Boston Globe*, April 23, 1998, pp. A5ff.

105. Ellen Goodman. "Kevorkian Isn't Helping 'Gentle Death.'" *Newsday*, August 4, 1992, p. 32.

106. Lance Morrow. "Time for the Ice Floe, Pop: In the Name of Rationality, Kevorkian Makes Dying—and Killing—Too Easy." *Time*, December 7, 1998, pp. 48ff.

107. Amir Muhammad. "Heard Any Good Books Lately?" *New Straits Times*, October 21, 1995, pp. 9ff.

108. Raymond Kurzweil. *The Age of Intelligent Machines*. Cambridge: MIT Press, 1990.

## ◆ CHAPTER 7

1. Negative effects other than the ones discussed here, such as racism and sexism, cannot be explained by this process. See Ester Reiter. *Making Fast Food*. Montreal and Kingston: McGill-Queen's University Press, 1991, p. 145.

2. Michael Schrage. "The Pursuit of Efficiency Can Be an Illusion." *Washington Post*, March 20, 1992, p. F3.

3. Richard Cohen. "Take a Message—Please!" *Washington Post Magazine*, August 5, 1990, p. 5.

4. Peter Perl. "Fast Is Beautiful." *Washington Post Magazine*, May 24, 1992, p. 26.

5. Bob Garfield. "How I Spent (and Spent and Spent) My Disney Vacation." *Washington Post/Outlook*, July 7, 1991, p. B5.

6. Bruce Horovitz. "The Price of Family Fun: Disney Raises Theme Park Admission Prices." *USA TODAY*, April 13, 1998, p. 8B.

7. Bob Garfield. "How I Spent (and Spent and Spent) My Disney Vacation." *Washington Post/Outlook,* July 7, 1991, p. B5.

8. Stan Luxenberg. *Roadside Empires: How the Chains Franchised America.* New York: Viking, 1985.

9. Julia Kay. "High-Tech Playground to Lure Families to Burger Restaurant." *Times-Picayune,* January 27, 1997, p. E14.

10. John Bowman. "Playing Around: Local Leaps and Bounds to Close in Wake of Discovery Zone Buying Chain." *Business First–Louisville,* January 9, 1995, sect. 1, p. 4.

11. Stephen Levine. "McDonald's Makes a Play to Diversify." *Washington Post,* August 30, 1991, pp. GI, G4.

12. Yomiuri Shimbun. "Golden Arches Better-Known in Japan." *The Daily Yomiuri,* January 26, 1995, p. 17. Here, Shimbun also states that McDonald's owned at the time 20% of the Japanese operations of Toys "R" Us; see also "Allying Toys and Fast Foods." *New York Times,* October 8, 1991, p. D15.

13. Stan Luxenberg. *Roadside Empires: How the Chains Franchised America.* New York: Viking, 1985, p. 116.

14. Burger King does the same thing to its fries. See Ester Reiter. *Making Fast Food.* Montreal and Kingston: McGill-Queen's University Press, 1991, p. 65.

15. Allen Shelton. "Writing McDonald's, Eating the Past: McDonald's as a Postmodern Space." Unpublished manuscript.

16. "Fast Food Speeds Up the Pace." *Time,* August 26, 1985, p. 60.

17. Planet Hollywood is bankrupt, although it appears to be emerging from it. See http://www.hotel-online.com/News/PR2003_2nd/Jun03_PlanetHollywood Vegas.html

18. Peter Carlson. "Who Put the Sunshine in the Sunshine Scent?" *Washington Post Magazine,* December 16, 1990, p. 20.

19. Dina ElBoghdady. "Kiddie Carts." January 30, 2003. See www.myrtle beachonline.com/mld/sunnews/2003/01/31/business/5063133.htm

20. Neil Postman. *Amusing Ourselves to Death: Public Discourse in the Age of Show Business.* New York: Viking, 1985, p. 3.

21. Ian Mitroff and Warren Bennis. *The Unreality Industry: The Deliberate Manufacturing of Falsehood and What It Is Doing to Our Lives.* New York: Birch Lane, 1989, p. 12.

22. William Severini Kowinski. *The Malling of America: An Inside Look at the Great Consumer Paradise.* New York: William Morrow, 1985.

23. William Severini Kowinski. *The Malling of America: An Inside Look at the Great Consumer Paradise.* New York: William Morrow, 1985, p. 371.

24. Jack Schnedler. "Mastering Mall of America: Full-Throttle Day of Shop-Hopping Tames Minnesota's Mighty Monster." *Chicago Sun-Times/Travel,* February 6, 1994, pp. 1ff.

25. Kara Swisher. "A Mall for America?" *Washington Post/Business,* June 30, 1991, pp. H1, H4.

26. Daniel Boorstin. *The Image: A Guide to Pseudo-Events in America.* New York: Harper Colophon, 1961.

27. Ian Mitroff and Warren Bennis. *The Unreality Industry: The Deliberate Manufacturing of Falsehood and What It Is Doing to Our Lives.* New York: Birch Lane, 1989.

28. Joel Achenbach. "The Age of Unreality." *Washington Post,* November 22, 1990, pp. Cl, C14.

29. Ester Reiter. *Making Fast Food.* Montreal and Kingston: McGill-Queen's University Press, 1991, p. 95.

30. Jill Smolowe. "Read This!!!!" *Time,* November 26, 1990, pp. 62ff.

31. Michael Schrage. "Personalized Publishing: Confusing Information with Intimacy." *Washington Post,* November 23, 1990, p. B13.

32. Mark A. Schneider. *Culture and Enchantment.* Chicago: University of Chicago Press, 1993, p. ix. Weber derived this notion from Friedrich Schiller.

33. Hans Gerth and C. Wright Mills. "Introduction." In Hans Gerth and C. Wright Mills, eds., *From Max Weber.* New York: Oxford University Press, 1958, p. 51.

34. Mark A. Schneider. *Culture and Disenchantment.* Chicago: University of Chicago Press, 1993, p. ix.

35. Virginia Stagg Elliott. "Fast-food Sellers under Fire for Helping Supersize People." April 21, 2003. See www.ama-assn.org/sci-pubs/amnews/pick_03/hlsc0421.htm

36. Maryellen Spencer. "Can Mama Mac Get Them to Eat Spinach?" In Marshall Fishwick, ed., *Ronald Revisited: The World of Ronald McDonald.* Bowling Green, OH: Bowling Green University Press, 1983, pp. 85–93.

37. Donald J. Hernandez and Evan Charney, eds. *From Generation to Generation: The Health and Well-Being of Children in Immigrant Families.* Washington, DC: National Academy Press, 1998.

38. Patty Lanoue Stearns. "Double-Sized Fast Foods Means Double the Trouble." *Pittsburgh Post-Gazette,* October 10, 1996, p. B6.

39. Patty Lanoue Stearns. "Double-Sized Fast Foods Means Double the Trouble." *Pittsburgh Post-Gazette,* October 10, 1996, p. B6.

40. Regina Schrambling. "The Curse of Culinary Convenience." *New York Times,* September 10, 1991, p. A19.

41. Regina Schrambling. "The Curse of Culinary Convenience." *New York Times,* September 10, 1991, p. A19.

42. "E. coli Outbreak Forces Closure of Meat Plant." *Independent* (London), August 22, 1997, p. 12.

43. Max Boas and Steve Chain. *Big Mac: The Unauthorized Story of McDonald's.* New York: E. P. Dutton, 1976.

44. Bill Bell, Jr. "Environmental Groups Seeking Moratorium on New or Expanded 'Animal Factories.'" *St. Louis Post-Dispatch,* December 4, 1998, p. C8.

45. Tim O'Brien. "Farming: Poison Pens." *Guardian* (London), April 29, 1998, p. 4.

46. Olivia Wu. "Raising Questions: Environmentalists Voice Concerns over Booming Aquaculture Industry." *Chicago Tribune*, September 9, 1998, pp. 7Aff; Colin Woodard. "Fish Farms Get Fried for Fouling." *Christian Science Monitor*, September 9, 1998, pp. 1ff.

47. Eric Lipton. "Visit to Groomer's Takes Deadly Turn." *Washington Post*, March 31, 1995, p. B1.

48. In many areas, there has been a simultaneous increase in reasonably authentic ethnic restaurants.

49. "The Grand Illusion." *The Economist*, June 5, 1999, pp. 2–18.

50. Ellen Goodman. "Fast-Forwarding through Fall." *Washington Post*, October 5, 1991, p. A19. There is another irrationality here. Those who buy things through catalogs find that their deliveries are often late or they never arrive at all. Said the president of the Better Business Bureau of Metropolitan New York, "With mail order, the biggest problem is delivery and delay in delivery." See Leonard Sloane. "Buying by Catalogue Is Easy: Timely Delivery May Not Be." *New York Times*, April 25, 1992, p. 50.

51. George Ritzer. *The McDonaldization Thesis*. London: Sage, 1998, pp. 59–70.

52. Ester Reiter. *Making Fast Food*. Montreal and Kingston: McGill-Queen's University Press, 1991, pp. 150, 167.

53. Leidner disagrees with this, arguing that McDonald's "workers expressed relatively little dissatisfaction with the extreme routinization." See Robin Leidner. *Fast Food, Fast Talk: Service Work and the Routinization of Everyday Life*. Berkeley: University of California Press, 1993, p. 134. One could ask, however, whether this indicates a McDonaldizing society in which people, accustomed to the process, simply accept it as an inevitable part of their work.

54. Eric Schlosser. *Fast Food Nation: The Dark Side of the All-American Meal*. Boston: Houghton Mifflin, 2001.

55. Robin Leidner. *Fast Food, Fast Talk: Service Work and the Routinization of Everyday Life*. Berkeley: University of California Press, 1993, p. 30.

56. Bob Garfield. "How I Spent (and Spent and Spent) My Disney Vacation." *Washington Post/Outlook*, July 7, 1991, p. 5.

57. Henry Ford. *My Life and Work*. Garden City, NY: Doubleday Page, 1922, pp. 105, 106.

58. Studs Terkel. *Working*. New York: Pantheon, 1974, p. 159.

59. Barbara Garson. *All the Livelong Day*. Harmondsworth, UK: Penguin, 1977, p. 88.

60. Studs Terkel. *Working*. New York: Pantheon, 1974, p. 175.

61. For a review of the literature on this issue, see George Ritzer and David Walczak. *Working: Conflict and Change*, 3rd ed. Englewood Cliffs, NJ: Prentice Hall, 1986, pp. 328–372.

62. Ray Oldenburg. *The Great Good Place*. New York: Paragon, 1987.

63. One exception to the general rule discussed here that diners do not linger is the tendency for retirees to use McDonald's as a social center, especially over

breakfast or coffee. Some McDonald's restaurants even allow seniors to conduct bingo games.

64. William R. Mattox, Jr. "The Decline of Dinnertime." *Ottawa Citizen,* April 30, 1997, p. A14.

65. Nicholas von Hoffman. "The Fast-Disappearing Family Meal." *Washington Post,* November 23, 1978, p. C4.

66. Margaret Visser. "A Meditation on the Microwave." *Psychology Today,* December 1989, p. 42.

67. Margaret Visser. "A Meditation on the Microwave." *Psychology Today,* December 1989, pp. 38ff.

68. "The Microwave Cooks Up a New Way of Life." *Wall Street Journal,* September 19, 1989, p. B1.

69. Margaret Visser. "A Meditation on the Microwave." *Psychology Today,* December 1989, p. 40.

70. Margaret Visser. "A Meditation on the Microwave." *Psychology Today,* December 1989, p. 42.

71. Peggy Gisler and Marge Eberts. "Reader Disagrees with Advice for Mom Too Tired to Read." *Star Tribune* (Minneapolis), July 3, 1995, p. 3E.

72. Mary Ficklen. "Love These Days Can Be So Viagravating." *Dallas Morning News,* June 8, 1998, p. 12C; Alison MacGregor. "Fountain of Sexual Youth Carries Risks for Couples: Sex Can Ruin Some Relationships, Therapists Warn." *Ottawa Citizen,* May 27, 1998, p. A8.

73. William H. Honan. "Professors Battling Television Technology." *New York Times,* April 4, 1995, p. D24.

74. Amy Goldstein. "AMA Votes to Unionize Doctors." *Washington Post,* June 24, 1999, pp. A1, A18.

75. Kris Hundley. "The Inpatient Physician." *St. Petersburg Times,* July 26, 1998, pp. 1Hff.

76. Sherwin B. Nuland. *How We Die: Reflections on Life's Final Chapter.* New York: Knopf, 1994, p. 149.

77. Philippe Aries. *The Hour of Our Death.* New York: Knopf, 1981.

78. Sherwin B. Nuland. *How We Die: Reflections on Life's Final Chapter.* New York: Knopf, 1994, p. xv.

79. Jean Baudrillard. *Symbolic Exchange and Death.* London: Sage, 1976/1993, p. 180.

80. Nancy Gibbs. "Rx for Death." *Time,* May 31, 1993, p. 34.

81. Sherwin B. Nuland. *How We Die: Reflections on Life's Final Chapter.* New York: Knopf, 1994, p. 254.

## ◆ CHAPTER 8

1. George Ritzer. *The Globalization of Nothing.* Thousand Oaks, CA: Pine Forge Press, 2004.

2. Frank Lechner. "Globalization." In George Ritzer, ed., *Encyclopedia of Social Theory*. Thousand Oaks, CA: Sage, forthcoming.

3. Others, closely related to McDonaldization, are Americanization and the global expansion of capitalism.

4. Roland Robertson. "Globalization Theory 2000+: Major Problematics." In George Ritzer and Barry Smart, eds., *Handbook of Social Theory*. London: Sage, 2001, pp. 458–471.

5. Roland Robertson. "Globalization Theory 2000+: Major Problematics." In George Ritzer and Barry Smart, eds., *Handbook of Social Theory*. London: Sage, 2001, p. 462.

6. Roland Robertson. "Globalization Theory 2000+: Major Problematics." In George Ritzer and Barry Smart, eds., *Handbook of Social Theory*. London: Sage, 2001, p. 461.

7. They deal with when globalization began, whether the nation-state is being undermined by globalization, and the relationship of the latter to modernity. These are all important issues, but they will not concern us here largely because of a desire to keep this book focused and because no book can cover everything. Furthermore, other observers would surely contest Robertson's list of central issues and come up with very different lists.

8. Roland Robertson. "Globalisation or Glocalisation? *Journal of International Communication* 1(1994):33–52.

9. For another, see Peter Berger and Samuel Huntington, eds. *Many Globalizations: Cultural Diversity in the Contemporary World*. Oxford, UK: Oxford University Press, 2002.

10. Roland Robertson. "Globalization Theory 2000+: Major Problematics." In George Ritzer and Barry Smart, eds., *Handbook of Social Theory*. London: Sage, 2001, pp. 458–471. Globalization is at the heart of Robertson's own approach, but it is central to that of many others. The most notable is Appadurai's view that the "new global cultural economy has to be seen as a complex, overlapping, disjunctive order" (see Arjun Appadurai. *Modernity at Large: Cultural Dimensions of Globalization*. Minneapolis: University of Minnesota Press, 1996, p. 32). While John Tomlinson uses other terms, he sees glocalization as "friendly" to his own orientation (see John Tomlinson. *Globalization and Culture*. Chicago: University of Chicago Press, 1999).

11. I feel apologetic about adding yet another neologism, especially such an ungainly one, to a field already rife with jargon. However, the existence and popularity of the concept of glocalization requires the creation of the parallel notion of grobalization to emphasize that which the former concept ignores or downplays.

12. I am combining a number of different entities under this heading (nations, corporations, a wide range of organizations, and so on), but it should be clear that there are profound differences among them, including the degree to which, and the ways in which, they seek to grobalize.

13. I have previously discussed the elements of McDonaldization; here, I discuss it as a process that is sweeping across the globe—as a centrally important grobalization process.

14. Roland Robertson. "Globalization Theory 2000+: Major Problematics." In George Ritzer and Barry Smart, eds., *Handbook of Social Theory*. London: Sage, 2001, p. 464. Note: italics in original.

15. George Ritzer. *The McDonaldization Thesis*. London: Sage, 1998, pp. 174–183.

16. However, there are some forms of nothing that are locally conceived and/or controlled.

17. That is, by, for example, the headquarters of a multinational corporation or a national government.

18. George Ritzer. *The Globalization of Nothing*. Thousand Oaks, CA: Pine Forge Press, 2004, p. 3.

19. Control, as we have seen, is also a basic dimension of McDonaldization.

20. As in the case of the caveat about the definition of nothing, there are some forms of something that are centrally conceived and/or controlled.

21. George Ritzer. *The Globalization of Nothing*. Thousand Oaks, CA: Pine Forge Press, 2004, p. 7.

22. For a critique of dichotomous thinking, see Elisabeth Mudimbe-Boyi, ed. *Beyond Dichotomies: Histories, Identities, Cultures, and the Challenge of Globalization.* Albany: State University of New York Press, 2002.

23. W. Delacoma. "Silk Road, CSO Explore the East." *Chicago Sun-Times,* October 26, 2002, p. 20.

24. An interesting example of the trend toward nothingness is the increasing use of audio guides and rented tape players at such shows and at museums more generally.

25. Gucci bags are nothing, as that concept is defined here, but they are certainly expensive. Grobalization as a process can also be seen in markets dealing with higher end, more expensive products as well. For example, Gucci bags, Benetton sweaters, and Prada shoes are certainly nothing, as that concept is defined here, and are also certainly considered expensive by most. Thus, the grobalization of nothing is not limited by cost considerations, although more affordable products do have more of an elective affinity with grobalization than do less affordable ones.

26. Those who emphasize glocalization are often critical of grobalization in general, and as a surrogate for it, one of its subprocesses, McDonaldization (see, for example, Arjun Appadurai, *Modernity at Large: Cultural Dimensions of Globalization*. Minneapolis: University of Minnesota Press, 1996, p. 29; Ulrich Beck. *What Is Globalization?* Cambridge, UK: Polity, 2000, p. 42; Roland Robertson. "Globalization Theory 2000+: Major Problematics." In George Ritzer and Barry Smart, eds., *Handbook of Social Theory*. London: Sage, 2001, p. 464; James L. Watson, ed. *Golden Arches East: McDonald's in East Asia*. Stanford, CA: Stanford University Press, 1997, p. 35).

27. Mike Featherstone. *Undoing Culture: Globalization, Postmodernism and Identity.* London: Sage, 1995.

28. Jonathan Friedman. *Cultural Identity and Global Processes.* London: Sage, 1994.

29. Michel De Certeau. *The Practice of Everyday Life.* Berkeley: University of California Press, 1984, p. 34.

30. Steven Seidman. "The End of Sociological Theory: The Postmodern Hope." *Sociological Theory* 9:131–146.

31. Robertson (1992) is one who is generally even-handed in his treatment of the grobal and the glocal, even though he is closely associated with the latter concept.

32. Salah Wahab and Chris Cooper, eds. *Tourism in the Age of Globalisation.* London: Routledge, 2001.

33. Grobal forms of nothing (e.g., McDonald's toys) can be transformed into something (either grobal or glocal) when, for example, they are transformed into collector's items.

34. Cited in James L. Watson. "Transnationalism, Localization, and Fast Foods in East Asia." In James L. Watson, ed., *Golden Arches East: McDonald's in East Asia.* Stanford, CA: Stanford University Press, 1997, p. 12.

35. Barbara Sullivan. "McDonald's Sees India as Golden Opportunity." *Chicago Tribune—Business,* April 5, 1995, p. 1.

36. Betsy McKay. "In Russia, West No Longer Means Best: Consumers Shift to Home-Grown Goods." *Wall Street Journal,* December 9, 1996, p. A9.

37. T. R. Reid. "Fish & Chips Meet Their Vindaloo." *Washington Post,* July 6, 1999, pp. C1, C10.

38. Jessica Steinberg. "Israeli Fast-Food Outlets Offer Passover Meals." *Times–Picayune,* April 26, 1997, p. A19.

39. Yunxiang Yan. "McDonald's in Beijing: The Localization of Americana." In James L. Watson, ed., *Golden Arches East: McDonald's in East Asia.* Stanford, CA: Stanford University Press, 1997, pp. 39–76.

40. Yunxiang Yan. "McDonald's in Beijing: The Localization of Americana." In James L. Watson, ed., *Golden Arches East: McDonald's in East Asia.* Stanford, CA: Stanford University Press, 1997, pp. 39–76.

41. James L. Watson. "McDonald's in Hong Kong: Consumerism, Dietary Change, and the Rise of a Children's Culture." In James L. Watson, ed., *Golden Arches East: McDonald's in East Asia.* Stanford, CA: Stanford University Press, 1997, pp. 77–109.

42. James L. Watson. "McDonald's in Hong Kong: Consumerism, Dietary Change, and the Rise of a Children's Culture." In James L. Watson, ed., *Golden Arches East: McDonald's in East Asia.* Stanford, CA: Stanford University Press, 1997, p. 91.

43. David Y. H. Wu. "McDonald's in Taipei: Hamburgers, Betel Nuts, and National Identity." In James L. Watson, ed., *Golden Arches East: McDonald's in East Asia.* Stanford, CA: Stanford University Press, 1997, p. 125.

44. James L. Watson. "Transnationalism, Localization, and Fast Foods in Asia." In James L. Watson, ed., *Golden Arches East: McDonald's in East Asia.* Stanford, CA: Stanford University Press, 1997, p. 6.

45. James L. Watson. "McDonald's in Hong Kong: Consumerism, Dietary Change, and the Rise of a Children's Culture." In James L. Watson, ed., *Golden Arches East: McDonald's in East Asia.* Stanford, CA: Stanford University Press, 1997, p. 80.

46. Emiko Ohnuki-Tierney. "McDonald's in Japan: Changing Manners and Etiquette." In James L. Watson, ed., *Golden Arches East: McDonald's in East Asia.* Stanford, CA: Stanford University Press, 1997, p. 173.

47. James L. Watson. "Transnationalism, Localization, and Fast Foods in Asia." In James L. Watson, ed., *Golden Arches East: McDonald's in East Asia.* Stanford, CA: Stanford University Press, 1997, pp. 1–38.

48. David Barboza. "Pluralism under Golden Arches." *New York Times,* February 12, 1999, pp. C1ff.

49. Shannon Peters Talbott. "Global Localization of the World Market: Case Study of McDonald's in Moscow." *Sociale Wetenschappen* (December 1996):31–44.

50. Marshall Ingwerson. "That Golden Touch to the Arches in Russia." *Ohio Slavic and East European Newsletter* 25(Spring 1997):1. (Originally published in the *Christian Science Monitor,* 1997.)

51. Lee Hockstader. "Attack on Big Mac." *Washington Post,* August 8, 1995, p. A13.

52. Yunxiang Yan. "McDonald's in Beijing: The Localization of Americana." In James L. Watson, ed., *Golden Arches East: McDonald's in East Asia.* Stanford, CA: Stanford University Press, 1997, p. 75.

53. Emiko Ohnuki Tierney. "McDonald's in Japan: Changing Manners and Etiquette." In James L. Watson, ed., *Golden Arches East: McDonald's in East Asia.* Stanford, CA: Stanford University Press, 1997, p. 165.

54. Mos Food Services Web site: www.mos.co.jp

55. Sangmee Bak. "McDonald's in Seoul: Food Choices, Identity, and Nationalism." In James L. Watson, ed., *Golden Arches East: McDonald's in East Asia.* Stanford, CA: Stanford University Press, 1997, pp. 136–160.

56. Sangmee Bak. "McDonald's in Seoul: Food Choices, Identity, and Nationalism." In James L. Watson, ed., *Golden Arches East: McDonald's in East Asia.* Stanford, CA: Stanford University Press, 1997, pp. 136–160.

57. T. R. Reid. "Fish & Chips Meet Their Vindaloo." *Washington Post,* July 6, 1999, pp. C1, C10.

58. James L. Watson. "McDonald's in Hong Kong: Consumerism, Dietary Change, and the Rise of a Children's Culture." In James L. Watson, ed., *Golden Arches East: McDonald's in East Asia.* Stanford, CA: Stanford University Press, 1997, pp. 77–109.

59. Emiko Ohnuki-Tierney. "McDonald's in Japan: Changing Manners and Etiquette." In James L. Watson, ed., *Golden Arches East: McDonald's in East Asia.* Stanford, CA: Stanford University Press, 1997, pp. 161–182.

60. Emiko Ohnuki Tierney. "McDonald's in Japan: Changing Manners and Etiquette." In James L. Watson, ed., *Golden Arches East: McDonald's in East Asia.* Stanford, CA: Stanford University Press, 1997, pp. 161–182.

61. Benjamin R. Barber. *Jihad vs. McWorld.* New York: Times Books, 1995; see also Thomas L. Friedman. *The Lexus and the Olive Tree: Understanding Globalization.* New York: Farrar, Straus, Giroux, 1999.

## ◆ CHAPTER 9

1. Joe Kincheloe. "The Complex Politics of McDonald's and the New Childhood: Colonizing Kidworld." In Gaile S. Cannella and Joe L. Kincheloe, eds., *Kidworld: Childhood Studies, Global Perspectives, and Education.* New York: Peter Lang, 2002, pp. 75–12.

2. Ironically and paradoxically, some aspects of the process of McDonaldization (for example, the Internet and cybershops) are allowing many people to do more things at home. This poses something of a threat to other rationalized aspects of society (for example, shopping malls).

3. Ester Reiter. *Making Fast Food.* Montreal and Kingston: McGill-Queen's University Press, 1991, p. 165.

4. Saul Hansell. "As Broadband Gains, The Internet's Snails, Like AOL, Fall Back." *New York Times,* February 3, 2003, p. C1.

5. Don Slater. "'You Press the Button, We Do the Rest': Some Thoughts on the McDonaldization of the Internet." Paper presented at the meetings of the Eastern Sociological Society, Boston, March, 1999.

6. Daniel Bell. *The Coming of Post-Industrial Society: A Venture in Social Forecasting.* New York: Basic Books, 1973.

7. Jerald Hage and Charles H. Powers. *Post-Industrial Lives: Roles and Relationships in the 21st Century.* Newbury Park, CA: Sage, 1992.

8. Jerald Hage and Charles H. Powers. *Post-Industrial Lives: Roles and Relationships in the 21st Century.* Newbury Park, CA: Sage, 1992, p. 10.

9. Although there are, as we have seen, efforts to automate them as well.

10. Jerald Hage and Charles H. Powers. *Post-Industrial Lives: Roles and Relationships in the 21st Century.* Newbury Park, CA: Sage, 1992, p. 50.

11. Simon Clarke. "The Crisis of Fordism or the Crisis of Social Democracy?" *Telos* 8(1990):71–98.

12. Pierre Bourdieu. *Distinction: A Social Critique of the Judgment of Taste.* Cambridge, MA: Harvard University Press, 1984.

13. Lorraine Mirabella. "Trouble Brews for Starbucks as Its Stock Slides 12 Percent." *Baltimore Sun,* August 1, 1998, pp. 10C; Margaret Webb Pressler. "The Brain behind the Beans." *Washington Post,* October 5, 1997, pp. H01ff.

14. Alex Witchel. "By Way of Canarsie, One Large Hot Cup of Business Strategy." *New York Times,* December 14, 1994, p. C8.

15. For more on postmodernism, see George Ritzer. *Postmodern Social Theory.* New York: McGraw-Hill, 1997; Jean Baudrillard. *Symbolic Exchange and Death.* London: Sage, 1976/1993; Fredric Jameson. "Postmodernism, or the Cultural Logic of Late Capitalism." *New Left Review* 146(1984):53–92; Fredric Jameson. *Postmodernism, or The Cultural Logic of Late Capitalism.* Durham, NC: Duke University Press, 1991; Jean-Francois Lyotard. *The Postmodern Condition: A Report on Knowledge.* Minneapolis: University of Minnesota Press, 1984; Steven Best and Douglas Kellner. *Postmodern Theory: Critical Interrogations.* New York: Guilford, 1991.

16. Smart argues that rather than viewing modernism and postmodernism as epochs, people can see them as engaged in a long-running and ongoing set of relationships, with postmodernity continually pointing out the limitations of modernity. See Barry Smart. *Postmodernity.* London: Routledge, 1993.

17. Allen Shelton. "Writing McDonald's, Eating the Past: McDonald's as a Postmodern Space." Unpublished manuscript.

18. David Harvey. *The Condition of Postmodernity: An Enquiry into the Origins of Cultural Change.* Oxford, UK: Basil Blackwell, 1989, p. 189.

19. David Harvey. *The Condition of Postmodernity: An Enquiry into the Origins of Cultural Change.* Oxford, UK: Basil Blackwell, 1989, pp. 284, 293.

20. Fredric Jameson. "Postmodernism, or the Cultural Logic of Late Capitalism." *New Left Review* 146(1984):53–92; *Postmodernism, or The Cultural Logic of Late Capitalism.* Durham, NC: Duke University Press, 1991.

21. Fredric Jameson. "Postmodernism, or the Cultural Logic of Late Capitalism." *New Left Review* 146(1984):78.

22. Fredric Jameson. "Postmodernism, or the Cultural Logic of Late Capitalism." *New Left Review* 146(1984):66.

23. Fredric Jameson. "Postmodernism, or the Cultural Logic of Late Capitalism." *New Left Review* 146(1984):64.

24. Fredric Jameson. "Postmodernism, or the Cultural Logic of Late Capitalism." *New Left Review* 146(1984):76.

25. Postmodern intensity also occurs when "the body is plugged into the new electronic media." See Martin Donougho. "Postmodern Jameson." In Douglas Kellner, ed., *Postmodernism, Jameson, Critique.* Washington, DC: Maisonneuve, 1989, p. 85.

26. Thus, attacks like the one on the McDonald's in Belgrade are exceptional events, although we will see later that there is a danger that such violence may become more common.

27. Fredric Jameson. "Postmodernism, or the Cultural Logic of Late Capitalism." *New Left Review* 146(1984):65–66.

28. Fredric Jameson. "Postmodernism, or the Cultural Logic of Late Capitalism." *New Left Review* 146(1984):65–66, 71.

29. Fredric Jameson. "Postmodernism, or the Cultural Logic of Late Capitalism." *New Left Review* 146(1984):68.

30. Fredric Jameson. "Postmodernism, or the Cultural Logic of Late Capitalism." *New Left Review* 146(1984):68.

31. Alex Callinicos. *Against Postmodernism: A Marxist Critique.* New York: St. Martin's, 1990, p. 4.

32. George Ritzer. *Enchanting a Disenchanted World: Revolutionizing the Means of Consumption.* Thousand Oaks, CA: Pine Forge, 1999.

33. Ian Heywood. "Urgent Dreams: Climbing, Rationalization and Ambivalence." *Leisure Studies* 13(1994):179–194.

34. Jon Krakauer. *Into Thin Air.* New York: Anchor, 1997, p. xvii.

35. Jon Krakauer. *Into Thin Air.* New York: Anchor, 1997, pp. 39, 353.

36. Jon Krakauer. *Into Thin Air.* New York: Anchor, 1997, p. 320.

37. Jon Krakauer. *Into Thin Air.* New York: Anchor, 1997, p. 320.

38. Jon Krakauer. *Into Thin Air.* New York: Anchor, 1997, p. 100.

39. Jon Krakauer. *Into Thin Air.* New York: Anchor, 1997, p. 86.

40. Jon Krakauer. *Into Thin Air.* New York: Anchor, 1997.

41. Mount Everest Web site: www.mounteverest.net/story/RecordEversetseason Jun22003.shtml

42. Yahoo Media Web site: http://media.yahoo.com/globalextremes

43. Barnaby J. Feder. "Where Have You Gone, Ray Kroc?" *New York Times,* June 5, 1997, pp. D1ff.

44. "As Hamburgers Go, So Goes America." *The Economist,* August 23, 1997.

45. Guy Dinmore. "Milosevic Playing Well at Home." *Chicago Tribune,* March 31, 1999.

46. Anne Swardson. "A Roquefort David Strikes a Coke Goliath." *International Herald Tribune,* August 23, 1999, p. 5; Roger Cohen. "Fearful over the Future, Europe Seizes on Food." *New York Times–Week in Review,* August 29, 1999, pp. 1, 3.

47. Peter S. Goodman. "Familiar Logo on Unfamiliar Eateries in Iraq." *Washington Post* May 26, 2003:A1, A14.

48. Margaret Pressler. "It's a Wrap: Stuffed-Tortilla Chain Falls Flat." *Washington Post,* June 2, 1998, p. C01.

49. Julia Llewellyn Smith. "French with Tears: Club Med Goes Mickey Mouse." *Sunday Telegraph,* July 27, 1997, pp. 19ff.

50. Andrew Clark. "City: Ailing Body Shop Gets a Makeover." *Daily Telegraph* (London), October 23, 1998, p. 33; Roger Cowe. "Blow for Body Shop." *Guardian* (London), May 25, 1998, p. 16.

51. Penny Parker. "Franchisees Left Holding the Bag: Boston Chicken's Financing Plan Took Toll on Restaurant Developers." *Denver Post,* October 26, 1998, pp. E01ff.

52. Lorraine Mirabella. "Trouble Brews for Starbucks as Its Stock Slides 12 Percent." *Baltimore Sun,* August 1, 1998, pp. 10C.

53. Bryan Wagoner. "They Have Grounds for Discontent." *Boston Globe,* February 8, 1998, pp. 1ff (City Weekly); Monte Williams. "The Local Flavor Only, Please." *New York Times,* October 23, 1996, pp. B1ff.

54. Ian King. "Burger King to Close in France as Grandmet Cuts Its Losses." *Guardian,* July 30, 1997, p. 18.

55. Edwin McDowell. "Holiday Inn, Passed By, Fights Ravages of Time." *International Herald Tribune,* March 30, 1998, pp. 11ff.

56. "Franchising: Rattling the Chains." *Brandweek,* April 21, 1997.

57. Paul Farhi. "McDonald's Customers: Made to Order Audience." *Washington Post,* November 19, 1991, pp. B1, B5.

58. Starbucks has recently sought to expand its offerings and types of outlets, but so far with little success.

59. George Ritzer. *The McDonaldization Thesis.* London: Sage, 1998, p. 181.

60. Robert Johnson. "Wouldn't It Have Been Simpler to Build a Quick Chick Brick Stack?" *Wall Street Journal,* April 13, 1999, p. B1.

61. Steven L. Goldman, Roger N. Nagel, and Kenneth Preiss. "Why Seiko Has 3,000 Watch Styles." *New York Times,* October 9, 1994, p. 9; Steven L. Goldman, Roger N. Nagel, and Kenneth Preiss. *Agile Competitors and Virtual Organizations: Strategies for Enriching the Customer.* New York: Van Nostrand Reinhold, 1995.

62. Joseph Pine. *Mass Customization: The New Frontier in Business Competition.* Cambridge, MA: Harvard Business School Press, 1993.

63. Connie Mok, Alan T. Stutts, and Lillian Wong. "Mass Customization in the Hospitality Industry: Concepts and Applications." At www.hotel-online. com/Trends/ChiangMaiJun00/CustomizationHospitality.html

64. Logo Softwear Web site: www.logosoftwear.com

65. "Agencies Vie for CNN Euro AD campaign." *Marketing Week,* June 5, 1997, p. 10.

66. Dow Jones News Service. "CNN, Oracle to Deliver Customized News." *Denver Rocky Mountain News,* June 5, 1997, p. 4B.

67. However, that is not to say that there could never be real threats to McDonaldization. For example, shopping and much else on the Internet shifts control away from McDonaldized systems and in the direction of the consumer.

## ◆ CHAPTER 10

1. Vic Sussman. "The Machine We Love to Hate." *Washington Post Magazine,* June 14, 1987, p. 33.

2. Kirk Johnson. "Bread: Satisfying a Need to Knead." *New York Times,* February 8, 1995, p. C1.

3. Vic Sussman. "The Machine We Love to Hate." *Washington Post Magazine,* June 14, 1987, p. 33.

4. Tanya Wenman Steel. "Have Time to Bake? What a Luxury!" *New York Times,* February 8, 1995, p. C4.

5. Weber, cited in Hans Gerth and C. Wright Mills, eds. *From Max Weber.* New York: Oxford University Press, 1958, p. 128.

6. The threefold typology presented here is not exhaustive. McDonaldized systems can also be seen as sets of "monkey bars." From this perspective, the iron cage is nothing more than a playground apparatus that can become anything the people involved with it want it to be. Thus, people can make it a velvet, rubber, or iron cage, if they so desire. While there is merit to this view, it probably overestimates the power of human beings. Cages, whether they are velvet, rubber, or iron, are structures, and therefore they (and those who support them) are often resistant to efforts to modify them. See Jay Klagge. "Approaches to the Iron Cage: Reconstructing the Bars of Weber's Metaphor." *Administration & Society* 29(1997):63–77.

7. Andrew Malcolm. "Bagging Old Rules to Keep a Food Co-op Viable." *New York Times,* November 8, 1991, p. B7.

8. Other examples include St. Mary's College in Maryland and Evergreen State College in Washington.

9. For other examples of shops such as Marvelous Market, see Marian Burros. "Putting the Pleasure Back into Grocery Shopping." *New York Times,* February 21, 1987, sec. 1, p. 54.

10. This quotation, as well as others in this section, are drawn from Marvelous Market's occasional newsletters.

11. "Eating Out Is In, and the Chains Add Variety to Lure New Diners." *Time,* August 26, 1985, p. 60.

12. Phyllis C. Richman. "Bread and Beyond." *Washington Post Magazine,* September 7, 1997, p. W21ff.

13. Rhonda M. Abrams. "It's Time for You Small Retailers to Get Real." *Des Moines Register,* April 6, 1998, p. 10.

14. Fred "Chico" Lager. *Ben & Jerry's: The Inside Scoop.* New York: Crown, 1994; Suzanne Alexander. "Oh, Wow, Man: Let's, Like, Hear from the Auditors." *Wall Street Journal,* June 28, 1991, pp. Al, A6.

15. Fred "Chico" Lager. *Ben & Jerry's: The Inside Scoop.* New York: Crown, 1994, p. 148.

16. Fred "Chico" Lager. *Ben & Jerry's: The Inside Scoop.* New York: Crown, 1994, p. 133.

17. Fred "Chico" Lager. *Ben & Jerry's: The Inside Scoop.* New York: Crown, 1994, p. 28.

18. Fred "Chico" Lager. *Ben & Jerry's: The Inside Scoop.* New York: Crown, 1994, p. 36.

19. Ben Cohen and Jerry Greenfield. *Ben & Jerry's Double-Dip.* New York: Fireside, 1998.

20. Ben & Jerry's Web site: www.benandjerrys.com/our_company/about_us/our_history/timeline/index.cfm

21. Ben & Jerry's 1990 annual report, p. 7.

22. Fred "Chico" Lager. *Ben & Jerry's: The Inside Scoop.* New York: Crown, 1994, p. 145.

23. Two preceding quotations from Maxine Lipner. "Ben & Jerry's: Sweet Ethics Evince Social Awareness." *COMPASS Readings,* July 1991, pp. 26–27.

24. Two preceding quotations from Carol Clurman. "More Than Just a Paycheck." *USA WEEKEND,* January 19–21, 1990, p. 4.

25. Ben & Jerry's Web site: www.benandjerrys.com/scoop_shops

26. Maxine Lipner. "Ben & Jerry's: Sweet Ethics Evince Social Awareness." *COMPASS Readings,* July 1991, p. 25.

27. Fred "Chico" Lager. *Ben & Jerry's: The Inside Scoop.* New York: Crown, 1994, p. 164.

28. Eric J. Wiffering. "Trouble in Camelot." *Business Ethics* 5(1991):16, 19.

29. Patricia Aburdene. "Paycheck." *USA WEEKEND,* January 19–21, 1990, p. 4.

30. Ben & Jerry's Web site: www.benjerry.com/our_company/press_center

31. June R. Herold. "B & B's Offer Travelers Break from McBed, McBreakfast." *Business First-Columbus,* May 15, 1991, col. 1, p. 1.

32. Betsy Wade. "B & B Book Boom." *Chicago Tribune,* July 28, 1991, pp. C16ff.

33. Paul Avery. "Mixed Success for Bed-Breakfast Idea." *New York Times,* July 28, 1991, pp. 12NJ, 8.

34. Eric N. Berg. "The New Bed and Breakfast." *New York Times,* October 15, 1989, pp. 5ff.

35. Harvey Elliott. "All Mod Cons and Trouser Presses 'Ruining B & Bs.'" *Times* (London), April 3, 1996.

36. George Ritzer. "Implications of and Barriers to Industrial Democracy in the United States and Sweden." In Irving Louis Horowitz, ed., *Equity, Income and Policy: A Comparative Developmental Context.* New York and London: Praeger, 1977, pp. 49–69.

37. John Vidal. *McLibel: Burger Culture on Trial.* New York: New Press, 1997.

38. McSpotlight Web site: www.mcspotlight.org/media/press/mclibel/theobserver 230303.html

39. McSpotlight Web site: www.mcspotlight.org

40. Danny Penman. "Judgment Day for McDonald's." *Independent* (London), June 19, 1997, pp. 20ff.

41. McSpotlight Web site: www.mcspotlight.org/campaigns/current/residents/index.html

42. McSpotlight Web site: www.mcspotlight.org/media/press/releases/msc 240903.html

43. Jacqueline L. Salmon. "McDonald's, Employees Reach Pact: Strike Ends." *Washington Post,* October 23, 1998, p. C3.

44. Ester Reiter. *Making Fast Food.* Montreal and Kingston: McGill-Queen's University Press, 1991, pp. 70ff.

45. Workers Online Web site: http://workers.labor.net.au/156/news83_maccas.html

46. James Brooke. "Two McDonald's in Darien Do Their Hiring in Bronx." *New York Times,* July 13, 1985, sec. 1, p. 24; Michael Winerip. "Finding a Sense of

McMission in McNuggets." *New York Times,* August 23, 1988, sec. 2, p. 1; "McDonald's Seeks Retirees to Fill Void." *New York Times,* December 20, 1987, sec. 1, p. 54; Jennifer Kingson. "Golden Years Spent under Golden Arches." *New York Times,* March 6, 1988, sec. 4, p. 26.

47.  Glenn Collins. "Wanted: Child-Care Workers, Age 55 and Up." *New York Times,* December 15, 1987, sec. 1, p. 1.

48.  Anthony Ramirez. "When Fast Food Goes on a Diet." *Washington Post,* March 19, 1991, pp. D1, D7.

49.  National Heart Savers Association Web site: www.heartsavers.org

50.  Marian Burros. "Fast-Food Chains Try to Slim Down." *New York Times,* April 11, 1990, pp. CI, C10.

51.  Leon Jaroff. "A Crusader from the Heartland." *Time,* March 25, 1991, pp. 56, 58.

52.  Marian Burros. "Eating Well." *New York Times,* March 2, 1994, p. C4.

53.  *Seattle Times,* May 5, 1997, p. E1.

54.  Anthony Ramirez. "When Fast Food Goes on a Diet." *Washington Post,* March 19, 1991, pp. D1, D7.

55.  Ross Kerber and Greg Johnson. "Getting Leaner." *Los Angeles Times,* February 9, 1995, p. D1.

56.  Denise Gellene. "Sales of Low-Fat Items Fall on Lean Times." *Los Angeles Times,* February 6, 1996, pp. 1Dff.

57.  Greg Johnson. "Fat. Sales: An Unpredictable Relationship." *Los Angeles Times,* March 20, 1996, p. 6D.

58.  Phyllis C. Richman. "Savoring Lunch in the Slow Lane." *Washington Post,* November 22, 1998, pp. M1ff.

59.  Phyllis C. Richman. "Savoring Lunch in the Slow Lane." *Washington Post,* November 22, 1998, p. M1.

60.  *Slow,* July-September 1998, np.

61.  Corby Kummer. *The Pleasures of Slow Food.* San Francisco: Chronicle Books, 2002, p. 26.

62.  Corby Kummer. *The Pleasures of Slow Food.* San Francisco: Chronicle Books, 2002, p. 23.

63.  Corby Kummer. *The Pleasures of Slow Food.* San Francisco: Chronicle Books, 2002, p. 23.

64.  Corby Kummer. *The Pleasures of Slow Food.* San Francisco: Chronicle Books, 2002, p. 25.

65.  Corby Kummer. *The Pleasures of Slow Food.* San Francisco: Chronicle Books, 2002, p. 25.

66.  ABC News Web site: http://abcnews.go.com/sections/world/DailyNews/slowcities000724.html

67.  ABC News Web site: http://abcnews.go.com/sections/world/Daily News/slowcities000724.html

68.  Sprawl-Busters Web site: www.sprawl-busters.com

69.  Sprawl-Busters Web site: www.sprawl-busters.com/victoryz.html

70. See Al Norman. *Slam-Dunking Wal-Mart: How You Can Stop Superstore Sprawl in Your Hometown.* Saint Johnsbury, VT: Raphael Marketing, 1999.

71. Hawke Fracassa. "Sterling Hts. Stops Burger King." *Detroit News,* August 14, 1998, p. C5.

72. Isabel Wilkerson. "Midwest Village; Slow-Paced, Fights Plan for Fast-Food Outlet." *New York Times,* July 19, 1987, pp. 1, 16.

73. Mary Davis Suro. "Romans Protest McDonald's." *New York Times,* May 5, 1986, p. C20.

74. Jane Perlez. "A McDonald's? Not in Their Medieval Square." *New York Times,* May 23, 1994, p. A4.

75. Dominic Kennedy. "Welcome to Burger-Free Heaven." *Times* (London), January 3, 1998.

76. Dominic Kennedy. "Welcome to Burger-Free Heaven." *Times* (London), January 3, 1998.

77. Steve Ginsberg. "Blockbusted: Neighborhood Merchants Produce Summer Flop." *San Francisco Business Times,* September 2, 1994, sec. 1, p. 3.

78. In one notable exception, the entire state of Vermont had, at least until the mid-1990s, been kept free of Wal-Marts. See Paul Gruchow. "Unchaining America: Communities Are Finding Ways to Keep Independent Entrepreneurs in Business." *Utne Reader,* January-February 1995, pp. 17–18. Now, however, and consistent with the idea of increasing McDonaldization, there are a number of Wal-Marts in that state. See www.store-search.com/walmart/vermont.html

79. Peter Pae. "Retail Giant Rattles the Shops on Main Street." *Washington Post,* February 12, 1995, p. B3.

80. Peter Kilborn. "When Wal-Mart Pulls Out, What's Left?" *New York Times/Business,* March 5, 1995, pp. 1, 6.

81. "Eating Out Is In, and the Chains Add Variety to Lure New Diners." *Time,* August 26, 1985, pp. 60–61.

82. Anthony Ramirez. "In the Orchid Room . . . Big Macs." *New York Times,* October 30, 1990, pp. DI, D5.

83. Jane Perlez. "A McDonald's? Not in Their Medieval Square." *New York Times,* May 23, 1994, p. A4.

84. Kate Connolly. "McCafe in Vienna? Grounds for War." *Observer,* August 30, 1998, p. 19.

85. John Holusha. "McDonald's Expected to Drop Plastic Burger Box." *Washington Post,* November 1, 1990, pp. A1, D19; John Holusha. "Packaging and Public Image: McDonald's Fills a Big Order." *New York Times,* November 2, 1990, pp. Al, D5.

86. "Michigan McDonald's: McNews You Can Use." PR Newswire, June 20, 2003.

87. Warren Brown. "Hardee's to Introduce Recycled Plastic in Area." *Washington Post,* March 22, 1991, pp. B1, B3.

88. Ron Alexander. "Big Mac with Chopin, Please." *New York Times,* August 12, 1990, p. 42.

89. Eric Maykuth. "Chock Full o' Nuts Restaurants Are Dying Quietly." *Washington Post*, September 16, 1990, p. H16.

90. Anna D. Wilde. "Just Like Ice Cream in the Sun: HoJo's Dominance Has Melted Away." *Patriot Ledger*, August 13, 1994, p. B25.

91. Thomas J. Peters and Robert H. Waterman. *In Search of Excellence: Lessons from America's Best-Run Companies*. New York: Harper & Row, 1982.

92. Thomas J. Peters and Robert H. Waterman. *In Search of Excellence: Lessons from America's Best-Run Companies*. New York: Harper & Row, 1982, p. 201.

93. Duayne Draffen. "Independent Video Stores Survive within Niches." *New York Times*, February 17, 1998, pp. B5ff; Edward Guthmann. "Vintage Video: Bay Area's Independent Video Stores Enjoy Blockbuster Success." *San Francisco Chronicle*, October 5, 1997, pp. 38ff.

94. Robert Nelson. "Chain Reaction Franchises Have Taken a Big Bite Out of Omaha's Sit-Down Restaurant Market. But There Is Still Room for the Savvy Independent Owner." *Omaha World-Herald*, March 1, 1998, pp. 1Eff.

95. Robert Nelson. "Chain Reaction Franchises Have Taken a Big Bite Out of Omaha's Sit-Down Restaurant Market. But There is Still Room for the Savvy Independent Owner." *Omaha World-Herald*, March 1, 1998, pp. 1Eff.

96. Carol Emert. "Between the Lines: Changes in Industry Will Have Big Impact on What We Read and Where We Buy Our Books." *San Francisco Chronicle*, May 5, 1998, pp. E1ff.

97. For a similar effort, see Neil Postman. *Technopoly*. New York: Knopf, 1992, pp. 183ff.

98. Peter Perl. "Fast Is Beautiful." *Washington Post Magazine*, May 24, 1992, pp. 10ff; Allen Shelton. "Writing McDonald's, Eating the Past: McDonald's as a Postmodern Space." Unpublished manuscript, p. 47; Eileen Schulte. "Breakfast Club Marks Member's 99th Birthday." *St. Petersburg Times*, November 22, 1998, pp. 11ff.

99. Regina Schrambling. "The Curse of Culinary Convenience." *New York Times*, September 10, 1991, p. A19.

100. All quotations in this paragraph are from Regina Schrambling. "The Curse of Culinary Convenience." *New York Times*, September 10, 1991, p. A19.

101. Warren Leary. "Researchers Halt Ripening of Tomato." *New York Times*, October 19, 1991, p. 7.

102. John Tierney. "A Patented Berry Has Sellers Licking Their Lips." *New York Times*, October 14, 1991, p. A8.

103. James Hamilton. "Fast Food Chains Playing Pie' Piper with Mr Men and Pokemon Freebies." Scottish Media Newspapers Limited–*The Sunday Herald*, August 19, 2001, p. 6.

104. Eric Schmuckler. "Two Action Figures to Go, Hold the Burger." *Brandweek*, April 1, 1996, pp. 38ff.

105. Chris Rojek. *Ways of Escape: Modern Transformations in Leisure and Travel*. London: Routledge, 1993.

106. Chris Rojek. *Ways of Escape: Modern Transformations in Leisure and Travel.* London: Routledge, 1993, p. 188.

107. Stanley Cohen and Laurie Taylor. *Escape Attempts: The Theory and Practice of Everyday Life,* 2nd ed. London: Routledge, 1992.

108. James Miller. *The Passion of Michel Foucault.* New York: Anchor, 1993.

109. Stanley Cohen and Laurie Taylor. *Escape Attempts: The Theory and Practice of Everyday Life,* 2nd ed. London: Routledge, 1992, p. 197.

110. Roger Cohen. "Faux Pas by McDonald's in Europe." *New York Times,* February 18, 1992, p. D1.

111. Two quotes from Sharon Waxman. "Paris's Sex Change Operation." *Washington Post,* March 2, 1992, p. B1.

112. Dylan Thomas. *The Collected Poems of Dylan Thomas.* "Do Not Go Gentle into That Good Night." New York: New Directions, 1952, p. 128.

# Index

# About the Author

**George Ritzer** is Distinguished University Professor at the University of Maryland, where he has also been a Distinguished Scholar-Teacher and won a Teaching Excellence Award. He was also awarded the 2000 Distinguished Contributions to Teaching Award by the American Sociological Association. He is perhaps best-known for *The McDonaldization of Society* (translated into over a dozen languages) and several related books, including *Expressing America: A Critique of the Global Credit Card Society* and *Enchanting a Disenchanted World: Revolutionizing the Means of Consumption*. His latest effort in this domain is *The Globalization of Nothing* (2004), and he has just completed a *Handbook of Social Problems* (2004). He is also cofounding editor of the *Journal of Consumer Culture*.